# Evidence-Based Mental Health Practice

More Advance Acclaim for
*Evidence-Based Mental Health Practice*

"This book is a timely supplement to the President's New Freedom Commission Report. Drake, Merrens, and Lynde present an invaluable resource for those seeking to understand what evidence-based mental health practice is as well those wanting to grasp the challenges of implementing evidence-based practices. In an accessible style with numerous case examples, *Evidence-Based Mental Health Practice* provides an in depth view of the six evidence based practices for persons with severe mental illness, including assertive community treatment, supported employment, and family psychoeducation. An essential read for practitioners, administrators, and students alike."

> — Phyllis Solomon, Ph.D., Professor, School of Social Work, and Professor of Social Work in Psychiatry, Department of Psychiatry, School of Medicine, University of Pennsylvania

---

**The New Hampshire-Dartmouth Psychiatric Research Center**

The editors are affiliated with the New Hampshire-Dartmouth Psychiatric Research Center (PRC). The PRC was established in 1987 as a public–academic liaison involving the New Hampshire Division of Behavioral Health and the Dartmouth Medical School. Current areas of research include:

- Implementation of Evidence-Based Practices
- Vocational rehabilitation/supported employment
- Services for homeless persons
- Integrated treatment of co-occuring substance abuse
- Services for the elderly
- Trauma and post-traumatic stress disorder
- Infectious diseases (including HIV and Hepatitis)
- Methodology of services research

The PRC conducts interdisciplinary research on services for individuals who have severe mental illness, primary schizophrenia spectrum, and bipolar disorders. The PRC specializes in developing effective interventions under research conditions, then translating these interventions into actual mental health services practices and evaluating their effectiveness in routine practice settings. PRC research incorporates multiple scientific perspectives, such as clinical, economic, and ethnographic.

The PRC is a major center for the Evidence-Based Practices Initiative, a national project initiated by the Substance Abuse and Mental Health Services Adminstration's Center for Mental Health Services and the Robert Wood Johnson Foundation.

# Evidence-Based Mental Health Practice
## A Textbook

Edited by
Robert E. Drake, M.D., Ph.D.
Matthew R. Merrens, Ph.D.
David W. Lynde, M.S.W, L.I.C.S.W.

W. W. Norton & Company
New York • London

For information about permission to reproduce selections from this book, write to Permissions, W. W. Norton & Company, Inc., 500 Fifth Avenue, New York, NY 10110

Production Manager: Leeann Graham
Manufacturing by Quebecor World Fairfield/Martinsburg

**Library of Congress Cataloging-in-Publication Data**

Evidence-based mental health practice : a textbook / edited by Robert E. Drake, Matthew R. Merrens, David W. Lynde.
    p.   cm.—(A Norton professional book)
Includes bibliographical references and index.
**ISBN 0-393-70443-2 (pbk.)**
1. Mental health services. 2. Evidence-based psychiatry. I. Drake, Robert E. II Merrens, Matthew R. III. Lynde, David W. IV. Series.

RA790.5.E8427 2005
362.2—dc22     2004057508

W. W. Norton & Company, Inc., 500 Fifth Avenue, New York, N.Y. 10110
www.wwnorton.com

W. W. Norton & Company Ltd., Castle House, 75/76 Wells St., London W1T 3QT

1  3  5  7  9  0  8  6  4  2

We dedicate this book to those individuals and organizations that have passionately and tirelessly advocated improving community mental health services.

# Contents

# Contents

# | Editors and Contributors

**Susan T. Azrin, PhD**, is a clinical psychologist and senior study director at Westat, a company that conducts mental health services research and program evaluation for adults with severe mental illness.

**Gary R. Bond, PhD**, is Chancellor's Professor of Psychology at Indiana University–Purdue University, Indianapolis, where he has been on the faculty since 1983. His research has been devoted to evidence-based practices for individuals with severe and persistent mental illness, with a primary focus on supported employment and assertive community treatment.

**Patrick Boyle, LISW, CCDC III-E**, is a licensed independent social worker with certification as a chemical dependency counselor. He serves as Director of Clinical Training for the Ohio Substance Abuse and Mental Illness Coordinating Center of Excellence.

**Christina M. Delos Reyes, MD**, serves as the medical consultant to the Ohio Substance Abuse and Mental Illness Coordinating Center of Excellence and also treats patients at Recovery Resources, Inc., a community mental health center in Cleveland.

**Barbara Dickey, PhD**, is Associate Professor, Department of Psychiatry, Harvard Medical School and the Cambridge Health Alliance. She has been studying patterns of care, costs of care, and treatment outcomes of the most seriously mentally ill for 25 years.

**Lisa Dixon, MD**, is Professor of Psychiatry at the University of Maryland School of Medicine. She serves as Director of the Division of Services Research in the school's Department of Psychiatry, and as Associate Director for Research of the VA Mental Illness Research, Education and Clinical Center, the Capitol Health Care Network.

**Robert E. Drake, MD, PhD**, is the Andrew Thomson Professor of Psychiatry and Community and Family Medicine at Dartmouth Medical School and Director of the New Hampshire–Dartmouth Psychiatric Research Center. His work is focused on developing and evaluating innovative community programs for persons with severe mental disorders.

**Mary E. Evans, RN, PhD, FAAN**, is a professor and Associate Dean for Research and Doctoral Study at the College of Nursing, University of South Florida. Her research has focused on children and families.

**Melinda Fox, MA, LADC**, is a research associate at the New Hampshire–Dartmouth Psychiatric Research Center and a faculty member in psychiatry at Dartmouth Medical School. She has worked extensively on several research projects examining the effectiveness of treatment for people with serious mental illnesses and substance use disorders.

**Kenneth J. Gill, PhD, CPR**, is Founding Chair and Professor of Psychiatric Rehabilitation and Behavioral Health Care at University of Medicine and Dentistry of New Jersey—School of Health Related Professions. He is Vice-President of the Certification Commission for *Psychiatric Rehabilitation* and Associate Editor of *Psychiatric Rehabilitation Skills*.

**Susan Gingerich** is an independent consultant, trainer, and an author of books, chapters, and treatment manuals. She has over 20 years of experience working directly with people with mental illness and their family members.

**Richard J. Goscha, MSW**, is Director of Training and Technical Assistance for the University of Kansas School of Social Welfare's Office of Mental Health Research and Training and a doctoral student in social welfare at the University of Kansas.

**Howard H. Goldman, MD, PhD**, is Professor of Psychiatry at the University of Maryland School of Medicine. He is the author of numerous publications and serves on the editorial boards of many journals. Dr. Goldman contributed to the Surgeon General's Report on Mental Health and was a consultant to the President's New Freedom Commission on Mental Health.

**Paul G. Gorman, EdD**, is Director of the West Institute at the New Hampshire–Dartmouth Psychiatric Research Center and a faculty member of Dartmouth Medical School. He has also held several senior management positions in a community mental health centers.

**Gretchen Grappone** is a research associate at the New Hampshire–Dartmouth Psychiatric Research Center and at Dartmouth Medical School. She is a NAMI–New Hampshire board member and has spoken extensively about her personal experience with depression, its treatments, and the stigma associated with the disease.

**Gary Haugland, MA**, is a research scientist at the Nathan S. Kline Institute for Psychiatric Research and on the faculty of Center for the Study of Issues in Public Mental Health. His current research interests include service system issues for persons from diverse cultural groups,

**Lon Herman, MA**, is Program Director for Residency, Training, and Learning for the Ohio Department of Mental Health and also Assistant Professor of Psychiatry with the

Medical College of Ohio, Department of Psychiatry. She is responsible for the development of seven statewide mental health Coordinating Centers of Excellence in Ohio.

**Amanda Jones** is a doctoral student in the clinical rehabilitation psychology program at Indiana University–Purdue University, Indianapolis.

**Richard A. Kruszynski, LISW, CCDC III-E**, is a licensed independent social worker and certified chemical dependency counselor. He has extensive experience in both mental health and substance abuse treatment programs.

**H. Stephen Leff, PhD**, is Senior Vice-President at the Human Services Research Institute and Assistant Professor of Psychology at Harvard Medical School. His work has focused on evaluation and planning in mental health systems.

**David W. Lynde, MSW, LICSW**, is the training manager for the West Institute at the New Hampshire–Dartmouth Psychiatric Research Center and faculty member of Dartmouth Medical School. He provides training and consultation regarding the implementation of evidence-based practices.

**Mike McKasson, MA, LCSW**, is Co-Director of the Assertive Community Treatment Center and Director of Adult Services at Adult and Child Mental Health Center. He has over 27 years of clinical experience working with adults who have serious and persistent mental disorders.

**Matthew R. Merrens, PhD**, is Visiting Professor of Psychiatry at Dartmouth Medical School and the New Hampshire–Dartmouth Psychiatric Research Center. He has extensive experience in clinical psychology and community mental health and has authored and edited a number of textbooks in psychology.

**Alexander L. Miller, MD**, is Chief of the Division of Schizophrenia and Related Disorders and Director of the Schizophrenia Module of the Texas Medication Algorithm

Project at University of Texas Health Science Center, San Antonio. His research has focused on examining the effects of new antipsychotics and on the long-term medication management of schizophrenia.

**Gary Morse, PhD**, is President of Community Alternatives: Innovations in Behavioral Care, a community health organization that specializes in services for low-income and homeless people, especially those with severe mental illness. He is Adjunct Professor of Psychology at the University of Missouri, St. Louis. He is also the national trainer and consultant for the EBP project on assertive community treatment.

**Kim T. Mueser, PhD**, is a licensed clinical psychologist and a Professor in the Departments of Psychiatry and Community and Family Medicine at the Dartmouth Medical School and at the New Hampshire-Dartmouth Psychiatric Research Center. His clinical and research interests include the psychosocial treatment of severe mental illnesses, dual diagnosis, and posttraumatic stress disorder. He has published extensively and given numerous lectures and workshops on psychiatric rehabilitation.

**Aaron Murray-Swank, PhD**, is a post-doctoral fellow at the VA Mental Illness Research, Education and Clinical Center, the Capitol Health Care Network. His work has focused on psychosocial rehabilitation for individuals with serious mental illness, with a particular speciality in developing and evaluating rehabilitation services.

**Phyllis Panzano, PhD**, is on the faculty at Ohio State University. Her research over the past 20 years reflects her commitment to applying industrial-organizational psychology and organizational behavior knowledge to the challenges facing individuals and organizations within the mental health domain. In addition, she operates Decision Support Services, Inc., a research and consulting firm.

**Carlos W. Pratt, PhD, CPRP**, is a professor and Director of Graduate Programs in Psychiatric Rehabilitation,

Department of Psychiatric Rehabilitation, School of Health Related Professions, University of Medicine and Dentistry of New Jersey. He has many years of experience designing and administering services for persons with severe mental illness.

**Charles A. Rapp, PhD**, is a professor at the University of Kansas School of Social Welfare and Director of the Office of Mental Health Research and Training. He is the codeveloper of the strengths model of case management and the client-centered performance model of social administration.

**Robert Schore, MS, CSW**, is a media consultant and writer at the Nathan S. Kline Institute for Psychiatric Research Center for Study of Issues in Public Mental Health. As a clinical social worker, he has worked extensively with culturally diverse populations in ethnic neighborhoods of New York City.

**Carole Siegel, PhD**, is Director of Statistics and Services Research Division at the Nathan S. Kline Institute for Psychiatric Research, a research professor of psychiatry at New York University School of Medicine, and an adjunct professor at the NYU Robert F. Wagner Graduate School of Public Administration. Research areas of interest are the development of services research methodologies, including mental health indices and performance measures, and quantitative policy analysis of financial and economic issues.

**David L. Shern, PhD**, is a professor and Dean of The Louis de la Parte Florida Mental Health Institute. As a college of the University of South Florida, the de la Parte Institute is one of the largest research and training Institutes in behavioral health in the United States. Dr. Shern's professional interests involve understanding the impacts of differing organizational, financing, and program approaches on the outcomes experienced by adults with severe mental illnesses.

**William C. Torrey, MD**, is Associate Professor of Psychiatry at Dartmouth Medical School, Research Director of the West Institute at the New Hampshire–Dartmouth Psychiatric Research Center and as Medical Director of Dartmouth's local community mental health center. His research interests have focused on supported employment for adults with severe mental illnesses and on strategies for implementing evidence-based practices.

Prologue

# | "Helpful" Mental Health Services

*David W. Lynde*

AS A BACHELOR'S LEVEL SOCIAL WORKER, I applied for a case manager position at a community mental health center in February 1987. I had recently resigned as the director of a small group home for adolescent females. One reason for my resignation was my frustration that the sole interest of the administration in the program appeared to be its financial viability. I wanted to be asked about the interventions or services that we were providing, or how our program was helpful to the residents, but instead I fielded constant questions about revenues and budgets. So I interviewed for a new position, hoping to return to the social work values that had attracted me to the field—primary among them, helping people.

I asked one of the case managers what the best part of the job was and he said, "You learn that people with mental illness are just people too." That response bounced around in my head for days, providing some assurance that I was returning to the right values, with the right peers and philosophy. In my first "supervision" meeting as a case manager, my supervisor told me, "You are the only tool that

This project is supported by an unrestricted grant from the Eli Lilly Foundation, the Johnson & Johnson Charitable Trust, the West Family Foundation, and the Robert Wood Johnson Foundation.

you have to do this job." So there I was, in a new position, with a new mission, and the only tool I had was myself.

As a new case manager, I received lots of information, support, and consultation from a committed, hard-working group of colleagues who were focused on being helpful and responsive to the needs of the "clients" with whom we had the privilege of working. It seemed that our mission could be described in a rather simple fashion; as case managers, clinicians, and other community support staff, our job was to help clients stay out of the hospital. We had the capacity to refer clients to inpatient hospital services when necessary, but most importantly, we strove to help people live in the least restrictive environments possible.

A key part of our mission was to help clients establish incomes that would enable them to live in independent, supported, or shared housing. Entitlement programs were a primary source of this income, and we all worked diligently to help clients apply for Medicaid, Aid to the Permanently and Totally Disabled (APTD), Supplemental Security Income (SSI), Social Security Disability Income (SSDI), and housing subsidies.

In the midst of establishing eligibility for permanent disability (a hope-robbing term) benefits with clients, work was a complicating factor. How could a person simultaneously apply for disability insurance and apply for employment? Furthermore, the concept of employment seemed to be more of an end goal of treatment than a meaningful therapeutic activity. I still shudder as I recall some conversations with clients. "Perhaps it would be better if you chose not to work right now," or "Let's see if we can get your symptoms under control first and then we can think about work." I worked with one client who managed to be hired for more than a dozen jobs in about a year's time. When I look back, with some embarrassment, I think I wanted him to work out his anger (which I thought was the problem) in therapy. Sadly, it never occurred to me that he needed help in the form of on-the-job support to develop skills and strategies to manage conflicts that arose with his coworkers.

Our Community Support Program director was
committed to providing staff with training and information
about what was happening in the field of mental health. We
had the opportunity to participate in trainings that challenged us to think about what we were doing in order to be
helpful to people with mental illness. During one statewide
conference, we were exposed to information about effective ways to work with clients who experience co-occurring
mental illness and substance use problems (also referred to
as *dual disorders*). Our state system began a major initiative
in cooperation with the New Hampshire–Dartmouth
Psychiatric Research Center for dual-disorder services.
Many of us had struggled with how to be helpful as we
worked with clients whose lives were complicated by dual
disorders. This project provided a chance to evaluate our
practices and learn new skills to be more effective.

During the course of the training, each community
mental health center was asked to designate an agency
"champion" for dual-disorders treatment. One of our clinicians, who had a strong interest in this area, attended
monthly training sessions in this model and disseminated
the information, along with research articles, to the rest of
our staff. We began to learn about assessment tools, stages
of change, and especially group treatment. The way we
provided services to clients with dual diagnoses improved as
a result of the commitment of the state system, the agency,
and one clinician's commitment to change. We also noticed
that as we provided more effective services, more of the
clients that we worked with also began to ask for these services, especially the stage-wise groups.

Of course, some of us stumbled through the learning
process. For example, I learned the importance of screening
for substance use disorders in clients long before I learned
the valuable information about matching interventions with
the appropriate stages of treatment. I was working with a
client who had undergone several hospitalizations as a result
of severe symptoms associated with schizophrenia. During
our first conversation about the use of alcohol and its impact

on his life, I suggested that he attend an Alcoholics Anonymous group in the community. At our next meeting, I asked him if anything had been useful to him in attending the meeting. "Yes, I learned that I need to stop taking all of these medications to get into recovery, and I learned that all of the problems in my life have to do with alcohol, and none of them have anything to do with any type of mental illness."

During the early 1990s a trend began to emerge as the conferences and trainings we attended focused more on client-centered services. We were exposed to "new" information about client empowerment and how to better understand and help clients to achieve their own goals. Annual statewide conferences facilitated by "Partners for Change," a coalition of consumers; state mental health authority people; community providers; and the state National Alliance for Mental Illness (NAMI) all emphasized this change. The philosophy of collaboration and client evaluation of services became more evident. We were exposed to new treatment ideas, including methods to use when working with clients who have trauma histories.

During my graduate social work training, I continued to receive more education about mental health services and methods by which to become an effective consumer of research information. The concepts of truly being with clients and learning to understand them as individuals, family members, and members of many different "systems" (some empowering, some oppressing) were stressed. Not surprisingly, one of the key concepts in most of our clinical courses was how to use the *Diagnostic and Statistical Manual* (Third Edition—Revised) for differential diagnosis and assessment.

I practiced signing my name with the initials *MSW* even before I was graduated. I wondered what was different about what I now knew regarding how to help clients. A funny thing happened on my way to "becoming" a clinician: I began to learn that a good deal of my learning came from the clients themselves. They were a good source of information about what was helpful, and they let me know when I made mistakes. I made plenty of them.

Good leadership produced some valuable improvements in our Community Support Program. Our director decided that we would provide family support services. Many of us invested in protecting boundaries and client confidentiality offered objections to this change. I, like many of my colleagues, thought this kind of shift would make things worse and undermine our "therapeutic" relationships with clients. We were on another learning curve. Family support services proved to be a great resource for clients, families, and the rest of our staff working to help clients achieve their goals.

Our state mental health system established agency reimbursement rates that were adjusted depending on the employment rate of clients at our agency. As a result, another new program, employment services, was introduced, engendering a new set of fears and a new set of reasons for some of us to resist this change. Clients were fearful of work, weren't they? Isn't that what I had been telling them? Years later our employment services coordinator would remind me of my reluctance. "For a long time, we didn't have any referrals from you for any of the clients that you were working with." She was right. Employment services became another useful service that helped clients achieve their goals.

A new client-driven concept was also on the horizon—the philosophy of, and commitment to, *recovery*. There was something significantly different about this perspective. Our old and familiar mission of keeping clients out of the hospital was being challenged. A new goal was set: help consumers to establish a meaningful sense of self, purpose, hope, and direction. One of our administrators commented on this new philosophy with some disdain, "Nothing really new . . . just what we have been doing for years with a different name." The clients with whom we worked were clear that there was indeed something very different about this perspective, and they were a big part of helping many of us to see what was important.

Effective system leadership can create effective system-based changes. Our state mental health authority supported the movement toward a recovery orientation. Providers were repeatedly told that providing community support services in consumers' communities was more effective than providing services at our center. We did not respond to that philosophical change until the state mental health authority changed the reimbursement incentives. The rate for community-based services was raised higher than the rate for center-based services. The mission was to provide illness management services with clients in their community. We did not have a structured or well-developed method of providing these services, but we were told *where* we would be providing those services—in the community.

As with many clinicians who had obtained state licenses, I was asked to provide clinical supervision at our agency. Again I asked myself, "What do I know now that would enable me to provide good supervision?" I tried to piece together what seemed useful from my exposure to several previous clinical supervisors. I gathered some articles to read, and even a book, but the information that I was looking for seemed to elude me.

Few things challenged what I thought I knew about mental health services more than preparing to teach in a university social work department. I wondered what it would take to be a good teacher and, more importantly, what were the most important things to teach that were actually effective in helping people with a mental illness. The next academic year I began to teach a course on social work and mental illness. I was quickly humbled by the realization that there was so much existing information on effective mental health treatments. I wondered why I had never bridged the gap between what I practiced and what the research described as effective. I stayed in this stage of contemplation for some time.

I worked in several positions in our Community Support Program (CSP), and eventually as CSP Director. Our program involved several components of "traditional" services, with case management at the core. One of these components was a day treatment program. Despite the lack of much good evidence that day treatment was useful, I fought to continue this program. As CSP director, one aspect of day treatment became very clear to me: It was a financial engine that could pull much of the CSP program. Without much thought or effort, I found myself thinking about finances rather than social work values. Our state Division of Mental Health contracted with some well-trained providers to develop a paper on "preferred practices" for community mental health services in the state. While attending a meeting regarding a draft of this document, I was angered to learn that they had not identified day treatment as a preferred practice. I even took the time to write to them with some suggested language about including day treatment. None of my suggestions was based on research: all were driven by my monetary-based desire to keep our "valuable" day treatment program in place.

After leaving my position as CSP director, I became aware of the wealth of scientific information about mental health services and felt embarrassed about what I had not implemented in my previous positions in community mental health. Some of the services I, or we, provided were good, because they were based on good models and were supported by the state mental health authority as a result of the collaboration with the New Hampshire–Dartmouth Psychiatric Research Center. Some of the services may have been moderately helpful because we were "lucky." Most of our luck, however, came from consumers who were patient enough to teach us; some came from good leadership and some came from a very dedicated and compassionate staff. Some of the services showed no evidence of being helpful for consumers and their families, but we contined them based on the "that is what we do here" model.

Our field is now challenged by another important evolution, known as evidence-based practices (EBPs). These are services, such as competitive employment, that have demonstrated their effectiveness in helping consumers to achieve their own goals. These practices are based on the values of supporting consumers in hopeful ways to achieve their own goals, to develop meaningful roles in the community, to establish identities beyond the symptoms and impairments of mental illness, and, most importantly, to support the recovery process. In the mental health field, we are now confronted with a sense of obligation, especially in our roles as public mental health authorities, community mental health agency administrators, and individual mental health practitioners, to understand these practices and to implement them in order to provide the best available services to consumers.

Economic difficulties and scarce resources are often identified as barriers to implementing evidence-based practices. Often people ask "How can we invest limited resources in evidence-based practices?" Perhaps we should ask "How can we afford to invest our increasingly limited mental health resources in services for which there is no evidence of effectiveness?"

Consumers have taught many of us valuable lessons about living with a mental illness and lessons about critical values and ingredients for mental health services. One of those lessons is that people with mental illness can, and do, achieve recovery, with support, hope, commitment, and hard work. Perhaps the same challenge holds true in our mental health system. With the combination of evidence-based practices, hope, hard work, and commitment, can our mental health system achieve recovery?

It is our intention, as the editors and authors of this book, to provide information regarding the evolution of evidence-based practices, including some of the currently identified EBPs. *Evidence-Based Mental Health Practice* explores some of the complex challenges involved in efforts to implement EBPs, and it highlights the meaningful opportunities that are inherent in this paradigm shift. We are grateful for the vast amount of time, energy, and hard work that has gone into the publication of this work and hope that we are contributing to the profound discussion regarding "effective helpers," as we work with individuals and families with mental illness in making progress in their recovery process.

*Part I*
# BACKGROUND

ONE

# | What Is Severe Mental Illness?

*Barbara Dickey*

THIS CHAPTER DESCRIBES THE NATURE OF severe mental illness (SMI), the history of its treatment, and the challenges to integrating the lives of individuals with serious mental illness into the social fabric of our society.

## Early History of Serious Mental Illness

Severe mental illness is not new. As early as Homer we have descriptions of those possessed by the gods: "*Entheos* refers to a god within who might speak only to the chosen one, exciting wild and uncoordinated movements or induce a frenzy as the sign of divine anger or lead the victim to speak in tongues" (Robinson, 1996, p. 9). Ulysses unsuccessfully feigned madness to avoid going to war with Troy. Even in classical Greek and Roman texts there are discussions of the culpability of individuals who, in the words of Plato, are in a state of madness and have committed a crime. The recorded treatment (or not) for thousands of years often depended on the interpretation of behavior within the social context: Were they healers, the voice of the Divine, or wicked witches doing the work of Satan? Depending on how behaviors were

Entheos

1

interpreted, the "treatment" might be anything from eleva-
tion to priesthood to burning at the stake.

Age of Enlightenment

The idea that mental illness was a disease began to grow
during the Age of Enlightenment, when reason began to
compete with superstition as the prevailing explanation of
human behavior. Where once "lunacy" was believed to be
caused by the gods or evil spirits and demonic possession
was the sign of witchcraft, the growth of geographic exploration spurred the advancement of science. One of the
earliest writings that attributed madness to a disease was
Robert Burton's *The Anatomy of Melancholy*, which declared
that the diseases arising from the brain include "phrenzy,
lethargy, melancholy, madness, weak memory, sleeping sick-
ness or insomnia" (Burton, 1628, as cited in Robinson,
1996, p. 108). The cures he prescribed for melancholy
included prayer, diet, medicine, laxatives, diuretics, fresh
air, exercise, games, shows, music, merry company, wine,
sleep, and bloodletting. By the early 1700s, the treatment of
those with mental disabilities was more institutional in this
country and in Europe. In colonial America, towns had the
power to assume responsibility for those who were seriously
mentally ill and the poor in their communities by establishing almshouses. Although the willingness of communities to support efforts on behalf of those among them who
were less fortunate marked an important step in social
reform, conditions were wretched and medical attention
almost nonexistent (Grob, 1994).

Emergence
of asylums

Gradually, special hospitals, called *asylums*, were built for
those with the means to pay for treatment in far more
acceptable settings. Here patients received "moral treatment," a movement begun in France by Philippe Pinel at
the end of the 18th century. He believed that afflicted
people with serious mental illness could recover because,
despite their madness, they retained a part of their brain
that could respond to reason. Asylum was an essential part
of the treatment, and as the popularity of moral treatment
spread, so did asylums. At the same time in England,
Quakers were establishing the York Retreat, where the envi-

ronment was designed to encourage internal self-restraint. Benjamin Rush, a noted physician in Philadelphia, was among those who believed that the treatment of the mentally ill should have a medical basis. But it was Dorothea Dix of Massachusetts who led the campaign in this country to move the indigent mentally ill out of the overcrowded and miserable almshouses to asylums, often outside of towns in the countryside. Worcester State Hospital, the first  of these built in 1833, still exists, high on a wooded hill overlooking the city of Worcester, Massachusetts.

## Defining Severe Mental Illness

Because mental illnesses vary in their manifestation in individuals, it is important to be able to identify those people who have the most severe forms of mental illness for several reasons. First, appropriate treatment then can be made available; some health plans have more generous reimbursement schedules for the treatment of serious mental illness. Second, disability, if it occurs, can be assessed and documented thereby entitling the individual to health benefits and supplemental income through government programs. Finally, accurate definitions of specific disorders are the sine qua non of clinical research that tests the efficacy of medications or other treatments.

Historical reports of mental illness describe it in ways that often linked it to superstition or religious beliefs. Efforts to make diagnoses more "scientific" have led to classification systems that describe moods and behaviors so that different disorders can be labeled and treated differentially. Early efforts at categorization of mental illnesses resulted in the *Diagnostic and Statistical Manual of Mental Disorders*, (*DSM*), first published in 1918 and updated repeatedly to reflect growing knowledge of the etiology and epidemiology of mental illnesses.

*Severe mental illness* is a broad term used to separate the "mad" from the "sad": Severe mental illness may require hospitalization and is characterized by episodes of illness

*Diagnostic and Statistical Manual (DSM)*

Defining SMI

that cause substantial disruption in everyday life. In this way SMI is unlike other mental illnesses that are emotionally painful but less disruptive and more transient. Considerable controversy still exists about just how to define severe mental illness and how those so afflicted are different from those who are not. However, there is universal agreement that the tragedy of severe mental illness is the number of people who suffer untreated, are treated inappropriately, or who lose their lives earlier than expected because of higher incidence of medical illnesses and suicide.

**New Freedom Commission definition**

The definition used in the recent report of the President's New Freedom Commission on Mental Health (NFCMH 2003) requires that three criteria be met: (1) the person has a mental, behavioral, or emotional disorder (2) of sufficient duration to meet diagnostic criteria specified within the current *DSM*, and (3) which has resulted in functional impairment that substantially interferes with or limits one or more major life activities (Section 1912 [c] of the Public Health Services Act, as amended by Public Law 102/321).

### Functional Impairment

*Functional impairment* is defined as difficulties that substantially interfere with, or limit, an individual's performance of basic daily living skills (e.g., eating, bathing, dressing), instrumental living skills (e.g., maintaining a household, managing money, getting around in the community, taking prescribed medication), and functioning in social, family, and vocational or educational contexts (NFCMH, 2003). Notice that the definition of SMI does not specify diagnostic categories, only that the disorder meets the criteria set forth in the *DSM*. There is general agreement that diagnoses, in and of themselves, do not provide criteria for the severity of a mental illness that a person experiences. Nevertheless, some definitions used to specify which individuals are eligible for special community support services exclude certain diagnostic categories that may result in disability. For example, in Massachusetts, to be eligible to receive Department of Mental Health continuing care services, an adult must have a mental illness that:

Massachusetts service criteria

1. Includes a substantial disorder of thought, mood, perception, orientation, or memory that grossly impairs judgment, behavior, capacity to recognize reality, or the ability to meet the ordinary demands of life; and
2. Has lasted, or is expected to last, at least 1 year; and
3. Has resulted in functional impairment that substantially interferes with, or limits, the performance of one or more major life activities, and is expected to do so in the succeeding year; and
4. Meets diagnostic criteria specified within the current edition of the *DSM*, which indicates that the individual has a serious, long-term mental illness that is not based on symptoms primarily caused by substance-related disorders, mental retardation, or organic disorders due to a general medical condition.

This definition is narrower than the one provided in the President's New Freedom report because it excludes certain primary diagnoses. This type of definition, which gives explicit criteria for an individual's eligibility to receive services, is designed to make it easier for government agencies to distinguish who among those people who seek treatment are in greatest need and are not able to access services elsewhere.

## Psychosis

The most common problem for people with severe mental illness is psychosis, which is a state of mind characterized by loss of contact with reality. Episodes of psychosis may be transient and are not specific to any given diagnosis; they are a hallmark of schizophrenia and may occur during the manic phase of bipolar disorder. Individuals suffering from psychosis may have perceptions of reality that are strikingly different from the reality perceived by others around them. They may be unable to distinguish what is real from what is not real because their experiences are distorted by hallucinations and delusions, with the result that they may feel frightened, anxious, and confused.

**Hallucinations** | *Hallucinations* are perceptions that are not connected to an appropriate source. Although hallucinations can occur in any sensory form—auditory (sound), visual (sight), tactile (touch), gustatory (taste), and olfactory (smell)— hearing voices that other people do not hear is the most common type of hallucination in schizophrenia. These voices may describe activities, carry on a conversation, warn of impending dangers, or even issue orders to the individual.

**Delusions** | *Delusions* are false beliefs, held by an individual, that are not subject to reason or contradictory evidence. For example, people suffering from paranoid-type symptoms often have delusions of persecution; that is, false and irrational beliefs that they are being cheated, harassed, poisoned, or conspired against. Delusions of grandeur, in which a person may believe he or she is a famous or important figure, also occur. Delusions can be quite bizarre; for instance, believing that a neighbor is controlling his or her behavior through magnetic waves; that people on television are directing special messages to him or her; or that his or her thoughts are being broadcast to others.

## Schizophrenia

Schizophrenia is a psychiatric disorder marked by hallucinations and delusions, disturbances in thought and emotion, and impaired interpersonal functioning and relationship to the outside world that lasts for at least 6 months. Onset is usually during adolescence or early adulthood. Researchers have found a slightly higher rate of schizophrenia among individuals who have first-degree biological relatives diagnosed with schizophrenia.

## Bipolar Disorder

Bipolar disorder, formerly called manic–depression, is a mood disturbance marked by alternating episodes of mania and depression. The essential feature of an episode of mania is a predominant mood that might be euphoric, expansive, or irritable. The disturbance is sufficiently severe to cause marked impairment in occupational functioning or in usual social activities. Associated symptoms may be delusions, decreased need for sleep, inflated self-esteem, and loud or rapid speech. Onset is usually in young adulthood. Bipolar disorder occurs more often among individuals who have first-degree biological relatives diagnosed with the same diagnosis.

## Major Depression

Major depression is a severe mood disorder marked by diminished interest or pleasure in activities of daily life. Symptoms (e.g., significant weight loss or gain, trouble sleeping, difficulty concentrating), may be so severe as to markedly interfere with working or relationships with others. In some cases, symptoms may include delusions or hallucinations.

## Epidemiology of Severe Mental Illness

*Epidemiology* is the branch of medicine that studies the distribution of diseases. Although estimates of the extent of serious mental illness vary depending on who is (and who is not) included in the definition, it is believed that in any given year 2–3% of the adult population suffers from the most severe forms of mental illness (Kessler, Berglund, & Shaw, 1996). Many others with serious mental illnesses are less disabled but have periodic episodes of illness that interrupt their day-to-day lives. These estimates are important because they are the foundation of congressional debate about continuing legislative support for health benefit programs and income support.

## Challenges to the Integration of People with SMI

Public health concerns

The treatment of persons with SMI is a major public health concern for several reasons. The disability associated with it SMI has an economic impact estimated to cost $79 billion

Costs

annually, which reflects lost productivity as well as treatment costs (Rice & Miller, 1996). Furthermore, most people with SMI are treated in the public sector; therefore, the services provided are directly or indirectly funded by tax revenues. Expenditures include health and long-term care benefits through Medicaid and related income support, Medicare, which includes health benefits and disability payments, and through state and local programs that provide mental health treatment and community support programs. The latter often include residential treatment programs. In addition to these categorical aid programs, the Department of Veterans Affairs treats military veterans with mental illness (treatment includes hospital and ambulatory care).

SMI and serious
health problems

Mental illness is also a public health concern because people with SMI often have serious medical problems. Research studies have shown that these medical problems may go undiagnosed or untreated for many individuals. People with SMI are sometimes unwilling to seek medical help or may have difficulty in describing their problems to a physician. Psychotic symptoms may interfere with a patient's ability to answer questions about the medical problem that brings him or her to the physician. These and other problems contribute to a disconcertingly higher than expected mortality rate for people with SMI (Dickey, Drembling, Azeni, & Normand, 2003).

SMI and substance
abuse

Finally, there is considerable evidence that adults with SMI often abuse alcohol and drugs at a higher rate than people in the general population. These substance abuse problems further complicate their lives and present increased challenges to providing effective services that help them in their recovery process. These individuals are often characterized as having a "dual diagnosis" or a "co-occurring disorder." Providing specially tailored services to people with co-occurring disorders is one of the most urgent issues in the mental health field today (Drake & Mueser, 1996).

In the following sections we review challenges that are widely discussed and that present vexing problems not easily resolved. Virtually all of these problems are linked, at least indirectly, to a larger question of how economic conditions and social class are related to the course of the lives of people with SMI. There are volumes of published studies on the higher rates of illness and death among people who are poor, especially, poor people from minority groups (Wilkinson & Marmot, 2003). Findings from mental health studies consistently report that this is also true for people with SMI. Research has also associated urbanization and industrialization with poorer outcomes of serious mental illness and there is some evidence that residents of rural areas or less developed countries have the benefit of the protective effect of life in less complex societies (Sugar, Kleinman & Heggenhousen, 1991).

*Challenging problems*

### Dementia Praecox versus Recovery

Ever since Emil Kraepelin, in 1878, described schizophrenia as *dementia praecox*, or dementia of early onset that reflects a decline of cognitive processes, clinicians have thought that this particularly severe disorder had a downward path that was irreversible. In the early 20th century, Eugen Bleuler was the first (but not the last) to disagree with this characterization of schizophrenia. His son, Manfred, carrying on his father's research, has written that many people with schizophrenia improved in later life and that 25–35% recovered from it. Since then there has been consistent evidence supporting this finding; unfortunately, the prevailing clinical view about recovery remains pessimistic about recovery. Consumers and mental health advocacy groups argue that this pessimistic view taints the view of clinicians in their work with consumers and family members. Without the concept of recovery, there is little incentive for professionals to offer hope to consumers and

*Social integration*

*Course of illness and recovery*

family members. The recovery movement has resurrected, and sometimes created, a sense of hope among those people with schizophrenia and other severe mental illnesses. Stories of recovery and developing a life that is integrated within the social fabric of the community have been published with increasing regularity. These stories rarely claim complete cures, and many are about individuals meeting and overcoming the challenges of living with SMI.

Recovery | According to the President's New Freedom Commission on Mental Health, recovery

> refers to the individual process in which people with serious mental illness are able to live, work, learn, and participate fully in their communities. For some people it is the development of a definition of life beyond being a person with a mental illness. For some individuals, recovery is the ability to live a fulfilling and productive life despite a disability. For others, recovery implies the reduction or complete remission of symptoms. Science has shown that having hope plays an integral role in an individual's recovery process. (NFCMH, Executive Summary, 2003, p. 5)

President's New Freedom Commission on Mental Health | The President's New Freedom Commission on Mental Health (2003) has taken direct aim at the notion that serious mental illness has a lifelong, debilitating course. Acknowledging the many challenges to treating serious mental illness, the report states that the goal of a transformed mental health system is recovery. The report concluded: "Because recovery will be the common, recognized outcome of mental health services, the stigma surrounding mental illnesses will be reduced, reinforcing the hope of recovery for every individual with a mental illness" (p. 6).

## Stigma

The actions and behaviors of some people openly draw attention to the presence of a mental illness. For others with SMI, their illness may be less visible. In either case, people with SMI often experience rejection, discrimination, and stigma. According to the New Freedom Commission on Mental Health, stigma

> refers to a cluster of negative attitudes and beliefs that motivate the general public to fear, reject, avoid, and discriminate against people with mental illnesses. Stigma about people with mental illness is widespread in the United States and other Western nations. Stigma leads others to avoid living, socializing, or working with, renting to, or employing people with mental disorders—especially severe disorders, such as schizophrenia. It leads to low self-esteem, isolation, and hopelessness. It deters the public from seeking and wanting to pay for care. Responding to stigma, people with mental health problems internalize public attitudes and become so embarrassed or ashamed that they often conceal symptoms and fail to seek treatment. (NFCMH Executive Summary, 2003, p.5)

In fact, even the label of mental illness is enough to stigmatize a person in both his or her personal and work life. The stigma of mental illness is inappropriate and demeaning, and it has a direct effect on the social integration of individuals with severe mental illness. Strauss and Carpenter (1981) have effectively captured the burden of stigma

Devastating impact of stigma

> Who can doubt the devastating impact on a fragile person of perceiving that the entire social milieu regards him (wittingly or not) as subhuman, incurable, unmotivated, or incompetent to pursue ordinary expectations . . . ? Can we doubt that a deteriorating course of disorder is fostered when fundamental roles are changed by social stigma and employment opportunities become limited? (p. 128)

The President's New Freedom Commission on Mental Health (2003), Mental Health: A Report of the Surgeon General (1999), and the National Health Consumer Association (1999) all identify discrimination and stigma as a barrier to recovery.

*Resilience*

The President's New Freedom Commission on Mental Health Executive Summary report also provides principles to guide the transformation of the mental health system. One of these principles incorporates the goal of recovery: "care must focus on increasing consumers' ability to successfully cope with life's challenges, on facilitating recovery and on building resilience, not just on managing symptoms" (p. 5). *Resilience* refers to the personal and community qualities that enable people to rebound from adversity, trauma, tragedy, threats, or other stresses and to go on with life with a sense of mastery, competence, and hope. Many people with SMI demonstrate profound resilience daily in their recovery process. We now understand from research that resilience is fostered by a positive childhood and includes positive individual traits (e.g., optimism, good problem-solving skills). Closely knit communities and neighborhoods are also resilient, and this quality allows them to provide supports for their members (NFCMH, 2003).

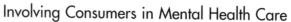

## Involving Consumers in Mental Health Care

Many factors—some historic, some contemporary—have led to the development of a stronger consumer voice in the delivery, research, planning, and policy development of mental health services. Consumers have long fought for active roles in their treatment process and for input as to what values, principles, and outcomes in treatment are most important. They make their point vividly by proclaiming "Nothing about us without us."

The nationwide pressure on cost containment and cost-reduction strategies, both in regard to managed care and budget cuts, has many mental health stakeholders concerned about the negative influence on the quality of mental health services. These concerns have grown as shrinking state tax revenues have placed an extra burden on the state public health system.

The active involvement of consumers in mental health services is important for many reasons. Consumers contend that their participation fosters accountability, increases consumer satisfaction, improves public confidence in the health-care system, provides an opportunity for collaboration, and improves decision making by incorporating consumer insights and firsthand information on service delivery. Hundreds, perhaps thousands, of consumers have become providers of mental health services in a variety of venues throughout this country, where they not only provide critical services but also function as poignant examples of hope and role models for other consumers.

| Advantage of consumer participation

One way that consumers have become involved in the health planning domain is by developing and implementing methods for monitoring the quality of health-care services (U.S. General Accounting Office, 1994). The result is a set of recommended indicators and measures for a mental health report card that is

| Mental health report card

- Consumer oriented
- Based on research and explicit values
- Focused on, but not limited to, serious mental illness
- Designed to emphasize the outcomes of mental health treatment

It remains to be seen how helpful such report cards, and other forms of consumer participation, are in improving the treatment of people with SMI.

## Involuntary Commitment

One of the thorniest problems in the mental health field is how to balance the individual rights of a person with SMI with those of society. The argument for involuntary treatment is that, when a person refuses treatment *and* is not competent to determine what is in his or her own best interest *and* presents an imminent threat to his or her own safety or the safety of others, the community has a responsibility to provide treatment. The legal process of making

| Balancing individual and social rights

| Imminent danger

this assessment varies from state to state; some require that a health-care professional make that judgment, others require a court to mandate, and some require a combination of the two. Just what constitutes "imminent danger" is a subjective judgement, and this subjective element has elicited opposition to any form of involuntary commitment. Many critics see such commitment as a blatant abuse of civil liberties, whereas others argue that, once the mental illness is treated and the person is better able to make judgments and speak for themselves, he or she will have increased opportunity for self-determination and a better quality of life. Commitment laws vary from state to state and do not always include forced treatment or the forced use of medications. That is, in some states a person can be involuntarily committed to a hospital to ensure his or her safety or that of others, but that person cannot be forced to accept treatment, including medications, while there. Those who oppose this approach describe individuals so committed as "rotting with their rights on" (Gutheil, 1980, p. 327). There have been some efforts to establish outpatient involuntary treatment to avoid institutional commitments, but there is uneven application of this approach from state to state.

## SMI and Homelessness

Perhaps the most common and controversial application of involuntary commitment occurs with people who are both seriously mentally ill and homeless. In a famous case in New York City, the mayor, Edward Koch, announced in 1987, "morally and legally we have an obligation to help those who can't or won't help themselves" (Rochefort, 1993, p. 150). City workers identified street people who were in "foreseeable danger" and hospitalized them against their will. The first person so identified brought a lawsuit against the city (with the help of the ACLU), and after the suit worked its way through the courts, her release from Bellevue Hospital was obtained almost 3 months later. It is shocking to learn that the number of homeless people has grown by 40% in the last decade, at a time when the United States is the most wealthy and powerful country in the world. The most reliable count comes from the Urban Institute (Burt, Aron, Lee, & Balente, 2001), which estimated the number of homeless people in 1996, based on interviews conducted in a representative sample of rural and urban areas. The estimate was derived from data gathered from people who were using some type of homeless service and thus provides a conservative figure: 842,000 adults and children, up from 600,000 in 1987 (Burt et al., 2001). This same study arrived at an annual prevalence ranging from 2.3 to 3.5 million people. It is thought that about one-quarter of this population has a severe mental illness and about half of those individuals have a history of, or are currently affected by, substance abuse problems.

Homeless head count

In searching for the roots of homelessness for people with SMI, several authors have made compelling arguments based on economic theory. No authors who have delved deeply and broadly into the problem point to deinstitutionalization as a root cause. Instead, they note the lack of community-based services for people with mental illness, the difficulty of coordinating social and medical services, and the lack of attention that mental illness receives in our larger social agenda. All of these factors contribute to the plight of those who are homeless and mentally ill. There is widespread agreement that the ravages of mental illness, inpatient commitment laws, and substance use contribute to homelessness as vulnerabilities or risk factors rather than as "causes." Among people with SMI who are homeless, there is a disturbingly high incidence of substance use disorders. Breakey and Thompson (1997), in their summary of the McKinney Homeless Research Demonstration Programs, reported "ubiquitous" problems that challenged every project. Providing specially tailored services to people with co-occurring disorders is one of the most urgent issues in the mental health field today (Drake & Meuser, 1996).

Roots of homelessness

## Inadequate Health Insurance

No discussion of treatment for people with SMI can be held without including the topic of health insurance, or the lack thereof. Many people with SMI are not eligible for employer-based health insurance coverage. State administered Medicaid programs provide some health-care insurance benefits for people disabled by severe mental illness, but eligibility for this program varies by states, and many states are restricting and reducing both eligibility and state-optional covered benefits. The federal program, Medicare, which is also not universally available to those with disabilities who have a work history, provides limited mental health services coverage for people with SMI. For both Medicaid and Medicare recipients, finding a health-care provider who is willing to accept these benefits is a significant challenge.

Work disincentives

Both Medicaid and Medicare disability programs contain practical work disincentives for people with SMI. For example, Gilda is a 28-year-old female with SMI who hopes to work and has a goal of being employed at a bookstore. She has Medicaid benefits that provide coverage for medication and treatments to help her manage her symptoms of schizophrenia. However, if Gilda is able to obtain a job in a bookstore, she may loose her Medicaid health-care coverage (because the income from her work will exceed the allowable amount, or, by working full time, she will fail the "disability" threshold required for eligibility) that has been paying for the services and medications that help her to manage her symptoms so that she can hold a job in the first place. Gilda is faced with a difficult decision; she may be forced to choose between not working and keeping her Medicaid to pay for services so that she is able to function better or pursuing her goal of working, which may not include the health benefits she requires but pays more than her disability income. This is a classic "double-bind" situation that forces the individual to lose something, whatever decision is made. Many people, without SMI, use employment as a means to provide health-care coverage for themselves and their families. For people with SMI, employment often means losing rather than gaining health-care coverage. There are a number of federal and state-based work incentive programs underway to address this significant problem, with varying degrees of success and access.

## Concluding Comments

Social inequality and poverty have direct impacts on the lives of people with SMI, placing ethical issues of justice and equality squarely within the arena of public health. No consideration of the plight of those with SMI can avoid acknowledging that factors other than treatment have a profound effect on the course and outcome of the disorders. Our societal response to SMI is complicated; not only do we not yet know what causes it or how to cure it, but the realities of social class and the economic structure of our society reduce the likelihood of recovery. There is considerable evidence that there is a social gradient to the health status of our citizens, particularly, people with SMI. To summarize volumes of research in a single sentence, those people with more financial and other resources have lower rates of morbidity and mortality. A report from the World Health Organization (WHO; Wilkinson & Marmot, 2003) summarized much of this research by noting that this finding is consistent in every country, regardless of its global economic standing. The report goes on to state that "material circumstances are harmful to health . . . being poor, unemployed, socially excluded or otherwise stigmatized also matters" (p. 9). Improving the chances for those with SMI to become socially integrated into our society must be a priority for all those who work in this field.

## References

Breakey, W. R., & Thompson, J. W. (Eds.). (1997). *Mentally ill and homeless: Special programs for special needs*. Amsterdam: Harwood Academic Publishers.

Burt, M., Aron, L. Y., Lee, E., & Balente, J. (2001). *Helping America's homeless: Emergency shelters or affordable housing?* Washington, DC: Urban Institute Press.

Dickey B., Dembling, B., Azeni, H., & Normand, S. L. (2003). Externally caused death rates for adults with substance use mental disorders. *Journal of Behavioral Health Services and Research, 30*(1), 75–85.

Drake R. E., & Mueser, K. T. (1996). Alcohol use disorder and SMI. *Alcohol Health and Research World, 20,* 87–93.

Grob G. N. (1994). *The mad among us.* Cambridge, MA: Harvard University Press.

Gutheil, T. G. (1980). In search of true freedom: Drug refusal, involuntary medication and rotting with your rights on. *American Journal of Psychiatry, 137,* 327–328.

Kessler R. C, Berglund, P. A., & Shaw, S. (1996). The 12-month prevalence and correlates of serious mental illness. In R. W. Mandersheid & M. A. Sonnenschein (Eds.), *Mental health, United States* (DHHS Publication No. [SMA] 96-3098, pp. 59–70). Washington DC: U.S. Government Printing Office.

O'Flaherty, B. (1996). *Making room: The economics of homelessness.* Cambridge, MA: Harvard University Press.

President's New Freedom Commission on Mental Health (NFCMH). (2003). *Achieving the promise: Transforming mental health care in America.* DHHS Publication No. SMA-03-3832, Rockville, MD.

Rice, D. P., & Miller, L. S. (1996). The economic burden of schizophrenia: Conceptual and methodological issues and cost estimates. In M. Moscarelli, A. Rupp, & N. Satorius (Eds.), *Schizophrenia* (pp. 321–334). Chichester, UK: Wiley.

Robinson, D. N. (1996). *Wild beasts and idle humours.* Cambridge, MA: Harvard University Press.

Strauss J. S., & Carpenter, W. T. (1981). *Schizophrenia.* New York: Plenum.

Sugar, J. A., Kleinman, A., & Heggenhousen, K. (1991). Development's downside: Social and psychological pathology in countries undergoing social change. *Health Transition Review, 1,* 211–220.

U.S. Department of Health and Human Services (DHHS). (1999). *Mental health: A report of the Surgeon General.* Rockville, MD: US Department of Health and Human Services, US Public Health Services.

U.S. General Accounting Office (GAO). (1994). *Health care reform: Report cards are useful but significant issues need to be addressed.* Washington, DC: Author.

Wilkonson, R., & Marmot, M. (2003). *Social determinants of health: The solid facts.* (Second Edition). Copenhagen: World Health Organization.

TWO

# What Are Community Mental Health Services?

*Carlos W. Pratt*
*Kenneth J. Gill*

THE DEINSTITUTIONALIZATION MOVEMENT BEGAN in the late
1950s, peaked in the 1970s and continues today in some
areas of the country. In response, the community mental
health system has developed and experimented with myriad
service models. Changes since 1960 have followed a pattern
similar to the course marked by personal computers, where
rapid change and obsolescence have been the rule.
Occasionally, treatment models and rehabilitation strategies became obsolete even before their outcomes were
studied. In some cases, agencies and systems have held on
to older, more provider-comfortable ways of service
delivery, despite increasing evidence of their ineffective-
ness. This chapter outlines the development of community-
based mental health services from deinstitutionalization
through the present. Many diverse service models still exist;
fortunately, we have entered an era of accountability in
which mental health programs are expected to provide
services of known effectiveness.

## From Institutionalization to Deinstitutionalization

As recently as the 1950s, many people in the United States
diagnosed with a severe mental illness, such as schizo-

Institutionalization
syndrome

phrenia, were institutionalized in large state-run psychiatric hospitals for years. Lengthy hospitalizations produced an institutional syndrome characterized by extreme dependency, despondency, and a loss of affect—symptoms similar to the negative symptoms of schizophrenia (Lehrman, 1961; Ridgway & Zipple, 1990; Schmieding, 1968). The inactivity and lethargy associated with this syndrome were difficult to distinguish from the symptoms of the original illness.

Advocacy movement | A growing mental health advocacy movement helped to increase public awareness of the plight of people residing in psychiatric institutions. In 1950, the National Association of Mental Health was formed through the merger of several similar longstanding organizations. These advocacy groups were effective at improving attitudes toward persons with mental illness and mental health services. During this period, public awareness of the plight of persons institutionalized in mental hospitals was also raised by books, such as *The Snake Pit,* and by movies, such as *Three Faces of Eve.* The media focus dramatized the fate of these individuals while emphasizing their essential humanity.

This time period also marked the discovery and initial applications of antipsychotic medications, such as chlorpromazine (Torrey, 2001). For many people with a mental illness, the new medications effectively reduced their symptoms.

Community mental health movement | Some notable examples of community mental health services also emerged. Partial hospital outpatient programs, modeled after inpatient services but without overnight stays, were developed in several settings. Former psychiatric hospital patients living in the community came together for mutual support in what would later emerge as the clubhouse movement. Nurses began to provide outreach services to help discharged patients function in the community. These activities all presaged the community mental health movement.

A case study of deinstitutionalization | The history of deinstitutionalization in New Jersey exemplifies the national experience. There were over 22,000 persons in New Jersey State Psychiatric hospitals before 1956. By 1994, even with a significant population growth, this number had shrunk to 3,400 persons (Torrey, 1997). Still, while this process was going on, each of the state's four large adult psychiatric institutions remained open. In his book *Out of the Shadows: Confronting America's Mental Illness Crisis*, Torrey (1997) discussed the fate of Ocean Grove, New Jersey, a small seashore town that was profoundly affected by deinstitutionalization. Much of Ocean Grove is comprised of large homes and seaside resorts from the Victorian era. The deinstitutionalization movement began to impact the town in the mid 1980s. "By 1992, there were 426 licensed boarding home beds for discharged psychiatric patients and approximately 200 more that were unlicensed" (Torrey, 1997, p. 63). In this small town of 5,600, about 600 individuals, more than 10% of the population, were discharged psychiatric patients, estimated to be proportionately the largest concentration of discharged patients in the country (Torrey, 1997). Ocean Grove stands out because of its small size relative to the influx of discharged patients. At the same time, the presence of large numbers of discharged patients is not unusual for large cities around the nation. For example, in the latter part of the 1970s, over 40,000 patients from New York State psychiatric hospitals were discharged to New York City (Kihss, 1980). In many cases across the country, planning for deinstitutionalized persons was woefully inadequate or entirely lacking. Living in a boardinghouse that did not provide adequate mental health services often did not offer any improvement over institutional care.

## The Community Mental Health Centers Construction Act

The shift from institutional to community-based services was accelerated when Congress passed the 1963 Community Mental Health Centers Construction Act (PL 88-164). This act provided a substantial amount of federal funding for the creation of comprehensive community mental health centers (CMHCs) around the nation.

Federally funded CMHCs were mandated to offer five essential services: outpatient treatment, inpatient treatment, crisis intervention services, consultation/education, and partial hospitalization programs. In most CMHCs the partial hospitalization program was the service of choice for recently deinstitutionalized individuals. Services often included psychiatric consultations, medication prescribing and monitoring, individual and/or group therapy, and other therapeutic modalities such as occupational therapy, skills training groups, recreation, and socialization. Whereas some CMHCs provided comprehensive services, others contracted with local clinics and other agencies to provide some of their services.

### Partial Hospitalization

The growth of partial hospitalization as a treatment approach was rapid and impressive, increasing nationally from 168 programs in 1963 to 1,280 programs in 1973, and serving approximately 186,000 patients per year (Taube, 1973). At the same time, state psychiatric hospitals around the country adopted more liberal discharge policies that affected nearly 90% of the patient population, or approximately 900,000 people, by 1995 (Torrey, 2001).

Inadequate services

Initially, most of the services available for the newly deinstitutionalized population were inappropriate, inadequate, and poorly staffed. A noted critic, Fuller Torrey, estimated that only about 5% of the 789 federally funded CMHCs seriously embraced the challenge of providing appropriate services for persons with severe mental illness (Torrey, 2001). Workers in traditional community mental health programs were unprepared for this challenge (Farkas, O'Brien, & Nemec, 1988; Stern & Minkoff, 1979; Torrey, 2001). Many professionals shunned people who were newly deinstitutionalized, because they were considered inappropriate subjects for the psychodynamic, insight-oriented treatments they had been trained to provide (Torrey, 1992). Possibly because of the low status associated with this population (Farkas et al., 1988), treatment programs for patients with severe mental illness were often staffed by persons without degrees in mental health. Because many of the deinstitutionalized persons had spent much of their adult lives in an institution, they presented with pervasive functional deficits and complex diagnostic, treatment, and management problems. They were often considered undesirable treatment cases and were therefore neglected (Amador & Johanson, 2000).

To further complicate matters, as community services for persons with lengthy institutional histories evolved, the services were found to be much less effective for the next generation of consumers, most of whom had not experienced the debilitating effects of long-term institutionalization (e.g., Pepper, Ryglewicz, & Kirshner, 1981; Ridgway & Zipple, 1990).

## The Federal Role

Since the mid-1800s, the care of people with mental illness in the United States has traditionally been the financial responsibility of the states, although some large cities and counties have also accepted this responsibility. Beginning with the Community Mental Health Centers Construction Act of 1963, the federal government assumed a larger role, and with the 1965 passage of Medicaid, the federal government took on a significant portion of the financial burden of providing services for this population. This change continues to have important ramifications for the types of services provided as well as the oversight of those services. Since each state is charged with designing how their Medicaid system will work and receives differing amounts of federal support, based on income formulas, there is significant diversity among states. Because many individuals with mental illness are disabled, unemployed, and poor, they are often eligible to receive federal entitlements such as Supplemental Security Income (SSI) or Social Security Disability Insurance (SSDI), which became available in 1972. These funds provide income support for the disabled people living in the community.

| Medicaid

Fee-for-service models | The increased availability of federal funds for the treatment of people with mental illnesses has had a profound effect on how states fund these services. Many states that had provided funding for services through various grant-in-aid formulas began switching to Medicaid fee-for-service models to maximize federal reimbursement and to reduce state expenditures. In such systems, a prominent emphasis on providing billable services strongly influences which services are offered to which consumers, and how these services are designed and implemented.

### The Influence of the Clubhouse Movement

Fountain House | A completely separate development, the clubhouse movement, which was started by former psychiatric hospital patients living in the community, has had a profound effect on the evolution of community-based services. Starting in the late 1940s, former patients banded together for mutual support and assistance and began to develop their own services. They emphasized quality-of-life issues, involving the need for social supports, work, and housing, rather than the treatment of symptoms. The first and most prominent clubhouse was Fountain House in New York City (Beard, Propst, & Malamud, 1982). With the support of community-based charitable associations and individuals, notably the National Council of Jewish Women and Elizabeth Schermerhorn, Fountain House residents were able to acquire their own building and hire some professional staff (Flannery & Glickman, 1996); this building, an old mansion, had a fountain, hence the name. Seeing themselves as a viable model for people with mental illness living in the community, and as a life-affirming alternative to the disease model approach of the CMHCs, the residents of Fountain House also offered their premises as an active training site for individuals interested in establishing new clubhouses around the country. This seeding of new clubhouses was instrumental in eventually creating a worldwide system of consumer-oriented programs, jointly operated by program members and staff. As the community-based system grew, the clubhouse movement was influential in its adoption of a more consumer-oriented, quality-of-life approach to services in contrast to the disease-oriented approach employed by many of the CMHCs. Today, the standards and philosophy of the clubhouse movement are maintained by the International Center for Clubhouse Development (ICCD). This group (*http://www.iccd.org/*) maintains and promulgates clubhouse standards, certifies programs as genuine clubhouses, holds meetings and conducts trainings for program members and professionals.

## The Emergence of Community Support Programs and Continuity of Care

As the deinstitutionalization movement progressed, the inadequacy of existing community-based services became increasingly apparent. Gradually, a national consensus emerged that the existing services were inadequate, unco-ordinated, and even nonexistent in many places. Innovative grass-roots initiatives, such as the clubhouse movement, were rare. In some aspects, many consumers were less well served in the community than they had been in the hospital. Community services were not well developed in many areas, in part because hospitals remained open and operating, precluding those financial resources from being redirected to develop needed community-based services.

National consensus

In response to the inadequacy of community services, the Congress acted again, this time passing the Comprehensive Mental Health Services Act (1973). This new act required each state to develop a plan for the provision of community-based services. In a further effort, in 1977 the National Institute of Mental Health (NIMH) created the Community Support Program (CSP; Turner & TenHoor, 1978). CSP funded demonstration projects around the country that emphasized case management as the central coordinating element in effective community-based services. The primary goal of these programs was to ensure the coordination and continuity of treatment services for consumers within a system that was fragmented and

Community support program

difficult to navigate. In addition, CSP case managers worked to ensure that consumers had access to services and that services were accountable and efficient.

### Training for Community Living and Assertive Case Management

Predecessor to ACT

Many of the early innovations in community treatment came about as the result of trial-and-error responses to persistent problems. For example, frustrated by the "revolving door" situation affecting many of the people they discharged, the staff at the Mendota Mental Health Institute, a large state psychiatric hospital in Wisconsin, began developing a new service strategy (Greenley, 1995). They observed that when workers followed discharged patients into the community to ensure that they were provided with adequate aftercare services, these patients were less frequently readmitted. These clients were more likely to connect with community services, continue to take their medications, and maintain stable housing arrangements. This strategy, begun in 1970, was called training in community living, an early version of assertive community treatment (ACT), which later evolved into one of the first evidence-based practices in psychiatric rehabilitation (Stein & Test, 1985). Of course, innovations do not emerge fully formed. Continuous refinement and constructive replications by other professionals eventually led to the evidence-based practice (EBP) we know today.

Assertive community<br>treatment—ACT

ACT represents a true paradigm shift from clinic-based services because it involves the provision of services in the environments where people live and work. Rather than requiring that individuals attend a clinic to receive services, the services are provided in the natural community settings where the individual resides. ACT services help to foster community integration. They are assertive in the sense that workers go into the community to meet their clients, making it more likely that medication is available when needed, housing problems are dealt with as they arise, and the problems of everyday life get the attention they need in a timely manner. ACT is described in detail in Chapter 14.

## Supported Employment

The low level of competitive employment of persons with severe mental illness, estimated to be between 0 and 30%, continues to be an important barrier to community integration and recovery (Anthony & Blanch, 1987; Anthony, Cohen, & Danley, 1988; Anthony, Cohen, Farkas, & Gagner, 2002). A number of strategies to increase employment has been utilized with minimal success, including sheltered workshops, skills training, transitional employment, and affirmative industries. The most successful strategy yet devised, supported employment, was given a boost by a 1986 amendment to the Rehabilitation Act. This amendment defined and authorized the federal funding of supported employment programs, making it a priority funded by 100% federal funds, meaning that no matching funds from states were required.

The supported employment strategy for improving employment outcomes was developed by professionals working with people who have developmental disabilities. Much of the initial work of adapting this strategy to community mental health was carried out at the Center for Psychiatric Rehabilitation at the Sargent College of Health and Rehabilitation Sciences, Boston University. Karen Danley, one of the founding members of the center, was one of the principle developers of the choose–get–keep model of supported employment (Danley & Anthony, 1987). The centerpiece of this strategy is its focus on the individual's interests, skills, and job preferences. This emphasis on client choice was combined with a place–train strategy, whereby individuals were aided in obtaining the job they wanted and then provided with supports and the on-the-job training necessary to keep the job. This approach was a marked improvement over the train–place strategies, usually called prevocational services, provided in partial hospital programs and other agencies. In a groundbreaking study, and contrary to the prevailing wisdom, Bond, Dietzen, McGrew, and Miller (1995) demonstrated that "train–place" strategies often resulted in a loss of motivation to work and poor vocational outcomes. By contrast,

Client choice and place–strategy

the place–train strategy of supported employment was found to be superior. Further developments and research refinements led to the development of the evidence-based supported employment approach, which is described in detail in Chapter 16.

## The Affordable Housing Problem

The process of deinstitutionalization pushed thousands of people with meager financial resources into communities and created immediate housing problems. People who were discharged from inpatient settings often lived in boarding homes, group homes, single-room occupancy residences (SROs), or foster care. Tragically, many became homeless. Most of the discharged psychiatric patients found their way to poorer neighborhoods in cities and towns that had an available supply of substandard housing. As large numbers of former patients moved in, many of these settings took on the characteristics of psychiatric hospital environments (Carling, 1995). These individuals were frequently confronted with social stigma, a lack of financial resources, and poor community living skills.

Residential services models

Some residential services models, notably the Fairweather Lodges, responded to this situation by developing essentially self-contained environments where individuals could both live and work in a sheltered setting (Onaga, 1994). These lodges included a group home, but unlike other group homes, individuals were often discharged *as a group* from hospitals directly into these settings. Residents typically worked together in small businesses, sometimes with other workers who did not have a mental illness. Probably due to their support characteristics, these lodges, which have some similarities with clubhouses, proved to be fairly effective at reducing recidivism (Onaga, 1994). Despite their cloistered nature, which is today seen as inconsistent with community integration and ultimately recovery, some lodges are still in operation.

Step-down system ineffective

The original residential services model was specifically designed to help people who were deinstitutionalized adjust to community living. The basic model was a linear continuum on which the first stop was a highly structured group setting with 24-hour staffing, similar to a hospital environment. As the individual acclimated to this setting and acquired some of the skills needed for community living, he or she would graduate to another setting that had less structure and less supervision, with the ultimate goal being independent living in the community. Although this approach appeared logical, this step-down system was rarely effective, especially for the population for which it was designed (Ridgway & Zipple, 1990). Individuals tended to resist moving out of housing situations in which they were comfortable. In addition, resident sometimes experienced increased difficulties from their psychiatric illness due to the stress of moving. Rehospitalized individuals would often be discharged into the same step-down system and have to start, once more, in the most structured and supervised setting.

The problems with this design became even more obvious as younger individuals who had not spent significant time in institutions moved into the system. These people were less tolerant of high levels of structure and staff control. Not surprisingly, surveys consistently confirm that persons with severe mental illness wanted the same types of housing options as people without mental illness (Tanzman, 1993; Yeich, Mowbray, Bybee, & Cohen, 1994).

**Desire for housing options**

The supported housing model rejected the idea of the linear continuum in favor of immediate placement in housing in which individualized supportive services are provided. This model supplanted the notion of placing individuals with severe mental illness in residential settings with its emphasis on individual choice. Supported housing consists of helping the individual obtain the best housing that fits his or her choices and resources, and then providing supports designed to help the person keep his or her home (Carling & Ridgway, 1991).

**Supported housing model**

## Self-Help and Consumer-Operated Services

It is not surprising that people with mental illnesses—all members of a highly stigmatized group that is openly shunned by society—would come together for mutual support. In fact, the self-help movement for persons with severe mental illness predates deinstitutionalization. Today the self-help movement is recognized as a viable support modality and receives significant public funding as well as research attention in some states (e.g., Meade, Hilton, & Curtis, 2001; Segal, Redman, & Silverman, 2000; Segal & Silverman, 2002). Peer-support programs provide safe and friendly places where individuals can experience support, socialization, advocacy, and recreation.

**Consumer providers**

Individuals with severe mental illness are also moving into the mental health profession. Known as consumer providers, peer advocates, or "prosumers," these self-identified persons with mental illness provide services to peers in a variety of settings (Manos, 1993). The concept of service recipients becoming service providers has been a long-standing one in the treatment of alcohol and substance abuse (Moxley & Mowbray, 1997). Employing consumer providers, often in advocacy roles, offers advantages for services (e.g., ACT) that require in-vivo contacts in a variety of settings. Moxley and Mowbray (1997) pointed out that in addition to their ability to relate well with peers, consumer providers are important role models for persons with severe mental illness. Limited research on the efficacy of consumer providers suggests that they compare favorably with nonconsumers in similar positions (Lyons, Cook, Ruth, Karver, & Slagg, 1996; Solomon & Draine, 1995). However, a recent review of the literature, conducted by Solomon and Draine (2001), stated that the evidence is insufficient to draw any conclusions about the effectiveness of these services. Despite the delay of including consumer providers in the community service delivery system, there is some evidence that the consumers themselves feel supported by the agencies where they are employed (Basto, Pratt, Gill, & Barrett, 2000). A potentially important yet untested phenomenon is the beneficial effect consumer providers may have on the culture of community-based services.

## Individual Interventions

Initially through trial and error and currently with the assistance of clinical trials, individualized services have been undergoing continuous refinement. This progress is demonstrated by the emergence of evidence-based practices (EBPs). There exists a significant lag time between the development of the evidence of a practice's effectiveness and its implementation in the mental health field. The President's New Freedom Commission on Mental Health (2003) quoted an Institute of Medicine report, which estimates that it takes 15–20 years for new treatments whose effectiveness has been established by clinical trials to become part of routine care.

### Medication Management

Medication is the most efficacious treatment yet available for the management of symptoms associated with severe mental illness. Collaboratively determining the most effective medication(s) at the correct dosage(s) to treat targeted symptoms and reduce or eliminate difficult side effects is the principle task of psychopharmacology. Additionally, providing education and discussion regarding the effective use of medications by individuals with mental illness to further their individual recovery process is important. One structured EBP method to accomplish this goal, illness management and recovery, is described in detail in Chapter 17.

### Supportive versus Psychodynamic Therapies

There is consistent evidence that psychodynamic insight-oriented strategies, whether in the form of individual or group therapy, are contraindicated for persons with severe mental illness (e.g., Linn, Caffey, Klett, Hogarty, & Lamb, 1979; May et al., 1981). Instead, therapies that focus on the development of skills and coping strategies to manage illness and daily life tasks, provided within a supportive context, tend to be effective.

The emphasis on practical coping strategies and on an individual's strengths and talents rather than deficits is the

Strengths model

central component of a perspective pioneered by Carl Rogers. This treatment orientation has been modified and championed as the strengths model by Charles Rapp and his colleagues at the University of Kansas (Rapp, 1997). This approach is based on the belief that a person with a severe mental illness has the capacity to learn, grow, and recover regardless of the severity of the illness. The strengths model emphasizes the achievement of meaningful consumer-centered goals in the individual's recovery process by building on strengths rather than focusing on deficits.

### Skills Training

One of the most widely employed rehabilitation strategies for persons with severe mental illness is that of skills training, provided to help people better navigate the challenges of daily living in the community. These strategies essentially employ a social learning theory to aid individuals in acquiring the skills they need to operate effectively in the environments of their choice (Anthony et al., 2002; Bandura, 1977; Liberman, DeRisi, & Meuser, 1989). Typical skill areas include (1) the activities of daily living, such as shopping, cooking, and cleaning; (2) illness management skills, such as taking medication and communicating with the psychiatrist; (3) social skills, such as making new friends and dating; and (4) vocational skills, such as filling out applications, interviewing, and interacting with coworkers. Illness management and recovery is an evidenced-based practice that includes significant skills training and is described, as noted, in Chapter 17.

### Environmental Modifications

Some people with psychiatric illnesses benefit from modifications that allow them to function effectively in the environments of their choice. Such accommodations might include a different scheduling of break times on the job, assistance with transportation, and the provision of active support from a mental health professional. The provision of these accommodations became a legal requirement in employment, schools, and public buildings with the passage of the Americans with Disabilities Act (ADA) in 1990.

## Emerging Trends

As is the case in general medicine, providing effective services in the early phase of mental illness has significant benefits for recovery. There is mounting evidence that early intervention strategies help to reduce both the severity and the intensity of impairments for people with schizophrenia and possibly mental illnesses in general. Evidence suggests that as the duration of untreated psychosis, which is estimated to range from one to two years on average, increased, the severity, chronicity, and resultant disabilities associated with the illness also increased (McGlashan, 1999).

| Early intervention strategies

### Supported Services

The development and growing adoption of services such as supported employment, supported education, supported housing, and ACT represent an important organizational and philosophical shift in the field of community services. These services share several characteristics that set them apart from traditional clinic-based services. Supported services are provided in one or more of the community-based environments in which the consumer lives, learns, or works, not in the clinic. At their core, supportive services are based upon the individual's goals and preferences, guided by consumer choices, and individualized.

| Philosophical shift in community services

Individual providers or teams working in the community usually offer supported services. To be effective, this service strategy requires a great deal more independent functioning, creativity, and flexibility on the part of the provider staff. The increased professionalism demanded by these services has important ramifications for old patterns of staff supervision, training, and assessment. Effective supported services workers may need more specific training and more experience than do clinic-based staff. Receiving services in the environments where they are needed tends to be less stigmatizing for the individual than requiring a person with

| Staff requirements and challenges

a mental illness to attend a partial hospital program or a mental health clinic. This service delivery strategy favors and encourages consumer choice because the possible options are unlimited, whereas clinic-based services are often designed to meet the needs of the service providers or large groups within the client population.

### EBPs

EBPs are services that have been empirically tested by independent researchers for their ability to reliably support consumers in reaching desired goals and outcomes. The degree to which a specific program or service adheres to the principles of the EBP model is termed *fidelity*. Programs that adhere closely to the EBP model are considered to have high fidelity, whereas programs that significantly diverge from the model are considered to have low fidelity. Not surprisingly, high-fidelity programs tend to have better outcomes than low-fidelity programs. *Fidelity scales* are instruments used to assess a program's fidelity with a specific EBP.

Fidelity scales

   The application of an EBP approach to community-based services extends the promise of several potential benefits. The regular use of fidelity scales offers an important tool for ongoing quality assessments and improvements for mental health agencies and systems. The use of outcome measures that are consistent with consumer goals and priorities provides the opportunity to better meet consumer needs and preferences. The adoption of EBPs also provides mental health systems with a mechanism with which to monitor and defend the use of increasingly scarce resources in meeting the treatment needs for individuals with mental illness. Despite the potential advantages, EBPs have not yet been widely adopted by community mental health delivery systems around the nation (Wang, Demler, & Kessler, 2002).

Advantages of EBPs

### Recovery

The concept of recovery provides individuals who experience mental illnesses with optimism, encouragement, and hope (Deegan, 1988). The essential idea is that recovery involves the gradual development of a new sense of self that incorporates the mental illness. This idea is similar to the use of concept in the substance abuse field, in which a person states that he or she is "in recovery" or "in the process of recovering." The recovery paradigm, strongly championed by many consumers, implies that each person's path to recovery is unique. This, in turn, lends credence to the tenet that services must be individualized (e.g., supported services), based on consumer choice, and not time limited (Anthony, 1993; Deegan, 1988).

### Early Intervention Strategies

There is mounting evidence that early intervention strategies help to reduce both the severity and the intensity of impairments for people with schizophrenia and possibly for people with mental illnesses in general. Evidence suggests that as the duration of untreated psychosis, which is estimated to average from 1 to 2 years, increases, the severity, chronicity, and resultant disabilities associated with the illness also increase (McGlashan, 1999). Longer durations of untreated psychosis may be the result of denial, lack of awareness of an illness, or withdrawal from social supports. Using neuropsychological and behavioral signs, McGlashan (2000) is studying the effects of treating people in the early and late premorbid (before the illness) phases of their illness—in short, before they demonstrate a full-blown active psychosis. This work holds some promise for reducing the severity of these illnesses and their associated long-term disabilities, as well as the possibility of preventing the more serious phases of these conditions.

### Summary

Although marked by fragmentation, today's community mental health system faces new opportunities for enhancing the recovery, quality of life, and community integration of people with severe mental illness. The growth of EBPs and the development of evidence for new and emerging practices offer the opportunity of providing effective and recovery-oriented services for people with mental illnesses—if the focused commitment needed is present in the community. Despite their idiosyncratic nature, most elements of the community mental health system are capable of implementing and adapting aspects of EBP. In some locations, new structures may be required to offer specific services such as ACT or supported employment. Considering the benefits for consumers and their families that can be reliably expected to accrue, universal investment in implementation and further refinement of these practices will be worth the expenditures. A collaborative advocacy movement of consumers, family members, mental health providers, and leaders of our mental health systems offers the best opportunity to improve services for people with mental illness.

## References

Amador, X., & Johanson, A. L. (2000). *I am not sick I don't need help*. Peconic, NY: Vida Press.

Anthony, W. A., & Blanch, A. (1987). Supported employment for persons who are psychiatrically disabled: An historical and conceptual perspective. *Psychosocial Rehabilitation Journal, II*(2), 5–23.

Anthony, W. A., Cohen, M., & Danley, K. S. (1988). The psychiatric rehabilitation model as applied to vocational rehabilitation. In J. A. Ciardiello & M. D. Bell (Eds.), *Vocational rehabilitation of persons with prolonged psychiatric disorders* (pp. 59–80). Baltimore: Johns Hopkins University Press.

Anthony W. A. (1993). Recovery from mental illness: The guiding vision of the mental health service system in the 1990s. *Psychosocial Rehabilitation Journal, 16*(4), 11–23.

Anthony, W. A., Cohen, M., Farkas, M. D., & Gagne, C. (2002). *Psychiatric rehabilitation* (2nd ed.). Boston: Boston University Center for Psychiatric Rehabilitation.

Bandura, A. (1977). *Social learning theory*. Englewood Cliffs, NJ: Prentice Hall.

Basto, P. W., Pratt, C. W., Gill, K. J., & Barrett, N. M. (2000). The organizational assimilation of consumer providers: A quantitative assessment. *Psychiatric Rehabilitation Skills, 4,* 105–119.

Beard, J. H., Propst, R. N., & Malamud, T. J. (1982). The Fountain House model of psychiatric rehabilitation. *Psychosocial Rehabilitation Journal, 5,* 47–53.

Bond, G. R., Dietzen, L. L., McGrew, J. H., & Miller, L. D. (1995). Accelerating entry into supported employment for persons with severe psychiatric disabilities. *Rehabilitation Psychology, 40,* 91–111.

Carling, P. J. (1995). *Return to community: Building support systems for people with psychiatric disabilities.* New York: Guilford Press.

Carling, P. J., & Ridgway, P. (1991). A psychiatric rehabilitation approach to housing. In M. D. Farkas & W. A. Anthony (Eds.), *Psychiatric rehabilitation programs: Putting theory into practice* (pp. 28–80). Baltimore: Johns Hopkins University Press.

Danley, K. S., & Anthony, W. A. (1987). The choose–get–keep approach to supported employment. *American Rehabilitation, 13,* 6–9, 27–29.

Deegan, P. E. (1988). Recovery: The lived experience of rehabilitation. *Psychosocial Rehabilitation Journal, 11,* 11–19

Farkas, M. D., O'Brien, W. F., & Nemec, P. B. (1988). A graduate level curriculum in psychiatric rehabilitation: Filling a need. *Psychosocial Rehabilitation Journal, 12,* 53–66.

Flannery, M., & Glickman, M. (1996). *Fountain House: Portraits of lives reclaimed from mental illness.* Center City, MN: Hazelden.

Greenley, J. R. (1995). Implementation of an innovative service in Madison, Wisconsin: The program of assertive community treatment (PACT). Madison, WI: Mental Health Research Center.

Kihss, P. (1980, November 3). Influx of former mental patients burdening city, Albany is told. *New York Times,* p. 50.

Lehrman, N. S. (1961). Do our hospitals help make acute schizophrenia chronic? *Diseases of the Nervous System, 22,* 489–493.

Liberman, R. P., DeRisi, W. J., & Meuser, K. T. (1989). *Social skills training for psychiatric patients.* Elmsford, NY: Pergamon Press.

Linn, M. W., Caffey, E. M., Klett, C. J., Hogarty, G. E., & Lamb, H. R. (1979). Day treatment and psychotropic drugs in the aftercare of schizophrenic patients. *Archives of General Psychiatry, 36,* 1055–1066.

Lyons, J. S., Cook, J. A., Ruth, A. R., Kraver, M., & Slagg, N. B. (1996). Service delivery using consumer staff in a mobile crisis assessment program. *Community Mental Health Journal, 32,* 33–40.

Manos, E. (1993). Prosumers. *Psychosocial Rehabilitation Journal, 16,* 117–120.

May, P. R., Tuma, A. H., Dixon, W. J., Yale, C., Thiele, D. A., & Kraude, W. H. (1981). Schizophrenia: A follow-up study of the results of five forms of treatment. *Archives of General Psychiatry, 38,* 776–784.

McGlashan, T. H. (1999). Duration of untreated psychosis in first-episode schizophrenia: Marker or determinant of course? *Biological Psychiatry, 46,* 899–907.

McGlashan, T. H. (2000). Treating schizophrenia earlier in life and the potential for prevention. *Current Psychiatry Reports, 2,* 386–392.

Meade, S., Hilton, D., & Curtis, L. (2001). Peer support: A theoretical perspective. *Psychiatric Rehabilitation Journal, 25,* 134–141.

Moxley, D. P., & Mowbray, C. T. (1997). Consumers as providers: Forces and factors legitimizing role innovation in psychiatric rehabilitation. In C. T. Mowbray, D. T. Moxley, C. A. Jaspers, & L. L. Howell (Eds.), *Consumers as providers* (pp. 2–34). Columbia, MD: International Association of Psychosocial Rehabilitation Services.

Onaga, E. F. (1994). The Fairweather Lodge as a psychosocial program in the 1990s. In The Publication Committee of IAPSRS (Eds.), *An Introduction to psychiatric rehabilitation* (pp. 206–214). Columbia, MD: International Association for Psychosocial Services.

Pepper, B., Ryglewicz, H., & Kirshner, M. C. (1981). The young adult chronic patient: Overview of a population. *Hospital and Community Psychiatry, 32,* 463–469.

President's New Freedom Commission on Mental Health. (2003). *Achieving the promise: Transforming mental health care in America.* Retrieved September 20, 2004, from *http://www.mental-healthcommission.gov.*

Rapp, C. A. (1997). *The strengths model: Case management with people suffering from severe and persistent mental illness.* New York: Oxford University Press.

Ridgway, P., & Zipple, A. M. (1990). The paradigm shift in residential services: From the linear continuum to supported housing approaches. *Psychosocial Rehabilitation Journal, 13,* 11–31.

Schmieding, N. J. (1968). Institutionalization: A conceptual approach. *Perspectives in Psychiatric Care, 6,* 205–211.

Segal, S., Redman, D., & Silverman, C. (2000). Measuring clients' satisfaction with self-help agencies. *Psychiatric Services, 51,* 1148–1152.

Segal, S., & Silverman, C. (2002). Determinates of client outcomes in self-help agencies. *Psychiatric Services, 53,* 304–309.

Solomon, P. S., & Draine, J. (1995). The efficacy of a consumer case management team: Two-year outcomes of a randomized trial. *Journal of Mental Health Administration, 22,* 135–146.

Solomon, P., & Draine. J. (2001). The state of knowledge of the effectiveness of consumer provided services. *Psychiatric Rehabilitation Journal, 25,* 20–28.

Stein, L. I., & Test, M. A. (1985). The evolution of the training in community living model. *New Directions for Mental Health Services, 26,* 7–16.

Stern, R., & Minkoff, K. (1979). Paradoxes in programming for chronic patients in a community clinic. *Hospital and Community Psychiatry, 30,* 613–617.

Tanzman, B. (1993). An overview of surveys of mental health consumers' preferences for housing and support services. *Hospital and Community Psychiatry, 44,* 450–455.

Taube, C. A. (1973). *Day care services in federally funded community mental health centers.* Statistical Note No. 96, Survey and Reports Section, Biometry Branch, National Institute of Mental Health, Rockville, MD.

Torrey, E. F. (1992). *Freudian fraud: The malignant effect of Freud's theory on American thought and culture.* New York: Harper Collins.

Torrey, E. F. (1997). *Out of the shadows.* New York: Wiley.

Torrey, E. F. (2001). *Surviving schizophrenia* (4th ed.). New York: HarperCollins.

Turner, J. C., & TenHoor, W. J. (1978). The NIMH community support program: Pilot approach to a needed social reform. *Schizophrenia Bulletin, 4,* 319–344.

Wang, P. S., Demler, O., & Kessler, R. C. (2002). Adequacy of treatment for serious mental illness in the United States. *American Journal of Public Health, 92,* 92–98.

Yeich, S., Mowbray, C. T., Bybee, D., & Cohen, E. (1994). The case for a "supported housing" approach: A study of consumer housing and support preferences. *Psychosocial Rehabilitation Journal, 18,* 75–86.

*Part II*
Principles

# THREE

# The Principles of Evidence-Based Mental Health Treatment

*Robert E. Drake*

THE MOVEMENT TO MAKE MEDICINE MORE scientific has evolved over many decades. At the beginning of the 20th century, United States medical schools were certified on the basis of the Flexner Report, which prescribed a scientific basis for medical care. During the middle of the 20th century, the discovery of effective medications for many diseases enhanced the potential to cure disease and to provide relief from symptoms. However, the specific term *evidence-based medicine* was introduced in 1990 to refer to a systematic approach to helping practitioners apply scientific evidence to decision making at the point of contact with a specific consumer (Drake, 2003; Guyatt & Rennie, 2002). As the philosophy, major tenets, and techniques of the movement have evolved, evidence-based medicine has strongly influenced individual health-care decision making, the practices offered in health-care programs, and the structure of medical and public health systems.

| Defining evidence-based medicine

## Evidence-Based Medicine and Mental Health

Evidence-based medicine has slowly begun to influence the field of mental health. Currently, we have extensive evidence of effective treatments for specific mental illnesses, but the evidence also shows that these evidence-based practices are typically not available to consumers seeking mental health treatment. The term *science-to-practice gap* refers to the discrepancy between what we know works and what we actually offer in routine community mental health settings. Policymakers, administrators, clinicians, advocates, insurers, and researchers generally agree that the gap between science and practice must be closed; mental health programs and practitioners have an obligation to provide the most effective treatments—that is, evidence based practices—to consumers and their family members (Institute of Medicine, 2001; National Advisory Mental Health Council, 1999; National Alliance for the Mentally Ill, 2001; President's New Freedom Commission on Mental Health, 2003; U.S. Department of Health and Human Services, 1999).

**Five principles of evidence-based medicine**

As support for evidence-based medicine grows in the mental health field, the need to clarify its fundamental principles also increases. Many stakeholders are attempting to understand its key concepts, including underlying values and basic tenets. The purpose of this chapter is to introduce the philosophy of evidence-based medicine and to discuss  its applicability to evidence-based mental health treatments. Evidence-based medicine encompasses five fundamental principles. First, it builds on basic health-care values. Second, it asserts that the scientific evidence should be considered as one important factor in making health-care decisions. Third, it assumes that the scientific evidence is complicated, hierarchical, often ambiguous, and usually limited. Fourth, it recognizes that factors other than scientific evidence, such as consumers' values, preferences, and choices, are also critically important contributors to medical decisions. Fifth, it recognizes that clinical expertise is a critically important contributor to decision making.

### Basic Health-Care Values

The philosophy and ethics of health care recognize a variety of basic values (Backlar & Cutler, 2002; Culver & Gert, 1982). Here are a few examples:

Consumers and their families should be treated with respect.

Health-care practitioners should be truthful.

Health-care practitioners should be helpful and avoid harming the consumer.

Health-care services should be consumer-centered, which means that practitioners should recognize consumers' rights to autonomy, choice, and self-determination in relation to health-care decisions.

Evidence-based medicine fully endorses these and other basic health-care values.

Knowing the scientific evidence and sharing it in a collaborative way with the consumer show respect. Without knowing the evidence, practitioners cannot be certain that they are avoiding harm and doing their best to help. Without understanding the evidence, consumers cannot be truly informed and thus cannot make informed decisions about their health care. Consider, for example, the consumer with a specific type of cancer. The clinician must know which forms of treatment (e.g., surgery, radiation, chemotherapy, immunotherapy), are available for this specific form of cancer, and what the expected outcomes and possible side effects of each treatment are, and be able to present all of this information to the consumer in an understandable fashion. After understanding and considering the relevant evidence, the consumer has the right to participate in making a decision about treatment or to choose to take the clinician's recommendation. A breakdown in any of these steps interferes with the consumer's basic right to respect and autonomy. In fact, adherence to these steps is considered essential in modern cancer centers.

There are, of course, unusual situations in which involuntary treatment or other exceptions to basic health-care values are justified. For example, imagine the consumer who is acutely confused because of metabolic toxicity (i.e., a sudden disturbance of blood chemistry that causes the

Justifiable exceptions

brain to malfunction) and who is not able to understand his or her current situation and medical needs. In this situation, relying on next-of-kin or a court-appointed guardian to give informed consent for an important medical decision is considered morally justified and is usually legally prescribed.

### Basic Values in Mental Health Treatment

Basic health-care values are mirrored in the mental health field. A consumer who seeks treatment from a primary care provider or from a mental health specialist for depression has a right to (1) receive full information about the illness, (2) to understand the available treatments and their expected outcomes and potential side effects, and (3) to make an informed choice and give consent regarding treatment. The consumer's rights may be overlooked only in specific circumstances, such as when he or she presents an immediate life-threatening risk to self or others because of mental illness. In such a life-threatening situation, such as immediate suicide risk, state laws typically provide for a process of decision making, for example, by a panel of doctors and lawyers or a judicial process, to protect the consumer or the threatened victim.

Fundamental
assumption

Within the current mental health system, treatment for people with severe mental illnesses is generally based on wide-ranging beliefs and values that are extensions of basic health-care values. The fundamental assumption is that people with mental illnesses should possess all of the rights and opportunities that accrue to other citizens. Consumers should be able to live independently in the community; they should be able to pursue their own goals; they should be able to make their own choices about health care, employment, education, and other important areas. Moreover, the central aim of the public mental health system should be to assist consumers in establishing meaningful lives and roles in their communities, like any other citizen. These rights should be put aside only when there is a situation of immediate danger. These beliefs and values are consistent with the consumer-centered care that is advocated in the rest of medicine. In the mental health field a variety of terms have emerged to convey these beliefs and values, such as *social inclusion, community integration, empowerment,* and *recovery.* Use of these terms is an attempt to counter longstanding attempts to segregate and institutionalize people with psychiatric disabilities.

## Scientific Evidence

This primary principle is so widely accepted by researchers, well-trained practitioners, and policymakers that it often goes without explicit statement. During the 20th century, the scientific study of disease and treatment became the keystone of modern health care. The scientific method is, in fact, what separates modern medicine from folk remedies, religious cures, and various other approaches to health that are not supported by evidence. Scientific approaches to understanding illness, such as epidemiological methods and randomized controlled trials of interventions, have solved hundreds of medical problems, saved millions of lives, separated numerous effective treatments from an even greater number of ineffective or harmful treatments, and helped society to save billions of dollars. The scientific method is valued because it offers the most reliable, efficient, and unbiased approach to establishing the causes of illness and the effectiveness of treatments. Common sense, logic, history, and research argue against other approaches, such as relying on authorities, traditions, religious ideas, or the anecdotal experience of individual clinicians (Sagan, 1995).

## Experience of Individual Doctors

Historically, as medicine replaced religious and folk treatments, the standard method of determining effectiveness was based on the experience of individual doctors and their patients. Unfortunately, the individual impressions of clinicians have proved notoriously inaccurate in judging the effectiveness of treatments. The medical literature is replete with examples of ineffective or harmful treatments that enjoyed great popularity, sometimes for centuries, before they were replaced by effective treatments. For example, the practice of pouring boiling oil into wounds to facilitate healing on the battlefield caused tremendous tissue damage, but nevertheless persisted for several hundred years as the standard of care in military medicine, before cleansing and gentle treatment of wounds were discovered (Madden & Arem, 1981). In the modern era, many other popular treatments have been determined to be ineffective or harmful when studied scientifically. Recent examples include hormone replacement therapy for postmenopausal women, arthroscopic cleansing of arthritic joints, and the use of certain medications to prevent abnormal heart rhythms after heart attacks.

At the same time, scientific methods have helped to identify and validate highly effective treatments that were initially rejected by doctors. For example, the theory that stomach ulcers were based on bacterial infection was very unpopular among skeptical physicians who had been taught for decades that ulcers were caused by excess acid secretion. Nevertheless, the bacterial theory was proved correct by scientific methods, and treatment of ulcers with antibiotics has proved to be much more effective than treatment with antacids.

### Scientific Evidence in Mental Health Treatment

Mental health treatment has a similar history. Many historical treatments, such as long-term hospitalization, megavitamin regimes, and psychosurgery, were proved to be harmful or ineffective by careful research. At the same time, scientific research has developed and confirmed the effectiveness of numerous mental health interventions, including medications, psychotherapies, social therapies, and rehabilitation approaches. In fact, current treatments for severe mental illnesses, such as depression, bipolar disorder, and schizophrenia, are as effective as current treatments for most other chronic medical illnesses. Thus,

**Scientific methods**

ensuring the availability of scientifically validated mental health treatments, or practices, can be enormously beneficial, even life saving, for individuals who have severe mental illnesses. This message is one of the central tenets of the Surgeon General's Report on Mental Health (U.S. Department of Health and Human Services, 1999) and the President's New Freedom Commission on Mental Health (2003). Many of the effective interventions for severe mental illness are reviewed in this book.

Critics of evidence-based medicine point out that (1) researchers often disagree about the scientific evidence, (2) the scientific evidence is often limited to specific types of consumers or settings, and (3) there is no strong research evidence (e.g., randomized controlled trials) to inform many common clinical decisions. All of these arguments are valid. In fact, one of the major assumptions of evidence-based medicinal practice is that the scientific evidence has many limits and must be used judiciously (Guyette & Rennie, 2002).

*Critical arguments*

*cite?*

## The Gold Standard of Scientific Evidence

The gold standard for scientific evidence regarding treatment is the systematic review (or *meta-analysis*) of several double-blind randomized controlled trials, in which consumers are randomly assigned to an experimental treatment or an alternative treatment. However, randomized controlled trials are rare, and systematic reviews are even rarer. Even when available, randomized controlled trials are usually conducted under constrained research conditions, such as using university research settings, highly selected consumers, highly trained clinicians, carefully monitored treatments, and other special conditions that limit the extent to which results can be assumed to apply to clinicians and consumers in routine health-care settings. For example, research trials often do not include specific settings (e.g., rural clinics), specific minority groups (e.g., Hispanic Americans), specific clinical populations (e.g., persons with multiple previous episodes or serious comorbidities), typical clinicians (e.g., those with large caseloads or limited training), or other features of routine practice. In other words, the available scientific evidence always has limits. How does the philosophy of evidence-based medicine address this problem?

### Hierarchy of Evidence

The assumption in evidence-based medicine is that there is always a hierarchy of evidence. Some clinical decisions can be guided by high-level, more reliable, and more extensive evidence than others. There are always limitations regarding the quality of the evidence, in general, and the applicability of the evidence to specific consumers and situations. At the same, time some evidence is almost always available. Even the unsystematic observations of a single clinician or consumer constitute evidence, albeit very weak evidence, due to the limits of individual human inferential abilities. There are different ways to construct the hierarchy of evidence, but they all converge on several criteria. One is the design of the pertinent research. The highest quality for making a decision about an individual consumer is actually the *N* of 1 randomized controlled trial, in which the consumer switches from active treatment to placebo several times under double-blind conditions (Guyatt & Rennie, 2002). In most clinical situations, this approach is not feasible, so the highest standard becomes the systematic review of randomized controlled trials. As we move down the hierarchy, the criteria involve designs with less control that allow less certainty of inference (e.g., quasi-experimental studies, followed by systematic observational studies, followed by unsystematic clinical observations), fewer studies, and less external validity (or generalizability; Drake et al., in press). Sometimes only quasi-experimental studies are available, so these constitute the best available evidence. Sometimes observational studies allow extremely strong inferences (e.g., hip replacement surgery for debilitating osteoarthritis was so dramatically effective that it was never tested in controlled trials), and randomized controlled trials

*Limitations regarding quality of evidence*

are unnecessary (Guyatt & Rennie, 2002). Furthermore, much of the evidence regarding harmful effects of treatments comes from large observational studies.

In the typical clinical situation, the available evidence, even if strong, does not match a specific consumer perfectly. For example, several randomized clinical trials show the effectiveness of a particular intervention, but the specific consumer differs from the average consumer in those trials because she is Asian American, over age 75, or diabetic. How do the clinician and consumer make use of the evidence in this situation? This is where clinical experience and understanding the effects of co-occurring illnesses, treatments, and other factors are critical. For example, a prescribing physician absolutely has to know that geriatric consumers are more vulnerable to certain side effects and require smaller dosages of many medications.

### Limitations of the Evidence in Mental Health

In mental health, the evidence is also complex and limited. Few interventions have been studied with multiple randomized clinical trials, and typical or routine consumers and mental health practitioners have often been excluded from the trials. The existing evidence has rarely been risk-adjusted for individual characteristics, such as the presence of co-occurring illnesses.

### Principles of Treatment
One solution to this dilemma has been to identify principles of treatment that are supported by research. Consider the following example. When we are attempting to help people with mental illness to recover from substance abuse, there is little controlled research to support the proposition that a particular type of group treatment is effective, even though most programs for consumers with a "dual diagnosis" include treatment groups. There is, however, ethnographic evidence as well as extensive testimonial evidence that people need to find social support from other people who are not substance abusers in order to maintain their

recoveries (Alverson & Drake, 2001). There is also extensive evidence that consumers have different preferences for
group approaches (Noordsy Schwab, Fox, & Drake, 1996)
and that those who participate in one type or another of a
peer-support group for at least a year are likely to recover
from substance abuse (Drake, Latimer, Leff, McHugh, &
Burns, 2004). As a principle of treatment, we would therefore recommend that a variety of peer-support groups be
offered to consumers who are working toward substance
abuse recovery and that, in the absence of evidence that
one particular type of group is more effective than others,
consumer preference should be emphasized in order to
individualize services (Mueser, Noorsdy, Drake, & Fox,
2003). This approach seems far preferable to saying that we
have no evidence regarding group interventions or to
recommending a particular type of group based on a single
study.

Evidence-based medicine recognizes that factors other
than scientific evidence, such as consumers' values, preferences, and choices, and the availability of local services are
critically important contributors to medical decisions.
Evidence-based medicine assumes that scientific evidence is
only one important component of decision making
(Haynes, Devereaux, & Guyatt, 2002). A second component involves including the consumer's values, goals, preferences, and participation in a shared decision making
process. A third component is the sum of local circumstances: the availability of hospitals, specialists, programs,
insurance, supports, and other resources that affect health-
care decisions. All of these areas must be considered to
make optimal decisions.

## Consumer Preferences and Scientific Data

Consumer preferences, local conditions, or societal decisions about resources often override the scientific evidence,
especially in situations in which the evidence is weak
(Wennberg, Fisher, & Skinner, 2002). Consider a few examples. One consumer understands the evidence that surgery

for an aneurysm is the most effective treatment but decides to decline surgery (as Albert Einstein did). Unless competence to make the decision is at issue, the consumer's preference always overrides the scientific evidence. An elderly consumer with Alzheimer's disease develops pneumonia, and antibiotic therapy clearly would be effective for his condition. But before developing severe dementia, this consumer expressed a strong preference for rejecting medical treatments to prolong his life. His physician therefore prescribes pain medications to prevent suffering but not antibiotics to treat the pneumonia. A third consumer has severe narrowing of a carotid artery, for which surgery (i.e., an endarterectomy) is clearly an effective treatment. However, in the local hospital this procedure is rarely performed, and there is a high rate of surgical mortality. The consumer's physician therefore recommends medications to prevent stroke rather than surgery, until the consumer can travel to a large medical center hospital where this procedure is performed regularly and has greater success.

The focus on consumer preferences assumes that consumers have access to accurate and understandable scientific information. As the medical field advocates for consumer preferences and shared decision making (Charles, Gafu, & Whelan, 1999), it is clear that truly informed choice requires access to accurate information (O'Connor et al., 2003). Otherwise, consumers are left to make choices that are based on the opinions of their social contacts, the biases of vested interest groups (e.g., marketing), or the individual knowledge and opinions of their local health-care providers. With access to accurate information, consumers can make choices that are highly differentiated. That is, their treatment choices often differ from what their providers might recommend, from what their peers choose, and from what they would choose in the absence of such information (Wennberg et al., 2002). Nevertheless, informed consumer choice, which is termed *shared decision making* in medicine, often leads to better

Consumer need for access to scientific data

outcomes—not just higher satisfaction and adherence with treatment but improved biomedical outcomes. Although standards are rapidly developing for how information should be synthesized and presented to consumers in an unbiased fashion, this is an area that needs further research (O'Connor et al., 2003).

Shared decision making | The emphasis on accurate information and shared decision making implies a fundamental shift away from the traditional model of medical authority, in which the physician decides what is the best treatment and tells the consumer what to do. Shared decision making means that the provider shares information about reasonable and available treatments and their likely effects, both benefits and side effects, based on scientific information, and engages the consumer in a process that involves the consumer taking as much responsibility as he or she is able and willing to take, in terms of understanding the treatments and outcomes, making informed choices, and learning to manage his or her illness.

Quality of life | One critical implication of the emphasis on consumer preferences and shared decision making is that it affords a different view of outcomes as well as of treatments. Typically, consumers value functional status and quality of life as much or more than they value symptom control, and certainly more than they value physiological measures. For example, urologists often prefer opening the urinary track (i.e., the urethra) surgically to increase urine flow as a treatment for benign prostatic hypertrophy, but consumers are likely to value avoiding surgery and the possible side effects of surgery, such as incontinence and impotence, more than they value improving urine flow (Wennberg et al., 2002).

### Role of Local Factors

Another critical implication of the shift to encompass consumer preferences in a shared decision making process is that the practitioner must understand local factors that may override the evidence. For example, hospitals have very different rates of mortality and morbidity for various surgical procedures, and these local conditions must be weighed when considering whether and where to have surgery. Similarly, a complex treatment may be the most evidence-based intervention for a condition but may be unavailable locally or may be prohibitively expensive. As an extreme example, the treatment of various infectious diseases differs greatly in developing countries and in the United States.

### Consumer Preference

One common misconception regarding evidence-based practice in the mental health field is that it prescribes a  standard, rigid approach for all consumers, thereby eliminating consumer choice and preferences. As the foregoing discussion makes clear, the philosophy of evidence-based medicine is that the available evidence is just one factor in the decision making process. This is likewise true in mental health practices; consumer choices, preferences, and goals are key determinants in the effective provision of evidence-based practices. Along with many consumer advocacy groups, the evidence-based practices movement supports the maximization of consumer choice and self-determination (Bond, Salyers, Rollins, Rapp, & Zipple, in press). A treatment with the strongest evidence may not be the optimal treatment for a particular individual, who may have specific risk factors that preclude the treatment, for whom the treatment may not be available or affordable in a given situation, or who may have a different preference. Consider the example of clozapine. This drug is an evidence-based alternative for consumers with schizophrenia who do not respond well to other antipsychotic medications (Kane, Honigfeld, Singers, & Meltzer, 1988). However, many factors might exclude clozapine as the treatment of choice for a particular consumer. For example, the consumer may have a history of medical problems that would make clozapine especially dangerous; the consumer may prefer not to have regular blood monitoring, which is necessary with clozapine; the consumer may choose to avoid the characteristic side effects of clozapine, such as severe sedation; or clozapine may not be available or affordable for a variety of reasons. In shared decision making, all of these factors would be considered carefully and weighed against potential benefits by the consumer and the practitioner.

Consumer preferences for outcomes as well as treatments

Evidence-based medicine prescribes attention to consumer preferences for outcomes as well as treatments. For example, a consumer may value avoiding medication side effects more than eliminating symptoms. This emphasis in medicine is totally congruent with what has been termed the philosophy of recovery in mental health. *Recovery* implies attention to functioning and quality of life, rather than just symptom control (Ralph, 2000). The same emphasis on functional outcomes and quality of life has been evident in general medicine for the past 20 years. Similarly, one key aspect of the recovery movement is consumer choice, which has been emphasized in evidence-based medicine as attention to consumer preferences. Practices that are identified as evidence-based in mental health typically have consumer preferences built in at several points of the decision making process because choice corresponds with better consumer outcomes (Bond et al., in press).

## Importance of Clinical Expertise

Working with the consumer to understand the scientific evidence, to adjust the evidence to the particular characteristics of the consumer and his or her circumstances, to incorporate the consumer's preferences and decisions, and to include the specifics of local factors requires a great deal of clinical judgment (Haynes et al., 2002). In fact, as the scientific evidence proliferates, as demands for consumer-centered care increase, and as health-care organizations constrain time and decisions, the need for clinical expertise has expanded dramatically. More than ever before, correct diagnosis and prescribing are related to improved outcomes. More than ever before, consumers are demanding information and a role in health care decision making. And more than ever before, attempts to control health care costs are impinging on health-care decision making. How can all of these pressures be managed at the point of contact between practitioner and consumer?

The simple answer is that there is no substitute for clinical expertise. The clinician must first understand the individual consumer and his or her illness. If the diagnosis is incorrect or if the clinician misunderstands the consumer's preferences, the scientific evidence will not help. For example, clinical skills are needed to diagnose chest pain correctly as coronary artery disease, and each time the physician makes a misdiagnosis of esophagitis, an unnecessary death from heart attack may be the result. Similarly, prescribing an evidence-based medication that causes sexual side effects to a consumer who finds these side effects intolerable is unlikely to be effective. A clinician that fails to make the correct diagnosis or to elicit information about the importance of the side effects to the consumer will not have helped the him or her.

Second, the better the clinician understands the scientific evidence, the better he or she can determine how it applies to a specific consumer. Because of the rapidity of medical developments, keeping up with evidence-based practice is exceedingly difficult. The clinician must master information technology and be able to locate and assimilate information rapidly. Consider, for example, the situation of a consumer with hepatitis C, a serious liver infection, complicated by depression. The randomized controlled trials of treatments for hepatitis C infection have shown efficacy but have excluded consumers with depression. Should the clinician recommend the treatment? In most cases, there will be additional (usually weaker) evidence regarding potential interactions between the treatment and the comorbid condition. In other cases, the clinician must use knowledge of these other conditions and good judgment to discuss with the consumer whether the treatment is likely to be tolerated and effective in these specific circumstances.

| Mastering information technology

Third, the clinician must understand the local health-care situation accurately. The elderly consumer who already has regular support from family and a visiting nurse, for example, may have a different capacity to monitor side effects and take medicines accurately than a similar consumer without local supports. What if there is no family and the local managed care organization will not pay for a visiting nurse? Clinical judgment is required to put all of the pertinent factors together.

## Clinical Expertise in Mental Health

The situation in mental health care is similar. In many common clinical situations, the scientific evidence is relatively weak, and the practitioner must exercise careful judgment to help the consumer make an informed decision regarding the most desirable course of action. Complex psychosocial treatments are constantly evolving, and randomized controlled trials are rare. In many cases the existing randomized trials are totally unhelpful because they address an intervention that is no longer used. Obviously, randomized controlled trials of discarded interventions are less helpful than quasi-experimental studies of current interventions. Consider the situation of housing for persons with severe mental illnesses. Although there are few randomized controlled trials of supported housing, there are many systematic observational studies that consistently indicate that the great majority of consumers prefer and do well in independent housing with supports rather than in group homes (Newman, 2001). In this situation, a practitioner must understand the consumer's preferences (e.g., how does he or she feel about shared housing?), which become even more important when the evidence is weak. Additionally, the practitioner must understand (1) the individual characteristics of the consumer (e.g., Are there any complications, such as severe medical comorbidities, that would make independent living difficult or dangerous?), (2) the consumer's goals (e.g., Does he or she want to live alone or with roommates?), and (3) the local circumstances (e.g., Is the available housing safe and decent? Will either choice affect the consumer's access to his or her family or support group?). Just as clinical judgment is critical to evidence-based medicine, sound clinical judgment anchored in effective assessment is essential for evidence-based mental health practice.

## Discussion

The philosophy of evidence-based medicine has numerous implications for the mental health field. Consider the different stakeholder groups. First, people who are consumers are always at the center of decision making and evaluating outcomes. They are considered people with illnesses who have basic rights to information, discussion, respect, choices, and autonomy. The doctrine of "people first" asserts that these individuals should never be identified by their illnesses: for example, a client is a "person with schizophrenia," not "a schizophrenic." And a person with a mental illness is like any other individual with an illness who has a right to full information about that illness, who has a right to understand effective treatment options and their side effects, and who has a right to make choices regarding treatments and expected outcomes based on his or her personal preferences, goals, and values.

"People first" doctrine

Second, family members are often part of an individual's support network. They too need respect, information, support, and guidelines in order to be as effective as possible in supporting the recovery process of their loved ones. Nevertheless, the individual consumer maintains rights to autonomy and privacy. The family can be full partners in treatment only if the consumer chooses that degree of involvement. Without the consumer's consent, family members can still benefit by receiving generic information about mental illness and effective treatments, but they cannot be given access to information about the consumer's individual treatment.

Family members

**Practitioners must understand the scientific evidence**

Third, individual practitioners have a moral and ethical obligation to understand and share the scientific evidence regarding treatments. Most mental health practitioners are confronted with the reality that the evidence regarding effective treatments that they learned in school or formal training programs has changed. Continuing to provide mental health interventions without an understanding of the most current available evidence is not acceptable. Providing treatments that practitioners find to be most familiar, or that they personally prefer, rather than mental health treatments that correspond to the scientific evidence, is likewise no longer acceptable. Providing an ineffective mental health treatment rather than referring the consumer to a practitioner who provides effective mental health treatment is also unacceptable. The United States legal system, health-care overseers, and professional organizations have asserted that treatment recommendations should be consistent with the scientific evidence in situations where the evidence indicates that some treatments are clearly more effective than others.

Considering the scientific evidence requires that practitioners be able to (1) access that information, (2) understand its content and limitations, (3) explain the information in an understandable fashion to consumers, (4) collaborate appropriately with consumers and family members, and (5) apply the evidence judiciously to specific situations. These activities require both clinical and analytic skills; the clinician must make accurate assessments of the diagnosis, the scientific evidence, the consumer's preferences, and the local situation—and all of these inputs must be shared with the consumer in the process of collaborative decision making. If the diagnosis is incorrect, randomized controlled trials will not help anyone make a decision about effective treatment. Similarly, misunderstanding the evidence base, the local circumstances, or the weighting process can lead to the wrong decision. Evidence-based medicine involves techniques that help physicians and other decision makers apply the evidence to specific situations.

Fourth, agency and system administrators have an ethical obligation to make sure that practitioners in their mental health centers and systems are trained and supervised in evidence-based decision making and practices, and to ensure that the actual services provided correspond to such guidelines. This process should include quality controls, including feedback from consumers and family members. These needs must be balanced with available resources, because implementing evidence-based practices often involves new practitioner skills, new forms of organizing services, and the modification of reimbursement mechanisms.

Role of agency and system administrators

Fifth, policymakers have an obligation to shift health-care systems toward evidence-based practices. This means that prioritization of resources, funding mechanisms, organizational structures, credentialing mechanisms, contracting, monitoring, quality assurance, training and development, and other procedures should all be aligned to facilitate the provision of evidence-based practices. Without these structural supports, it is impossible for agencies, practitioners, and consumers to participate in their roles optimally and to achieve the best possible outcomes.

Role of policymakers

The philosophy of evidence-based medicine provides a set of ideals for the health-care system. In all areas of medicine, evidence-based approaches are honored more in the breach than in routine practice. In mental health care, the situation is probably worse, because evidence-based practice has just begun to be part of the discussion. The field of mental health would do well to avoid its tendency to develop arcane internal jargon that isolates mental health from the rest of medicine and reduces consumers' and the public's ability to understand and actively participate in the further development of scientifically validated mental health treatments. The mental health field has a moral and ethical obligation to learn from the experiences in other areas of medicine and to adopt the philosophy and practices of evidence-based medicine in order to optimize the benefit that people with severe mental illnesses receive from mental health services.

## References

Alverson, H., Alverson, M., & Drake, R. E. (2001). Social patterns of substance use among people with dual diagnoses. *Mental Health Services Research, 3*, 3–14.

Backlar, P., & Cutler, D. L. (2002). *Ethics in community mental health care.* New York: Plenum Press.

Bond, G. R., Salyers, M. P., Rollins, A. L., Rapp, C. A., & Zipple, A. M. (in press). How evidence-based practices contribute to community integration. *Community Mental Health Journal.*

Charles, C., Gafu, A., & Whelan, T. (1999). Decision making in the professional–patient encounter: Revisiting the shared decision making model. *Social Science in Medicine, 47*, 651–661.

Culver, C. M., & Gert, B. (1982). *Philosophy in medicine: Conceptual and ethical issues in medicine and psychiatry.* New York: Oxford University Press.

Drake, R. E. (2003). Evidence-based practices in mental health care. In R. E. Drake (Ed.), *The Psychiatric Clinics of North America* (4 ed., Vol. 26, pp. xiii–xiv). Philadelphia: W. B. Saunders.

Drake, R. E., Latimer, E. A., Leff, S., McHugo, G. J., & Burns, B. J. (in press). What is evidence? *Psychiatric Clinics of North America.*

Drake, R. E., McHugo, G. J., Xie, H., & Shumway, M. (2004). Three-year outcomes of patients with severe bipolar disorder and substance use disorder. *Biological Psychiatry.*

Guyatt, G., & Rennie, D. (2002). *Users' guides to the medical literature: A manual for evidence-based clinical practice.* Chicago: American Medical Association.

Haynes, R. B., Devereaux, P. J., & Guyatt, G. H. (2002). Clinical experience in the era of evidence-based medicine and patient choice. *American College of Physicians Journal Club, 136*, A11.

Institute of Medicine (IOM). (2001). Building a bridge to cross the chasm. *Joint Commission Perspective, 21*, 1–3.

Kane, J., Honigfeld, G., Singer, J., & Meltzer, H. (1988). Clozapine for the treatment-resistant schizophrenic. *Archives of General Psychiatry, 45*, 789–796.

Madden, J. W., & Arem, A. J. (1981). Wound healing: Biological and clinical features. In D. C. Sabiston (Ed.), *Textbook of surgery* (pp. 265–286). Philadelphia: W. B. Saunders.

Mueser, K. T., Noordsy, D. L., Drake, R. E., & Fox, M. (2003). *Integrated treatment for dual disorders: A guide to effective practice.* New York: Guilford Press.

National Advisory Mental Health Council (NAMHC). (1999). *Bridging science and service.* Rockville, MD: Author.

National Alliance for the Mentally Ill. (2001). *NAMI strategic plan 2001–2003.* Alexandria, VA: Author.

Newman, S. J. (2001). Housing attributes and serious mental illness: Implications for research and practice. *Psychiatric Services, 52,* 1309–1317.

Noordsy, D. L., Schwab, B., Fox, L., & Drake, R. E. (1996). The role of self-help programs in the rehabilitation of persons with severe mental illness and substance use disorders. *Community Mental Health Journal, 32,* 71–81.

O'Connor, A. M., Stacey, D., Erstwistle, V., Llewellyn-Thomas, H., Rovner, D., Holmes, E. P., et al. (2003). Decision aids for people facing health treatment or screening decisions. *Cochrane Database of Systematic Reviews, 1,* 1.

President's New Freedom Commission on Mental Health. (2003). *Achieving the promise: Transforming mental health care in America.* DHHS Publication No. SMA-03-3832, Rockville, MD.

Ralph, R. O. (2000). *Review of recovery literature: A synthesis of a sample of recovery literature 2000.* Portland, ME: Edmund S. Muskie Institute of Public Affairs, University of Southern Maine.

Sagan, C. (1995). *The demon-haunted world: Science as a candle in the dark.* New York: Random House.

U.S. Department of Health and Human Services (DHHS). (1999). *Mental health: A report of the Surgeon General.* Rockville, MD: U.S. Department of Health and Human Services, U.S. Public Health Services.

Wennberg, J.E., Fisher, E.S., & Skinner, J.S. (2002). Geography and the debate over Medicare reform. *Health Affairs* (Suppl.), Web Exclusives, W96–114.

FOUR

# | Evidence-Based Practice Emerges

*Susan T. Azrin*
*Howard H. Goldman*

EVIDENCE-BASED PRACTICE HAS EMERGED as the dominant practice model for mental health care. According to William Anthony, an internationally recognized leader in rehabilitation and recovery from mental illness, and his colleagues at Boston University's Center for Psychiatric Rehabilitation, "The influence of evidence-based practices has drastically changed how mental health systems are being planned at the beginning of the 21st century. No longer will system planning be done under the guidance of theory and opinion without major input from research on evidence-based practices" (2004). Most mental health care stakeholders—federal agencies, professional organizations, and consumer and family advocacy groups—endorse the evidence-based practice approach and promote its adoption. Evidence-based practice is clearly here to stay, and as Anthony and his colleagues proclaimed, the mental health care system will never be quite the same again.

*Evidence-based practice* means employing clinical interventions that research has shown to be effective in helping consumers recover and achieve their goals. This chapter explores the origins of the evidence-based practice concept and introduces the reader to some important figures in the history of evidence-based practice. We then examine the status of evidence-based practice today, including current evidence-based practice initiatives and the barriers that impede more widespread implementation of evidence-based practice. Finally, we identify specific strategies and tactics for overcoming those barriers and advancing evidence-based practice into the mental health field.

Surgeon General's report on mental health

The U.S. Surgeon General's 1999 report on mental health found that effective treatments are well documented for most mental disorders (U.S. Department of Health and Human Services, 1999). Individuals who experience a mental disorder or mental health problem are encouraged to seek help by choosing from this range of effective treatments to suit their preferences. However, the Surgeon General's report also alerted the public, mental health advocates, and policymakers to the gap between the practices that have demonstrated effectiveness and the reality of everyday practice. The treatment needs of individuals with mental illnesses often go unmet because services based on research are not routinely available. The report advises that mental health systems and agencies should offer evidence-based practices (EBPs) to all individuals who seek treatment for mental disorders. By asserting that an established scientific basis for the effective treatment of most mental illnesses exists and in calling for the mental health field to make these evidence-based practices available to all who seek treatment, the Surgeon General's report marks a turning point in mental health services delivery. With the availability of documented effective mental health treatments, it now becomes incumbent on practitioners, programs, and mental health systems to offer these evidence-based practices to consumers. Following the Surgeon General's report, the term evidence-based practice is increasingly used in the mental health field to refer to treatments that have a substantial science base supporting their effectiveness.

## What Constitutes Evidence and Evidence-Based Decision Making

In describing a practice as *evidence-based*, we mean that a body of research evidence supports the practice's effectiveness. According to the Institute of Medicine, "Effectiveness refers to care that is based on the use of systematically acquired evidence to determine whether an intervention, such as a preventive service, diagnostic test, or therapy, produces better outcomes than alternatives—including the alternative of doing nothing" (2001, p. 46). Thus, an evidence-based practice requires evidence of effectiveness. *Evidence-based decision making* refers to the use of available evidence to make treatment decisions. Evidence-based decision making assumes that consumers should receive treatments based on the best available scientific knowledge (Institute of Medicine, 2001). Although evidence-based practice has historic roots dating back to the 1950s, interest in it has grown rapidly over the last decade (Evidence-Based Medicine Working Group, 1992; Muir Gray, 1997; Risdale, 1995; Sackett, Strauss, Richardson, Rosenberg, & Haynes, 2000). The term *evidence-based practice* is derived from *evidence-based medicine*, which refers to the practice of evidence-based decision making in the medical field. The term *evidence-based practice* addresses the broader health field and is usually preferred over *evidence-based medicine* when discussing care of psychiatric disorders.

Davidoff (1999) argued that evidence has always contributed to clinical decision making; however, the standards for evidence have shifted over the past few decades. Reports of individual cases were the mainstay of clinical "evidence" prior to 1950. Since then, findings from 131,000 randomized controlled trials have been published. *Randomized controlled trials* are treatment studies with intervention and control groups to which participants are randomly assigned. Study designs and methodology are also much more sophisticated today. For example, *meta-analysis*, a method of statistically analyzing a large collection of indi-

| Randomized controlled trials

| Meta analysis

vidual studies' results in order to integrate the findings, was unheard of in 1950. In addition, Davidoff explains, prior to 1990, practitioners were trained to employ an evidence-based decision making process of limited utility. The four-step approach directed practitioners to:

Four-step approach

1. Formulate a clinical question for the problem.
2. Search for relevant information from the best available sources.
3. Evaluate that evidence for validity and usefulness.
4. Implement the findings.

Although this approach sounds logical, practitioners (i.e., clinicians providing treatment) experienced a number of problems with it (Davidoff, 1999; Guyatt et al, 2000; McColl, Smith, White, & Fields, 1998). In particular, how could a practitioner find the relevant information when it might reside in a multitude of possible locations? On what basis should the validity and clinical usefulness of the information in treatment be evaluated? Furthermore, most practitioners lacked the time, training, and resources to undertake this rather unwieldy approach to clinical decision making for each consumer.

## The Founders of Evidence-Based Practice

Although evidence-based practice as we know it today seems new, this is not really the case. One of the earliest proponents of the evidence-based practice approach was the late British epidemiologist Archie Cochrane. In the 1950s and 1960s, Cochrane, known as "the godfather of evidence-based medicine," devoted his career to promoting the importance of conducting randomized controlled trials to upgrade the quality of medical evidence (Mechanic, 1998). Cochrane viewed randomized controlled trials as the most reliable source of evidence. Almost two decades ago, Cochrane pronounced that only 15–20% of medical practice was based on scientifically sound research. He urged the evaluation of

Archie Cochrane

health services based on their scientific evidence, rather than on clinical impression, anecdotal experience, expert opinion, or "standard and accepted practice" (Cochrane, 1979). In his book *Effectiveness and Efficiency: Random Reflections on Health Services* (1972), he maintained that scarce health-care resources should be devoted to providing health-care practices that have been proven effective in well-designed evaluations. Cochrane also pointed out the difficulties in effectively disseminating clinically relevant research findings to practitioners. As a tribute to his pioneering efforts, the Cochrane Collaboration (1999) was established in 1992 as an international source of the highest quality, clinically relevant research evidence on a range of health disorders, which practitioners can easily access to inform their clinical decisions (*www.cochrane.org*).

| Cochrane Collaboration

David Eddy coined the term *evidence-based medicine*. A pioneer in applying mathematics to practitioner decision making, Eddy also insisted that practitioners employ evidence-based medicine, and he offered specific strategies on how to do so. Halfway through his surgical residency at Stanford University, Eddy abandoned his medical training. He had become disillusioned with medicine after discovering how little data informed physicians' decision making. He found the entire approach to medical practice haphazard, with little regard for individual patients' unique histories or circumstances. This led him to the study of physician decision making and a search for mathematical models of this process. He developed a series of practice guidelines for numerous medical disorders, many still in effect today, including guidelines for cancer screenings. He also built an elaborate software program, which he called *Archimedes* (named after the Greek god who boasted he could move the world with a single lever if only he had a place to stand), to simulate patients, diseases, and their interactions and outcomes. Akin to airline cockpit simulation, Archimedes brings the digital age to the practice of evidence-based medicine by providing the means of simulating clinical trials that would otherwise take years to run.

| David M. Eddy

| Archimedes

David L. Sackett

David Sackett's name is associated with evidence-based medicine the world over. He is credited with the early definition of evidence-based medicine as "the conscientious, explicit, and judicious use of current best evidence in making decisions about the care of individual patients" (Sackett, Rosenberg, Muir Gray, Haynes, & Richardson, 1996, p. 71). This definition implies that evidence-based medicine involves not only research evidence but also clinical judgment and attention to the individual consumer. The addition of clinical judgment and consideration of the consumer as a unique person broadened the concept of evidence-based medicine beyond care based solely on empirical data, as conceived by Archie Cochrane. While at Oxford University in 1994, Sackett founded the world's first Centre for Evidence-Based Medicine. His *Evidence-Based Medicine: How to Practice and Teach EBM* (Sackett et al., 2000) is the leading text on the topic.

Definition of
evidence-based
medicine

## Qualities of Evidence-Based Practice

Aside from the emerging evidence base supporting the use of evidence-based practice, as noted in the Surgeon General's (U.S. Department of Health and Human Services, 1999) report on mental health, the desire for increased quality and accountability in mental health services delivery has further fueled interest in evidence-based practice. Quality and accountability have become the watchwords of health and mental health services (Institute of Medicine, 2001). Implementing evidence-based practice is a means to achieving both ends. In this context *quality* refers to positive outcomes obtained by using cost-effective services, and *accountability* refers to documentation of adherence to evidence-based practice. *Fidelity* of a practice refers to whether the practice remains faithful to the treatment model that research has demonstrated to be effective. Evidence-based practice offers accountability by monitoring the fidelity of services to evidence-based practice models. Programs faithful to the evidence-based models generally produce

Quality

Accountability

Fidelity

good outcomes (though not necessarily for all individuals or in all circumstances). Helping consumers to achieve consistently positive outcomes is the goal of evidence-based practice, and implementing evidence-based practice offers a quality-improvement process toward that end.

The Institute of Medicine (2001) offered one of the most widely accepted definitions of evidence-based practice, adapted from Sackett and colleagues (2000):

> Evidence-based practice is the integration of best research evidence with clinical expertise and patient values. *Best research evidence* refers to clinically relevant research, often from the basic health and medical sciences, but especially from patient-centered clinical research into the accuracy and precision of diagnostic tests (including the clinical examination); the power of prognostic markers; and the efficacy and safety of therapeutic, rehabilitative, and preventive regimens. *Clinical expertise* means the ability to use clinical skills and past experience to rapidly identify each patient's unique health state and diagnosis, individual risks and benefits of potential interventions, and personal values and expectations. *Patient values* refers to the unique preferences, concerns, and expectations that each patient brings to a clinical encounter and that must be integrated into clinical decisions if they are to serve the patient. (p. 47)

Readers should note that, unlike Cochrane's definition of evidence-based medicine, the Institute of Medicine's definition of evidence-based *practice* balances the importance of randomized controlled trials with the clinical relevance of the research evidence. The new definition stresses the relevance of the research to the consumer in addition to the importance of a particular research design. Finally, in this new definition, the values of consumers now factor into decision making along with evidence and clinical judgment.

## Evidence-Based Practice in Routine Clinical Care

As the Surgeon General's (U.S. Department of Health and Human Services, 1999) report on mental health

*Contemporary definition of evidence-based practice*

*Science to service*

concluded, well-documented evidence-based practices exist for a number of mental health disorders. Yet, too often, these practices go unimplemented, even when consumers, practitioners, and policymakers fully understand the benefits and agree on desired outcomes. Clearly, a problem exists in moving effective mental health treatments from "science to service," that is, from research into actual practice. This gap between routine mental health care and evidence-based practice represents a significant public health problem that characterizes not only mental health treatment but also overall health care. According to the Institute of Medicine (2001), the lag time between discovering effective forms of treatment and incorporating them into routine patient care is 15–20 years.

Although most in the field would now agree that mental health treatment should rely on research that supports evidence of effectiveness, rather than solely on theory or individual practitioner judgment, moving evidence-based practice into routine mental health treatment remains a formidable task. In a population-based study, Wang, Berglund, and Kessler (2000) found that only 25% of the respondents with a serious mental illness received treatment consistent with evidence-based practice recommendations or guidelines. Likewise, in another study Lehman (2001) found that few consumers with schizophrenia received treatment consistent with the evidence-based practices recommended by the Schizophrenia Patient Outcomes Research Team (known as the Schizophrenia PORT).

## Evidence-Based Practice Initiatives

Supported employment

The good news is that EBP implementation activities exist in nearly every state in this country. (NASMHPD Research Institute, 2002). Supported employment, an intervention to help consumers obtain competitive, integrated employment, is the most frequently implemented EBP, with some type of implementation activity ongoing in 43 states. The bad news is that states usually do not implement the EBPs statewide or employ fidelity measures to assure quality. Below, we describe major national initiatives sponsoring the implementation of EBP.

In recognition of the growing importance of evidence-based practice to the psychiatry field, the journal of the American Psychiatric Association, *Psychiatric Services*, dedicated 2001 to evidence-based practices, publishing over a dozen articles on those practices in a range of treatment settings and populations. (Drake and Goldman [2003] offer most of these articles in a single volume.) The series addressed the following topics, among others:

*Psychiatric Services 2001 evidence-based practice series*

- Strategies for disseminating evidence-based practice to front-line providers
- Policy implications of evidence-based practice
- Ways to integrate evidence-based practice into the recovery model
- Evidence-based practice in child and adolescent psychiatry
- Evidence-based practice in services for family members of persons with psychiatric disorders
- Evidence-based pharmacological treatment guidelines and algorithms

This series continues to inform providers, administrators, policymakers, and consumers of the availability of a range of effective treatments and services for persons with serious mental disorders.

The largest national EBP initiative in the mental health field, the Evidence-Based Practice Project, is being coordinated by the New Hampshire–Dartmouth Psychiatric Research Center. It receives financial support from the Robert Wood Johnson Foundation, the Federal Center for Mental Health Services, and numerous other national, state, local, private, and public organizations. The project has three goals:

Evidence-based practices project

1. Ensure that more consumers and families can access effective services;

2. Assist mental health practitioners in developing the skills necessary to deliver effective services; and
3. Help administrators build the infrastructure to support and maintain these effective services.

Phase 1 of the project involved the identification of six current evidence-based practices and the collaborative development of the implementation resource kits for each of these practices. The project has developed a website at *www.mentalhealthpractices.org.* Phase 2 of the project, an eight-state field testing of the implementation resource kits, combined with the provision of consultation and technical assistance, is currently underway. Each step of the project has been a collaborative effort with many stakeholder groups involved (i.e., consumers, family members, practitioners, program leaders, and the public mental health authorities).

**President's New Freedom Commission on Mental Health**

In the first comprehensive study of the nation's mental health service delivery system in 25 years, following an executive order from President George W. Bush, the President's New Freedom Commission on Mental Health released their final report, *Achieving the Promise: Transforming Mental Health Care in America* (President's New Freedom Commission on Mental Health, 2003). The report documents the need to develop, expand, and implement evidence-based practices across all populations. The commission uses the term *evidence-based practice,* its abbreviation *EBP,* or *evidence-based treatment* 61 times in this influential report. In addition, the commission formed a subcommittee specifically to examine and offer policy recommendations on evidence-based practices.

In its report the commission not only emphasized the expansion of EBPs but also discussed strategies and tactics for implementing EBPs in the field: "The mental health field must expand its efforts to develop and test new treatments and practices, promote awareness of and improve training in evidence-based practices, and better finance those practices" (2003, p. 73). The importance of moving from science to service with the best available evidence pervades the commission's report. For example, "As promising new findings are conveyed from the research community into the hands of front-line providers, policies and financing criteria at the Federal, State, and local levels must provide incentives to support adopting and using these new findings" (p. 69). The commission's report largely sets the mental health field's agenda for the next decade, and its mandate to make EBPs available in routine mental health services will likely prove highly influential.

## Barriers to Implementing Evidence-Based Practice

Researchers have identified a discouragingly long list of rules, regulations, and policies that serve as barriers to implementing EBP in routine mental health care (Bond et al., 2001; Dixon et al., 2001; Drake et al., 2001; Hoagwood, Burns, Kiser, Ringelsen, & Schoenwald, 2001; Mellman et al., 2001; Torrey et al., 2001). Policies and administrative practices themselves can create both incentives and disincentives that shape the mental health service system. Identifying the policy interventions that facilitate implementation of EBP while minimizing implementation barriers represents a major challenge.

Despite the current barriers, states and local mental health systems, both public and private, have begun to move forward in their EBP implementation, even though levels of commitment and success have been variable. Unfortunately, even when service systems have attempted to implement EBP, they have not always done so by using mechanisms that ensure sustained adherence to fidelity. And even when EBPs have been implemented with fidelity, some systems have struggled with questions of how the EBPs coordinate with each other and with services that lack a strong evidence base. Many factors contribute to these implementation problems, including (Goldman et al., 2001):

- Lack of a long-term vision for the service system
- Lack of agreement on desired outcomes of the service system
- Lack of incentives for evidence-based practices
- Short-term horizons for policy planning
- Political mandates or competing priorities
- Resource limitations
- Uncertainty associated with change and untoward events

Below we discuss four specific barriers that must be overcome for EBP to become part of routine mental health services:

1. Lack of a workforce trained in EBPs
2. Lack of financing for EBPs
3. Lack of a comprehensive research base on EBPs and effective implementation
4. Lack of infrastructure to support EBP

### Lack of a Workforce Trained in EBP

According to the Surgeon General (U.S. Department of Health and Human Services, 1999) and experts on specific EBPs, there exists a shortage of trained practitioners able to provide EBPs. The President's New Freedom Commission on Mental Health specifically identified a general shortage of qualified practitioners trained in EBP as a key obstacle to improving the quality of the nation's mental health care, warning that this lack of training leads to a workforce "ill-equipped to use the latest breakthroughs in modern medicine" (2003, p. 70). Rural areas especially lack practitioners trained in EBP, with particularly acute shortages in practitioners who serve children, adolescents, and older adults.

Assertive community treatment—ACT

Traditional training practices do not facilitate the learning of EBPs. For example, many EBPs require multidisciplinary team approaches, such as occur in assertive community treatment (ACT). Community-based ACT is an integrated, multidisciplinary approach to providing persons with severe mental illnesses with a comprehensive array of medical, psychosocial, and rehabilitative services. (See Chapter 14 for a detailed discussion of ACT.) A world that emphasizes disciplinary training impedes the learning and implementing of multidisciplinary training and EBPs. In addition, some EBPs, for example, family psychoeducation (explored in Chapter 18), require that consumers, practitioners, and family members receive special training.

## Lack of Financing for EBP

Current mental health-care financing policies often stand as system barriers to implementing EBPs, according to the Surgeon General (U.S. Department of Health and Human Services, 1999), the President's New Freedom Commission on Mental Health (2003), and numerous researchers of mental health services delivery researchers (Drake et al., 2001; Goldman et al., 2001; Torrey et al., 2001). In its final report, the commission observes, "Fee-for-service reimbursement systems for Medicaid, Medicare, and other payers do not allow providers to bill for essential components of many EBP programs" (2003, p. 69). The commission cites complex reimbursement policies as a hindrance to getting EBPs to the people who need them:

Reimbursement policies

> The complexities and limitations in paying for many well-established evidence-based practices for children and adults cause the quality of mental health services to vary greatly. In particular, Medicaid, Medicare, and private payers must keep current with advances in evidence-based practices, continuously examining practice to inform reimbursement policies. (p. 69)

Depending upon the source of funding for mental health services, however, the EBP implementation barriers differ. As an example, private health-care insurance rarely includes mental health services more complex than an outpatient office visit. Some services, including EBPs, simply fall outside the scope of traditional health insurance.

Parity

The lack of parity for mental health-care benefits (as compared to other medical benefits) in private health-care insurance further reduces the likelihood of private insurance plans offering EBPs coverage. *Parity* refers to the provision of health insurance coverage with the same benefits for mental disorders as are allotted to other medical disorders. Individuals in the public mental health system may have the greatest access (though still limited) to some of the EBPs.

Medicaid and
Medicare

As the largest funder of mental health services in the nation, Medicaid is the most important potential payer for EBPs for individuals with severe mental disorders. However, Medicaid does not currently specifically cover many accepted EBPs. Even when Medicaid does cover a particular EBP, states and providers often find it difficult to understand how to bill Medicaid for the EBP. (Medicare views many of the EBP services as outside their rigid coverage rules entirely.) The commission explains the difficulty for states in trying to use Medicaid funds for EBPs: "While it is possible for Medicaid to cover a number of EBPs, the only way to access reimbursement presently is to navigate the system expertly enough to obtain approval to provide those services under an option or waiver" (2003, p. 70). For example, some states have managed to establish a Medicaid billing process for supported employment, whereas other states are still struggling with this issue. Most mental health systems cannot afford to offer EBPs without Medicaid reimbursement mechanisms.

## Lack of a Comprehensive Research Base

Lack of research
generalizability

Although the Surgeon General (U.S. Department of Health and Human Services, 1999) concluded that a range of effective treatments exists for most mental disorders, for some serious clinical problems—such as youth suicide, post-traumatic stress disorder, and borderline personality disorder—a rigorous research base does not yet exist; however, the evidence base for each of these problems continues to grow. In many cases, evidence comes from clinical trials that may not be generalizable to typical treatment settings without modification. For example, practitioners in the effectiveness studies may have had specific types of training or supervision, or the consumers participating in the studies may not have been representative. Argyris (1993) warns that treatment effectiveness studies simply cannot capture the inherent complexity of actual clinical practice.

Once identified, it is important to implement EBPs with expediency in the field. At the current time, we have yet to identify the best mechanisms for facilitating this rapid deployment of science to service. Although thousands of studies have investigated dissemination and implementation of best practices in health care and mental health care, specifically, very little data exist on how to implement specific EBPs (Torrey et al., 2001).

| Lack of dissemination of EBP knowledge base

## Lack of Infrastructure

The move from science to services requires strong national leadership if EBP is to become a national priority for treatment. Currently, architects of the mental health system are under pressure to organize services within the context of quality improvement. Leadership is often a critical force in removing barriers to the implementation of EBPs at all levels.

| Lack of national leadership

The technology and communications infrastructure of mental health care lags far behind that of other health care sectors, according to the Institute of Medicine (2001). Practitioners and policymakers today lack universal access to the latest scientific advances and other health information that would promote the use of EBPs in routine mental health services. This information is rarely available. Consumers and their family members, too, want up-to-date information on effective treatments and support services, yet this information is seldom available to them (President's New Freedom Commission on Mental Health, 2003). The further development of EBPs and their integration into routine mental health services requires a national strategy and a corresponding technological infrastructure.

| Lack of an information technology infrastructure

No one-size-fits-all remedy

In discussing the barriers to implementing EBPs, one barrier is frequently overlooked: Not every mental health problem has an evidence-based solution (Goldman et al, 2001). Furthermore, even with an available EBP for a specific consumer objective and problem, no guarantee exists that the EBP will prove effective for everyone with similar symptoms, history, and objectives. Effective EBP requires a consumer-centered assessment of each individual's strengths, goals and needs. EBPs are not designed as a one-size-fits-all remedy for all persons with mental illnesses.

## Meeting the Challenges of Implementing Evidence-Based Practice

What actions can we take to overcome the barriers to implementing EBP? Here we consider the following specific action strategies that can be applied to meet the challenge of successfully implementing EBP in routine mental health care:

- Improve public awareness of EBPs
- Provide technical assistance for EBP Implementation
- Ensure the supply of practitioners trained in EBP
- Reduce financial barriers to EBP
- Continue to build the science base for new EBPs
- Establish leadership in implementing EBPs
- Build the technology infrastructure to support EBPs
- Tailor EBPs to age, sex, race, and culture

These action strategies require the involvement of both the public and private sectors, federal, state, and local levels of government, mental health-care practitioners, administrators, policymakers, and consumers and families. Discussed in detail below, the strategies and derived from the work of Goldman and Azrin (2003), the President's New Freedom Commission on Mental Health (2003), and the Surgeon General's Report on mental health (U.S. Department of Health and Human Services, 1999).

## Improve Public Awareness of EBPs

Although awareness of EBP alone is not adequate for implementation, it constitutes a necessary first step. Evidence from general medical care supports the strategy of raising awareness to effect change in mental health services delivery (Reiser, 1992). Consumers and family members informed of the benefits associated with EBPs can create a powerful demand for these services (Frese et al., 2001). Practitioners and policymakers who are aware of, and understand, the EBPs and their utility will be more likely to adopt them.

## Provide Technical Assistance

*Technical assistance* means providing direct guidance to mental health program administrators, providers, policymakers, and other stakeholders on how to build the infrastructure for successful EBP implementation in a particular program setting. The Evidence-Based Practice Project (discussed earlier in this chapter) is finding that technical assistance is essential to effective EBP implementations, especially when the implementation process actively involves all the stakeholders, including consumers and families, in this process (Drake & Goldman, 2003). This technical assistance encompasses consultations with agency and system administrators in preparation for implementing the EBP and teaching the needed skills to those personnel who will provide the EBP. This assistance has been available to those sites involved in the Evidence-Based Practices Project, and it is currently available to other sites through a limited number of implementation centers across the country (www.mentalhealthpractices.org).

## Ensure the Supply of Trained Practitioners

A consensus has emerged that the existing mental health workforce must be offered updated knowledge and skills through quality improvement and continuing education. The mental health-care field lags in its efforts to train practitioners in newer practices, particularly EBPs. Practitioners have not shown an unwillingness or lack of interest in learning EBPs. Rather, too many structural barriers exist to absorbing and implementing EBPs in everyday services. Developing mechanisms for training the current workforce and influencing the training curriculum of new professionals and paraprofessionals will ensure an adequate supply of practitioners trained in the EBPs. To improve and expand the work force that provides EBPs, the President's New Freedom Commission on Mental Health (2003) specifically recommended that graduate and continuing education programs train more mental health practitioners in EBPs and emerging best practices. The commission suggests that Department of Health and Human Services spearhead this effort and lead a public–private partnership to develop a comprehensive strategic plan aimed at improving workforce recruitment, retention, diversity, and skills training. Finally, because many EBPs involve a multidisciplinary treatment approach (e.g., supported employment and ACT), the infrastructure for a national multidisciplinary mental health practitioner training program must be established.

### Reduce Financial Barriers

Realistically, an EBP is not available to an individual if he or she cannot afford it, or if a program cannot afford to provide it for the price offered by payers. The failure of most mental health service financing mechanisms to pay adequately for EBPs creates a major barrier to their implementation. Concurring, the President's New Freedom Commission on Mental Health "encourages public and private payers to reframe their reimbursement policies to better support and widely implement EBPs" (2003, p. 81).

Mental health financing barriers

Resources in mental health agencies must support the transition from traditional practice to EBP. When non-EBPs generate income for an agency, it is difficult to motivate practitioners and administrators to implement EBPs instead. Offering practitioners and administrators incentives for implementing and sustaining EBPs will likely facilitate EBP implementation. Although permanent resource increases will not necessarily accompany the move to EBP, one-time-only resources to support the transition to EBP have proven beneficial (Goldman et al., 2001).

*Parity for Mental and Medical Disorders*
Currently, no national parity law mandates full parity for mental health-care benefits. Consequently, health insurance benefits for the diagnosis and treatment of mental disorders typically do not measure up to the amount of coverage for other medical disorders. In many private health insurance plans, the benefits for mental disorders involve higher copayments (i.e., the amount the insured individual owes for the service), lower annual and lifetime dollar limits, and fewer allowed outpatient visits and inpatient hospital days than for other medical disorders. For example, an individual with schizophrenia might find that, in many private health insurance policies for diagnosis and treatment of the schizophrenia:

Health insurance for schizophrenia and diabetes

- The co-payment is $50 for each office visit.
- Office visits are limited to 25 per year.
- The annual limit is $200,000.
- The lifetime limit is $500,000.
- Hospital inpatient days are restricted to 30 per year.

Contrast this coverage with health insurance benefits for treatment of another medical disorder requiring long-term care, diabetes:

- The copayment is only $10 for each office visit.
- Office visits are unlimited.
- The annual limit is $1 million.
- The lifetime limit is $10 million.
- Hospital inpatient days are unlimited.

Unfortunately, some individuals with mental disorders find that not only does their private health insurance *not* cover EBPs, but also that the plan covers very few services of any type to treat mental illnesses. Additionally, Medicare provides *no* parity for mental disorders and *no* prescription benefits at all. Lack of parity for mental health care limits the availability of treatment for these disorders—including evidence-based treatments—and increases treatment costs to the individual. This disparity in health insurance benefits for mental health care amounts to discrimination against persons with mental disorders. Full national parity should extend to all Americans, ending this discriminatory insurance practice.

**Medicaid and Medicare financing of EBPs**

Medicaid and Medicare benefits should cover EBPs, and the rates paid to practitioners must create an incentive for them to deliver EBPs. For example, in some settings, Medicaid does not reimburse for the EBP-supported employment at a rate that compares favorably with that for far less effective sheltered workshop or train-and-place rehabilitation interventions (this point is discussed further in Chapter 16). The Centers for Medicare and Medicaid Services constitute the nation's largest single payer for mental health services through their Medicare and Medicaid funding. Given this influential role, the Centers for Medicare and Medicaid Services should remove unreasonable financial barriers to implementing EBPs in the Medicaid and Medicare programs. The centers should also offer comprehensive guidance and technical assistance to states on effectively financing EBPs in mental health under the existing regulations. For example, until very recently, Medicaid policy almost uniformly discouraged the EBP implementation of ACT. However, with a sophisticated understanding of Medicaid payment mechanisms, states can finance most (if not all) of the key components comprising ACT. Medicare offers no drug benefits for outpatients, does not cover rehabilitation services, and requires higher copayments for outpatient psychotherapy than for other outpatient medical services.

**Mental health services block grant**

In an era of scarce resources for public mental health services, the federal Mental Health Services block grant (administered by the Center for Mental Health Services within the Substance Abuse and Mental Health Services Administration) represents one of the most important existing funding streams available for mental health service innovations. Although relatively small in dollar size, the block grant gives state mental health authorities broad latitude in the use of these federal funds to pay for the provision of community-based mental health services, including EBPs. Block grant resources could be used to shift services from existing (non-evidence-based) practices to EBP, *without* the federal government increasing block grant funding. Several states have already implemented EBPs using block grant money. State legislators want evidence of effective services and accountability for the services funded through the block grant. These two characteristics—effectiveness and accountability—are the hallmarks of EBP, as discussed earlier in this chapter. Modifying requirements of the block grant by, for example, mandating that the block grant or a certain portion of it be used only for EBPs, could make it easier for states to implement EBP.

## Continue to Build the EBP Science Base

We must continue to build our understanding of what constitute EBPs, refining this understanding as new research evidence emerges. Then we must bring these effective new practices to practitioners in the field, evaluating the earliest EBP implementation efforts as we go and using the lessons learned to inform future EBP implementation activities. Likewise, dissemination projects and funding are needed to determine the best ways to disseminate the new practices to practitioners in the field. Involving all stakeholders—consumers, family members, and practitioners in psychiatry, psychology, social work, primary practice, and nursing—in the planning, fielding, and evaluation of EBP implementation and research will enhance its effectiveness.

As noted earlier, only a limited knowledge base for the effectiveness of EBPs exists. The steady development of new treatments to add to this knowledge base, especially regarding those disorders for which EBPs do no yet exist, must continue. Moreover, research to determine whether identified EBPs are effective in all ethnic subpopulations, among persons who have multiple disorders, and in all practice settings—for example, rural as opposed to urban settings—is needed. As Anthony and his colleagues (2003) pointed out, the treatment-effectiveness knowledge base must expand as our understanding of what constitutes EBP evolves. Medicaid demonstration initiatives, in particular, are critical to informing the Centers for Medicare and Medicaid Services about the effectiveness and cost implications of EBPs.

### Establish Leadership in Implementing EBPs

Although a leadership infrastructure will play a vital role in promoting the development and implementation of EBPs, national leadership on the EBP front is even more of an imperative. Currently, no central point of coordination on EBP-related matters exists. This situation promotes fragmentation and limits collaboration and efficiency in all EBP endeavors.

Public–private partnership |
The emergence of national leadership is the most promising structure for creating a public–private partnership. The federal government should initiate and sustain an EBP public–private partnership with all key mental health services stakeholders: states, local governments, and the private sector, including consumer and family advocacy groups, as well as payer, provider, and professional groups. This partnership would aim to advance EBP knowledge, disseminate EBP findings, facilitate the development of a workforce trained to deliver EBP, and ensure the implementation of EBPs with adequate financial support. The President's New Freedom Commission (2003) recommended a similar EBP public–private partnership.

To accomplish these goals, the proposed partnership might sponsor and support a center or collaborative network to review potential EBPs and the research supporting their effectiveness. The partnership could encourage multiple perspectives on what constitutes evidence and evidence-based practice and who makes these decisions. Opinions differ on these matters, and perhaps there will never be complete consensus. But, there exists no national leadership on these issues, to facilitate healthy discourse or collaboration. Who should recognize the treatments and services that become designated as EBPs? An EBP public–private partnership represents the ideal body to carry out this responsibility. The partnership might also develop quality improvement tools, conduct training, and provide ongoing consultation and support to systems and organizations that implement EBPs.

Quality improvement programs—licensing, credentialing, accreditation, and professional associations' standards for empirically supported treatments and practice guidelines—represent important mechanisms for moving EBPs into the field. The public–private partnership could serve as a coordinating point or clearinghouse for these activities, which would involve numerous organizations at the national, state, and local levels and in both the public and private sectors.

| Quality improvement
| programs

## Build Information Technology Infrastructure

It is essential to develop an effective information technology infrastructure to give practitioners and consumers easy access to the most recent scientific advances in mental health services. The New Freedom Commission on Mental Health stated that: "With the explosion of scientific advances, new treatments, breakthroughs in promoting health, and medical information, all providers must have high-speed electronic access to the latest evidence-based practice guidelines, best practice models, ongoing clinical trials, scientific research, and other health information" (2003, p. 81). Recall the problems inherent with the four-step approach to clinical decision making that required practitioners to search for relevant clinical information across all available sources. This model proved unworkable because practitioners could not possibly locate all the relevant evidence pertaining to each consumer. Building an information technology infrastructure that allows universal access for all practitioners and consumers would surmount that obstacle. A decade ago, we would have dismissed this effort as impractical. But today, with Internet access commonplace, a technology infrastructure to support the development, dissemination, and implementation of EBPs in routine mental health care represents a readily achievable goal.

### Tailor EBPs to Age, Sex, Race, and Culture

Disparities in mental health services

Traditionally, the mental health system has not served culturally diverse groups well. According to the President's New Freedom Commission on Mental Health, "The mental health system has not kept pace with the diverse needs of racial and ethnic minorities, often underserving or inappropriately serving them. Specifically, the system has neglected to incorporate respect or understanding of the histories, traditions, beliefs, languages, and value systems of culturally diverse groups" (2003, p. 49). We must eliminate the disparities in mental health services for these groups. This problem especially deserves consideration given the census figures indicating that by the year 2005, racial and ethnic minorities will comprise more than 40% of the United States population (Bureau of the Census, 2001). As such, the mental health field must consider how well current and future EBPs address the mental health treatment needs of individuals from culturally diverse groups.

Surgeon General's report on culture, race, and ethnicity

Unfortunately, the current research base cannot support the use of all the EBPs with each of the culturally diverse groups—based on ethnic or racial identity, age, gender, or other cultural influences—that practitioners may encounter in actual practice. Encouragingly, in his report on culture, race, and ethnicity (U.S. Department of Health and Human Services, 2001), the Surgeon General concluded that the existing research on EBPs with various racial, cultural, and ethnic groups generally finds positive outcomes. While the evidence base on EBPs with culturally diverse populations evolves, practitioners must tailor evidence-based treatments to meet the needs of consumers from culturally diverse groups. For example, to engage members of linguistic minority groups in treatment and EBPs, practitioners must offer language-appropriate services. When using medications with culturally diverse groups, practitioners and consumers should understand how variations in physiology, beliefs about medicines, and other attitudes might affect the course of treatment. Finally, practitioners must carefully reconcile fidelity to an EBP program model with the need to engage everyone in a community who might need or benefit from the available services.

## References

Anthony, W., Rogers, E. S., & Farkas, M. (2003). Research on evidence-based practices: Future directions in an era of recovery. *Community Mental Health Journal, 39*, 101–114.

Argyris, C. (1993). *Knowledge for action: A guide to overcoming barriers to organizational change.* San Francisco: Jossey-Bass.

Bond, G. R., Becker, D. R., Drake, R. E., Rapp, C., Meisler, N., Lehman, A., et al. (2001). Implementing supported employment as an evidence-based practice. *Psychiatric Services, 52*, 313–322.

Bureau of the Census. (2001). *Profiles of general demographic characteristics 2000: 2000 census of population and housing.* Washington, DC: U.S. Department of Commerce.

Cochrane, A. L. (1972). *Effectiveness and efficiency: Random reflections on health services.* London: Nuffield Provincial Hospitals Trust.

Cochrane, A. L. (1979). 1931–1971: A critical review, with particular reference to the medical profession. In G. Teeling-Smith & N. Wells (Ed.), *Medicines for the year 2000* (pp. 1–11). London: Office of Health Economics.

Cochrane Collaboration. (1999). *Cochrane brochure.* Retrieved September 5, 2003, from http://*www.cochrane.org/*.

Davidoff, F. (1999). In the teeth of the evidence: The curious case of evidence-based medicine. *The Mount Sinai Journal of Medicine, 66*(2), 75–83.

Dixon, L., McFarlane, W., Lefley, H., Lucksted, A., Cohen, M., & Falloon, I. (2001). Evidence-based practices for services to families of people with psychiatric disabilities. *Psychiatric Services, 52,* 903–910.

Drake, R. E., & Goldman, H. (2003). *Evidence-based practices in mental health care.* Washington, DC: American Psychiatric Association.

Drake, R. E., Goldman, H. G., Leff, H. S., Lehman, A., Dixon, L., Mueser, K. T., et al. (2001). Implementing evidence-based practices in routine mental health service settings. *Psychiatric Services, 52,* 179–182.

Evidence-Based Medicine Working Group. (1992). Evidence-based medicine: A new approach to teaching the practice of medicine. *Journal of the American Medical Association, 268*(17), 2420–2425.

Frese, F. J., III, Stanley, J., Kress, K., & Vogel-Scibilia, S. (2001). Integrating evidence-based practices and the Recovery Model. *Psychiatric Services, 52,* 1462–1468.

Goldman, H. G., & Azrin, S. T. (2003). Public policy and evidence-based practice. *Psychiatric Clinics of North America, 26,* 1–19.

Goldman, H. G., Ganju, V., Drake, R. E., Gorman, P., Hogan, M., Hyde, P., et al. (2001). Policy implications for implementing evidence-based practices. *Psychiatric Services, 52,* 1591–1597.

Guyatt, G. H., Meade, M. O., Jaeschke, R. Z., Cook, P. J., & Haynes, R. B. (2000). Practitioners of evidence-based care: Not all clinicians need to appraise evidence from scratch but all need some skills. *British Medical Journal, 320,* 954–955.

Hoagwood, K., Burns, B., Kiser, L., Ringelsen, H., & Schoenwald, S. (2001). Evidence-based practice in child and adolescent mental health services. *Psychiatric Services, 52,* 1179–1189.

Institute of Medicine. (2001). *Crossing the quality chasm: A new health system for the 21st century.* Washington, DC: National Academy Press.

Lehman, A. (2001). Quality of care in mental health: The case of schizophrenia. *Health Affairs, 18,* 52–65.

McColl, A., Smith, H., White, P., & Field, J. (1998). General practitioners' perceptions of the route to evidence based medicine: A questionnaire survey. *British Medical Journal, 316,* 361–365.

Mechanic, D. (1998). Bringing science to medicine: The origins of evidence-based practice. *Health Affairs, 17,* 250—251.

Mellman, T., Miller, A., Weissman, E., Crismon, M., Essock, S., & Marder, S. (2001). Evidence-based pharmacologic treatment for people with severe mental illness: A focus on guidelines and algorithms. *Psychiatric Services, 52,* 619–625.

Muir Gray, J. A. (1997). *Evidence-based healthcare: How to make policy and management decisions.* London: Churchill Livingstone.

NASMHPD Research Institute (National Association of State Mental Health Program Directors). (2002). *State mental health agency profiling system.* Retrieved September 5, 2003, from *http://nri.rdmc.org/profiles01/Report01.cfm.*

President's New Freedom Commission on Mental Health. (2003). *Achieving the promise: Transforming mental health care in America. Final report.* (DHHS Pub. No. SMA-03-3832). Rockville, MD: U.S. Government Printing Office.

Reiser, S. J. (1992). Consumer competence and the reform of American health care. *Journal of the American Medical Association, 267,* 1511–1515.

Risdale, L. (1995). *Evidence based general practice.* Philadelphia: W. B. Saunders.

Sackett, D. L., Rosenberg, W., Muir Gray, J. A., Haynes, R. B., & Richardson, W. S. (1996). Evidence-based medicine: What it is and what it isn't. *British Medical Journal, 312,* 71–72.

Sackett, D. L., Strauss, S. E., Richardson, W. S., Rosenberg, W., & Haynes, R. B. (2000). *Evidence-based medicine: How to practice and teach EBM.* (2nd ed). London: Churchill Livingstone.

Torrey, W. C., Drake, R. E., Dixon, L., Burns, B., Flynn, L., & Rush, J., et al. (2001). Implementing evidence-based practices for persons with severe mental illnesses. *Psychiatric Services, 52,* 45–50.

U.S. Department of Health and Human Services (DHHS). (1999). *Mental health: A report of the Surgeon General.* Rockville, MD: U.S. Department of Health and Human Services.

U.S. Department of Health and Human Services (DHHS). (2001). *Mental health: Culture, race, and ethnicity. A report of the Surgeon General.* Rockville, MD: U.S. Department of Health and Human Services.

Wang, P. S., Berglund, P., & Kessler, R. C. (2000). Recent care of common mental disorders in the United States: Prevalence and conformance with evidence-based recommendations. *Journal of General Internal Medicine, 15,* 284–292.

# FIVE

# Clinical Decision Making and the Evidence-Based Practitioner

*Kenneth J. Gill*
*Carlos W. Pratt*

tHE EVIDENCE-BASED MENTAL HEALTH PRACTITIONER, a relatively new professional, is guided primarily by relevant research on interventions that are available to help consumers reduce impairments associated with mental illness and achieve their goals. To this end, every evidence-based practitioner must be an informed student of the professional literature, capable of assessing, understanding, and applying the quality of evidence therein. The evidence-based practitioner informs consumers of treatment and rehabilitation options, including information concerning the relative merits of each option in producing desired outcomes, as well as its drawbacks, such as side effects.

This chapter presents a critical examination of the current state of mental health practices and the associated education and training processes. It is not meant to focus excessively on the flaws of any one profession; rather, it highlights the limitations in practitioner decision making found across mental health fields. Although there is some evidence that professionals with different educational preparation differ in their decision making approaches (Falvey, 2001), many of the mental health professions share an overreliance on what is described as "intuition" and personal experience. These criticisms certainly apply to psychiatric rehabilitation and psychology, the professions to which we belong.

## Introduction

Consumerism, a recovery orientation, and the philosophy of empowerment exert overlapping influences on the evolution of treatment services for people with severe mental illness (SMI). Each has a different emphasis but similar implications for the implementation of treatment strategies. In the last two decades, one of the most important and positive developments in the mental health field has been the influence of consumerism, as the recipients of mental health services have increased their expectations for access to a range of high-quality interventions (Hoge, Jacobs, Belitsky, & Migdole, 2002). Consumerism implies that real choice is available. Traditionally, however, professionals have not been trained to appreciate this concern (Hoge et al., 2002). Parallel to the development of consumerism among persons with SMI is the philosophy of recovery (Deegan, 1988; Ralph, 2002), which acknowledges the life journey of the individual with severe mental illness, coping and thriving, while incorporating the reality of a mental illness into his or her self-image. Integral to the notion of recovery is the evidence that individuals with SMI often find or create satisfying and meaningful lives. Related to consumerism and recovery is the construct of empowerment, which refers to an individual's efforts to enhance a sense of self-efficacy in managing his or her own life and to experience success in important environments (Bandura, 1997; Pratt, Gill, Barrett, & Roberts, 1999).

All of the evidence-based practices (EBPs) covered in this volume are practical approaches aimed at helping consumers achieve meaningful goals. All seek to help consumers improve their quality of life and promote their integration in the community. A number of these approaches involves sharing information and coping strate-

Consumerism

Recovery orientation

Empowerment

The goal of all EBPs

gies with consumers and their families to empower them with knowledge and skills. Other strategies are aimed at relieving psychiatric symptoms or addictions to substances in order to help promote recovery. All EBPs seek to promote consumer self-sufficiency and interdependence.

## Respect for Consumer Input

In light of the values of consumerism, recovery, and empowerment, one of the most important characteristics of the evidence based-practitioner or, more precisely, a practitioner guided by the research evidence, is to respect consumer input and preferences. This worthy aim is more easily stated than achieved. A simple affirmation of this value is not enough. Nor is it appropriate to take a "hands-off" approach, leaving consumers without information or guidance about the best course of treatment. Indeed, such an approach could be interpreted as an abdication of professional responsibility.

Like any other consumer of health-care service, a person with severe mental illness should have sufficient knowledge to make informed choices about effective treatment services and to avoid harmful ones. To be truly respectful of consumer choice, a practitioner must ensure that the consumer has the opportunity to understand and consider the best information available. As a familiar advertisement for men's discount clothing states, "An educated consumer is our best customer." To help an individual make the most informed choice possible, consumers and their families need to be educated about the specifics of each of their options, including knowledge of the outcomes, benefits, and drawbacks of each possible intervention.

Consider an example of another long-term, serious, life-threatening disorder: coronary artery disease. What if you or one of your family members was diagnosed with this disorder, which is the leading cause of heart attacks? What type of recommendations would you want to be given regarding treatment? Would you want recommendations

Educating consumers

based solely on the doctor's personal opinions and preferences, regardless of current research? Or would you prefer recommendations that were influenced by the accumulated science on the subject, such as the relative efficacy of different treatments and procedures in terms of survival rates, therapeutic effects, and side effects? Do persons with severe and persistent mental illnesses deserve anything less when considering their treatment and rehabilitation options (Torrey et al., 2001)?

**Evidence-driven attitude and skills**

Developing an evidence-driven attitude, in which services and treatment recommendations are primarily guided by an understanding of science, is essential. Developing the skills to provide specific interventions is equally critical and is discussed throughout this text. The EBP practitioner knows that the best way to develop a meaningful, collaborative partnership with consumers is to help them become educated regarding their illnesses and effective treatment options. Therefore, the practitioner will need to develop the communication skills to determine the type of everyday language and the complexity of explanation that will be understandable for each individual consumer, and his or her families, when appropriate. An effective practitioner must be open to questions and discussion. Listening carefully to a consumer's preferences, concerns, and comments and observing body language can help determine if the explanations regarding treatment and potential outcomes are being understood.

An individual's self-report about the effectiveness of past treatments, side effects, and personal preferences is essential. For example, the fact that a particular medication caused serious side effects is important data, as is a family member's report that his or her relative is experiencing the early signs of increased symptomatology, foreshadowing relapse.

**Research evidence on SMI treatment**

Some have raised the objection that there is not enough research evidence on the treatment of SMI to make informed recommendations. Clearly, such individuals lack information. In fact, a great deal of research now exists on EBPs that successfully reduce symptomatology, prevent

unnecessary hospitalization, incarceration, or homelessness, and enhance coping, improve skills of daily living, and
promote employment (Lehman & Steinwachs, 2003;
Satcher, 2000). Additional information on promising practices continues to emerge. Yet, even though this information is available, it does not mean that routine mental
health programs are providing evidence-based practices. In
fact, less than 10% of individuals with schizophrenia receive
services that could be considered best practices, according
to the Surgeon General's Report (Public Health Service,
1999), the Schizophrenia Patient Outcomes Research Team
(Lehman & Steinwachs, 2003), and the report from the
President's New Freedom Commission on Mental Health
(2003). Thus, it is very reasonable for any consumer or
concerned family member to ask:

> "What is the likelihood that this practice will help me to
> do what I want with my life?"
> "What is the best way to keep me from getting sick
> again?"
> "What can you do to help us cope with this illness
> better?"
> "How will I be able to get and keep a job?"

To begin to answer these questions, each practitioner and
his or her agency will need to become informed students of
research, evaluating the quality of evidence regarding
particular clinical issues and the interventions designed to
address them (Olney, Strohmer, & Kennedy, 2002). This
task involves thinking like a scientist and understanding
hypothesis testing in both the clinical and research realms
(Spaulding, Sullivan, & Poland, 2003). It also means understanding the limitations of research evidence.

## Recommended Outlook for Practitioners

Practitioners and program leaders should be able to think
scientifically, which is described by Paul Meehl (1993) as
"the passion not to be fooled and not to fool anyone else"

Practitioner as
scientist

(1993, p. 728). That is, as a learner, a current or future practitioner should have the skills and knowledge to avoid being misled by people in authority or other sources of so-called knowledge. This entails learning about what the best evidence is and how to evaluate it. The second part of Meehl's statement implies that practitioners should actively share this knowledge with their consumers.

A thorough understanding of research methods will help the EBP practitioner assess which studies are capable of providing causal explanations and which provide only evidence of associations or correlations among variables. Being guided by research is a matter of professional responsibility and is central to ethical practice. Indeed, "practitioners have a professional responsibility to keep abreast of new findings and policy changes that may affect consumers" (Olney et al., 2002, p. 2). Like most of the mental health-related disciplines, rehabilitation counselors include this perspective in their code of ethics. Thus, practitioners must "maintain a reasonable level of awareness of current scientific and professional information . . . They will take steps to maintain competence in the skills they use; they will be open to new techniques" (Commission on Rehabilitation Counselor Certification, 2002, p. 7). As Olney and colleagues (2002) pointed out, for many students, understanding theoretical analyses, research designs, statistics, and ambiguous findings are not the highlights of their professional education. Yet all the major professional education accreditation agencies require mental health practitioners to study statistics and research. The rationale of each profession varies slightly, but the main thrust is that the student, and later the practitioner, must decide what research findings mean and whether they are relevant (Olney et al., 2002).

Empirical methods | Furthermore, armed with an understanding of the relevant science, the EBP practitioner can use hypotheses and deductive processes similarly to a researcher (Spaulding et al., 2003). The research evidence should guide both assessments and interventions. According to Garb and

Boyle, "Mental health professionals should not use an assessment instrument or treatment method solely because it seems to work in clinical practice. Instead, practitioners should become familiar with the research literature to learn if the assessment instrument or treatment method is supported by empirical research" (2003, p. 31). When helping a consumer pursue his or her goal, a practitioner considers the empirical evidence. Interventions with empirical support are considered along with their probability for helping the consumer to achieve his or her goal. Once interventions are tried, their effectiveness is assessed in terms of measurable outcomes. Based on the results of the interventions, new hypotheses may be formed, perhaps new interventions are warranted, and the process continues (Spaulding et al., 2003).

Each clinical step is based on research findings and evaluated in terms of observable results. Yet the EBP practitioner should also be aware that this process is prone to certain biases. Individual clinical work does not have the methodological controls against bias that are present in research studies. EBP practitioners understand that their own experience can be biased and misleading. (This point is discussed in more detail later in this chapter.)

| Bias propensity

## Traditional Clinical Decision Making

Existing practices in the mental health field are typically based on tradition, convenience, practitioners' preferences, political correctness, and so-called clinical "wisdom" (Drake et al., 2001). At times, historical clinical practice in mental health has proven to be both unhelpful and tragically harmful. Practitioners who learn to think like scientists and then share this thinking with consumers are in significant contrast to those who still employ traditional methods of clinical decision making (Drake et al., 2001; Spaulding et al., 2003).

The traditional approach to clinical decision making relies on the clinical judgment or intuition of the practi-

| Clinical judgment

tioner, informed by experience or the policies and procedures of the program or agency. Occasionally, the practitioner consults with a supervisor or colleague who may be asked to assert his or her authority or clinical judgment. Here again, the primary guide is the experience of the practitioner and his or her supervisor. This approach rarely engages consumers and family members in informed discussions of treatment options. Typically, the individual practitioner (or team of practitioners) does not consider whether his or her experience is representative of all of the knowledge relevant to the problem. Nor does the practitioner consider whether the inferences drawn from this prized experience are as unbiased as possible (Lynn, & Lohr, 2003b; Meehl, 1973). In fact, there is strong evidence that the experience of a given practitioner is usually *un*representative (Gilje & Kloset, 2000; Lilienfeld et al., 2003b). The identification of this problem is not new. In 1954, psychologist Paul Meehl published a small but seminal book, *Clinical versus Statistical Prediction: A Theoretical Analysis and a Review of the Evidence*, which pointed out the problems inherent in employing "clinical judgment" when making predictions. Almost 50 years later, books such as Lilienfeld, Lyn, and Lohr's *Science and Pseudo-Science in Clinical Psychology* (2003a) and Spaulding, Sullivan, and Poland's *Treatment and Rehabilitation of Severe Mental Illness* (2003) are still calling for a more scientific approach to clinical practices.

Intuition versus observation

Many practitioners rely on what they call intuition, defined as immediate apprehension without reasoning, immediate insight, or knowing something without knowing how it is known (Cioffi, 2001; Gilje & Klose, 2001). Many nurses reportedly described their decision making as partly intuitive and strongly endorsed the statement, "I can see changes in a patient's condition but I am not always able to explain how I know this" (Gilje & Klose, 2000). There is the possibility that intuition may actually bea product of over-learning (Bandura, 1997), similar to riding a bicycle, such that the experienced individual no longer tracks all the steps involved and is simply unaware of the steps when he or she performs them. Consider the following anecdote:

> A case manager reported that he could use his intuition to predict psychiatric relapses before they became apparent. Believing he was bragging, his colleagues tracked his predictions. He did seem to be fairly good at predicting who would soon be hospitalized, and he rarely said that someone was experiencing increased symptoms when they were not. When pressed on how he achieved such accuracy, he said he noted some "small signs, almost nothing." When pressed further, he said, "When I notice one of our consumers looking more disheveled, lacking energy, and losing sleep, I suspect an impending relapse." What he attributed to intuition was, in fact, based on the observation of signs that have been empirically demonstrated to be early warning signs of relapse in many psychiatric disorders.

For educational and training purposes, the idea of intuition is not very helpful. However, development of observational skills has obvious value (Spaulding et al., 2003). Unfortunately, the interpretation of these very observations may be prone to bias. Bias is a preference or inclination, especially one that inhibits impartial judgment. Generally speaking, experience is highly valued in clinical training by both practitioners and educators. The experience and clinical judgment of faculty, field supervisors, and senior colleagues are often integral to the training curriculum. Although the preceding vignette was an instance of a practitioner using his experience very effectively, Lilienfeld et al. (2003a) summarized research showing that the decision making behavior of experienced practitioners often differs little from that of relatively inexperienced students. Occasionally, clinicians' predictions are no better than those of laypersons educated in nonmental health fields (Lilienfeld et al., 2003b, c)!

*Bias of overvaluation*

A large survey of nurses found that they primarily base their treatment plans on experience with others patients whom they see as similar to the present case, rather than on

*Reliance on experience and heuristics*

scientific evidence (Gilje & Klose, 2001). In practice, this certainly seems reasonable. It is a sound use of the heuristic of representativeness, in which one instance is treated as representative of a class (Tversky & Kahneman, 1974). A heuristic is a strategy, approach or "rule of thumb" used to guide decision making under conditions of uncertainty.

Yet, despite its efficiency, this thinking is not individualized to each consumer's situation, it does not take into account any research evidence that may have accumulated related to the topic, nor does it consider how well those previous interventions worked (Spaulding et al., 2003). Favoring experience over science has enormous risks. According to Lilienfeld and associates:

> Once we abdicate our responsibility to uphold high scientific standards in administering treatments, our credibility and influence are badly damaged. Moreover, continuing to ignore the imminent dangers posed by questionable mental health techniques, we send an implicit message to our students that we are not deeply committed to anchoring our discipline in scientific practice or to combating potentially unscientific practices. (2003b, p. 9)

The danger of reliance on experience rather than research is seen in the history of medicine. In the 19th century, most surgeons, *based on their experiences,* rejected Lister's discovery of antiseptic surgery for decades. This misguided action had predictably disastrous results for patients.

Practitioners' faith in the experience of their senior colleagues and themselves seems to be associated with an aversion to the importance of research evidence. Meehl (1973) noted that mental health practitioners tend to think that being "softhearted" allows them to be "softheaded." There is, however, no logical reason why concern for the suffering of the individual patient (being softhearted) should be associated with a tendency to commit logical or empirical mistakes (being softheaded). Meehl found that practitioners, in their efforts to function in a caring manner, can become illogical or even irrational. Meehl and

Aversion to
research evidence

Softheaded versus
hardheaded

we would like to see genuinely softhearted practitioners whose compassion leads to an exhaustive search for the most empirically sound methods for relieving pain and suffering. In fact, true empathy should engender a search for effective treatments.

## Evaluating Evidence: All Sources of Information Are Not Equally Good

Meehl found that many mental health practitioners, particularly psychologists, believe that "all evidence is equally good" (1973, p. 228). In contrast, the evidence-based practitioner understands that some evidence is *clearly better* than other evidence.

Understanding which type of evidence is best is perhaps the strongest argument for developing a working understanding of research design and statistics. This understanding, in turn, helps a practitioner to be more effective in working with people with SMI. When practitioners and those responsible for clinical programs are able to understand and evaluate research, they are better able to incorporate research findings into services and clinical programs.

Assessing the evidence requires understanding the concepts of internal and external validity (Campbell & Stanley, 1963; Rosnow & Rosenthal, 1996). *Internal validity* is the ability to make defensible causal inferences from the data—that is, that the probability of a particular outcome is increased due to a specific treatment. The classic design for inferring internal validity involves randomly assigning individuals to different conditions that receive different levels or types of specified treatments (the independent variable). The control group receives the usual treatment, an alternative treatment, or no treatment. The group(s) of individuals assigned to the new treatment is known as the experimental group(s). The results of the treatments, or outcomes, are dependent variables. Evaluators, who are unaware of either the hypothesis or the group to which a subject belongs,

*Internal and external validity*

*Control group*

*Experimental group*

*Dependent variables*

known as "blind" evaluators, gather these results, and investigators analyze the results using standard and unbiased statistical procedures.

Unless a study or a series of studies has strong internal validity, we should be skeptical about any inferences made regarding causation. The information needed to make this judgment is often found in the "Method" section or "Design" subsection of research reports.

*External validity* is the ability to generalize or apply findings from one setting to another setting in another place or time. Studies that employ samples of individuals similar to the population a practitioner serves have the potential to be generalized to the practitioner's clients. This information is found in the "Participants" or "Subjects" area of the "Method" section. An additional way to ensure external validity is to confirm that the stimuli that constitute the independent variable, in this case, the treatment methods, can be generalized (Maher, 1978). Can the treatments employed in the study actually be applied in similar dose, frequency, duration, and quality in the setting under consideration?

Randomized trial

A randomized controlled trial (RCT) is the comparison of two or more interventions in which the participants have been randomly assigned to a treatment group, meaning that each participant has an equal probability of being assigned to either the control or experimental group. This strategy has the best chance of producing equivalent groups for comparison. At best, alternate interventions should be comparable in all aspects except for the active ingredient of the different treatments. If the interventions are designed in this manner and the subjects are randomly assigned, the investigator has done his or her best to ensure internal validity (Campbell & Stanley, 1963). This type of design is used in controlled clinical trials and is considered a true experiment.

Quasi-experiment

Sometimes, random assignment studies are not possible and preformed treatment groups or other designs must be used. Such "quasi-experiments" may be employed, as well as correlational studies, which examine the association among important variables (Anthony, Rogers, & Farkas, 2003). Already existing groups formed for another purpose may be used to compare treatments. Because these groups were not formed by random assignment, we cannot assume that they are comparable, and therefore the internal validity of the study is weaker. Similarly, post-hoc (after the fact) groups developed in the course of the study do not meet the standard of a true experiment, because selection factors may account for between-group differences. This is clearly a lower standard of evidence because a variety of confounding or alternative factors may be present. Nevertheless, there are a number of reputable quasi-experimental designs that employ comparison groups and yield interpretable results. The classic reference is Campbell and Stanley's (1963) *Experimental and Quasi-Experimental Designs.* Sometimes the best available evidence is based on quasi-experimental studies, because some questions are difficult to address in randomized studies.

Clinical trials without comparison groups provide much weaker research evidence. Their major flaw lies in the fact that there is no basis for comparison. This design contrasts with both experiments and quasi-experiments that have control or comparison groups. The observed effects may be due solely to the passage of time, or may not be any different from the effect of alternative interventions. Clinical observation, expert opinion, and case studies are not considered research evidence, but may be sources of speculation and hypotheses. Such information may lay the groundwork for future research.

Although RCTs provide the best evidence, a single RCT study, by itself, does not constitute strong evidence. It is always necessary to replicate, or repeat, the findings. Independent investigators should be able to produce similar results. This need for replication by independent researchers is one of the most basic tenets of science, because replication provides the best corroboration of evidence, helping to ensure that findings were not the result of chance events, unintentional biases, or even intentional misrepresentation.

Trials lacking comparison groups

The need for replication

## An Example of a Randomized Controlled Study

An example of a randomized controlled study is provided by Drake and colleagues, who compared the effects of supported employment with enhanced vocational rehabilitation services (Drake et al., 1999). A clearly defined and representative sample of individuals with SMI were randomly assigned to one of two vocational rehabilitation conditions: individual placement and support (IPS; another term for supported employment) or enhanced vocational rehabilitation similar to the services offered by state vocational rehabilitation agencies. Each offered intensive services but differed in terms of the program model. The study results provided evidence of the superiority of the IPS approach in terms of both employment and quality-of-life outcomes for the consumers involved. This was one of the studies that contributed to the body of evidence establishing supported employment and the IPS approach as an evidence-based practice. This study replicated earlier findings and subsequent studies have replicated these results.

## An Example of a Quasi-Experiment

In an example of a preformed groups design, Drake, Becker, Biesanz, and Torrey (1994) compared the success of a supported employment program to day treatment in promoting vocational outcomes and the potential side effects of the treatment approaches. The study compared a day treatment program in New Hampshire, which was converting to an IPS supported employment program, to another program nearby that was not converting. Although the researchers demonstrated that the two groups were comparable (a common feature of good quasi-experimental studies), in terms of many relevant variables, they could not control for other factors that might have been controlled by random assignment. The positive outcomes associated with supported employment found in this study were later replicated in other quasi-experimental and experimental designs.

## *An Example of a Correlational Study*

Correlational studies can be useful for identifying associations among variables, which in turn can be helpful in developing hypotheses for further exploration. For example, Torrey, Mueser, McHugo, and Drake (2000) investigated the correlation between self-esteem and vocational outcomes. The study found a modest positive correlation, though weaker than expected. This study raised some interesting questions about the nature of the self-esteem measure and whether job satisfaction is perhaps a mediating variable that influences self-esteem. Other investigators picked up on this hypothesis and conducted another correlational study that found that self-esteem and job satisfaction were positively correlated (Casper & Fishbein, 2002).

## Peer-Reviewed Journals

Peer-reviewed journals require that peers of the researchers review articles before they are accepted for publication. Journals usually include original research reports, which are known as primary sources. Both original reports of a quantitative nature and those of a qualitative nature may be published. These journals also offer secondary sources, which are articles that review primary research reports in a given area. For example, reviews might catalog all the experimental, quasi-experimental, and nonexperimental designs on a given topic about a given population or intervention. Additionally, review articles provide judgments regarding internal and external validity. Some examples of review articles include:

Content of journals

- Mueser, Bond, Drake, and Resnick's (1998) review of case management practices and assertive community treatment
- Bond, Drake, Mueser, and Becker's (1997) review of supported employment studies in *Psychiatric Services*
- Mueser and colleagues (2002) review of illness management in *Psychiatric Services*

**Cochrane Database**

Probably the most rigorous reviews available are found in the *Cochrane Databases of Systematic Reviews* (Cochrane Collaboration, 2004). These provide relatively frequent and very thorough updates of the research literature and are available online at *www.cochrane.org*. Typically there is a very detailed analysis of the article, particularly the method and results, and usually a *meta-analysis* of effect size, which is a statistical indicator of practical significance. The Cochrane reviews indicate whether or not the author(s) of the review may have a conflict of interest or vested interest in the studies being reviewed. So, for example, if the author of the review was an investigator on any of the projects reviewed, this conflict of interest would be noted. Cochrane reviews are an excellent resource for evaluating the quality of experimental and quasi-experimental evidence. In fact, there is now a Cochrane review of all the established evidence-based practices, as well as many other related areas of psychiatry.

**Tertiary sources**

Tertiary sources include popular media, encyclopedia, and textbooks such as this. Tertiary sources can be scholarly or not, based on the extent to which they draw on primary and secondary resources and how carefully the analysis of the evidence has been conducted.

## The Persistence of Cognitive Errors and Biases

Maintaining an evidence-based orientation does not necessarily make us immune to cognitive errors and biases. *Cognition* refers to the faculties of knowing, including awareness, perception, reasoning, and judgment. Everyone is prone to making cognitive errors when interpreting experience. Meehl wrote, "it is absurd, as well as arrogant, to pretend that acquiring a Ph.D. somehow minimizes me from the errors of sampling, perception, recording, retention, retrieval, and inference to which the human mind is suspect" (1973, p. 278). We are all familiar with the phenomena of racial, gender, religious, and ethnic biases. Less familiar are more subtle biases, including (1) the avail-

ability heuristic (strategy) bias, (2) the self-serving attributional bias, (3) the pessimism or pathologizing bias, (4) the
confirmatory bias, and (5) the overconfidence bias.

A common practitioner bias regarding the interpretation of experience is embodied in the *availability heuristic.*
This is the tendency to believe that a prominent or available
example is actually representative of an entire population
of events or individuals (Tversky & Kahneman, 1974).
Availability is influenced by how dramatic, recent, or
unique an event happens to be, rather than by the actual
frequency or known probabilities. The availability heuristic,
for example, is evident in the stigma regarding mental
illness. This bias explains why some individuals believe
persons with SMI are extremely dangerous. They are influenced by real and fictional accounts from the media,
including television, newspapers, and the Internet,
describing violent incidents committed by individuals who
are said to be psychotic. These incidents are much more
"available" to people than other less dramatic instances. So,
for example, information about a homeless man in New
York City who pushes someone in front of a subway train is
more available than examples from daily life of the many
strangers, homeless persons, acquaintances, or perhaps
family members with SMI who have never committed such
acts. After all, the presence of violence, in itself, is more
remarkable than its absence. Although there are differences in the patterns and frequency of violence among
persons with SMI and the general population, few individuals are aware of the actual research findings on the subject
(Solomon, 2003). The data show that the greatest risk of
violence is not a random, homicidal act against a stranger
(the most "available" scenario) but isolated verbal assaults
against a person's own relatives in his or her home
(Solomon, 2003).

The availability heuristic operates subtly in clinical
settings. Similar to the dramatic example of violence noted
above, practitioners have a tendency to remember remarkable instances and to recall them as part of their experi-

Availability heuristic

ence. What often makes an example dramatic, however, is *not* that it is characteristic or representative, but that it is uncharacteristic or unrepresentative. That is part of what makes it memorable; it sticks out. A common form of this bias is the *illusory correlation* (Tversky & Kahneman, 1974), which grows out of the belief that the co-occurrence of two indicators, even when relatively rare, is believed to be common. Consider this example:

Members of a clinical team were convinced that individuals with SMI who returned to work were at increased risk for psychiatric relapses due to the stress of working. They vividly recalled instances in which a consumer had experienced an increase in symptoms after going back to work. They had more difficulty recalling that for every individual who obtained employment and experienced an increase of symptoms, or a relapse, many more consumers obtained employment without increased symptoms or relapses. Similarly, it went unnoticed that even more individuals who never obtained employment had increased symptoms or experienced relapses. In fact, despite the convictions of all the team members, relapsing after returning to work was a relatively rare co-occurrence, *not* a common one. Oddly enough, this team also seemed indifferent to the evidence that long-term poverty, idleness, and isolation associated with unemployment are very stressful and may lead to increased symptoms and relapse (Marrone & Golowka, 1999). At the same time, these team members remained unaware of research suggesting that increased symptoms are not *positively* correlated with employment but *negatively* correlated. In fact, people with serious mental illness who become employed subsequently have fewer symptoms and are hospitalized less frequently, although the causal direction is yet to be established (Bond et al., 2001; Mueser, Becker, Torrey, & Xie, 1997).

Generally, most individuals, including mental health practitioners, tend to be biased in their own favor, exhibiting a *self-serving attributional bias* (Campbell & Sedikides, 1999). That is, we tend to attribute success to our

*Illusory correlation*

*Example of illusory correlation*

*Self-serving attributional bias*

own efforts and intelligence, whether or not luck or favorable circumstances were involved. Conversely, we attribute failures to bad luck and negative circumstances rather than to our own lack of effort or poor performance. The following is an example from an ACT (assertive community treatment) team:

When discussing the history of a consumer who remained out of the hospital and in stable housing for a long period of time, the team talked about all the great, effective services they had provided to bring about this desirable outcome. However, when a consumer experienced increased symptoms and impairments that required inpatient treatment in the hospital, this outcome was attributed to the consumer's lack of motivation and noncompliance with medication. The ACT team members tended to take full credit for the consumer successes but shifted the responsibility for lack of success elsewhere.

| Example of self-serving attributional bias

In contrast to the self-serving bias, with the *pessimism* or *pathologizing bias*, practitioners overemphasize negative outcomes and develop unnecessarily low expectations for consumers. Harding and Zahniser (1994) recounted a common tendency of many practitioners to overemphasize negative outcomes for persons with severe and persistent mental illness. This tendency is related to the availability heuristic, because it is based on what is available or prominent in memory. Often, staff expend a great deal of effort to help individuals who are relapsing, but consumers who are experiencing fewer difficulties get much less notice. Consider the following example:

| Pessimism or pathologizing bias

In order to study the outcomes of a psychiatric rehabilitation program, we informally asked program staff what they believed to be the annual rate at which consumers in their program required inpatient treatment in a hospital. The staff at the rehabilitation program estimated that the annual rate was between 25% and 60% of the consumers served by the program. When the data were collected, the actual rate of consumers in the program requiring treatment in the hospital was only 8% annually. The practitioners clearly over-

| Example of pessimism or pathologizing bias

estimated the frequency of what they considered a negative outcome for consumers, possibly resulting in negative expectations and perhaps unnecessary pessimism.

Confirmatory bias | A *confirmatory bias* is the tendency that we all have to seek, find, and confirm the observations we expect to find, and ignore or deemphasize information we do not expect to find. A typical report from nurses, for example, is: "'I ascertain the accuracy of my first impressions by seeking clear signs in the client's behavior that support those impressions'" (Gilje & Klose, 2000, p. 297). At first glance, this observational approach is the most reasonable of strategies. Indeed, it is an empirical strategy based on the procedure of forming a hypothesis and gathering data to see if it is supported (Spaulding et al., 2003). One might even be tempted to ask, "How else should a practitioner act?" Still, this approach may lead to the exclusion of other explanations. Confirmatory bias is present when other probable explanations are not considered. The practitioner seeks out and finds only information that confirms his or her initial impression, ignoring information or observations that do not. The following anecdote illustrates the risks:

Example of confirmatory bias | The psychiatrist was struck by "Ralph's" vivid reports of hearing voices and some of Ralph's very unusual, apparently irrational ideas. Ralph was exhibiting the classic symptoms of schizophrenia: auditory hallucinations and delusions. Conferring with other members of the team, everyone concurred on the presence of these symptoms and a preliminary diagnosis of schizophrenia, which later became the final diagnosis. Ralph was treated in the standard manner, with a series of antipsychotic drugs, but over a period of many months, he did not appear to get better. He also developed a number of side effects. A new nurse assigned to the team noted that Ralph experienced marked mood swings consisting of periods when he was "high" and periods when he was very "blue."'" He certainly had hallucinations and delusions, but these usually went along with his current mood: grandiose delusions when he was "up," persecutory delusions when he was "down." Still, the team persisted in its assessment, maintaining that Ralph had schizophrenia. Finally, the psychiatrist decided to change the diagnosis for Ralph to bipolar disorder with psychotic features and prescribed a mood stabilizer. Ralph had a much-improved clinical response.

The fact that Ralph received the wrong treatment for months may have been due not only to the *confirmatory* bias, but also to a related error, the *overconfidence bias*. Once an expectation is confirmed, we tend to have *overconfidence* in our initial judgment and stick by it, ignoring new and contradictory facts. Once the team formed the initial hypothesis that Ralph had schizophrenia, they continued to collect evidence that supported their original diagnosis, focusing on his symptoms of delusions and hallucinations but apparently ignoring the symptoms of mood swings. Although this anecdote is just one example, there are actually a number of controlled studies in this area (Garb & Boyle, 2003).

| Overconfidence bias

In this section we have reviewed the many common types of bias that can, and often do, interfere with the process of making informed clinical decisions. The ubiquitousness of these biases underscores the importance of the need for decision making to be based on evidence and research. An evidence-based orientation should be a fundamental component of the clinician's thinking and behavior.

## Research on the Role of Practitioners

Given that there is such an emphasis on personal experience, you might wonder if there is any empirical evidence for what practitioners actually do. In fact, most of the mental health professions have conducted role delineation studies to define the knowledge and skills that are requisite to competent practice in the discipline. A unique, interdisciplinary example comes from *Role Delineation of the Psychiatric Rehabilitation Practitioner* study, completed by the International Association of Psychosocial Rehabilitation

Services (IAPSRS, 2001; now USPRA—the United States Psychiatric Rehabilitation Association), with input from several hundred practitioners in the United States and Canada. A summary of this study is available in the certification section of the USPRA website (*http://www.uspra.org*) and can be obtained in full from USPRA.

**Prominence of interpersonal competence**

The IAPSRS study highlighted the fact that whereas knowledge and skill in interventions are critical to effective practice, other domains are important as well. They found that skilled interventions are needed and should follow from thorough assessment and planning. Practitioners, however, gave the greatest weight to interpersonal competence, including listening and using expressive language that is clear and understandable to consumers and their families. Interpersonal competence is critical to the role of the EBP practitioner, not only for the delivery of the EBPs, but also in explaining treatment alternatives. Active listening, speaking to consumers in language that they understand, using reflective responses and paraphrasing, and observing whether this communication appears to be understood by consumers are all essential skills (IAPSRS, 2001). These skills are critical to being a fluent "translator" of scientific findings to "lay" individuals. Xavier Amador and his colleague (Amador & Johanson, 2000) also highlight the paramount role of communications skills. They have found that many persons with severe mental illness are literally unaware of their symptoms or are unaware that these symptoms are part of an illness. They suggest that consumers must be engaged in a dialogue that helps them both understand and notice symptoms as part of an illness. This type of dialogue requires very refined communication skills (Amador & Johanson, 2000).

**Professional role**

Integrating a sense of professional role, defined as a commitment to lifelong learning, continuing education, ethical practice, and the ongoing development of skills, is essential (IAPSRS, 2001). In addition, there is a need for commitment to both formal and informal teamwork and collegiality. The competent practitioner respects and draws on the unique expertise of professional and nonprofessional colleagues. He or she offers unique expertise and is happy to assist colleagues.

Strong collegial relationships are warranted, in the interests of consumers, but practitioners must not suspend critical judgment. Collegial relationships should be mutually respectful and able to tolerate reasonable disagreement.

The IAPSRS role delineation study includes other domains that are instructive to the EBP practitioner, such as a thorough appreciation of community and system resources and the skills to access them. In addition, attention to diversity and respect for individual differences associated with ethnic and cultural factors are stressed (IAPSRS, 2001).

## Review of Practical Implications

It is worth reviewing the practical implications of the issues raised in this chapter. As a practitioner guided by evidence, you should:

- Acquire and practice the skills of EBP interventions in a collaborative way with consumers.
- Be an informed student of research in your readings.
- Be skeptical of your own inferences and aware of biases; ask yourself, "Is my past experience really applicable to this new situation?"
- Maintain an intellectually critical stance that fosters awareness of other sources of bias.
- Be a good listener and communicator, with strong interpersonal skills.
- Learn how to learn, attending conferences and presentations, seeking out research reports in the programs or proceedings, asking presenters about their method and results, and asking them to highlight limitations.
- Participate as a team player on your own team, in your own agency, and outside your agency (Liberman, Hilty, Drake, Tsang, & Hector, 2001).

## Conclusion

A large body of research has demonstrated that consumers of mental health services and their families are very capable of making informed choices, particularly after engaging in some of the leading evidence-based practices, such as illness management (Mueser et al., 2002) or family education and support. Indeed, there have been reports of mental health consumers themselves examining research evidence in a very informed manner (Pratt & Gill, 1990). When practitioners, consumers, and their families are well informed, true consumer choice and collaboration are possible. Hoge et al. (2002) highlight the necessity for students to appreciate consumerism from both the primary consumer's perspective and the family members' perspective. The consumer-driven, evidence-based approach contrasts sharply with the intuitive-experience-based approach, which relies solely on expert opinion and is often pseudoscientific (Drake et al., 2001; Lilienfeld et al., 2003a). The EBP perspective is consistent with the recovery movement, in which individuals participate actively in regaining their own lives. It is the practitioner's role to inform consumers of the range of available and effective options that support the his or her goals and preferences, and the relative merits and drawbacks of each approach. This method requires the practitioner to be an informed student of research throughout his or her career.

## References

Amador, X. & Johanson, A. L. (2000). *I am not sick, I don't need help!* Peconic, NY: Vida Press.

Anthony, W., Rogers, E. S., & Farkas, M. (2003). Research on evidence-based practices: Future directions in an era of recovery. *Community Mental Health Journal, 39,* 101–114.

Bandura, A. (1997). *Self-efficacy: The exercise of control.* San Francisco: Freeman.

Bond, G. R., Drake, R. E., Mueser, K. T., & Becker, D. R. (1997). An update of supported employment for people with severe mental illness. *Psychiatric Services, 48,* 335–346.

Bond, G. R., Resnick, S. G., Drake, R. E., Xie, H., McHugo, G. J., & Bebout, R. R. (2001). Does competitive employment improve nonvocational outcomes for people with severe mental illness? *Journal of Consulting and Clinical Psychology, 69*, 489–501.

Campbell, D. T., & Stanley, J. C. (1963). *Experimental and quasi-experimental designs for research.* Boston: Houghton Mifflin.

Campbell, K. W., & Sedikides, C. (1999). Self-threat magnifies the self-serving bias: A meta-analytic integration. *Review of General Psychology, 3*, 23–43.

Casper, E. S., & Fishbein, S. (2002). Job satisfaction and job success as moderators of the self-esteem of people with mental illnesses. *Psychiatric Rehabilitation Journal, 26*, 33–42.

Cioffi, J. (2001). A study of the use of past experiences in clinical decision making in emergency situations. *International Journal of Nursing Studies, 38*(5), 591–599.

Cochrane Collaboration. (2004). Cochrane database of systematic reviews (3rd quarter,). *Cochrane Library.* Retrieved September 5, 2004, from *http://www.cochrane.org.*

Commission on Rehabilitation Counselor Certification (CRCC). (2002). *Code of professional ethics for rehabilitation counselors.* Retrieved September 20, 2004, from *http://www.crccertification.com/code.html.*

Deegan, P. E. (1988). Recovery: The lived experience of rehabilitation. *Psychiatric Rehabilitation Journal, 11*, 11–19.

Drake, R. E., Becker, D. R., Biesanz, J. C., & Torrey, W. C. (1994). Rehabilitative day treatment vs. supported employment: I. Vocational outcomes. *Community Mental Health Journal, 30*, 519–532.

Drake, R. E., Goldman, H. E., Leff, H. S., Lehman, A. F., Dixon, L., Mueser, K. T., & Torrey, W. C. (2001). Implementing evidence-based practices in routine mental health service settings. *Psychiatric Services, 52*, 179–182.

Drake, R. E., McHugo, G. J., Bebout, R. R., Becker, D. R., Harris, M., Bond, G. R., & Quimby, E. (1999). A randomized clinical trial of supported employment for inner-city patients with severe mental disorders. *Archives of General Psychiatry, 56*, 627–633.

Falvey, J. E. (2001). Clinical judgment in case conceptualization and treatment planning across mental health disciplines. *Journal of Counseling and Development, 79*, 292–303.

Garb, H. N., & Boyle, P. A. (2003). Understanding why some clinicians use pseudoscientific methods: Findings from research on clinical judgment. In S. O. Lilienfeld, S. J. Lynn, & J. M. Lohr (Eds.), *Science and pseudoscience in clinical psychology* (pp. 17–38). New York: Guilford Press.

Gilje, F., & Klose, P. (2000). A study of decision making among U.S. psychiatric nurses. *Archives of Psychiatric Nursing, 14*(6), 296–299.

Harding, C. M., & Zahniser, J. H. (1994). Empirical correction of seven myths about schizophrenia with implications for treatment. *Acta Psychiatrica Scandanavica, 90,* 140–146.

Hogan, M. (2002, October). *Mental health reform from 30,000 feet.* The State Mental Health Olmstead Coordinators. 2nd Annual Training Institute, Arlington, VA.

Hoge, M. A., Jacobs, S., Belitsky, R., & Migdole, S. (2002). Graduate education and training for contemporary behavioral health practice. *Administration and Policy in Mental Health, 29,* 335–357.

International Association of Psychosocial Rehabilitation Services (IAPSRS). (2001). *Role delineation report for the certified psychiatric rehabilitation practitioner.* Morrisville, NC: Columbia Assessment Services.

 Lehman, A. F., & Steinwachs, D. M. (2003). Evidence-based psychosocial treatment practices in schizophrenia: Lessons from the Patient Outcomes Research Team (PORT) project. *Journal of the American Academy of Psychoanalysis and Dynamic Psychiatry, 31,* 141–154.

Liberman, R. P., Hilty, D. M., Drake, R. E., & Tsang, Hector W. H. (2001). Requirements for multidisciplinary teamwork in psychiatric rehabilitation. *Psychiatric Services, 52,* 1331–1342.

Lilienfeld, S. O., Lynn, S. G., & Lohr, G. M. (2003a). *Science and pseudoscience in clinical psychology.* New York: Guilford Press.

Lilienfeld, S. O., Lynn, S. J., & Lohr, J. M. (2003b). Science and pseudoscience in clinical psychology: Concluding thoughts and constructive remedies. In S. O. Lilienfeld, S. J. Lynn, & J. M. Lohr (Eds.), *Science and pseudoscience in clinical psychology* (pp. 461–465). New York: Guilford Press.

Lilienfeld, S. O., Lynn, S. J., & Lohr, J. M. (2003c). Science and pseudoscience in clinical psychology: Initial thoughts, reflections, and considerations. In S. O. Lilienfeld, S. J. Lynn, & J. M. Lohr (Eds.), *Science and pseudoscience in clinical psychology* (pp. 1–14). New York: Guilford Press.

Maher, B. A. (1978). Stimulus sampling in clinical research: Representative design reviewed. *Journal of Consulting and Clinical Psychology, 46,* 643–647.

Marrone, J., & Golowka, E. (1999). If work makes people with mental illness sick, what do unemployment, poverty, and social isolation cause? *Psychiatric Rehabilitation Journal, 23*, 187–194.

Meehl, P. E. (1954). *Clinical versus statistical prediction: A theoretical analysis and a review of the evidence.* Minneapolis: University of Minnesota Press.

Meehl, P. E. (1973). *Psychodiagnosis: Selected papers.* Minneapolis: University of Minnesota Press.

Meehl, P. E. (1993). Philosophy of science: Help or hindrance? *Psychological Reports, 72*, 707–733.

Mueser, K. T., Becker, D. R., Torrey, W. C., & Xie, H. (1997). Work and nonvocational domains of functioning in persons with severe mental illness: A longitudinal analysis. *Journal of Nervous and Mental Disease, 185*, 419–426.

Mueser, K. T., Bond, G. R., Drake, R. E., & Resnick, S. G. (1998). Models of community care for severe mental illness: A review of research on case management. *Schizophrenia Bulletin, 24*, 37–74.

Mueser, K. T., Corrigan, P. W., Hilton, D. W., Tanzman, B., Schaub, A., Gingerich, S., et al. (2002). Illness management and recovery: A review of the research. *Psychiatric Services, 53*, 1272–1284.

Olney, M., Strohmer, D., & Kennedy, J. (2002). Why research matters: Forging a reciprocal relationship between the researcher and the practitioner. *Rehabilitation Counseling Bulletin, 46*, 2–4.

Pratt, C. W., & Gill, K. J. (1990). Sharing research knowledge to empower people who are chronically mentally ill. *Psychosocial Rehabilitation Journal, 13*(3), 75–79.

Pratt, C. W., Gill, K. J., Barrett, N. M., & Roberts, M. M. (1999). *Psychiatric rehabilitation.* San Diego, CA: Academic Press.

President's New Freedom Commission on Mental Health. (2003). *Achieving the promise: Transforming mental health care in America.* Retrieved September 20, 2004, from *http://www.mentalhealthcommission.gov.*

Public Health Service. (1999). *Mental health: A report of the Surgeon General.* Retrieved November 17, 2004, from *http://www.surgeongeneral.gov/library/mentalhealth/home.html.*

Ralpr, R. O. (2000). Recovery. *Psychiatric Rehabilitation Skills, 4*(3), 480–517.

Rosnow, R. L., & Rosenthal, R. (1996). *Beginning behavioral research: A conceptual primer* (2nd ed.). Englewood Cliffs, NJ: Prentice-Hall.

Satcher, D. (2000). Mental health: A report of the Surgeon General—executive summary. *Professional Psychology: Research and Practice, 31*(1), 5–13.

Solomon, P. (2003, August). *Violence of persons with severe mental illness towards family caregivers.* Paper presented at the meeting of the World Association for Psychosocial Rehabilitation, New York, NY.

Spaulding, W. D., Sullivan, M. E., & Poland, J. S. (2003). *Treatment and rehabilitation of severe mental illness.* New York: Guilford Press.

Torrey, E. F. (2003, August). *Human rights: Balancing patient, families, and the community.* Paper presented at the meeting of the World Association for Psychosocial Rehabilitation, New York, NY.

Torrey, W. C., Drake, R. E., Dixon, L., Burns, B. J., Flynn, L., Rush, A. J., et al. (2001). Implementing evidence-based practices for persons with a severe mental illnesses. *Psychiatric Services, 52*, 45–50.

Torrey, W. C., Mueser, K. T., McHugo, G. H., & Drake, R. E. (2000). Self-esteem as an outcome measure in studies of vocational rehabilitation for adults with severe mental illness. *Psychiatric Services, 51*, 229–233.

Tversky, A., & Kahneman, D. (1974). Judgment under uncertainty: Heuristics and biases. *Science, 185*, 1124–1131.

SIX

# The Importance of Research in Mental Health Service Delivery

*David L. Shern*
*Mary E. Evans*

MENTAL HEALTH SERVICES RESEARCH (MHSR) is the systematic study of the organization, delivery, and outcomes of services for persons with severe mental illness (SMI). As such, MHSR is an interdisciplinary field that includes economists, psychologists, sociologists, psychiatrists, social workers, nurses, public health specialists, and others involved with understanding human behavior at the levels of the person, community, and society. In MHSR we are interested in identifying and understanding the factors that influence the need for treatment, the impact of treatment on the consumer, as well as those factors associated with effective services.

Definition of mental health services research

## Types of MHSR

There are two types of MHSR: service system research and clinical services research. *Service systems research* focuses on the relationships among components that together comprise the service system; issues of financing and regulation, for example, might be the objects of study. *Clinical services research* investigates the service interventions and the people who deliver and receive them. Clinical services research is more closely related to the helping relationship,

123

whereas service system research studies the factors that surround and influence that relationship.

Service system research examines the influences of organizational, legal, and financial factors on services. These include variables such as the effects of differing types of insurance coverage on access to treatment. Recently, for example, the federal government and many state governments have considered laws that would require insurance coverage for mental health benefits to be at parity with coverage for general health services. Debate has focused on the estimated costs of parity in insurance benefits, with some early cost estimates for offering equivalent services based on the RAND health insurance experiments of the 1970s. These experiments indicated that the demand for mental health services is affected by consumers' out-of-pocket expenses (i.e., less out-of-pocket expenses were associated with greater use of services) and that parity would be a very expensive social policy option (see McGuire, 1989, for a discussion). However, use of these early estimates failed to anticipate the changes in access to treatment that occurred with managed care. When calculations were completed that included more recent data reflecting the effects of demand-side management, parity in coverage was estimated to have only modest effects on increasing overall costs. This example hints at the complexity of service system research, because it can involve legal, organizational, financial, and regulatory mechanisms that may impact access to treatment. In a later section of this chapter, we present a framework for thinking about the complex nature of service system research.

Clinical services research focuses on the variables that affect services at the client level. These researchers are interested in the factors that influence people to seek treatment, the factors that encourage them to become engaged in a change process through a helping relationship, and those factors that directly influence the clinicians who provide services. For example, the training that clinicians receive in college and through continuing education is one factor that may influence their approach to providing treatment. We have come to realize, though, that training alone is not a very effective tool for changing clinician behavior and that using the "train and hope'" methodology to improve the quality of services is not likely to be successful. Systematic feedback about the relationship of clinician behaviors to treatment guidelines and outcomes of care, supportive organizational climates, and reimbursement systems that reward desired behaviors are all variables that may influence clinician performance, quality of treatment, and outcomes. In turn, consumer knowledge, attitudes, and opinions might influence treatment seeking. If having a mental illness is stigmatized in our culture, people may be embarrassed to admit having such a problem and therefore fail to seek help. The degree to which individuals do not recognize that their thoughts or feelings are symptoms of mental illness and do not know that there are effective strategies for changing how they feel, they will not seek treatment.

Both service system and clinical services research help us understand the factors that influence service need, use, and outcome. Clinical research is focused more directly on the service encounter, and systems research is focused on more distal factors related to financial, organizational, and legal structures. Ultimately, the purpose of both is to provide information on how to design services that work for consumers.

| Joint purpose

## Why Is It Important to Study Mental Health Services?

The premise of evidence-based practices (EBPs) is that mental health services should have a scientific base. By *scientific base* we mean evidence that researchers have systematically collected that the services provided to consumers and families are beneficial. Although the need for this base may seem obvious, the fact is that much of our current practice is not based on scientific evidence. Simply observing that individuals who receive services get better

| Establishing a science base through MHSR

over time is not an adequate science base on which to conclude that the services received were associated with their improvement. Years ago Hans Eysenck (1952) demonstrated that the rate at which people with "psychoneurosis"' improved was as great for individuals who received custodial treatment (i.e., essentially, no active treatment) as for those who were treated with psychotherapy. In fact, individuals in the custodial treatment group improved at a slightly *greater* rate than those receiving psychotherapy. And although the psychotherapists attributed their clients' improvement to psychoanalysis, without a comparison group (i.e., individuals with similar problems who were not receiving psychoanalysis and who did not improve), there was no scientific basis for their conclusion. Likewise, studies decades later by Bickman and his colleagues (Bickman, Summerfelt, & Noser, 1997) challenged the widely held belief that child outcomes would be superior in sites that provided services based on a system of care principles and values (Stroul & Friedman, 1986) than in sites that provided care that was not based on these values and principles. His research demonstrated that child outcomes were not superior in the system of care sites. The importance of research in mental health services, therefore, is to verify that the conclusions we draw from theories, common beliefs, traditions, or the observation of single treatment populations are accurate.

An example of MHSR

A poignant example of the importance of systematic observation comes from the work of Courtney Harding. Building on the work of her colleague George Brooks, Harding conducted an important long-term follow-up of consumers with schizophrenia in the United States (Harding, Brooks, Ashikaga, Strauss, & Breier, 1987). Her work relied on the meticulous records kept by Brooks when he was the psychiatrist in charge of treating people with SMI at the Vermont State Hospital. Brooks's client records allowed Harding to successfully contact these patients many years after their release from the hospital. These patients were among the last of the long-term patients to be released from the hospital during the deinstitutionalization of Vermont's hospitals in the 1960s. They were considered the most severely impaired of the patients, and most mental health professionals would have predicted that very few of them would ultimately recover in the community. A belief among some professionals at the time was that the course of schizophrenia was one of persistent deterioration throughout the lifetime.

Some 30 years after their discharge from the hospital, Harding and her team located these patients. Although approximately one-third of the patients was deceased, the research team was successful in contacting over 90% of those still living. When they located the individuals, they used a structured interview protocol to assess the clinical and functional status of the former hospital patients. They also collected data from individuals who knew the patients well. If the client was deceased, collateral reports were used to help understand the status of the individual prior to his or her death. The researchers were shocked by what they found. The majority of these long-term hospital patients had either improved or substantially recovered from their illnesses. Many were indistinguishable from others of their age in their community. Several other investigators throughout the world have replicated Harding's work (Harding, 1992), and although debate continues regarding the measurement of recovery and the proportion of individuals who will recover (Harrow, Sands, Silverstein, & Goldberg, 1997), there is now no doubt that a significant number *will* recover.

The previously held belief that individuals with schizophrenia could not recover was largely derived from observing them in state hospitals. Patients who were institutionalized for the majority of their adult life showed progressive deterioration. However, without either systematically verifying what happens to long-term patients (as occurred in the Harding study) or comparing their outcomes to individuals who received an alternative treatment regimen, it was incorrect to conclude that the experi-

| Reasons for
| conducting MHSR

ence of state hospital patients adequately represented all persons with schizophrenia. Unfortunately, because of these faulty observations, thousands of people with schizophrenia and their family members were advised that they would never recover from their illness, and many lost all hope of improvement. Therefore, one of the most important reasons for MHSR is to assure that we base our practices and policies on data that have been collected in such a way as to merit our assertions. Observations made without comparison conditions do not meet these standards and are not adequate for concluding which treatments are effective.

**Internal and external validity**

A second reason for MHSR is to understand how to translate scientific findings into real-world settings. Years ago, Donald Campbell and Julian Stanley (1963) identified two types of validity that can be used to characterize scientifically derived information: internal and external validity. *Internal validity* refers to the ability to draw causal inferences from a set of observations. The greater control present in a particular research design, the greater the ability to draw causal inferences. *Control* in a research design involves the degree to which we can rule out alternative interpretations of the findings from research projects. The more control researchers have in a project, the greater their ability to rule out alternative explanations. *External validity* refers to the degree to which scientific findings from a particular experiment can be generalized to other situations.

**Randomized controlled trials**

The most internally valid scientific evidence is derived from well-conducted randomized controlled trials (true experiments). In these, investigators attempt to control all of the "extraneous" variables that may influence a particular outcome, so that they will be in a strong position to conclude that the differences in outcome are attributable to the treatments. In addition, if the researchers fail to find an effect of their treatment, they want to be sure that the absence of the desired outcome is not due to factors that are extraneous to their hypotheses. Typically, clinical interventions are designed to work for people who have specific mental disorders or problems that impede goal obtainment (e.g., getting a competitive job). Often, only individuals with one condition, or mental illness, are included in a study. Importantly, research participants (consumers, in this case) agree to participate in the study and subject themselves to the risks of experimental research. Furthermore, great care is exercised in the study to be certain that the experimental interventions are delivered in an exacting way, with ongoing assessments conducted to verify that the practice protocol is followed (i.e., fidelity). All of these control measures are designed to maximize the internal validity of the research. Conclusions drawn from well-executed randomized controlled trials, therefore, are clear regarding the linkage of the practice to the outcome.

The findings, however, from these internally valid studies are often much less clear when generalized to populations and settings outside the parameters investigated in the clinical trial. Although it is desirable, from a control perspective, to have a homogeneous population, often treatment populations in nonexperimental situations are heterogeneous. Limiting research populations to individuals who have a single disorder does not comport with the composition of ordinary clinical populations, whose constituents often have multiple disorders, including multiple mental health and substance abuse problems. Although strictly controlling the characteristics of the intervention is essential in order tobe able to attribute effects to the intervention, this degree of control is difficult, if not impossible, to achieve in ordinary clinical settings. The very characteristics that maximize internal validity, therefore, might compromise our ability to generalize our findings to real-world clinical settings, such as community mental health centers. Because randomized controlled trials that have a high internal validity are a central element of our evidence base, Hoagwood, Burns, and Weisz (2002) noted the challenges that remain in connecting the evidence base, once established, to actual clinical practice in everyday settings. Studies with a high degree of internal

Generalizability

control can demonstrate the efficacy of a practice. The effectiveness of a practice, on the other hand, is determined by its ability to produce a positive effect in a real-world setting with real-world populations. Ideally, mental health practices are both efficacious and effective.

Summary of
importance of
MHSR

Mental health services research is important for at least two reasons. First, it enables us to study the outcomes of the practices that we are providing in a more systematic manner. This information helps us to understand the conditions and circumstances in which individuals are able to recognize their problems and seek help for them as well as understanding the effectiveness of the help that is delivered. As such, the information that is developed through systematic research is essential for the competent, and some would say, ethical delivery of mental health treatments. Additionally, MHSR has implications for the design of mental health service systems in order to assure that consumers and families have maximum access to practices that promote positive outcomes. The second reason that MHSR is important is to navigate the difficult territory between efficacy and effectiveness. The evidence for the efficacy of a practice means that a benefit for consumers may occur as a result of receiving the practice. Services research is needed to ensure that these benefits of treatment, in fact, occur in real-world settings by understanding how *efficacious* treatments can be *effective* treatments.

## How Can We Study the Complex Factors That Influence Mental Health Services?

As is clear from even the few brief examples that have been provided in this chapter, multiple variables must be considered when attempting to understand mental health services in real-world settings. These variables involve not only the characteristics of the people who need or seek care but also the characteristics of caregivers and the settings in which they work.

We have developed a model, shown in Figure 6.1, to help us understand the complex influences on help-seeking behavior, service delivery, and outcomes (Shern, Evans, & Veysey, 1992). We call this a *heuristic* model because it is intended to guide services research and to help us discover important relationships between the domains that are included in the model. We identify five domains that influence the outcomes experienced by individuals, as well as the overall outcomes experienced in the service system: consumer characteristics, organizational characteristics, practitioner (caregiver) behavior and characteristics, services environment, and service system characteristics. We identify two types of outcomes: system and consumer outcomes (on the far right of the figure). Consumer outcomes may include changes in clinical status, such as symptom level, changes in level of community functioning, or status changes such as those related to employment or disability. System-level outcomes include changes in the resources devoted to differing types of treatment (e.g., inpatient vs. outpatient or emergency service use), waiting times to receive services, proportion of facilities meeting external accreditation standards, and other outcomes related to organization and delivery of services.

A heuristic model for MHSR

### FIGURE 6.1
**Heuristic model for mental health services research**

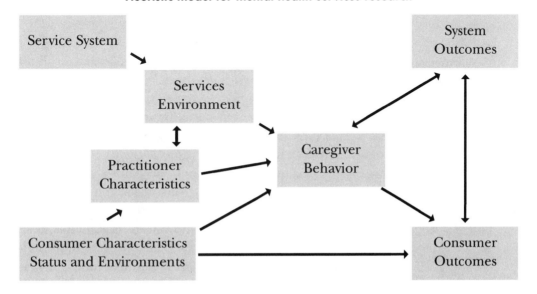

**Consumer and
system outcomes**

In the model, arrows indicate where we expect effects to occur. Consumer outcomes are expected to be influenced directly by the services that the consumer receives from a practitioner (i.e., caregiver behavior) as well as by the characteristics of the consumer. Although caregiver behavior directly influences consumer outcomes, caregiver behavior is, in turn, directly influenced by caregiver characteristics (e.g., knowledge, attitudes), by the service environment in which the caregiver works and, of course, by the characteristics and needs of the consumers. We expect, therefore, that the influences in the service setting will have an indirect effect on consumer outcomes that is mediated by caregiver behavior. Finally, our model predicts that the characteristics of the service setting will be directly affected by systems-level variables such as financing and regulation. The double-headed arrow between services environment and caregiver characteristics indicates the reciprocal influence: The people who work in the service environment will impact it, and conversely, differing types of service environments will attract differing types of practitioners. Similarly, system outcomes are expected to be influenced by consumer outcomes and practitioner behaviors and to influence practitioner behaviors and consumer outcomes as well.

### Domains in the Heuristic Model

**Consumer
characteristics**

Consumer characteristics include a range of variables. Both demographic and physical characteristics (e.g., age, race, ethnicity, and height and weight) as well as marital, socioeconomic, and employment status are included in consumer characteristics. Additionally, we consider clinical and functional status in this domain. *Clinical status* refers to the symptoms that individuals experience and the degree to which they find the symptoms uncomfortable or painful. *Functional status* refers to the degree to which individuals can perform important social and interpersonal tasks, such as performing activities of daily living, maintaining interpersonal relations, and successfully contributing to their community through work or school. Consumer characteristics also include variables related to their environment, such as housing status. Other characteristics of the environment might include the degree of discrimination against consumers as a result of having a mental illness. Individual characteristics, therefore, form a wide-ranging set of variables that describes the individual in his or her environment.

Literally hundreds of studies have related individuals' characteristics to the reception of services and to the outcomes that individuals with mental illnesses experience. Individual characteristics are known to be related to rates of mental illness. Men, for example, are much more likely to be diagnosed with a substance abuse disorder than women, whereas women are more likely to have a diagnosis of depression or anxiety disorder than men. Individuals from some ethnic or racial minority groups in the United States are less likely to seek and use mental health outpatient services than individuals from other ethnic or racial groups.

An individual's genetic makeup and life experiences are also important individual characteristics. During the last several years, for example, we have become increasingly aware of the importance of trauma as a correlate of mental illness. As part of this developing awareness, we have also learned that practitioners often do not inquire about consumers' trauma histories. As a result, the behavior of the practitioner is not likely to be responsive to the needs of someone who has experienced trauma. The lack of trauma-informed care is an example of a practitioner behavior that is not sensitive to consumer characteristics and needs.

Practitioners are persons who provide mental health services. They may be formal or informal practitioners. *Formal practitioners* are individuals who have a paid position or role, such as clinical or case management staff, that explicitly involves the provision of help. *Informal practitioners* (often called supporters or caregivers) may be family members or even friends. Often in MHSR we concentrate on formal practitioners and the specific types of help that

| Examples of consumer characteristics

| Practitioner characteristics and behaviors

they provide. These services, which are intended to aid others, comprise an important component of the evidence-based practices that are the topic of this text.

**Consumer characteristics**

In our heuristic model we predict that practitioner behaviors will be directly influenced by three factors. The first factor is the characteristics of the individual who is seeking help. For example, assertive community treatment (ACT) is designed for individuals who have severe impairments from mental illnesses and who require intensive support in the community. To determine who is likely to be helped by ACT requires a careful assessment by the practitioner of the consumer's characteristics and needs.

**Practitioner characterisitcs**

The second factor that we predict will impact practitioner behavior is the sum of the practitioner's own characteristics, which include attitudes, knowledge, and beliefs in addition to demographic characteristics and statuses. In turn, the practitioner's preservice and inservice training influences his or her attitudes, knowledge, and beliefs. Hopefully, this training will impart knowledge regarding the elements of EBP and thorough assessment techniques to help practitioners understand which practices may be most effective in helping consumers achieve their goals.

**Services environment**

The third factor that may impact practitioner behavior is the characteristics of the work environment. Environmental factors include all of the work rules and regulations as well as the culture. The culture of the services environment is reflected in the cumulative attitudes, values, and beliefs of the staff as well as the general organizational climate. Rules include all of the formal and informal mechanisms that are used to control individuals' conduct in the work environment. Formal rules include the procedures that are used to regulate work behavior (e.g., attendance requirements, dress codes, regulations that control hiring and disciplinary action), whereas informal rules, the organization's norms, involve expectations regarding how individuals will behave in the setting—literally, what is expected of the agency's employees as well as its clients. Culture and climate can have an important effect on how a work environment functions and the outcomes produced for consumers and the service system.

The final domain of the heuristic model involves the characteristics of the mental health service system, including financial, legal, and organizational components. Many service organizations (which can, themselves, involve multiple service settings) are regulated by federal, state, or local governments as well as by the requirements of other entities (both public and private) that provide reimbursement for services. These requirements can become directly embodied in the work setting rules; federal antidiscrimination laws are prime examples. All of these external regulations, of which employment laws are only one component, directly affect the rules of service settings. Civil liability for poor practices and the damage that they cause to consumers (or employees) creates risk for an organization. Management of this risk is a strong determinant of the behavior of organizations.

*Service system characteristics*

In addition to these laws and related regulations, the relationships between purchasers of service (e.g., insurance companies) and service agencies are also very important. For example, state Medicaid authorities are the major source of reimbursement for public mental health services. What Medicaid buys has a profound effect on what service settings will provide. If, for example, Medicaid pays only for services that are provided in a clinic, it will be very difficult to provide service to an individual that requires practitioners to work in the community (e.g., outreach, case management, classroom aide). Similarly, if insurance only reimburses in-office psychotherapy services and not rehabilitative services, it will be difficult to implement some EBPs. Understanding these funding variables is essential to understanding the incentives under which service settings operate and the rules that are developed to regulate practitioner behavior.

*Funding variables*

This heuristic model provides a framework for thinking about the domains that are important to the functioning of a mental health services system. It helps us to manage the

*Advantages of using the heuristic model*

complexity of the environment by identifying the domains that we can consider in describing a particular practitioner behavior or consumer outcome. It may also be helpful to identify the points of intervention for implementing and sustaining an EBP. The model can guide mental health services researchers in selecting the variables that they wish to study in any given service setting, as well as explicitly identifying the variables they are not studying but that may nevertheless influence the services on which they are most focused.

**Service setting characteristics**

In a study that illustrates the importance of MHSR, Glisson and his colleagues (Glisson & Hemmelgarn, 1998) demonstrated that characteristics of the service setting (including organizational climate) had an important impact on consumer outcomes for children. Glisson and Hemmelgarn assessed the organizational climate and interorganizational coordination of 32 public children's service offices in 24 counties in Tennessee. The experimental intervention in this MHSR study involved the introduction of new interorganizational case management teams to coordinate services from multiple systems for children entering state custody. Half of the counties received the new case management services and half did not.

Glisson and Hemmelgard hypothesized that increasing the coordination of services in the 12 pilot counties (a service-system-level intervention) would directly affect the climate of the organizations that provided services (service-setting variable). Increased coordination of services would also directly affect the quality of services provided (practitioner behavior) and the interorganizational relationships among the service-providing organizations (systems variables), relative to the 12 comparison counties. In their study, therefore, they wished to examine the effects of an organizational variable (new case management teams) on service settings, practitioner behavior, and consumer outcomes.

**Need for positive organizational climate**

Interestingly, they found that the introduction of the new services did not impact the service settings, the quality of services, or consumer outcomes as anticipated. This finding again illustrates the importance of MHSR, because most everyone would have expected that this type of coordination would affect services and outcomes. In conducting the study, however, they learned that children served by offices (service settings) with more positive climates experienced greater improvements in their psychosocial functioning than children served in offices with less positive climates. Glisson and Hemmelgarn concluded that service effectiveness was related more to organizational climate (service-setting variable) than to service-system configurations (systems variable). The outcome of their research suggests that efforts to improve public service systems should be focused on creating positive organizational climates rather than increasing interorganizational services coordination. Their study illustrates the importance of testing the impact of interventions that seem to have great appeal from a commonsense perspective (i.e., everyone knows that they are important). In the process of testing the formal hypothesis, they uncovered an important, previously undocumented finding, that organizational climate is related to consumer outcomes.

Their work also suggests the need for further research to help us understand how organizational climate impacts consumer outcomes. The heuristic model would suggest that the effects of organizational climate would have to be expressed by practitioner behaviors. The research questions involve identifying which practitioner behaviors (e.g., attitudes, knowledge, beliefs, skills) might be affected or if there are unanticipated factors causing the improved outcomes in settings with more positive organizational climate. For example, these environments might attract a clientele with better prognoses; more resources, consumer characteristics, and these cited characteristics, rather than practitioner behaviors, might explain the differences in consumer outcomes.

The above discussion illustrates the ways in which the heuristic model can help to organize thinking about the multiple influences that can affect consumer outcomes. Additionally, it provides an example of how variables from differing domains in the model impact consumer outcomes.

## Summary

In this chapter we have defined mental health services research, distinguished between two types of services research (service system and clinical services research), and presented a heuristic model to help guide mental health services research. We have also emphasized the importance of mental health services research in identifying factors related to accessing services, exploring consumer and system outcomes of services, and debunking myths about consumer and practitioner behaviors and consumer outcomes. MHSR helps us to assess the effectiveness of services that are provided in routine community mental health settings, the challenges involved in implementing services that have been shown to be efficacious in clinical trials research (balancing internal and external validity), and developing an approach to practice that helps us to continually develop evidence regarding the effectiveness of our interventions. An ongoing challenge for the field of MHSR is to develop and refine models and methods that foster the testing of promising practices, whether related to financing mechanisms or to improvements in the delivery and types of mental health services.

## References

Bickman, L., Summerfelt, W. T., & Noser, K. (1997). Comparative outcomes of emotionally disturbed children and adolescents in a system of services and usual care. *Psychiatric Services, 48*, 1543–1548.

Campbell, D. T., & Stanley, J. C. (1963). *Experimental and quasi-experimental designs for research.* Chicago: Rand McNally.

Eysenck, H. J. (1952) The effects of psychotherapy: An evaluation. *Journal of Consulting and Clinical Psychology, 16*, 319–323.

Glisson, C., & Hemmelgarn, A. (1998). The effects of organizational climate and interorganizational coordination on the quality and outcomes of children's service systems. *Child Abuse and Neglect, 22,* 401–421.

Harding, C. M., Brooks, G. W., Ashikaga, T., Strauss, J. S., & Breier, A. (1987). The Vermont longitudinal study of persons with severe mental illness, I: Methodology, study sample, and overall status 32 years later. *American Journal of Psychiatry, 144,* 718–726.

Harding, C., Strauss, J. S., & Zubin, J. (1992). Chronicity in schizophrenia: Revisited. *British Journal of Psychiatry, 161,* 27–37.

Harrow, M., Sands, J. R., Silverstein, M. L., & Goldberg, J. F. (1997) Course and outcome for schizophrenia versus other psychotic patients: A longitudinal study. *Schizophrenia Bulletin, 23,* 287–303.

Hoagwood, K., Burns, B. J., & Weisz, J. R. (2002). A profitable conjunction from science to service in children's mental health. In B. J. Burns & K. Hoagwood (Eds.), *Community treatment for youth: Evidence-based interventions for severe emotional and behavioral disorders* (pp. 327–338). New York: Oxford University Press.

McGuire, T. G. (1989). Financing and reimbursement for mental health services. In C. A. Taube, D. Mechanic, & A. Hohmann (Eds.), *The future of mental health services research* (pp. 87–111; DHHS Pub. No. [ADM] 89-1600). Washington, DC: U.S. Government Printing Office.

Shern, D. L., Evans, M. E., & Veysey, B. M. (1992). Human resource, program and client correlates of mental health outcomes. In J. W. Jacobson, S. N. Burchard, & P. J. Carling (Eds.), *Community living for people with developmental and psychiatric disabilities* (pp. 263–283). Baltimore MD: Johns Hopkins University Press.

Stroul, B. A., & Friedman, R. M. (1986). *A system of care for seriously emotionally disturbed children and youth.* Washing, DC: CASSP Technical Assistance Center, Georgetown University Child Development Center.

# SEVEN

# | Evidence in Intervention Science

## *H. Stephen Leff*

THIS CHAPTER EXPLORES HOW WE PUT the evidence into psychosocial interventions. In the chapter I:

- Discuss why evidence is important
- Define psychosocial interventions as socially complex services
- Define evidence
- Describe and briefly trace the history of intervention science, a particular type of science that produces evidence about interventions
- Discuss the intervention science guidelines that are most difficult to follow in studies of psychosocial interventions
- Consider the concerns of mental health stakeholders regarding basing mental health systems on evidence
- Envision the role that evidence will play in mental health systems in the future

## Why Evidence Is Important

Health-care systems throughout the United States are adopting evidence-based treatments because it is widely believed that basing health care on evidence is the best way to bring safe and effective treatments to the public. As Millenson noted (1997):

A health care delivery system characterized by idiosyncratic
and often ill-informed judgments must be restructured
according to evidence-based medical practice, regular assessment of the quality of care and accountability. The alternative is a system that makes life and death treatment decisions
based on conflicting anecdotes and calculated appeals to
emotion. (p. 6)

Many mental health services researchers, clinicians, and
policymakers have reached the same conclusion for mental
health as well as physical health treatments and systems
(Rotter, 1971).

## Socially Complex Services Interventions

Psychosocial interventions use psychological, interpersonal,
and social approaches to improve the cognitive, emotional,
and daily functioning of individuals. In this chapter we
focus on psychosocial interventions for persons with severe
mental illness. Wolff (2000) referred to these interventions
as socially complex services (SCS). SCS interventions coordinate and deliver a variety of services and service sectors
that is responsible for assisting consumers in improving the
quality of their lives in a number of different areas.
Compared to clinical interventions, SCS interventions have
properties that make it difficult, but not impossible to
produce evidence about their effectiveness (Wolff, 2000).

Wolff summarized these properties elegantly by
describing SCSs as characterized by complex arrangements
and soft boundaries. These differences are summarized in
Table 7.1.

As this table shows, SCS interventions have multiple
components for delivering and coordinating services and
service systems to enhance role performance and quality of
life as well as change effects and cognitions. They have soft
boundaries in that their implementation requires
addressing aspects of the intervention context (e.g., administrative policies, provider training, consumer interactions
with employers and landlords) that would be considered

outside the bounds of traditional clinical interventions. Below, we discuss the implications of these characteristics for producing evidence.

| TABLE 7.1 | | |
|---|---|---|
| A Structural Taxonomy of Types of IC Interventions | | |
| **Key inputs of intervention** | **Ideal clinical interventions** | **Socially complex service interventions** |
| Staffing arrangements | Single provider Professional staff Standardized expertise Highly motivated staff | Many providers Mix of lay and professional staff Nonstandardized expertise Differently motivated staff |
| Protocol specificity | Concrete and measurable | Ambiguous and hard to measure |
| Subject involvement | Illness/problem with low level of professional uncertainty High insight into illness  High understanding of benefit and risks  Health is valued | Illness/problem with high level of profes sional uncertainty Variable insight into illness Variable under standing of benefits and risks Mental health has mixed value |
| Environmental boundaries | Hard external boundaries | Soft external boundaries |

Adapted from "Using Randomized Controlled Trials to Evaluate Socially Complex Services: Problems, Challenges and Recommendations," by N. Wolff, 2000, *The Journal of Mental Health Policy and Economics*, Volume 3, pp. 97–109.

## The Definition of Evidence

Intervention science produces and assesses the evidence of treatment effectiveness under real-world conditions. Evidence about an intervention, or intervention evidence, is a body of assertions about causal relationships between practices and the consumer outcomes of interest. We call

Evidence-based practice

these causal relationships *effects*. When the evidence favors the conclusion that a practice has a desired effect, we speak of it as *evidence-based*.

Basic versus real-world research

Intervention evidence can come from one or more studies that follow the guidelines of intervention science, which investigates the effects of interventions implemented under real-world conditions. The goal of intervention science is to improve public access to practices that have proven to be safe and have clinically important effects. It differs from basic science in that the goal of basic science is to develop and test theories and research methods. Basic science characteristically tests interventions under ideal conditions that are usually very different from real-world conditions. For example, in a community mental health center, real-world conditions may include the delivery of the intervention by staff members who have a variety of educational and training backgrounds, or within the context of a program where staff turnover is consistently high. These conditions may not be simulated in laboratory conditions, where designated providers are chosen based on their interest, education, and experience. Basic research is one source of ideas for interventions and a source of research methods.

## A Brief History of Intervention Science

Intervention science may be viewed as a fairly recent invention. Figure 7.1 illustrates a timeline, beginning with the creation of the Food and Drug Administration (FDA) in 1906 and highlighting a selection of other significant events in the history of intervention science. These events include:

**FIGURE 7.1**

**A timeline of important developments in intervention science**

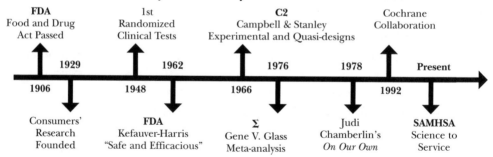

- The passing of the Food and Drug Act leading to the establishment of the Food and Drug Administration (FDA) and its mission to test the safety and effectiveness of medical interventions.
- The establishment of Consumers' Research, an organization that evolved into Consumers' Union and established the interest of consumers in evidence-based reviews of products of all kinds.
- The first randomized clinical trial was conducted, a study of the efficacy of streptomycin in treating tuberculosis, and reported in a 1948 issue of the *British Medical Journal* (Millenson, 1997). The randomized clinical trial placed clinical judgment within a new scientific framework (Millenson, 1997).
- The passage of the Kefauver–Harris bill, following the tragic birth defects caused by thalidomide, which gave the FDA increased authority to ensure the safety and efficaciousness of medications.
- The publication of Campbell and Stanley's book (Campbell & Stanley, 1966) on quasi-experimental research designs that showed that rigorous research could be conducted under real-world conditions.
- The speech, and later the publication of an article, by Gene V. Glass, showing how the results of individual studies can be combined in a systematic and quantitative manner, and marking the beginning of the "meta-analysis movement" (Hunt, 1997).
- The publication of Judi Chamberlin's book, *On Our Own* (1978), which was a founding event in the mental health consumer movement and its interest in consumer participation in all aspects of the mental health system, including research and evaluation.
- The founding of the Cochrane Collaboration in 1992, named after Archibald Cochrane, a highly influential British epidemiologist. The collaboration provides systematic reviews and meta-analyses for a large number of physical and mental health interventions. It also provides guidance on how to conduct research trials and syntheses.

- The current pursuit of a "science-to-services" agenda by the Substance Abuse and Mental Health Services Administration (SAMHSA; discussed in the final section).

As intervention science has evolved, we have learned important lessons. These lessons are as follows.

### Stakeholder Participation

Intervention science is intended to meet public needs. As such, it should be, and increasingly has been, guided by stakeholder participation, including consumers and family members. Consumers, in particular, have provided valuable direction both in terms of positive outcomes to be sought and negative outcomes to be avoided in intervention studies. Consumers often identify critical values to investigate that are different from those of scientists. Consumer values should influence which practices are investigated, how risks and desired outcomes are defined, and other aspects of research methods. Gomory pointed out, "professionally defined expectations of client change can be coercive and patronizing, and ultimately harmful" (1999, p. 7). Most consumers of mental health services have not been trained in research methods. Nevertheless, they can play a role in setting the direction and boundaries of psychosocial interventions (Kitcher, 2001).

### Phased Process

The experience of the FDA teaches us that intervention science is best thought of as an ordered process, involving multiple phases, like rungs on a ladder, beginning with discovery and ending with postdissemination monitoring (Food and Drug Administration [FDA]/Center for Drug Evaluation and Research, 1998). One important aspect of this phased process is that different types of evidence are acceptable at different stages in the evidence generation process. The phases in intervention science for psychosocial interventions are as follows.

*Phase 1: Discovery*

In this phase psychosocial interventions should be identified for further testing under controlled conditions and in real-world settings. Some practices may have been shown to work under laboratory conditions but not when applied in real-world settings. Some practices in this phase have only subjective, anecdotal evidence supporting their effectiveness. Phase 1, provides an opportunity for practices believed to be safe and effective by providers and consumers, who have experience with them, to be tested and possibly moved up the evidence ladder. This type of evidence has been referred to as "practice-based evidence."

Practice-based evidence

*Phase 2: Intervention Development*

This phase of intervention science should address whether practices are feasible and safe when implemented under real-world conditions. Phase 2 studies also should be used to work out the research and evaluation design issues that are pertinent to intervention testing and monitoring. *Feasibility* refers to whether the intervention can be reliably produced. In regard to psychosocial interventions, establishing feasibility involves providing evidence that an intervention can be "manualized" or otherwise taught and delivered with fidelity to the described principles of the practice. Exploring *safety* involves defining adverse events that could be associated with the intervention, estimating their likelihood, and evaluating their acceptability to consumers and other stakeholders. Evidence of feasibility for this phase can be primarily preexperimental, produced by focus groups, key informant interviews, and related approaches. Simple pre–post intervention assessments of consumer change may suggest, but not provide, definitive evidence of effectiveness. These preliminary tests are conducted with small numbers of people to minimize burden and risk to participants.

*Phase 3: Effectiveness Studies*

Effectiveness studies investigate the effects of practices on targeted outcomes, under real-world conditions. Because

Effectiveness versus efficacy research

psychosocial interventions consist of complex arrangements and have soft boundaries, the intervention in effectiveness studies should be broadly conceived to include all
essential services and environmental supports.

A number of authors has compared what is commonly
referred to as efficacy and effectiveness research (Glasgow,
Lichtenstein, & Marcus, 2003; Weisz, Weiss, & Donenberg,
1992). Conventionally, it is argued that efficacy research
tests interventions under conditions that are somehow
more controlled and rigorous than effectiveness research
(Glasgow, Lichtenstein, & Marcus, 2003). Weisz and others
have noted, however, that both types of research can be
equally controlled and rigorous, and that the conditions of
efficacy research exclude so much of the real-world that
they are "artificial," whereas effectiveness research studies
interventions under real-world conditions. (Carroll &
Rounsaville, 2003; Glasgow et al., 2003; Weisz, Weiss, &
Donenberg, 1992).

*Phase 4: Generalizability Studies*
Phase 3 tests of psychosocial interventions may be restricted
to certain types of consumers, service settings, or
geographic areas. If these tests are encouraging, inevitably
questions are raised about whether a practice is applicable
to other consumers, service settings, and geographic areas.
For these reasons, it is sometimes necessary to conduct tests
of psychosocial interventions involving types of consumers
(e.g., persons of color), service settings (e.g., primary care
clinics), and geographic areas (e.g., rural environments)
that were not included in phase 3 studies. It is important to
note that funding for this type of research is often difficult
to secure and therefore becomes a barrier to the development of specific generalizability research.

*Phase 5: Disseminability Studies*
A goal of intervention science is making interventions that
are safe and effective broadly accessible to the public.
Accomplishing this goal requires learning how any given
practice can be widely disseminated. It is one thing to show
that an intervention is effective in varying environments. It

is another task to convince agency administrations, mental health system leaders, and practitioners to adopt new interventions and implement these practices throughout a state or the nation. Considerable evidence exists that disseminating new interventions at this scale is a difficult and poorly understood process (Hays, 1996; Rogers, 1983). This barrier has led to the recognition of the need for studies of various dissemination methods.

*Phase 6: Postdissemination Quality-Improvement Studies*
After a psychosocial practice has been widely implemented, data should be collected on the long-term experiences of consumers who receive the intervention (FDA/Center for Drug Evaluation and Research, 1998). This type of monitoring can discover adverse or positive effects that can only be detected when interventions are in widespread and prolonged use. Such data fit nicely into the quality assurance and improvement systems that should be a part of the mental health system.

Psychosocial interventions can have negative as well as positive effects (Beutler, 2000). Identifying the negative effects of interventions, particularly medical ones, has driven the development of intervention science more than the desire to find positive ones (Hilts, 2003). As Glasgow and colleagues (2003) suggested, intervention science is about finding interventions that do more good than harm.

## Multiple Studies
The history of intervention science has taught us that single studies, even when they are of high quality, can be misleading. A high-quality individual study may indicate, by chance, that an ineffective practice is effective (Type I error) or that an effective practice is ineffective (Type II error). Truly chance findings should not repeat. Multiple studies also increase our understanding of how intervention effects vary. Finally, multiple studies by investigators who have no allegiance for or against a specific practice can eliminate the unintended bias that creeps into studies by intervention developers and advocates.

Type I and Type II errors

At the same time, the results of multiple studies can be confusing, particularly to the public. For this reason intervention science has developed requirements and methods for analyzing multiple studies. Clarke and Chalmers (1998) noted:

> The public is often confused by the conflicting messages it
> receives as a result of piecemeal reporting of research. . . .
> Those who turn to reports of trials to help guide treatment
> deserve nothing less than a discussion of the totality of the
> relevant evidence. . . . To paraphrase John Donne, No trial is
> an island, entire of itself; every trial is a piece of the conti-
> nent. A part of the main. (pp. 280–281)

## Organizational Support

The history of intervention science also teaches us that to develop, test, disseminate, and monitor the uses of evidence requires supporting organizations. Pharmaceutical companies and the FDA have played these roles in the development of medications and medical devices, with federal agencies and universities playing supporting roles. There is much less organizational support for intervention science as it is applied to psychosocial interventions. In mental health, the Substance Abuse and Mental Health Services Administration, over time, has developed a "science to services" mission that does support intervention science. Other federal agencies, private foundations, states, and universities also provide some support. The importance of enhancing this support is discussed further in the last section of this chapter.

## Guidelines for Evidence of Intervention Effectiveness

We have just seen that building the evidence base requires conducting multiple phase 3 and 4 studies that meet certain quality criteria. As studies accumulate, their results are combined through systematic reviews and meta-analyses that weight the findings in terms of their size and quality. There is no magic number of agreed-upon studies that is needed to show that a practice is effective in facilitating specified outcomes. But as the number of studies mount, eventually the field reaches consensus that an intervention is, or is not, effective in causing certain outcomes (West et al., 2002). Various guidelines have been developed and translated into scorable criteria for rating study quality (Lohr & Carey, 1999).* These guidelines have been based on the logic of basic and intervention science of eliminating threats to validity. Below, we focus on the most critical guidelines for psychosocial interventions.

## Guideline 1. Psychosocial intervention studies should make meaningful comparisons by selecting appropriate control conditions.

The evidence for the effectiveness of a practice is most convincing when it is the result of a study in which the intervention was compared to a placebo or a control treatment that has already been proven to be effective (International Conference on Harmonisation, 1998). *Placebos* are activities that appear to be like interventions but lack the "active ingredients" theorized to cause the desired outcomes. We compare interventions to placebos because research has shown that people sometimes improve when they receive attention, irrespective of which intervention is provided. In psychosocial interventions a placebo may impact consumers by engendering hope and positive self-regard that may result in positive clinical change (Healy, 1999; Parloff, 1986; Shapiro & Morris, 1978). It is therefore vital to compare a new intervention with a placebo-only group to evaluate actual intervention-related treatment benefits. This approach is used in pharmaceutical evaluation trials

| Placebo control

---

*The U.S. Food and Drug Administration Center for Drug Evaluation and Research (1998), the International Conference on Harmonisation (1998), and the American Psychological Association (2002) provide comprehensive and detailed descriptions of important guidelines for developing evidence in intervention science. The guidelines provided by the FDA probably have been used, reviewed, and debated more widely than any similar writings on intervention science.

when a new medicine is compared against an inert agent (e.g., sugar pill) to determine effectiveness.

Minimal control

In addition to the placebo control condition, Strayhorn (1987) has identified a number of other comparisons. The *minimal but useful treatment control* and the *alternative treatment control* both provide something of benefit to consumers, but not the critical ingredients of the psychosocial intervention. The *dismantling control* approach involves crafting multiple alternatives, each of which has only one or some, but not all, of the active ingredients of the targeted psychosocial intervention. These alternatives are contrasted with the full intervention. The *no-treatment control* withholds any intervention. An example of this design would be the use of a waiting list control group, in which consumers are monitored for changes while they are waiting for services to be available to them.

Alternative treatment control

Dismantling control

No treatment control

*Placebo, minimal services, alternative services,* and *no treatment controls* are difficult to develop and implement (Strayhorn, 1987). At a technical level, the problem is to identify the active ingredient of a practice and to craft a credible alternative "treatment" that withholds all of these elements and that also has no negative effects. Such interventions do address the ethical issue, because consumers in control groups do receive proven services.

Control conditions that consist of so-called standard or usual services have come to be widely used in psychosocial intervention research. This method is similar to the alternative services approach. It is crucial to clearly define what is meant by standard or usual services and to demonstrate that such services do not contain the critical ingredients of the practice being tested. Given that investigators often fail to accomplish these tasks, the *standard-and-usual-services* approach is usually neither technically nor ethically satisfactory. In addition, usual services vary by site.

Standard and usual services as a control

Investigations using no-treatment control groups are easier to conceptualize. This approach provides evidence of whether or not the intervention is better than nothing. This approach is critical if we wish to avoid doing harm and wasting resources. If the length of the research is short enough so as not to put consumers at substantial risk, the ethical issues can be mitigated by offering the practice to the no-treatment control group at the end of the study, if it was shown to be effective. However, psychosocial intervention studies are often too long for this option to be a meaningful way to address the ethical issue of withholding services. When fully informed consumers volunteer to participate in such studies, for altruistic reasons, certain protections can be implemented to identify study participants in control conditions who need to be withdrawn from the study because they are at risk.

### Guideline 2. Psychosocial intervention studies should control for the possibility of baseline differences between study groups.

Randomization is the gold standard of methods for assigning persons to conditions in research on intervention practices. This design element involves assigning research participants to various groups by chance methods. It should be used whenever possible in phases 3 and 4 of intervention studies. There is now evidence that randomization can be used in studies of psychosocial interventions if time and resources permit (Leff, Mulkern, Drake, Allen, & Chow, 2002).

Limits of randomization

However, randomization does not ensure that groups assigned to conditions are equivalent (Hsu, 1989). This is especially true with small samples. Moreover, even with large samples, randomization will fail in a small percentage of replication studies. Often, the evidence for psychosocial interventions consists of a relatively small number of small sample replications, making it important to examine differences between the groups and to identify whether or not the differences are important.

There are methods for statistically controlling for group differences in data analyses of psychosocial intervention studies when participants were not randomized or the randomization failed (Campbell & Stanley, 1966;

Rosenbaum & Rubin, 1985). Many intervention scientists have used these techniques, particularly when analyzing large administrative databases and clinical records. When randomization is not an option, well-designed quasi-experimental studies should be used for phases 3 and 4.

### Guideline 3. Fidelity measures demonstrate that the practice was implemented as designed.

Dissemination research has shown that even when practices are elaborately specified, as in the case of manualized treatments, local programs and providers often change them to meet what are perceived to be local conditions (Hays, 1996; Rogers, 1983). If these changes are not well described, we can mistakenly infer that intervention effects are varied, when, in fact, it is the intervention itself that is varied. *Fidelity measurement* refers to measuring the degree to which interventions are implemented and sustained *as specified* by practice experts, in manuals, or in other materials. Any valid study of a practice should implement fidelity measures and provide evidence that the intervention was delivered as defined. These measures should include measures of how contextual factors (e.g., administrative and financing issues) were addressed. Ideally, studies should use fidelity scales designed specifically to assess the implemented practice.

### Guideline 4. Practice studies should use outcome measures that directly address, or have known relationships to, primary outcomes.

Proxy versus primary outcome measures

Studies of psychosocial interventions often include secondary or surrogate variables (i.e., proxy measures). These variables "stand in for," or are of lower priority than, the desired clinical and rehabilitation outcomes (International Conference on Harmonisation, 1998). For example, some practices employ reduced psychiatric hospitalizations as a surrogate measure for symptom reduction. Since the relationship between symptoms and hospitalizations can be affected by administrative and funding policies, studies should not interpret reduced hospitalizations as a sign of symptom reduction. In fact, there have been instances when treatments showing a highly positive effect on a secondary or surrogate outcome have ultimately been shown to be detrimental to a primary clinical outcome, and vice versa (International Conference on Harmonisation, 1998). Ideally, studies should measure primary outcomes.

## Guideline 5. Psychosocial intervention studies should identify key outcomes in advance and distinguish between planned and unplanned analyses.

Dar, Serlin, and Omer (1994) found that unplanned "data mining" was present in a large proportion of psychotherapy studies. There are reasons to believe the same is true of studies of psychosocial practices, including the availability of large data sets and ease of computer-implemented statistical analysis, (Drake & McHugo, 2003). It is essential to have theory-driven evaluation and testing of a priori hypotheses (i.e., hypotheses specified prior to initiation of research) both within and across studies to avoid capitalizing on chance associations. Studies without a priori hypotheses do not constitute formal proof of effectiveness, and unplanned analyses should be used sparingly (International Conference on Harmonisation, 1998). Studies should always distinguish between planned and unplanned analyses.

*Avoid unplanned analyses*

## Guideline 6. Studies should identify outcomes that have clinical, rehabilitation, or policy significance.

Not all statistically significant differences have significant clinical or policy ramifications. As technological improvements make larger studies possible, the probability of studies finding statistically significant, but otherwise trivial, differences becomes greater (Drake & McHugo, 2003; International Conference on Harmonisation, 1998; Rogers, Howard, & Vessey, 1993). Several procedures are available to define clinical significance, such as choosing variables that are widely accepted to be important consumer

*Statistical significance is not enough*

outcomes (e.g., mortality), and the use of statistical methods for operationally defining clinical meaningfulness (Jacobson & Truax, 1991.

### Guideline 7. Practice studies should measure long-term impacts.

Practices that target outcomes such as improved consumer functioning and improved quality of life can take more than 1 year to demonstrate substantial positive effects. On the other hand, short-term effects, such as symptom reduction may not persist after the psychosocial intervention is withdrawn. For these reasons studies of practices should be as long as possible. Characteristically, studies track outcomes for 1 year, although long-term follow-up periods are sometimes added to clinical trials.

### Guideline 8. Practice studies should give providers, those who assess outcomes, and consumers as little information as possible about study hypotheses and assignments to study conditions.

"Blinding" the research participants

Research shows that when providers, researchers, and intervention recipients (i.e., consumers) are aware of the study hypotheses and of which consumer is in which study condition, the study results can be biased. Ideally, intervention studies should withhold this information from all three groups. This is referred to as "blinding." In most cases it is impossible for providers to be unaware of what intervention they are providing. However, it should be possible to avoid letting the providers know which practice the researchers hypothesize will work best. It is equally difficult for consumers to be unaware of what practice they are receiving, but likewise, it is possible to keep the study hypotheses from them. This procedure works best when the alternative interventions are delivered in different sites. In many cases it may be possible to keep those who assess outcomes unaware of both assignment and hypotheses.

*Guideline 9. Psychosocial intervention studies should correct for analyses of multiple measures of the same outcome.*

Dar and colleagues (1994) found that a high proportion of the psychotherapy research studies they reviewed did not adequately correct for testing the same hypotheses with multiple measures of the same outcomes, with the risk of accepting chance findings as valid intervention effects (Bangert-Drowns, 1986; Dar et al., 1994; International Conference on Harmonisation, 1998). Because studies of psychosocial interventions focus on multiple outcomes analyzed with large data sets and the availability of easy to use computer-implemented statistical analyses, there is the potential for using multiple measures of the same outcome. Studies should avoid this problem by focusing on a small number of key impacts chosen because of their grounding in theory or psychometric properties (Dar et al., 1994).

A statistically significant result by chance

*Guideline 10. Practice studies should analyze data for all persons assigned to study conditions and take into account missing data and other protocol violations.*

Studies of psychosocial interventions often focus on populations of consumers that are difficult to engage in treatment and frequently leave treatment prematurely. This reality raises issues about how to handle dropouts and missing data. For most psychosocial interventions, engaging and retaining persons in treatment is part of what the intervention is intended to achieve. Therefore, even when persons drop out of treatment, they should be retained in studies and their data should be included in "intent-to-treat" data analyses (International Conference on Harmonisation, 1998). Any data missing because persons dropped out of the research should be accounted for in the analyses. There are various techniques for handling the issue of missing data (Gibbons & Hedecker, 1994). If substantial amounts of data are missing and there is no credible way to impute the data, study results should be given minimal confidence. Additionally, changes in study design can be made for other reasons, including problems

Intent-to-treat analyses

related to recruiting consumers and breakdowns in randomization procedures. The potential of these incidents to bias study results should be carefully evaluated, sometimes by independent groups (data safety monitoring boards), and addressed in data analyses.

### Guideline 11. Practice studies should collect information on the dissemination of the practice.

Collecting and analyzing information such as intervention costs and the quality of intervention manuals and training materials are important components when evaluating the dissemination characteristics of the interventions. Therefore, studies should collect such information and report it along with evidence of effectiveness. This type of information sets the stage for dissemination and phase 5 research.

## Additional Important Concerns

Evidence versus the recovery vision

Despite the benefits of basing services on evidence, consumers, providers, persons of color and other minority groups, as well as researchers may still voice concerns about using evidence as the basis for mental health services. One concern articulated by consumers is that the evidence about psychosocial practices does not necessarily address the outcome that is *their* primary goal-recovery. As Anthony noted: "much of the existing, published, evidence-based practice research was conceived without an understanding of the recovery vision and/or implemented prior to the emergence of the recovery vision" (2001, p. 5). This concern assures that recovery is a definable, unidimensional, and measurable construct, which has thus far not been shown.

If measures of recovery can be developed, future studies might investigate how these measures relate to previous measures of symptoms, functioning, and quality of life. If these measures are found to be related, it would provide at least indirect support for interventions shown to affect the earlier measures. A second way to approach this concern would be to conduct new phase 3 and 4 studies of the evidence-based practices, with measures of recovery, when they are developed, as outcomes.

Another consumer concern is that mental health policy-makers will direct all financial resources exclusively to the delivery of evidence-based practices. In this scenario, resources would not be available to support practices such as peer-support programs and consumer-operated services. In fact, it may be that consumer-operated services and existing evidence-based services will not compete for the same resources. Existing psychosocial services require research at phases 3–5, whereas newly emerging consumer-operated psychosocial interventions still need research at phases 1 and 2. Hopefully, political and policy decision makers would allocate resources to all of the intervention science phases to foster the growth and development of the evidence base for the practice. This concern may reflect the phenomenon of true partners fighting over inadequate resources rather than collaborating to advocate for more adequate funding.

Practitioners who do not provide evidence-based interventions are concerned that the services they render will not be reimbursed, that they might be vulnerable to malpractice suits for not delivering evidence-based services, and that the manualized aspect of evidence-based practices will not permit them to respond to individual consumer needs (Chambless & Ollendick, 2001; Clinicians for the Restoration of Autonomous Practice, 2003). The concern is that the state or the policymakers will provide reimbursement (e.g., Medicaid) only to support practices based on evidence. Many states are currently engaged in this very process with varying degrees of success. The concern about legal action for failure to provide services based on evidence of effectiveness has not materialized. The concern about consumer needs is being addressed by individualized consumer assessments and honors consumer preferences and goals. Individualizing services based on consumer preferences is at the core of the identified evidence-based practices.

| Funding concerns

| Practitioner concerns

Concerns of people of
color and other
minority groups

There is a concern that there is a that lack of evidence to demonstrate that practices that are effective with the majority of the population are also effective with specific minority, racial, ethnic, and culturally diverse groups. Bernal and Scharro-del-Rio (2001) noted that, given rigorous guidelines for what constitutes evidence, there is little in the existing literature about the effectiveness of services delivered to people of color. Understandably, funding for this type of evaluation is essential to make certain that evidence-based practices are appropriate for diverse populations of consumers.

Concerns of
researchers

Mental health services researchers are concerned about the challenges of producing evidence based on the guidelines discussed above. They are also concerned about the resources and organizational support provided by pharmaceutical companies and the FDA, in the case of medications and medical devices, for the phased process described to meet these challenges. One answer comes from the disjointed system we now have, in which multiple federal agencies, service providers, journals, and academic organizations pursue separate and often nonintegrated research agendas (Hunt, 1997). We have described this problem elsewhere as a serious game with multiple players, multiple sets of rules, no league, and no umpires (Leff, 2003). Under this system it can take over a decade to move scientific findings into practice. An alternative approach would be to appoint a federal agency to provide resources and organizational support to make the psychosocial intervention development process more orderly and efficient.

## A Vision for the Future

Science to services
initiative

The current science-to-services initiative of SAMHSA is a step in the right direction. A federal agency that adopts policies to support the development and dissemination of evidence-based practices in a more organized and expeditious manner is greatly needed. Under this initiative, SAMHSA is expanding its National Registry of Effective

Programs (NREP), which currently comprises substance abuse prevention services, to include substance abuse treatment and mental health prevention and treatment services. The registry is accessible on the Internet at *http://modelprograms.samhsa.gov*. NREP uses intervention science guidelines similar to the ones cited above, expressed as scorable criteria, to rate the quality of evidence for services that apply to be listed on NREP. Three raters who function like peer reviewers, rate each applicant. Review teams do not currently have consumers or other stakeholders as members, but it is hoped that they will be included in the future. Based on their scores, applicants are either not listed, listed as promising services, or listed as effective (evidence-based) services. Effective services with materials that make them disseminable are listed as model services. The plan is to provide technical assistance and resources to services that desire to move up the evidence ladder, so that they can conduct studies that address the intervention science guidelines. Thus the initiative promotes movement from science to services as well as services to science. Additionally, SAMHSA grant mechanisms are being redesigned to identify and develop services for NREP and to use NREP to identify disseminable services. Finally, SAMHSA is working with the National Institute of Mental Health, the Agency for Healthcare Research and Quality, and other federal agencies to pool resources for implementing this science-to-services agenda.

**Acknowledgments**
Work on this paper was supported by a cooperative agreement from the Center for Mental Health Services, Substance Abuse and Mental Health Services Agency: SM53128-01-1.

## References

American Psychological Association (APA). (2002). Criteria for evaluating treatment guidelines. *American Psychologist, 57*, 1052–1059.

Anthony, W. A. (2001, November 5). The need for recovery-compatible evidence-based practices. *Mental Health Weekly*. Retrieved November 30, 2004, from *http://global.factiva.com*

Bangert-Downs, R. L. (1986). Review of developments in meta-analytic method. *Psychological Bulletin, 99*(3), 388–399.

Bernal, G., & Scharro-del-Rio, M. R. (2001). Are empirically supported treatments valid for ethnic minorities? Toward an alternative approach for treatment research. *Cultural Diversity and Ethnic Minority Psychology, 7,* 328–342.

Beutler, L. (2000). David and Goliath: When empirical and clinical standards of practice meet. *American Psychologist, 55,* 997–1007.

Campbell, D. T., & Stanley, J. C. (1966). *Experimental and quasi-experimental designs for research.* Skokie, IL: Rand McNally.

Carroll, K. M., & Rounsaville, B. J. (2003). Bridging the gap: A hybrid model to link efficacy and effectiveness research in substance abuse treatment. *Psychiatric Services, 54,* 333–339.

Chambless, D., & Ollendick, T. H. (2001). Empirically supported psychological interventions: Controversies and evidence. *Annual Review of Psychology, 52,* 685–716.

Clarke, M., & Chalmers, I. (1998). Discussion sections in reports of controlled trials published in general medical journals: Islands in search of continents? *Journal of the American Medical Association, 280,* 280–282.

Clinicians for the Restoration of Autonomous Practice (CRAP) Writing Group (2002). EBM: Unmasking the ugly truth. *British Medical Journal, 325,* 1496–1498.

Dar, R., Serlin, R., & Omer, H. (1994). Misuse of statistical tests in three decades of psychotherapy research. *Journal of Consulting and Clinical Psychology, 62,* 75–82.

Drake, R. E., & McHugo, G. J. (2003). Large data sets can be dangerous! *Psychiatric Services, 54,* 133.

Food and Drug Administration/Center for Drug Evaluation and Research. (1998). *The CDER handbook.* Washington, DC: U.S. Department of Health and Human Services.

Gibbons, R. D., & Hedecker, D. (1994). Application of random-effects probit regression models. *Journal of Consulting and Clinical Psychology, 62,* 285–296.

Glasgow, R. E., Lichtenstein, E., & Marcus, A. C. (2003). Why don't we see more translation of health promotion research to practice? Rethinking the efficacy-to-effectiveness transition. *American Journal of Public Health, 93,* 1261.

Gomory, T. (1999). Programs of assertive community treatment (PACT): A critical review. *Ethical Human Sciences and Services, 1*, 147–163.

Hays, A. P. (1996). Influences on reinvention during the diffusion of innovations. *Political Research Quarterly, 49*, 631–650.

Healy, D. (1999). *The anti-depressant era.* Cambridge, MA: Harvard University Press.

Hilts, P. J. (2003). *Protecting America's health, the FDA, business, and one hundred years of regulation.* New York: Knopf.

Hsu, L. M. (1989). Random sampling, radomization, and equivalence of contrasted groups in psychotherapy outcome research. *Journal of Consulting and Clinical Psychology, 57*(1), 131–137.

Hunt, M. (1997). *How science takes stock: The story of meta-analysis.* New York: Russell Sage Foundation.

International Conference on Harmonisation. (1998). Guidance on statistical principles for clinical trials. *Federal Register, 63*, 49583–49598.

Jacobson, N., & Truax, P. (1991). Clinical significance: A statistical approach to defining meaningful change in psychotherapy research. *Journal of Consulting and Clinical Psychology, 59*, 12–19.

Kitcher, P. (2001). *Science, truth, and democracy.* Oxford, UK: Oxford University Press.

Leff, H. S. (2003, June). *A brief history of evidence-based practice and a vision for the future.* Paper presented at the NREP Mental Health Prevention Meeting, Washington, DC.

Leff, H. S., Mulkern, V., Drake, R. E., Allen, E., & Chow, C. M. (2002). *Knowledge assessment: A missing link between knowledge development and knowledge application.* Unpublished manuscript.

Lohr, K., & Carey, T. S. (1999). Assessing "best evidence": Issues in grading the quality of studies for systematic reviews. *Journal of Quality Improvement, 25*, 470–479.

Millenson, M. L. (1997). *Demanding medical excellence: Doctors and accountability in the information age.* Chicago: University of Chicago Press.

Parloff, M. (1986). Placebo controls in psychotherapy research: A sine qua non or a placebo for research problems? *Journal of Consulting and Clinical Psychology, 54*, 79–87.

Rogers, E. M. (1983). *Diffusion of innovation* (3rd Ed.). New York: Free Press

Rogers, J., Howard, K., & Vessey, J. (1993). Using significance tests to evaluate equivalence between experimental groups. *Psychological Bulletin, 113*, 553–565.

Rosenbaum, P. R., & Rubin, D. B. (1985). Constructing a control group using multivariate matched sampling methods that incorporate the propensity score. *The American Statistician, 39*, 33–38.

Rotter, J. (1971). On the evaluation of methods of intervening in other people's lives. *The Clinical Psychologist, 24*, 1–2.

Shapiro, A. K., & Morris, L. A. (1978). Placebo effects in medical and psychological therapies. In S. L. Garfield & A. E. Bergin (Eds.), *Handbook of psychotherapy and behavior change: An empirical analysis* (2nd Ed.). New York: Wiley.

Strayhorn, J. M. (1987). Control groups for psychosocial intervention outcome studies. *American Journal of Psychiatry, 144*, 275–282.

Weisz, J. R., Weiss, B., & Donenberg G. R. (1992). The lab versus the clinic: Effects of child and adolescent psychotherapy. *American Psychologist, 47*, 1578.

West, S., King, V., Carey, T. S., Lohr, K. N., McKoy, N., Sutton, S. F., et al. (2002). *Systems to rate the strength of scientific evidence.* Evidence Report/Technology Assessment No. 47 (AHRQ Publication No. 02-E016), Rockville, MD: Agency for Healthcare Research and Quality.

Wolff, N. (2000). Using randomized controlled trials to evaluate socially complex services: Problems, challenges and recommendations. *The Journal of Mental Health Policy and Economics, 3*, 97–109.

*Part III*
Implementation

EIGHT

# Closing the Gap between What Services Are and What They Could Be

*William C. Torrey*
*Paul G. Gorman*

MOST PEOPLE CARE DEEPLY ABOUT the health-care services that
they or their family members receive. Understandably,
people want and expect high-quality, professional services.
They are often surprised and disappointed when their
experience of health care does not meet this expectation.
In its recent publication, *Crossing the Quality Chasm: A New
Health System for the 21st Century*, the Institute of Medicine
(Committee on Quality Healthcare in America, 2001)
recommends that the whole health-care system dedicate
itself to improving the quality of care in the United States.
It is noted that high-quality care is characterized by services
that are effective, safe,patient-centered, timely, efficient,
and equitable. The Institute of Medicine observed that the
health-care system has a great deal of room for improvement on each of these dimensions of quality. The institute's
conclusion is that there is not just a "gap" between the
health-care services provided and the ideal high quality of
care, there is a "chasm."

People want high-
quality health care

Despite the hard work of many dedicated and caring
providers, the mental health care system joins the rest of
the health-care industry in falling far short of the ideal. The
movement to promote the widespread implementation of
evidence-based practices for adults with severe mental

Help people achieve
desired outcomes

167

illness (SMI) is an effort to improve the effectiveness of services that are offered by mental health professionals. The basic logic is that consumers and families are more likely to achieve the outcomes they desire if they have access to services that have been demonstrated to work in helping them achieve those outcomes.

This chapter begins by providing a historical context for community services, and then reviews the findings of studies that assess the access to, and the quality of community mental health services for, adults with SMI in this country. The chapter closes with a summary of the research on promoting change in health care, using a case example to illustrate the process of implementing an evidence-based practice.

## Historical Context of Mental Health Service

Stakeholders affect services

The current community mental health service system is the result of diverse and complex responses to the treatment needs of adults with SMI. Over the years, many different stakeholders have influenced the types of services that have been offered. Stakeholders who play essential roles include legislators who write laws and appropriate money; public mental health authorities who create administrative rules and financial incentives; insurers who structure benefits; community mental health center administrators who set priorities and organize care; and mental health clinicians who provide direct services. Thanks, in large part, to continued self-advocacy, there has been a substantial increase in the recognition of consumers and their family members as critical stakeholders.

Government responsibile for services

Unlike most other areas of health care, government agencies at the local, state, and federal level have long assumed responsibility for providing services to adults with SMI. Before the era of large state-built asylums, local governments often sheltered adults with severe mental illnesses in poorhouses and jails. In the early 1800s Dorothea Dix advocated for the construction of state institutions to provide humane treatment for people with mental illnesses. By the time of the Civil War, nearly every state had one or more asylums. States gradually took over the financial responsibility from local governments for the costs of housing people in these institutions. Consequently, the local communities sent more people to asylums leading to the growth of the inpatient facilities. By the 1950s, when institutionalization peaked, the inpatient population in the United States had reached 550,000 people (Grob, 1996).

The shift toward community care was the result of many factors. The emergence of the civil rights movement brought attention to the population in state hospitals who were being deprived of their civil rights without due process. Some success with mental health treatments during World War II had fostered a growing belief in the potential of community-based interventions. During that time, medical science began the process of discovering and developing psychiatric medications that reduced some of the symptoms of mental illnesses. However, research studies of the large institutions began to show that inpatients were not improving relative to the impairments of their illnesses. The process of deinstitutionalization, starting in the 1950s and lasting into the 1970s, moved many people with SMI out of the large state asylums but, unfortunately, not necessarily into better circumstances. Many people experienced difficult and oppressive conditions in their local communities. Little was known about how to effectively provide social services and treatment. Commonly, people were shifted from hospitals to other institutions such as nursing homes, jails, and segregated residential settings where they were no better off—a phenomenon known as "transinstitutionalization." Many became homeless. Observers concluded that the particular needs of adults with SMI were not being met (General Accounting Office, 1977; Turner & TenHoor, 1978). It became increasingly clear that institutionalization was not helpful and, indeed, was actually detrimental to the very people it was intended to help. This perspective, combined with the benefits from early psychiatric medica-

*Community care*

*Institutionalization*

*Deinstitutionalization*

*Transinstitutional-
ization*

tions as well as the high cost of inpatient facilities, provided incentives for the passage of the Community Mental Health Centers Act of 1963. This act, in concert with other federal legislation that provided grants to build community facilities and included mental health benefits in the Medicaid and Medicare programs, led to the development of our community mental health system (Grob, 1996; National Council for Community Behavioral Healthcare, 2003; U.S. Department of Health and Human Services, 1999).

With no significant research base upon which to develop community programs, each state created its own community mental health system, resulting in a significant amount of variation in treatment models, methods, and orientations. The early goal of many community support systems of treatment was simply to keep consumers from entering or returning to inpatient programs. As community-based models began to evolve, so did the focus on providing treatment with an orientation toward rehabilitation. This perspective, when combined with improved medications, fostered the emergence of a new goal that went beyond simply helping people with SMI stay out of psychiatric hospitals, began to evolve. Community-based models not only began to support the idea of empowerment but also to provide choices regarding types of services received and the goals pursued. Consumers, themselves, began to identify the goals they wanted to achieve. With more advances in treatment models and increased benefits from psychiatric medications, the concept of recovery—the process of establishing a definition of oneself beyond mental illness—emerged as a goal in some of the more progressive mental health systems in the 1990s. This movement was championed by consumers and bolstered by the spread of their success stories.

A fundamental challenge for community mental health systems has been to understand what types of services, within the wide array of available services, have been useful in helping consumers achieve their goals. The good news is that there now exists a significant body of knowledge about

*Marginal notes:*

Evolution of community-based models of service

Rehabilitation treatment

Consumer empowerment

Recovery

Core set of effective practices

how to help people with SMI and their families achieve specific goals and support them in their recovery process. Numerous reviews of the research evidence identify a core set of effective community mental health practices (Drake, Goldman, et al., 2001; Fenton & Schooler, 2000; Kane, 1999; Lehman, Steinwachs, & co-investigators, 1998b; Miller et al., 1999). This research strongly supports psychosocial interventions such as supported employment, various approaches to illness self-management, family psychoeducation, case management based on the principles of assertive community treatment, substance abuse treatment that is integrated with mental health treatment, and the use of specific medications prescribed in specific ways. These services can help consumers obtain the outcomes they desire, such as increased independent housing, competitive employment, improved quality of life, decreased homelessness, decreased hospitalizations, decreased symptoms of mental illness, and decreased substance use (Dixon et al., 2001; Drake, Essock et al., 2001; Mellman et al., 2001; Mueser et al., 2002; Phillips et al., 2001). When services with demonstrated effectiveness are widely available to people with SMI, they are able to lead more satisfying lives (Drake et al., 1998).

## The Nature of Current Services

Unfortunately, many people with SMI are not benefiting from mental health services. A national survey shows that only about one in every three people with any type of diagnosable mental disorder receives treatment in a given year (Reggie et al., 1993). Even in studies that only consider adults with SMI, only 40–50% receive treatment each year (Kessler et al., 1996; Wang, Demler, & Kessler, 2002). Multiple factors impede people's access to services. Mental health services are not available in all communities, and when they are available, the cost of services can often be prohibitive. Many people with SMI do not have health insurance, and for those with private insurance, the mental

Lack of service access

health benefits are often very limited. Furthermore, language and cultural barriers can interfere with access. Lastly, the stigma that is associated with mental disorders keeps many from seeking help (U.S. Department of Health and Human Services, 1999).

Current services do not reflect what is known to work

PORT

When people with severe mental illnesses are able to access services from the community mental health system, they generally are not offered services that have been validated by strong research support. The Schizophrenia Patient Outcome Research Team (PORT) provides the most extensive demonstration of this problem. Based on an exhaustive review of the treatment outcome literature, the team articulated 30 evidence-based treatment recommendations for people with schizophrenia (Lehman et al., 1998b). The investigators then examined how often the usual services in two state mental health systems followed the PORT recommendations. The PORT study revealed that consumers with the diagnosis of schizophrenia were highly unlikely to receive effective services (Lehman, Steinwachs, & co-investigators, 1998a). Even simple medication practices fell within standards of effectiveness 50% or less of the time. A minority of patients received effective psychosocial interventions. For example, only 9.6% of the consumers and their families received family psychoeducation, and only 22.5% of consumers in outpatient programs received any vocational services. One accompanying commentary summed up the study findings by saying that it "documents the abysmally poor care that the majority of patients receive" (Flynn, 1998, p. 30).

Evidence from other sources supports the PORT findings. An American Psychiatric Association study of usual practices came to similar conclusions (West et al., 2003), and a large national survey estimated that only 15.3% of adults with SMI receives minimally adequate services (Wang et al., 2002). As examples, Anderson and Adams (1996) noted that family psychoeducation is rarely available in routine practice settings, and Tashjian and colleagues (1989) reported that fewer than 5% of persons with SMI received supported employment services.

If practices with demonstrated effectiveness are usually not provided, what practices are offered to adults with SMI in the community? Mental health services vary widely from state to state, and from agency to agency within the same state, and even from one clinician to another within the same agency. The types of services offered depend on a number of factors, including the regulations and reimbursement structures of the state or public mental health authority, the leadership of a community mental health agency, and the training, background and education of the clinician.

Current services vary widely

Public mental health authorities play a significant role, by way of financial incentives and specific policies and procedures, in determining which practices are provided by agencies in a mental health system. Some state public mental health authorities have structured their funding and regulations to promote the provision of evidence-based practices. For example, New York and Indiana are currently creating and monitoring assertive community treatment teams to provide services for consumers with specific needs. However, many mental health authorities do not explicitly require providers to offer practices that are strongly supported by research. Indeed, many authorities expend significant financial resources annually on mental health services that have no demonstrable effectiveness, such as rehabilitative day treatment programs. Financial reimbursement structures can also become barriers to the implementation of evidence-based practices. Currently, Medicaid programs fund 80% of mental health services provided for adults with severe mental illness (National Council for Community Behavioral Healthcare, 2003). Because Medicaid reimbursement for services is usually based on a fee-for-service model, it creates the need for community mental health agencies to keep their clinicians as busy as possible producing billable units of time (productivity). When clinicians are participating in training, supervision, or service coordination, they are not meeting financial productivity requirements. This reimbursement mechanism creates a financial disincentive for the agency to

Public mental health authorities' influence on practice

Financing services

provide training, supervision, and coordination. Without these activities, clinicians will not be able to advance their skills, and services will be fragmented. The challenge is the mental health authorities to create more appropriate incentives.

Local factors can also strongly affect which practices are offered to consumers and families. For example, consumers and families can organize to advocate for better services. Some agencies have been able to implement new practices due, in large part, to the support of an agency "champion" for the practice. This process is more effective when the champion has the public support and backing of administrative leadership in the agency. Other agencies have been able to implement new practices with the persistent leadership and commitment of the agency director. Perceptions and attitudes of clinicians regarding practices influence which services are provided to consumers. Some clinicians are in the mental health field to be "therapists." This self-concept is likely to promote the implementation of an evidence-based practice if that practice has a therapy-like structure (e.g., cognitive–behavioral treatment of depression). The same clinicians, however, may strongly oppose the implementation of an evidence-based practice if it does not have the feel of office-based therapy (e.g., assertive community treatment or integrated dual disorders treatment), even when the practice also requires complex therapeutic skills.

In summary, only a minority of adults with a SMI is able to access treatment, and an even smaller minority receives treatment shown to be effective. After reviewing this state of affairs, members of the President's New Freedom Commission on Mental Health delivered their report to President Bush in July 2003. In his cover letter, the Commission's Chair, Michael Hogan, wrote:

> For too many Americans with mental illness, the mental
> health services and supports they need remain fragmented,
> disconnected and often inadequate, frustrating the oppor-
> tunity for recovery. Today's mental health care system is a

patchwork relic—the result of disjointed reforms and policies. Instead of ready access to quality care, the system presents barriers that all too often add to the burden of mental
illnesses for individuals, their families, and our communities.
(President's New Freedom Commission of Mental Health,
2003, p. 1)

## Closing the Chasm

In order for adults with mental illness to access mental
health services that are evidence based, these practices need
to be routinely available in community mental health
settings. Implementing an evidence-based practice (EBP)
requires the application of generalizable scientific knowledge in a particular context. The process first involves
promoting change in the behavior of groups of mental
health-care providers. What methods effectively promote
change in health-care providers? Theorists suggest that
behavior changes when intention to change is combined
with the necessary skill and the absence of environmental
constraint (Fishbein, 1995). One of the most cited models
(Green & Krueter, 1991) for promoting change prescribes
three elements: (1) predisposing or disseminating strategies
(e.g., educational events or written material), (2) enabling
methods (e.g., as decision support), and (3) reinforcing
strategies (e.g., as practice feedback mechanisms).

> EBP implementation
> involves promoting
> behavioral change
> in providers

Business theorists from outside the health-care field also
advocate a stage-wise approach to behavior change, noting
that users of innovations move through a series of stages:
from awareness of the opportunity to change, to selection,
adoption, implementation, and, finally, incorporation of
the innovation into their routine daily behavior (Klein &
Sorra, 1996). Efforts to promote change require different
interventions depending on the user's stage in the process.
For example, a social marketing (Andreasen, 1995) effort
may be needed to make providers aware of, and motivated
to use, an EBP, whereas a system of clinical supervision may
be what is needed to get a desired practice into daily effective use at a specific site. In summary, theorists suggest that

> Theory of change

change occurs in stages and that addressing motivation to change (why change?), enabling the change (how to change?), and reinforcing the change (how to maintain and improve the gains?) are all important to practice implementation.

**Research on practice change in general health-care**

General health care, like behavioral health care, faces the challenge of transferring research findings into routine practice (Bero et al., 1998). Reviews of the research on practice change conclude that passive educational approaches, such as the dissemination of clinical practice guidelines and didactic educational meetings, are ineffective and unlikely to result in practice change (Grimshaw et al., 2001). Taking a class on EBP does not translate directly into offering an EBP. One author remarked that lecture-hall efforts to change practice behavior are as effective as "shouting out the window" (Mazmanian & Davis, 2002).

**Adults learn through active participation**

Adults learn better when they actively participate in the learning process. Continuing education that includes interactive workshops, small-group discussions, and skills practice appears to be more effective than lectures and presentations alone (Thomson O'Brien, Freemantle, Oxman, et al., 2002). Auditing a practice and receiving direct feedback from clinicians is sometimes effective (Thomson O'Brien, Oxman, Davis, et al., 2002). And educational outreach visits, in which academics come to clinical sites and help tailor the practice to the particular context, can improve discrete measurable behavior, such as prescribing and test ordering (Thomson O'Brien, Oxman, Haynes, et al., 2002).

**Routine flow of work must support the desired practice**

Implementing a complex new practice requires a restructuring of the flow of daily work. The aim is to redesign the routine procedures of work so that it becomes natural for the clinician to provide services in the desired fashion and hard to do it in the manner to be avoided (Batalden & Stoltz, 1993). Even educated and motivated providers can have difficulty practicing in the desired manner without daily environmental supports. In one illustrative study, researchers were able to improve the primary care treatment of depression by using an intensive, multi-faceted program that included extensive physician education and restructuring of services (Katon et al., 1995). They found, however, that the improved care did not generalize to depressed clinic patients seen outside the restructured intervention program (even when the patients were seen by the same physicians), and the improved care did not endure after the research infrastructure that sponsored the implementation was withdrawn (Lin, Katon, & Simon, 1997).

Overall, the general medical literature on making changes in practice consistently supports the conclusion that there are "no magic bullets" for changing provider behavior in health care (Oxman, Thomson, & Davis, 1995). What does appear clear is that combining multiple strategies to overcome challenges is more likely to be effective than using just one intervention (Grimshaw & Russell, 1993). In studies of practice change, intensity of effort appears directly related to success (Davis, Thompson, Oxman, & Haynes, 1992). In addition, changing complex practice behavior, such as implementing a complicated mental health EBP, requires a higher level of effort than that needed to effect a relatively simple change, such as influencing a prescription choice.

The research that relates directly to efforts to implement EBPs in behavioral health is sparse, but the findings are consistent with the general medical literature. Training clinicians alone, even when it is fairly intensive, appears to increase knowledge but to have a limited impact on practice (McFarlane, McNary, Dixon, Hornby, & Cimett, 2001; Miller & Mount, 2001; Milne, Gorenski, Westerman, Leck & Keegan, 2000). Researchers have reported that promoting the use of EBPs generally requires an intensive effort over about a year that includes training, administrative consultation, and practice feedback (Torrey et al., 2001). Current national efforts to implement evidence-based behavioral health practice combine these elements. The National Evidence-Based Practices Project, for example, is field

No magic bullet

Research on practice change in mental health

testing an implementation process that attempts to predispose, enable, and reinforce practices. The project is designed to encourage mental health authorities, program leaders, clinicians, family members, and consumers to align their efforts to implement effective practices (Mueser, Torrey, Lynde, Singer, & Drake, 2003).

Changing practice is hard work |

In summary, the literature on health-care improvement stresses that different interventions are needed at different phases of practice implementation, and that using multiple interventions is more effective than using just one strategy. Because implementing an EBP is a relatively complex activity, an intensive effort over an extended period of time is often required. Implementing and sustaining high-quality, EBPs requires many ingredients, including committed and consistent leadership within an agency or a public mental health system.

## Implementing an EBP: A Case Vignette

Three-phase implementation |

The state public mental health authority, where East Costal Services (ECS; a fictitious name for a community mental health center) is located, identified competitive employment for consumers as a priority for the state system. In response, the administration at ECS reviewed the services they were providing and ways to help consumers obtain competitive employment. Mental health services provided at ECS incorporated a variety of "usual" programs, including a "day treatment program." The agency leadership made a decision to phase out their day treatment program and reallocate those resources toward a supported employment program. They developed an implementation process based on the following phases: (1) building momentum for change (why do it?), (2) enacting the change (how to do it?), and (3) maintaining and extending the gains (how to sustain the gains?).

Building momentum for change |

In response to the state's desire to facilitate competitive employment for consumers, the ECS leadership proposed to the mental health authority the idea of converting their day treatment program into supported employment and tracking the outcomes. In exchange, the mental health authority agreed to make provisions to reduce the financial risk for ECS in making this change. Although East Costal Services' leadership was convinced that the change was a good idea, the program staff was not. They were fully invested in their current program. Many staff expressed their concern about the potential poor outcomes for consumers without the day treatment program, and some staff were angry that they had not been consulted earlier in the decision making process. The ECS leadership needed to find a way to convince other stakeholders to support the change.

A few key members of the agency leadership began meeting weekly to strategize about ways to support the change. They organized a staff retreat to review the literature on supported employment, read consumer testimonials regarding employment to reflect the role that work plays in people's lives, and engaged staff in planning the change. Meetings were held with family members at the local chapter of the National Alliance for the Mentally Ill. Additional informational and discussion meetings were held for consumers. The work group at ECS developed a collaborative effort to address concerns that were raised regarding consumers. One key idea was the development of a consumer drop-in center at a local church for individuals who were not working. Some consumers helped the process by expressing an interest in the proposed employment supports.

After readjusting the implementation plan and spending more time addressing the why-change question and responding to concerns, it was clear that many changes were still needed. These included:

- *Facilities change.* Once the day treatment program was closed, the SMI program no longer needed a big

| Administration working with staff and consumers

building, and consumers were no longer bused to a central location where they spent the day. Now many services were delivered to individuals in the community. The program moved to a less expensive, smaller facility that better supported the new activity.

- *Staffing changes.* Some day treatment staff transferred to other jobs in the agency. Some could not support the change and chose to leave the agency. The day treatment program coordinator was initially opposed to the implementation of supported employment services, but remained open to its benefit. Eventually, she became an employment specialist. As she worked with consumers who were experiencing positive outcomes, she became an enthusiastic promoter of supported employment services. New employment specialists were hired to provide supported employment services.

- *Workflow changes.* The new program required regular meetings between employment specialists, case managers, and psychiatrists. The mental health treatment team meeting structure was redesigned to support the program needs. The new program required a shift in the billing and support staff functions. The scheduled hours for medication management services and integrated dual-disorders treatment groups were changed to accommodate the schedules of working consumers.

- *Training needs.* A structured and regular group supervision process was scheduled to promote skills acquisition and practice-centered supervision. The psychiatrist and team leaders provided the supervision; they first needed to become active learners, reading articles and attending conferences to acquire the knowledge and skills to lead the clinical team.

- *Maintaining and extending gains.* Many new programs wither over time as staff return to old habits. To prevent this undesirable outcome, even now, many years later, the ECS program leaders continue to devote attention to sustaining and improving the supported employment program. Strategies include:

- *Telling success stories.* What really sold the program to staff, families, and consumers was the positive impact the program had on the individuals it served. Many staff members assumed that many consumers who attended the day treatment program were too ill to work. When these consumers began to obtain competitive employment, the program focus shifted to employment supports. As consumers began working, they felt better about themselves. They appeared and felt more like community members and less like patients. As more stakeholders observed the benefits, they became interested in, and supportive of, the change.

- *Collecting and reporting outcome data.* By regularly collecting a few simple outcome measures, the program demonstrated that it was meeting and exceeding expectations. The number of consumers engaged in paid, integrated, competitive employment increased from less than 15% to around 40%. Data also showed that the closure of day treatment did not lead to an increase in hospitalizations, suicide attempts, or homelessness. The only identified downside to the change was that some consumers missed the social benefits of day treatment (Torrey, Clark, Becker, Wyzik, & Drake, 1997). In response, the CMHC facilitated the development of a local consumer-run program that appears to serve the social needs of many consumers (as well as provide other benefits) (Torrey, Mead, & Ross, 1998).

- Measuring program fidelity. The fidelity of a program to the principles of a practice model can easily drift over time. To address this issue, ECS designed a process involving outside evaluation of their adherence to evidence-based supported employment, using the supported employment fidelity scale. Program leaders meet to review the results and to plan adjustments in the program. The consumer employment outcomes and fidelity scores are also reported to the agency's management group and to the quality subcommittee of ECS's Board of Directors.

Strategies for success

In the case of ECS, the implementation process did not flow smoothly from phase to phase. For example, many questions about "why change" persisted even as the agency was implementing changes. A critical component in effecting the change was the ability of ECS leadership to assess the situation and make needed course adjustments during the implementation process. Throughout the implementation process the leadership of ECS remained committed to the goal of improving their services to support consumers who wanted to achieve competitive employment.

## Conclusion

Redesigning the mental health system is very important, especially to the vast numbers of people whose lives are complicated by the presence of a mental illness. As one expert on quality improvement readily noted, "Every system is perfectly designed to achieve the outcomes it is achieving" (Batalden, 1997). In general terms, our mental health services system is not designed to achieve the results that it has the potential to achieve. If the current mental health system is to provide services that have demonstrated their effectiveness in helping consumers achieve their desired outcomes, it will require active leadership and collaboration from all stakeholder groups to make this opportunity a reality.

## References

Anderson, J., & Adams, C. (1996). Family interventions in schizophrenia: An effective but underused treatment. *British Medical Journal, 313*, 505–506.

Andreasen, A. R. (1995). *Marketing social change: Changing behavior to promote health, social development, and the environment.* San Francisco: Jossey-Bass.

Batalden, P. B. (1997, May). *Systems and leadership.* Paper presented at the Hitchcock Alliance Leadership Learning Seminars, Dartmouth–Hitchcock Medical Center, Lebanon, NH.

Batalden, P. B., & Stoltz, P. K. (1993). A framework of the continual improvement of health care: Building and applying professional and improvement knowledge to test changes in daily work. *Joint Commission Journal on Quality Improvement, 19*, 424–445.

Bero, L. A., Grilli, R., Grimshaw, J. M., Harvey, E., Oxman, A. D., & Thomsom, M. A. (1998). Getting research findings into practice: Closing the gap between research and practice: An overview of systematic reviews of interventions to promote the implementation of research findings. *British Medical Journal, 317*, 465–468.

Committee on Quality Healthcare in America. (2001). *Crossing the quality chasm: A new health system for the 21st century.* Washington, DC: National Academy Press.

Davis, D. A., Thompson, M .A., Oxman, A. D., & Haynes, B. (1992). Evidence for the effectiveness of CME: A review of 50 randomized controlled trials. *Journal of the American Medical Association, 26*, 1111–1117.

Dixon, L., McFarlane, W. R., Lefley, H., Lucksted, A., Cohen, M., Falloon, I., et al. (2001). Evidence-based practices for services to families of people with psychiatric disabilities. *Psychiatric Services, 52*, 903–910.

Drake, R. E., Essock, S. M., Shaner, A., Carey, K. B., Minkoff, K., Kola, L., et al. (2001). Implementing dual diagnosis services for clients with severe mental illness. *Psychiatric Services, 52*, 469–476.

Drake, R. E., Fox, T. S., Leather, P. K., Becker, D. R., Musumeci, J. S., Ingram, W. F., et al. (1998). Regional variation in competitive employment for persons with severe mental illness. *Administration and Policy in Mental Health, 25*, 493–504.

Drake, R. E., Goldman, H. H., Leff, H. S., Lehman, F., Dixon, L., Mueser, K. T., et al. (2001). Implementing evidence-based practices in routine mental health service settings. *Psychiatric Services, 52*, 179–182.

Fenton, W. E., & Schooler, N. R. (2000). Editor's introduction: Evidence-based psychosocial treatment for schizophrenia. *Schizophrenia Bulletin, 26*, 1–3.

Fishbein, M. (1995). Developing effective behavioral change interventions: Some lessons learned from behavioral research. In T. E. Backer, S. L. David, & C. Soucy (Eds.), *Reviewing the behavioral science knowledge base on technology transfer. NIDA Research Monograph 155*. Rockville, MD: National Institute of Mental Health.

Flynn, L. M. (1998). Commentary on patterns of usual care for schizophrenia: Initial results from the Schizophrenia Patient Outcomes Research Team (PORT) client survey. *Schizophrenia Bulletin, 24,* 30–32.

General Accounting Office (GAO). (1977). *Returning the mentally disabled to the community: Government needs to do more.* Washington, DC: Author.

Green, L., & Krueter, M. (1991). *Application of precede/proceed in community settings: Health promotion planning—an educational and environmental approach.* Mountain View, CA: Mayfield.

Grimshaw, J. M., & Russell, I. T. (1993). Effect of clinical guidelines of medical practice: A systematic review of rigorous evaluations. *The Lancet, 342,* 1317–1322.

Grimshaw, J. M., Shirran, L., Thomas, R., Mowatt, G., Fraser, C., Bero, L., Grilli, R., Harvey, E., Oxman, A., & O'Brien, M. A. (2001). Changing provider behavior: An overview of systematic reviews of interventions. *Medical Care, 39,* II-2–II-45.

Grob, G. N. (1996). The severely and chronically mentally ill in America: A historical perspective. In S. Soreff (Ed.), *Handbook for the treatment of the seriously mentally ill.* Seattle, WA: Hogrefe & Huber.

Kane, J. M. (1999). Pharmacologic treatment of schizophrenia. *Biological Psychiatry, 46,* 1396–1408.

Katon, W. J., Von Korff, M., Lin, E. H., Walker, E., Simon, G. E., Bush, T., Robinson, & P., Russo, J. (1995). Collaborative management to achieve treatment guidelines: Impact on depression in primary care. *Journal of the American Medical Association, 273,* 1026–1031.

Kessler, R. C., Berglund, P. A., Zhao, S., Leaf, P. J., Kouzis, A. C., Bruce, et al. (1996). The 12-month prevalence and correlates of serious mental illness. In R. W. Manderscheid & M. A. Sonnenschein (Eds.), *Mental Health, United States* (DHHS Publication No. [SMA] 96-3098, pp. 59–70). Washington DC: U.S. Government Printing Office.

Klein, K. J., & Sorra, J. S. (1996). The challenge of innovation implementation. *Academy of Management Review, 21,* 1055–1080.

Lehman, A. F., Steinwachs, D. M., & co-investigators. (1998a). Patterns of usual care for schizophrenia: Initial results from the schizophrenia patient outcomes research team (PORT) client survey. *Schizophrenia Bulletin, 24,* 11–20.

Lehman, A. F., Steinwachs, D. M., & co-ivestigators. (1998b). Translating research into practice: The schizophrenia patient outcomes research team (PORT) treatment recommendations. *Schizophrenia Bulletin, 24,* 1–10.

Lin, E. H., Katon, W. J., & Simon, G. E. (1997). Achieving guidelines for the treatment of depression in primary care: Is physician education enough? *Medical Care, 35,* 831–842.

Mazmanian, P. E., & Davis, D. A. (2002). Continuing medical education and the physician as a learner: Guide to the evidence. *Journal of the American Medical Association, 288,* 1057–1060.

McFarlane, W. R., McNary, S., Dixon, L., Hornby, H., & Cimett, E. (2001). Predictors of dissemination of family psychoeducation in community mental health centers in Maine and Illinois. *Psychiatric Services, 52,* 935–942.

Mellman, T. A., Miller, A. L., Weissman, E. M., Crismon, M. L., Essock, S. M., & Marder, S. R. (2001). Evidence-based pharmacologic treatment for people with severe mental illness: A focus on guidelines and algorithms. *Psychiatric Services, 52,* 619–625.

Miller, A. L., Chiles, J. A., Chiles, J. K., Crismon, M. L., Rush, A. J., & Shon, S. P. (1999). The Texas Medication Algorithm Project (TMAP) schizophrenia algorithms. *Journal of Clinical Psychiatry, 60,* 649–657.

Miller, W. R., & Mount, K. A. (2001). A small study of training in motivational interviewing: Does one workshop change clinician and client behavior? *Behavioral and Cognitive Psychotherapy, 29,* 457–471.

Milne, D., Gorenski, O., Westerman, C., Leck, C., & Keegan, D. (2000). What does it take to transfer training? *Psychiatric Rehabilitation Skills, 4,* 259–281.

Mueser, K. T., Corrigan, P. W., Hilton, D. W., Tanzman, B., Schaub, A., Gingerich, S., et al. (2002). Illness management and recovery: A review of the research. *Psychiatric Services, 53,* 1272–1284.

Mueser, K. T., Torrey, W. C., Lynde, D., Singer, P., & Drake, R. E. (2003). Implementing evidence-based practices for people with severe mental illness. *Behavior Modification, 27,* 387–411.

National Council for Community Behavioral Healthcare (NCCBH). (2003). *The quest for survival.* Rockville, MD.

Oxman, A. D., Thomson, M. A., & Davis, D. A. (1995). No magic bullets: A systematic review of 102 trials of interventions to improve professional practice. *Canadian Medical Association Journal, 153,* 1423–431.

Phillips, S. D., Burns, B. J., Edgar, E. R., Mueser, K. T., Linkins, K. W., Rosenheck, R. A., et al. (2001). Moving assertive community treatment into standard practice. *Psychiatric Services, 52,* 771–779.

President's New Freedom Commission on Mental Health. (2003). *Achieving the promise: Transforming mental health care in America.* DHHS Publication No. SMA-03-3832, Rockville, MD.

Regier, D. A., Narrow, W. E., Rae, D. S., Mancerscheid, R. W., Locke, B. Z., & Goodwin, F. (1993). The de facto U.S. mental and addictive disorders service system: Epidemiologic catchment area prospective 1-year prevalence rates of disorders and services. *Archives of General Psychiatry, 50,* 85–94.

Tashjian, M. D., Hayward, B. J., Stoddard, S., & Kraus, L. (1989). *Best practice study of vocational rehabilitation services to severely mentally ill persons.* Washington, DC: Washington Rehabilitation Services Administration, U.S. Department of Education, 1989.

Thomson O'Brien, M. A., Freemantle, N., Oxman, A. D., Wolf, F., Davis, D. A., & Herrin, J. (2002). Continuing education meetings and workshops: Effects on professional practice and health care outcomes. *The Cochrane Library.* Retrieved November 17, 2004, from *http:// www.cochrane.org.*

Thomson O'Brien, M. A., Oxman, A. D., Davis, D. A., Haynes, R. B., Freemantle, N., & Harvey, E. L. (2002). Audit and feedback: effects on professional practice and healthcare outcome. *The Cochrane Library.* Retrieved November 17, 2004, from *http://www.cochrane.org.*

Thomson O'Brien, M. A., Oxman, D. A., Haynes, R. B., Freemantle, N., & Harvey, E. L. (2002). Educational outreach visits: Effects on professional practice and health care outcomes. In *The Cochrane Library.* Retrieved November 17, 2004, from *http://www.cochrane.org.*

Torrey, W. C., Clark, R. E., Becker, D. R., Wyzik, P. F., & Drake, R. E. (1997). Switching from rehabilitative day treatment to supported employment. In L. L. Kennedy (Ed.), *Continuum: Developments in ambulatory mental health care* (Vol. 4, pp. 27–38). San Francisco: Jossey-Bass.

Torrey, W. C., Drake, R. E., Dixon, L., Burns, B. J., Rush, A. J., Clark, R. E., et al. (2001). Implementing evidence-based practices for persons with severe mental illnesses. *Psychiatric Services, 52,* 45–50.

Torrey, W. C., Mead, S., & Ross, G. (1998). Addressing the social needs of mental health consumers when day treatment programs convert to supported employment: Can consumer-run services play a role? *Psychiatric Rehabilitation Journal, 22,* 73–75.

Turner, J. C., & TenHoor, W. J. (1978). The NIMH community support program: Pilot approach to a needed social reform. *Schizophrenia Bulletin 4,* 319–348.

U.S. Department of Health and Human Services (DHHS). (1999). *A report of the Surgeon General.* Washington, DC: Author.

Wang, P. S., Demler, O., & Kessler, R. C. (2002). Adequacy of treatment for serious mental illness in the United States. *American Journal of Public Health, 92,* 92–98.

West, J., Olfson, M., Narrow, W. E., Rae, D., Wilk Marcus, S., & Reier, D. A. (2003, June). *The treatment of schizophrenia in routine psychiatric practice.* Paper presented at the Academy of Health Annual Meeting, Nashville, TN.

# NINE

# What Are the Common Features of Evidence-Based Practices?

*Charles A. Rapp*
*Richard J. Goscha*

MIKE IS A 22-YEAR-OLD MALE who was diagnosed with schizophrenia 2 years ago. Since that time he has been in treatment at his local community mental health center. Mike always had a strong desire to work and develop a good career for himself. Upon entering services, he made it clear to his treatment providers that work was important to him and his future. Today, Mike just completed his third transitional employment slot and was scheduled to meet with his treatment providers to discuss "work." Mike's pre-allocated time in this transitional position ended last week because the position only allows consumers to work there for a maximum of 3 months. Even though he found the job rather boring and not challenging, he showed up for work every day and did all he was assigned and then some. He states that he wants to look for a full-time job that "belongs to" him, not to the mental health center. He is told that he is not yet ready and that he needs to work more on his social skills and his hygiene. His treatment providers inform Mike that he needs to continue attending groups at the psychosocial day treatment program for another 3 months to prepare him for work and then try another transitional employment job.

Traditional vocational services

Medication
management issues

JUANITA, A 28-YEAR-OLD MOTHER OF TWO, states that she wants to regain custody of her two daughters, that she wants a safe place to live, and that she would like to be working in the field of computers. Juanita has been receiving services from the local mental health center for a year. Today, at a "treatment-planning meeting," Juanita's case manager showed her where, on the treatment plan, she should sign. Once again, every 90 days, they get together to update her goals. As she looked over the plan, she saw the familiar goals: "stay out of the hospital," "improve socialization skills," and "take medications as prescribed." She complains to her case manager that she does not like the medications because they cause her to want to keep moving all the time, even when she tries to sit still, and she doesn't understand why she needs to take them. "I just want to get my kids back," she says. The case manager replies, "If you want any chance at getting your kids back, you'll need to take your medications." Reluctantly, Juanita signs the treatment plan.

Traditional
non-integrated
treatment

FOR THE SECOND TIME IN JUST UNDER A YEAR, ALAN was asked to leave an inpatient alcohol treatment program before completing the program. Alan had twice asked to be admitted to the program to help him learn to manage his problems with drinking alcohol. He was initially admitted a year and a half ago, then asked to leave shortly thereafter because the program was not "equipped" to deal with his type of problems. The reasons cited this time were the same as last: His constant conversations with himself were disruptive to the groups. Alan was told he needed to get his mental illness and the voices caused by that illness under control before he could return for treatment. At the same time, his mental health treatment providers told Alan that they would not prescribe medications to help manage the symptoms of schizophrenia until he was free of all alcohol use.

TINA HAS LIVED IN HER PARENTS' HOME for the past 2 years. They agreed to let her live there if she were willing to be a

contributing member of the household. This agreement
included Tina helping with the household chores, shopping, and paying something toward the household
expenses. During a recent review of her current medications, Tina tells the psychiatrist that she appreciates living
with her parents and that she wants to perform in the tasks
to which she has agreed, but that the medications she is
taking are making her feel too tired to do anything around
the house, and her weight gain is unbearable. She states
that she doesn't want to take the medications any longer.
Her psychiatrist tells her that the medications are the only
thing that have kept her out of the hospital this year, that
she is not aware of how helpful these medications are to
her, despite her complaints, and that if she quits she will
risk being hospitalized again. Tina later tells her parents
about not feeling heard at the meeting. Out of concern,
Tina's mother calls her daughter's case manager. The case
manager informs her that the problem is most likely Tina's
lack of motivation to do household chores and suggests that
Tina's parents confront her failure to do what she should
do around the home.

*Family issues in treatment*

JERRY IS A 22-YEAR-OLD ATHLETIC AND HANDSOME young man
who dreams of playing basketball at the state college, for
which he had been given a full scholarship. He attended
college for 1 year and did well in his course work as well as
basketball. During the summer following his first year of
college, things began to change for Jerry. He spent
increasing amounts of time alone in his room, sometimes
for days at a time. He started talking and yelling at people,
even when no one else was talking to him. He began to
insist that he only eat meals from sealed cans that he could
open and cook himself. Jerry's deteriorating state eventually required that he be hospitalized and treated for an
emerging mental illness. Jerry's parents steadily distanced
themselves from him when he began to experience hallucinations during the summer. They did not understand what
had happened to their son, who had excelled in high

*More family issues in treatment*

school both academically and socially. The doctor at the mental health center gave Jerry the diagnosis of schizophrenia and began to prescribe medications. Jerry's parents were never invited to meetings about their son at either the hospital or the mental health center. They were both scared and confused by what was happening with Jerry. Never having been given any direct information on the mental illness with which their son was struggling, and having never been told how they could be helpful, they began to limit their interactions and their attempts to be supportive to their son. A social work student (from the college that Jerry had once attended) who was doing her internship at the community mental health center wrote in her internship journal, "Jerry's parents don't seem to care. They are so caught up in their disappointment with their son and their own stuff that they cannot find a way to be helpful to him."

Current state of mental health services

Although these types of experiences do not occur at every community mental health center or agency, the case vignettes do depict the types of services that are provided every day in mental health services. The vast majority of mental health professionals and paraprofessionals are well-intentioned, hard-working, and undercompensated people. They are, however, forced to rely on a confusing variety of sources, including agency traditions, conflicting or minimal training, and questionable service design structures, to guide their provision of mental health services. Sadly, the result is often a paternal if not despotic mental health treatment system. Too often, mental health services ignore the voices, desires, and preferences of the very consumers that they are meant to serve. Services often blame, neglect, or alienate people who have caring, loving, and supporting relationships with consumers. Services may also insist on incompatible or impossible prerequisites for admission. As one consumer wisely commented, "If I could have stayed sober to remain in the substance abuse treatment program, I would not have needed to go there in the first place." Most profoundly, many mental health services often reinforce little or no expectation of hope and recovery, but rather reinforce ideas and values consistent with low expectations and lifelong disability.

## Six Common Features of Evidence-Based Practice

Evidence-based practices (EBPs) are those that have demonstrated positive results in helping consumers to achieve their goals. Currently, six evidence-based practices for adults with severe mental illness (SMI) are part of a national evaluation demonstration: assertive community treatment, supported employment, integrated dual-diagnosis treatment, family psychoeducation, illness management and recovery, and medication management. Each of these practices is discussed in a separate chapter in this text, and each contains specific interventions that target specific outcomes for people with psychiatric disabilities. Nevertheless, six features are common to all of them:

- Primary focus on recovery
- Facilitating empowerment and choice
- The recognized role of relationship
- The importance of in-vivo service delivery
- Utilization of the environment as a resource
- Primary focus on teamwork and integration of helping

### *Primary Focus on Recovery*

In the history of mental health, the diagnosis of schizophrenia or other severe mental illness was accompanied by a prognosis of lifelong disability. For example, in a recent New Zealand study all the subjects diagnosed with bipolar disorders were told that, "they would never be well and would always have to rely on medication" (Lapsley, Nikora, & Black, 2002, p. 30). In many ways, mental health systems have institutionalized low expectations and the notion that consumers need to be protected from real life and shel-

Bleak future

tered from stress. Jobs and careers, school and college degrees, apartments and homes were not only regarded as impossible goals, but were considered stressors that could worsen symptoms and outcomes.

**Defying the forecasts**

In the last 20 years, attitudes regarding chronicity and recovery have changed dramatically. Three separate bodies of research support the view that people with psychiatric disabilities can, and often do, recover. First are studies of people with SMI (mostly schizophrenia Bleuler, 1978; Ciompi, & Muller, 1976; DeSisto, Harding, McCormick, Ashikaga, & Brooks, 1995a, 1995b; Harding, Brooks, Ashikaga, Strauss, & Breier, 1987; Huber,Gross, & Schuttler, 1975; Ogawa et al., 1987; Tsuang, Woolson, & Fleming, 1979). Across these studies, people with SMI were followed (on average) for almost 30 years, and 55.4% recovered or improved significantly.

Second are thousands of first-person accounts of recovery and ethnographic studies of people living with SMI. Both approaches document the pain and despair of mental illness but also demonstrate the ability of people afflicted with SMI to overcome barriers and to develop satisfying, meaningful lives that are not dominated by illness.

Third are numerous mental health services research studies. The research supporting the six features described here, and other promising EBP features, demonstrates that people with psychiatric disabilities can learn to manage their illnesses, work in real jobs, control their substance abuse, and improve their relationships with the people who are supportive to them. Moreover, professionals using these methods can help in the recovery process.

Recovery is the primary foundation of each EBP. Helping people recover their lives is the overarching goal of the EBPs, and each is based on the philosophy and the reality that people with SMI can and do develop lives beyond the disabling effects of mental illness. With recovery as a focus, each of the EBPs offers effective strategies with which persons who have mental illness can overcome the barriers that have prevented them from reaching their personal goals.

Though each of the EBPs targets different areas of a person's life, they share a common view that consumers can and do become active participants in their own recovery process. The practices offer a collection of strategies that promote the recovery-oriented goals of consumers.

JADE WAS DIAGNOSED WITH SCHIZOPHRENIA over 8 years ago, during her second semester at a technical institute. Her desire was to eventually become a nurse, but when the voices she heard became unbearable, she dropped out of school, was hospitalized several times, and stopped taking care of herself. Although she was prescribed medications in the hospital, she usually stopped taking them when she returned home because they made her feel tired and gain weight. Jade had given up on herself and didn't care whether she was hospitalized or not. She had repeatedly contemplated suicide.

During another hospitalization, a nurse at the mental health center met with Jade after reading in her chart that she had been studying to become a nurse. The nurse acknowledged Jade's goal and invited her to attend an illness management and recovery (IMR) program that she helped facilitate at the center. The program might help Jade to understand her illness, learn ways to cope with her symptoms, and return to school. Jade told the nurse that a psychiatrist had said that going back to school was probably not an option for her anymore. The nurse respectfully disagreed. She could see that Jade was bright and again invited her to come to a few classes before giving up on the idea of returning to school. Jade agreed to attend two classes.

Jade was introduced to the concept of recovery and was told that mental illness need not be a lifelong disability. After talking about her symptoms with other consumers who had similar experiences, Jade learned to identify her own triggers, learned specific coping skills, and developed a wellness plan so that she could reduce the dosage of medications she was currently taking.

After 3 months, Jade had forgotten about her initial insistence on only attending two classes. The IMR program

Illness management and recovery

was instrumental in helping her to gain control of her life, and this past semester she re-enrolled in school.

## Facilitating Empowerment and Choice

Options and power

The last 20 years have witnessed considerable scholarly and practice-related activity focused on exploring empowerment as a central construct of mental health and social work. The concept is discussed both as a process and as an end goal or state. Empowerment is a state to which people aspire and that consumers and professionals collaborate in achieving. Despite the diversity of concepts, theories, and methods, the two consistent themes of empowerment research are options and power. Each of these themes has an objective and a subjective reality. The interplay of elements and the two realities help define the components of empowerment, as seen in Table 9.1.

| TABLE 9.1 The Interplay of Elements and Realities | | |
|---|---|---|
| | Objective reality | Subjective reality |
| Options | Choices or options | Perception of choices |
| Power | Authority | Confidence |

Authority as the power to choose

An empowered person or group requires an environment that provides options and ascribes authority to the person to choose. We could hypothesize that the more options available to a person, the greater that person's empowerment. *Authority* refers to the person's actual power to make a choice from the available options. For example, many people with SMI do not have the authority to decide when they will be discharged from the hospital, group home, or nursing home; that power has been granted to the hospital or the nursing home.

Limitations of subjective reality

Empowerment is also affected by the subjective reality of the person. A person could have many options but perceive only limitations. Most people are not aware of all the options available to them. For people with SMI, whose lives have been sheltered and segregated, a limited view of options is common.

Power is part authority and part confidence or perception of authority. A person can have the formal authority to make a choice or decision, but feel otherwise. For example, in most mental health systems consumers have the authority to decide where they will live and what services they will receive. The perception, or subjective reality, of many consumers, however, is that the authority is vested in the mental health personnel. Sometimes people lack the confidence to choose or to act on the options available to them. For example, a consumer may want to choose a competitive job but settle for a sheltered job due to lack of confidence.

*Empowerment Through Education*

EBPs contribute to increasing each of these components: choices, authority, perception of choices, and confidence. EBPs also facilitate the taking of action. In other words, they empower people by increasing available choices, providing education to facilitate informed choice, and placing the authority to choose in the hands of consumers. Among all the EBPs the most common method of fostering these components of empowerment is *through education*. Each of the evidence-based practices provides an educational component because consumers and family members rarely have basic or accurate information about mental illness or effective means of managing symptoms, medications, employment, and dual-diagnosis treatment. Lacking accurate information, consumers and family members are unable to make informed choices with regard to treatment options.

Each of the EBPs aims to offer consumers and family members the best available information to enable them to make fully informed decisions. In family psychoeducation (FPE), family members gain empowerment through increased knowledge about mental illness and the mental health system. IMR provides education about the effective use of medication as a means of managing symptoms and also to enable consumers to make informed choices about which medications to take. Psychoeducational programs, part of integrated dual-diagnosis treatment (IDDT), help to dispel misconceptions about dual diagnosis so that consumers and their family members can actively partici- pate in the recovery process. Information sessions, within supported employment (SE) programs, help consumers to choose jobs they prefer. Information sessions also address key concerns of consumers, such as how holding a job will impact the benefits they receive. Armed with accurate information, consumers can make informed decisions about such issues as benefits and health insurance coverage. As for all of us, knowledge is power.

*Enhance Consumer Skills*

Education alone is not sufficient to fully empower individ- uals. Many of the EBPs enhance skills and confidence to enable consumers to make active choices in their lives. IMR programs, for example, can empower individuals by teaching them more about self-care techniques. Mueser and colleagues stated, "Critical to people's developing hope for the future and formulating personal recovery goals is helping them gain mastery over their symptoms and relapses" (2002, p. 1273). Many IMR programs go beyond a focus on psychopathology and strive to improve self-efficacy and self-esteem, two important components of individual empowerment. Empowerment through skills building is also emphasized in assertive community treatment (ACT) and IDDT. To empower families, provision of information must be accompanied by skills training, ongoing guidance about management of mental illness, and emotional support. While SE does not require consumers to acquire a predetermined set of skills prior to finding a job, these programs do help consumers to capitalize on educational and training opportunities so that they may qualify for skilled jobs and develop satisfying careers.

*Consumers' Ability to Choose*

An important aspect of empowerment is the *consumer's ability to choose.* Though some critics claim that ACT is coercive (especially when its services are mandated), many elements of ACT are empowering. Consumer choice is a highly regarded component of ACT programs. Services are not limited to a predetermined set of interventions; rather, they are flexible and take into account consumer preferences, thereby making the consumer the director of the helping process. Phillips and colleagues (2001) viewed ACT services as one choice among many. Individuals who do not want to use ACT services should be able to select alternative services. IDDT also provides individual empowerment. An important component is to help consumers become more aware of their own power in making decisions that affect the attainment of their personal goals. Through motivational interviewing, individuals identify their personal goals and examine how various choices or behaviors facilitate or interfere with attaining these goals. The power to make choices is left in the hands of the consumers.

| Motivational interviewing

SE programs support the wide variety of competitive employment goals described by consumers. Traditional vocational programs offered a predetermined range of work opportunities that were often menial and usually paid less than minimum wage. SE services support the work goals of consumers who want real jobs, based on the reality that most people with SMI want to work (McQuilken, et al., 2003; Mueser, Salyers, & Mueser, 2001; Rogers, Walsh, Masotta, & Danley, 1991), that most prefer competitive employment to sheltered workshops (Bedell, Draving, Parrish, Gervey, & Guastadisegni, 1998), day treatment (Bond et al., 1995), and that most can work competitively (Bond et al., 2001). Instead of using traditional linear and mechanistic vocational strategies, SE helps consumers find meaningful competitive jobs in their communities, in keeping with their own preferences, strengths, and past work experiences. Unlike other vocational approaches, SE

| Supported employment programs

programs do not assess people for work readiness, but rather provide employment services to all consumers who demonstrate an interest in working.

The goal is to help place consumers in competitive employment based on consumer choice, without the artificial requirements of extended assessments, placements, transitional positions, trainings, and demonstrations of motivation. These traditional prerequisites are not only disempowering for consumers but also lack any research basis. Vocational interventions that do not target jobs directly have little impact on employment outcomes (Vandergoot, 1987).

FOR MOST OF HIS LIFE, HECTOR HEARD VOICES. To make matters worse, he also suffered from a co-occurring substance use problem. Because the shelters that provided some refuge in his city would not allow him to stay overnight when he was intoxicated, he spent many nights throughout the year sleeping on the streets. The staff at the mental health center had sought court orders to require treatment for his mental illness and substance abuse many times. Although these orders for mandatory treatment had been granted on a few occasions, they had had no impact on keeping Hector engaged in treatment. Each time he was released from the involuntary commitments to the psychiatric hospital, he failed to follow through with treatment and fell victim to his substance abuse and mental health symptoms. Eventually, Hector developed a deeply seated mistrust of the mental health system and went to great lengths to avoid any contact with mental health professionals. The mental health center that had tried several times to get Hector into treatment decided to implement an IDDT team, which provided outreach to individuals such as Hector. An outreach case manager made contact with Hector at the city's drop-in center and asked what things he would like help with. Hector was both surprised by and suspicious of such a question. Although initially he was resistant to talking to the case manager, he finally agreed to accept some blankets in case it got cool outside that evening.

Over the next several weeks, the case manager continued to make contact with Hector, slowly building a trusting relationship with him in a nonthreatening manner. Within 2 months, Hector agreed to allow the case manager to help him with housing. Although the case manager periodically discussed other services and supports that were available, he put no formal conditions upon Hector for receiving housing or other services. Three months later Hector agreed to meet with an addictions counselor at the program. He is now approaching 1 year of sobriety and credits the relationship he established with the outreach case manager as one of the keys to his recovery.

## The Recognized Role of Relationship

The relationship between the consumer and professional is seen as a cornerstone in virtually all approaches to casework, psychotherapy, and counseling. Some approaches view the relationship as the crucial therapeutic ingredient (Rogers, 1959), whereas other approaches see it as the context for practice, thereby enhancing the effectiveness of techniques (Fisher, 1978). Some empowerment models underscore the importance of the relationship (Dodd, & Gutierrez, 1990; Lee, 1994; Simon, 1994). Although recovery is highly individual, first-person accounts commonly point to the hopeful presence of a friend, a professional, a family, a teacher, a self-help group, or at times the staff of a particular program that helps trigger and sustain the recovery process. This element parallels one of the seven resiliencies, identified by Wolin and Wolin (1993): that of relationship.

Despite the importance of relationship, and the awareness of some professionals of its critical nature, there are characteristics of many mental health systems that undermine it. Large caseloads and confounding productivity standards, especially for case managers and psychiatrists, prevent the formation of a sufficiently close relationship. Furthermore, the lack of efficiently dedicated resources often contributes to a crisis-to-crisis mode of working that interferes with establishing a relationship. Low salaries and

*Factors that undermine relationship*

other conditions cause high turnover among staff, with the result that relationships are often severed.

**Assertive outreach and engagement stage**

The primacy of the helping relationship is evidenced most clearly in ACT, IDDT, and SE. Each practice devotes time and energy to building a trusting relationship between the consumer and provider. This relationship enhances the effectiveness of the practice in helping consumers to achieve their goals. For example, because of high program dropout rates and the difficulties of engaging persons with co-occurring disorders in treatment, dual-diagnosis interventions have advocated for an assertive outreach approach that allows time to develop a trusting relationship between staff and consumers. This is known as the engagement stage. Up to 75% of staff time in IDDT can be dedicated to assertive outreach. ACT also employs assertive outreach for individuals who have had difficulty developing treatment relationships and are suspicious of the mental health system. *Assertive outreach* means meeting with people where they are, physically and psychologically, in order to develop a trusting, positive, working relationship.

**Continuity of relationship and treatment**

Continuity is another important element in the helping relationship and is emphasized in many EBP approaches. Consumers, whose recovery may take a long time, need access to a consistent program over months and even years. In IDDT, consumers are able to work with the same clinician or team of clinicians for both mental health and substance abuse treatment. ACT promotes the continuity of the relationship by ensuring that services are available 24 hours a day, 7 days a week, by the same team members. High fidelity to ACT and IDDT programs also means that no specific program time limits are placed on consumers, allowing them to maintain consistent relationships with programs over an extended period of time. ACT also facilitates continuity in the relationship through shared caseloads, thereby minimizing disruption to services in the event of staff turnover. Similarly, follow-along supports after employment are maintained indefinitely in SE programs.

**Low caseloads**

ACT, IDDT, and SE all emphasize low caseloads to allow adequate time with each consumer. In order for staff to build positive working relationships with consumers, guidelines suggest caseloads of no more than 25 consumers for employment specialists (SE), 20 consumers per IDDT team member, and 10 consumers per ACT team member. Similarly, to avoid diluting the time and resources of SE programs, care should be taken to avoid assigning ancillary, nonvocational case management responsibilities to employment specialists.

ACT also makes provisions for consumers to be employed as ACT team members, thereby offering the opportunity for consumers to build a trusting relationship with a peer. Personal experience with mental illness affords these individuals a unique perspective on the mental health system.

CARLOS IS A 32-YEAR-OLD HISPANIC MAN who has spent most of his life living with family. Seven years ago he moved into a group home after his mother experienced health problems. A requirement for Carlos to live in the group home was that he attend the day treatment program at the mental health center and participate in daily groups to learn skills to live in the community, such as cooking, hygiene, recreation, and medication and money management. Carlos frequently heard voices and experienced racing thoughts that made it difficult for him to pay attention in the groups, especially while surrounded by 20 other consumers. He looked forward to the smoking breaks halfway through each group, so he could get outside and have a few minutes to himself. Carlos enjoyed eating and learning how to cook. Despite this interest, he had difficulty trying to apply what he was learning about cooking for 50 consumers at the day treatment program to cooking for one person. Carlos frequently asked the day treatment staff when he would be able to make the transition from the group home to his own apartment in the community. The consistent response was that until he demonstrated that he would take his medications, keep himself clean, and cook, living independently was not an option.

During a 1-year period, Carlos was hospitalized three times. During the third admission, the hospital case

*Need for assertive community treatment*

manager referred him to a local ACT program. Carlos agreed to join this program when he was told that the goal was to help him live in his own apartment. The ACT helped Carlos learn how to shop for food and prepare basic meals in his kitchen so that he could move into a studio apartment and ACT team members also helped Carlos to find ways to remember when and how to take medications and how to do different tasks in his apartment. Though team members continue to visit Carlos, they do so now now less frequently and less intensively because he has grown in independence.

### The Recognized Importance of In-Vivo Service Delivery

In-vivo services are community-based rather than agency-based. Services are delivered in the consumer's natural environment (e.g., homes, businesses, parks, restaurants) instead of the artificial environment of the mental health center. The purpose is to provide services and interventions where they are most needed and most used to help consumers fully integrate those supports into their own communities. There are many benefits to in-vivo services. When staff are immersed in the everyday lives of consumers, it provides opportunities for them to learn about and observe personal and environmental strengths, thereby allowing a more thorough assessment (Rapp, 1998; Witheridge, 1991). In-vivo services also reduce the barriers associated with the transfer of learning from one environment to another (Witheridge, 1991). Skills learned inside agencies do not necessarily generalize to more normalized settings (Gutride, Goldstein, & Hunter, 1973; Jaffe, & Carlson, 1976; Liberman, Massel, Mosk, & Wong, 1985). With ACT, 80% of total service time is spent in the consumer's community, in the settings and contexts in which problems arise and where support or skills are needed (Phillips et al., 2001). In SE programs, the employment specialist spends 70% or more time in the community (Bond et al., 2001).

Consumer retention rates

In-vivo services contribute to consumer retention (Bush, Langford, Rosen, & Gott, 1990) and are especially well suited to meeting the needs of high-priority individuals: those who continue to experience prolonged hospitalizations or have high readmission rates (Witheridge, 1991). The average retention rate of consumers for at least a year is 84% across ACT studies. This rate greatly exceeds traditional aftercare, whose retention rates seldom exceed 50% for even 6 months (Bond, McGrew, & Fekete, 1995). This is no small achievement, given the historical difficulty of engaging people with significant impairments due to the presence SMI in services. Bond commented that "one program using office visits because of a reluctance to make home visits had minimal success until it changed its treatment strategy" (1991, p. 75).

Services delivered in the community have been correlated with higher consumer satisfaction and service accessibility (Huxley, & Warner, 1992). Rapp (1992) added that consumer self-determination, if taken seriously, would alone make outreach visits the norm, because most people prefer it. Family members also strongly prefer in-vivo services to hospital-based services (Hoult, Reynolds, Charbonneau-Powis, Weekes, & Briggs, 1983).

| Consumer satisfaction

In-vivo services have an impact on outcomes such as reducing hospitalization (Bush et al., 1990). McGrew and Bond (1995) found nearly unanimous agreement among ACT experts on the importance of outreach and in-vivo service delivery. In a study of veterans at 10 sites, Rosenheck, Neale, Leaf, Milstein, and Frisman (1995) noted that one site had provided intensive services but did not provide them in community settings—and both inpatient usage and costs increased by more than 50%. Bond and colleagues found that "among consumers who are frequently hospitalized, those who do not become involved in treatment often continue their revolving-door pattern" (1990, p. 885).

| Reduced
| hospitalization

Family psychoeducation models vary in their delivery location, with some based in people's homes or in other community settings as well as traditional clinics (Dixon et al., 2001). Dixon and associates recommended holding family psychoeducation sessions in the home as a means of overcoming barriers of stigma (Dixon et al., 2001).

| Family psychoeducational delivery

Effective programs engage consumers and members of their support system by providing assertive outreach, usually through some combination of intensive case management and meeting in the consumer's home (Drake et al., 2001). Effective dual-diagnosis programs also focus on linking consumers to naturally occurring community resources and strengthening their social networks.

HARRY, A 30-YEAR-OLD CAUCASIAN MAN, grew up on a ranch in rural Kansas. Three years ago, within a 9-month period, both his parents died. With the help of his aunt and uncle who owned the contiguous ranch, Harry continued to operate a large farming operation. After a while the relatives began to notice that Harry was "forgetting" his responsibilities or doing them wrong. He began not eating, not bathing, and talking strangely. A visit to the mental health center resulted in Harry being diagnosed with schizophrenia. He was admitted into the state psychiatric hospital.

Upon discharge, Harry was placed in a group home with services provided by the local mental health center. Although not disruptive, Harry failed to meet the group home's hygiene and cleaning requirements. He did not attend mental health services, and resisted taking his medications. Over the next 2 years, Harry's stay at the group home was punctuated with three admissions to the state psychiatric hospital.

Harry was referred to a community mental health center where he was assigned a case manager. The case manager slowly began to appreciate Harry's knowledge and skill in farming. The case manager, who had a background in social work, took seriously Harry's expression of interest in farming and began working with him to find a place where he could use his skills.

They located a ranch on the edge of town where the owner was happy to accept Harry as a volunteer. Harry and the owner became friends, and Harry soon established himself as a dependable and reliable worker. After a few months Harry was able to save enough money from his work to recover his truck, which was being held by his conservator. Given this opportunity to drive his own vehicle again, Harry renewed his driver's license and began to drive to the farm daily. To the delight of the community support staff, Harry began to communicate with others, and everyone noticed his improvements in his hygiene and his sense of purpose in his life. Harry became an important role model for other consumers, as they observed the positive changes in his life.

### Utilization of the Environment as a Resource

The environment can be viewed as the place where people live, the resources available and used, and the people who populate that place. In short, it's everything outside of the person. Many mental health systems traditionally viewed the environment as "harmful" and void of resources for people with SMI. According to this view, communities are filled with stigma and discrimination and lack opportunities for people with SMI to build meaningful lives. One of the goals, therefore, of treatment becomes protecting consumers from the environments in which they want to live. For many years, families were seen as a cause of mental illness (Halter, Bond, & Graaf-Kaser, 1992).

*Traditional view as harmful*

The pathological view of the environment fostered an approach that sought to protect the consumer from exposure to this toxicity. The growth of asylums in the 19th century was viewed as a means of removing the "patient" from the chaos of urban life. Unhealthy social conditions were replaced with new therapeutic environments located in less stressful rural settings (Rothman, 1971). This effort to protect and segregate can still be seen in current community programs such as day treatment, group homes, and sheltered employment. The programs do not seek to change existing environments but rather replace them with artificial environments, and in this way, further impede community integration.

*Effort to protect and segregate*

By contrast, in evidence-based practices the environment is viewed as a resource: the place where consumers (1) develop relationships, careers, and educational pursuits, (2) gain freedom from substance impairments,

*Effort to empower, support, and integrate*

and (3) encounter opportunities to practice the skills of illness management. The community is, therefore, *the* environment in which the work and the practice of EBPs are focused and underscores the important role of families or other supportive individuals. FPE provides a forum and a structure whereby families and others can enhance their ability to provide support by increasing their understanding and by employing a problem-solving orientation. ACT prescribes that team members work with landlords, employees, teachers, coaches, and families so that they are able to support consumers as they create the type of life in the community that they desire. SE focuses on assisting consumers in the process of obtaining and keeping regular, competitive jobs in the community. Many of the practices, such as job development, job accommodations, and follow-along supports, are directed to work with employers.

Making new friends | IDDT prescribes work with consumers' social network and families as necessary to help consumers modify their behavior. Finding new friends who are not substance abusers is often key to recovery. IMR addresses the environment in two ways. First, it encourages family members or friends to have contact with the IMR practitioner to discuss their role in helping the consumer pursue goals or his or

Behavioral tailoring | her choice. Second, it uses behavioral tailoring, which is the development of strategies tailored to each person's needs, motives, and resources. Some behavioral tailoring strategies involve creating environmental cues to remember to take medications (e.g., notes strategically placed, audio cues from alarm clocks, or pairing the timing of taking medication with other daily routines such as brushing teeth).

NANCY, AN EMPLOYMENT SPECIALIST who works on the SE team, regularly attends the weekly group supervision for case managers at the mental health center. Before employment specialists became regular members of the mental health center treatment teams, employment goals or employment possibilities were rarely discussed at team supervision meetings. Instead, employment was viewed as something that happened outside of the purview of the mental health team. With Nancy at the team meetings, employment is now a primary focus. The treatment team, in collaboration with the employment specialist, has been able to help consumers achieve their employment goals at a rate that is 50% greater than last year. More consumers are staying engaged in SE longer since the service has been fully integrated with the case management program. Employment is no longer seen as a separate service but as an integral function of the team. Team members now discuss how employment can actually help, rather than hinder, consumers with their recovery process. The team has begun to view the work of supporting the employment goals of consumers as everyone's task, not just one person. Nancy is continuously available to case managers to discuss referrals to SE, to explain the impact of work on benefits, and to discuss ways they can work together to support consumers. The team has become an invaluable resource to the employment specialist in helping to identify consumers' strengths, talents and abilities.

### Primary Focus on Teamwork and Integration of Helping

Mental health services should be clear, consistent, and coordinated. For too long, services have been fragmented by separate agencies, specialists, funding streams, and nonintegrated treatment programs. Arranging for benefits is the responsibility of the case manager, housing is managed by the housing specialist, daytime activity and skill development are delegated to the day treatment or psychosocial program, medications are the responsibility of psychiatrists and nurses, employment is coordinated by vocational rehabilitation, substance abuse problems are referred to the designated separate agency, and so on. In such a scattered and segregated service environment, it is difficult or impossible for any well-meaning staff to develop a holistic approach to helping. Separate providers rarely meet to communicate with each other and often practice in separate domains.

> Separate providers and fragmented services

   The problems created by this model of services are considerable. People are not neatly compartmentalized. If a consumer with an existing substance use disorder suddenly loses her housing, she should be considered at increased

> Conflicting goals, requirements, and procedures

risk for substance abuse relapse. Or, a change in medications accompanied by a side effect of increased morning sedation may have a significant impact on a consumer's ability to work. The scattered approach to treatment often requires that a consumer develop working relationships with a host of providers and that the consumer coordinate the activities of an uncoordinated group of professionals. In many mental health systems, the gap in services is even greater when services are provided not only by separate individuals, but also by separate agencies, with conflicting goals, admission and discharge requirements, and procedures. For example, some mental health programs (e.g., group homes) require a person to be substance free and take psychiatric medicine, as prescribed, to be eligible for services, whereas some substance abuse services require a person to be free of all medicines to be eligible for services! Most consumers are unable to navigate the separate systems or make sense of disparate messages about treatment and recovery (Drake et al., 2001). In this complex model, many consumers have difficulty knowing which staff or which agencies to contact in times of crisis.

**Integrated versus broker model case management**

Integrated services are significantly more effective. This factor is present in most studies of effective case management, in contrast to the broker model of case management, which relies on referral and which is ineffective (Rapp & Goscha, in press). ACT programs that have had the most success in assisting consumers with goals related to independent living and employment (Marx, Test, & Stein, 1973; Mulder, 1982; Stein & Test, 1980) are the ones in which team members worked directly with consumers to achieve their goals. Similarly with regard to dual-diagnosis services, "in effective programs attention to substance abuse as well as mental illness is integrated into all aspects of the program" (Drake et al., 2001, p. 472).

**Seamless services**

IDDT was developed to counter the "system" in which separate mental health and substance abuse systems deliver fragmented and ineffective care to individuals with co-occurring disorders. The same team of practitioners provides dual-diagnosis treatments, which combine mental health and substance abuse interventions, in a coordinated and collaborative manner. Helping consumers overcome complicated impairments to work on recovery becomes the focus of services. With a consistent approach, philosophy, and set of recommendations available to the consumer, services become seamless and the need to navigate separate systems disappears (Drake et al., 2001). IDDT also recommends that those who work at all levels of the mental health system acquire the basic skills for working with persons with substance abuse problems, because substance use affects the lives of a large majority of consumers with mental illness.

ACT integrates fragmented services for consumers by having a team of professionals assume direct responsibility for providing the specific mix of services needed by each consumer, for as long as needed. ACT teams often include a psychiatrist, nurse, case managers, peer specialists, as well as substance abuse and vocational specialists, who collaborate to integrate the various interventions provided to a consumer. To better facilitate their work as a team, team members are cross-trained in each other's areas of expertise, and they assist and consult with each other. This team approach is facilitated through a daily review of each consumer's status and joint planning of the team member's daily activities (Phillips et al., 2001).

| Cross-tracking of team members

In SE, the SE team is closely integrated with the mental health treatment team. Considering that most consumers would like to work, this integration of services offers consumers more exposure and accessibility to vocational opportunities.

## Conclusion

The EBPs discussed in this chapter have been derived from separate lines of research conducted by different teams of investigators over the last 20 years. On the surface, the practices are quite distinctive and address unique aspects of the lives of people with SMI. Despite the unique characteristics of each EBP, however, they share several critical features:

- Practices should be based on the foundational belief that people can, and do, recover from mental illness.
- Practices should support and enhance consumer choice and control over life directions.
- As the bedrock of helping, practices should support and encourage close working relationships between consumers and practitioners.
- Services should be provided in the life space of the consumer.
- Practices should be focused on helping each consumer with the process of acquiring, mobilizing, and retaining natural community resources to help build a life he or she desires.
- Practices should be integrated through a team approach to service delivery.

## References

Bedell, J. R., Draving, D., Parrish, A., Gervey, R., & Guastadisegni, P. (1998). A description and comparison of experiences of people with mental disorders in supported employment and paid vocational training. *Psychiatric Rehabilitation Journal, 21,* 279–283.

Bleuler, M. (1978). *The schizophrenic disorders, long-term patient and family studies* (S. M. Clemens, Trans.). New Haven, CT: Yale University Press.

Bond, G. R. (1991). Variations in an assertive outreach model. *New Directions in Mental Health Services, 52,* 65–80.

Bond, G. R., Becker, D. R., Drake, R. E., Rapp, C. A., Meisler, N., Lehman, A. F., et al. (2001). Implementing supported employment as an evidence-based practice. *Psychiatric Services, 52,* 313–321.

Bond, G. R., McGrew, J. H., & Fekete, D. (1995). Assertive outreach for frequent users of psychiatric hospitals: A meta-analysis. *Journal of Mental Health Administration, 22,* 4–16.

Bond, G. R., Witheridge, T. F., Dincin, J., Wasmer, D., Webb, J., & De Graaf-Kaser, R. (1990). Assertive community treatment for frequent users of psychiatric hospitals in a large city. American *Journal of Community Psychology, 18,* 865–891.

Bush, C. T., Langford, M. W., Rosen, P., & Gott, W. (1990). Operation Outreach: Intensive case management for severely psychiatrically disabled adults. *Hospital and Community Psychiatry, 41*, 647–649.

Ciompi, L., & Muller, C. (1976). *The life-course and aging of schizophrenics: A long-term follow-up study into old age.* Berlin: Springer.

DeSisto, M. J., Harding, C. M., McCormick, R. J., Ashikaga, T., & Brooks, G. W. (1995a). The Maine Vermont three-decades study of serious mental illness: I. Longitudinal course comparisons. *British Journal of Psychiatry, 167,* 338–342.

DeSisto, M. J., Harding, C. M., McCormick, R. J., Ashikaga, T., & Brooks, G. W. (1995b). The Maine Vermont three-decades study of serious mental illness: I. Matched comparisons of cross-sectional outcome. *British Journal of Psychiatry, 167,* 331–338.

Dixon, L., McFarlane, W. R., Hefley, H., Lucksted, A., Cohen, M., Falloon, I., et al. (2001). Evidence-based practices for services to families of people with psychiatric disabilities. *Psychiatric Services, 5,* 903–910.

Dodd, P., & Gutierrez, L. M. (1990). Preparing students for the future: A power perspective on community practice. *Administration in Social Work, 14*(2), 63–78.

Drake, R. E., Essock, S. M., Shaner, A., Carey, K. B., Minkoff, K., Kola, L., et al. (2001). Implementing dual diagnosis services for consumers with severe mental illness. *Psychiatric Services, 52,* 469–476.

Fisher, J. (1978). *Effective casework practice.* New York: McGraw-Hill.

Gutride, M. E., Goldstein, G. P., & Hunter, G. R. (1973). The use of modeling and role playing to increase social interaction among asocial psychiatric patients. *Journal of Consulting and Clinical Psychology, 40,* 408–415.

Halter, C. A., Bond, G. R., & Graaf-Kaser, R. D. (1992). How treatment of persons with serious mental illness is portrayed in undergraduate psychology textbooks. *Community Mental Health Journal, 28,* 29–42.

Harding, C. M., Brooks, G. W., Ashikaga, T., Strauss, J. S., & Breier, A. (1987). The Vermont longitudinal study of persons with severe mental illness. *American Journal of Psychiatry, 144,* 718–735.

Hoult, J., Reynolds, I., Charbonneau-Powis, M., Weekes, P., & Briggs, J. (1983). Psychiatric hospital versus community treatment: The results of a randomized trial. *Australian and New Zealand Journal of Psychiatry, 17,* 160–167.

Huber, G., Gross, G., & Schuttler, R. (1975). A long-term follow-up study of schizophrenia: Psychiatric course and prognosis. *Acta Psychiatrica Scandinavica, 52,* 49–57.

Huxley, P. J., & Warner, R. (1992). Case management for long-term psychiatic patients: A study of quality of life. *Hospital and Community Psychiatry, 43,* 799–802.

Jaffe, P. G., & Carlson, P. M. (1976). Relative efficacy of modeling and instructions in eliciting social behavior from chronic psychiatric patients. *Journal of Consulting and Clinical Psychology, 44,* 200–207.

Lapsley, H., Nikora, L., & Black, R. (2002). *"Kia Mauri Tau!" Narrative of recovery from disabling mental health problems.* Wellington, New Zealand: Mental Health Commission.

Lee, J. A. B. (1994). *The empowerment approach to social work practice.* New York: Columbia University Press.

Liberman, R. P., Massel, H. K., Mosk, M. D., & Wong, S. E. (1985). Social skills training for chronic mental patients. *Hospital and Community Psychiatry, 36,* 396–403.

Marx, A. J., Test, M. A., & Stein, L. I. (1973). Extrahospital management of severe mental illness: Feasibility and effects of social functioning. *Archives of General Psychiatry, 29,* 505–511.

McGrew, J. H., & Bond, G. R. (1995). Critical ingredients of assertive community treatment: Judgment of the experts. *Journal of Mental Health Administration, 22,* 113–125.

McQuilken, M., Zahniser, J. H., Novak, J., Starks, R. D., Olmos, A., & Bond, G. R. (2003). The work project survey: Consumer perspectives on work. *Journal of Vocational Rehabilitation, 18,* 59–68.

Mueser, K. T., Corrigan, P. W., Hilton, D. W., Tanzman, B., Gingerich, S., Essock, S. M., et al. (2002). Illness management and recovery and recovery: A review of the research. *Psychiatric Services, 53*(10), 1272–1284.

Mueser, K. T., Salyers, M. P., & Mueser, P. R. (2001). A prospective analysis of work in schizophrenia. *Schizophrenia Bulletin, 27*(2), 281–296.

Mulder, R. (1982). *Evaluation of the Harbinger Program.* Unpublished manuscript.

Ogawa, K., Miya, M., Watari, A., Nakazawa, M., Yuasa, S., & Utena, H. (1987). A long-term follow-up study of schizophrenia in Japan, with special reference to the course of social adjustment. *British Journal of Psychiatry, 151,* 758–765.

Phillips, S. D., Burns, B. J., Edgar, E. R., Mueser, K. T., Linkins, K. W., Rosenheck, R. A., et al. (2001). Moving assertive community treatment into standard practice. *Psychiatric Services, 52,* 771–779.

Rapp, C. A. (1992). *The strengths perspective of case management with persons suffering from severe and persistent mental illness.* In D. Saleebey (Ed.), The strengths perspective in social work (pp. 45–58). New York: Longman.

Rapp, C. A. (1998). *The strengths model: Case management with people suffering from severe and persistent mental illness.* New York: Oxford University Press.

Rapp, C. A., & Goscha, R. J. (in press). The principles of effective case management. *Psychiatric Rehabilitation Journal.*

Rogers, C. (1959). A theory of therapy, personality, and interpersonal relationships as developed in the consumer-centered framework. In S. Koch (Ed.). *Psychology: A study of science* (Vol. 2; pp. 184–256). New York: McGraw-Hill.

Rogers, E. S., Walsh, D., Masotta, L., & Danley, K. (1991). *Massachusetts survey of consumer preferences for community support services: Final report.* Boston: Center for Psychiatric Rehabilitation.

Rosenheck, R., Neale, M., Leaf, P., Milstein, R., & Frisman, L. (1995). Multisite experimental cost study of intensive psychiatric community care. *Schizophrenia Bulletin, 21,* 129–140.

Rothman, D. (1971). *The discovery of the asylum.* Boston: Little & Brown.

Simon, B. L. (1994). *The empowerment tradition in American social work.* New York: Columbia University Press.

Stein, L. I., & Test, M. A. (1980). Alternative to mental hosptial treatment: I. Conceptual model, treatment program, and clinical evaluation. *Archives of General Psychiatry, 37,* 392–397.

Tsuang, M. T., Woolson, R. F., & Fleming, M. S. (1979). Long-term outcome of major psychosis. *Archives of General Psychiatry, 36,* 1295–1301.

Vandergoot, D. (1987). Review of placement research literature: Implications for research and practice. *Rehabilitation Counseling Bulletin, 31,* 243–272.

Witheridge, T. F. (1991). The "active ingredients" of assertive outreach. *New Directions in Mental Health Services, 52,* 47–64.

Wolin, S. J., & Wolin, S. (1993). *The resilient self.* New York: Villard Books.

TEN

# How Does a Practice Become Evidence-Based?

*Kim T. Mueser*
*Robert E. Drake*

THE PAST SEVERAL DECADES HAVE WITNESSED a tremendous growth in the theory, technology, and research, both basic and applied, regarding treatments for a wide range of severe mental illnesses. Fifty years ago there were few well-established interventions, either psychological or pharmacological, for improving any of the major mental illnesses that had been clinically described over the previous century, including depression, bipolar disorder, schizophrenia, and anxiety disorders. Since that time, numerous pharmacological and psychosocial interventions have been shown to have a dramatic effect on both the symptoms of different mental illnesses and their functional impairments on people's lives (Nathan & Gorman, 1998). Whereas early research gains, beginning in the 1950s and continuing up through the 1970s, focused mainly on single approaches to pharmacology, psychotherapy, or rehabilitation, progress in recent years has expanded to include the integration of multiple approaches (Jindal & Thase, 2003; Kopelowicz & Liberman, 2003; Lenroot, Bustillo, Lauriello, & Keith, 2003).

The word *evidence* has a number of different definitions, but in health care it typically means factual information

Recent history

What is evidence?

217

that has been developed using scientific methods. Scientific information, as opposed to opinion or anecdotal information, is systematically and deliberately obtained under conditions that are designed to minimize the effect of either observer bias (i.e., when the information obtained is observable) or self-rating bias (e.g., as when a person's responses to questions are influenced by his or her attempts to appear desirable to others). When data are gathered scientifically, they are often collected with standardized assessment procedures that have been shown to be reliable and accurate, by evaluators who are trained and deliberately kept unaware, or "blind," as to which treatment the patient, client, or consumer has been receiving. This process of blind assessment minimizes the possibility that the evaluator's bias regarding which treatment is more effective will influence his or her ratings. When evidence regarding treatment effects is obtained under these conditions, it tends to be reproducible and to predict what will happen when other clients receive similar treatments.

**Scientific versus other evidence**

Scientific evidence can be distinguished from other types of evidence that are often used to advocate for specific clinical interventions. For example, an individual consumer may have personal experience receiving an intervention that he or she found helpful, and based on that personal evidence, argue for the effectiveness of the intervention. The growing literature by consumers on the experience of recovery is replete with such personal accounts (Deegan, 1988; Leete, 1989). Similarly, an individual may observe others benefit from an intervention, or hear stories of other consumers using an intervention, and use these perceptions or accounts to advocate for its effectiveness. Another type of nonscientific evidence are assertions by an established authority (e.g., a respected clinician, consumer, spiritual advisor, celebrity, or other opinion leader) asserts that a practice is effective based on personal experience using the intervention. Still another type of nonscientific evidence is the use of theory to justify an intervention in the absence of actual data. One last type of nonscientific evidence is the use of feelings or intuition to select an intervention (e.g., if it "feels right"). Table 10.1 summarizes these types of scientific and non-scientific evidence.

**TABLE 10.1**
**Scientific and Nonscientific Evidence**

Scientific evidence:

- Is empirical (i.e., information is actually collected and not simply conjectured)
- Is collected systematically, purposefully, and based on a plan
- Strives to be objective and free of investigator bias

Examples of nonscientific evidence:
- Personal experience
- Personal observation
- Anecdotal reports
- Assertions by "authorities"
- Speculations based on theory
- Feelings or intuition (it "feels right")

The primary problem with relying on personal experience, personal observation, or anecdotal reports is that these types of evidence are highly subject to bias and systematic distortion (Kahnemann, Slovic, & Tversky, 1982). For example, people tend to attend to and remember information that supports their beliefs, and to minimize and forget information that does not support their beliefs, leading to increased certainty about, and confidence in, their preexisting convictions. Personal experience and observation are also limited by the common assumption that what worked for one person will work for most, it not all, others. Several potential problems influence experiential evidence from practitioners, even respected authorities. When authorities rely on personal experience and observations for making expert recommendations to

Problems with
nonscientific data

others, they are overlooking the fact that their observations may be vulnerable to the same distortions reviewed above. In addition, because of the special role afforded by experts, their recommendations may be influenced by their potential for personal gain, as interventions they endorse become more widely adopted. Evidence based on feelings and intuition, while personally meaningful, has little basis in fact because subjective experiences can be influenced by a host of factors unrelated to the intervention itself. Finally, although theories can make useful predictions, the predictions themselves are not a form of evidence; they are merely conjectures.

**Value of nonscientific data**

Although the types of evidence described above are not scientific, they may nevertheless be useful as careful observations and may lead to the development of effective interventions. Personal experience, observations, and anecdotal reports all provide valuable insights about potentially effective interventions. Science often makes use of accidental discoveries by one person. Similarly, speculations based on theories of psychopathology, functioning, or behavior change may lead to helpful interventions. New interventions are often developed from nonscientific evidence, such as clinical experience, or based on theoretical considerations. But *evidence for the effectiveness of new interventions* must be confirmed scientifically, through the collection of objective evidence in a carefully controlled manner. Many apparent discoveries are not reproducible. Learning to study interventions scientifically takes commitment and practice.

**Evidence-based practices versus best practices**

The terms *evidence-based practices* (EBPs) and *best practices* are often used synonymously with one another, but they actually have significantly different meanings. EBPs refer to interventions for which there is a solid scientific basis demonstrating their effectiveness at helping consumers to improve outcomes in specific areas. Best practices, on the other hand, usually refer to interventions deemed most effective by a consensus of individuals in the field. Although EBPs and best practices sometimes overlap, best practices can be biased by the current beliefs or theories of experts, by the prejudices of guild organizations (e.g., professional groups), or by the successful marketing of industry. Best practices are often proven incorrect by scientific research. Thus, compelling scientific evidence is needed to refer to an intervention as an EBP, whereas an intervention can be widely agreed upon to be a best practice before compelling scientific evidence has been gathered to support its effectiveness.

## Criteria for Establishing EBPs

A variety of different groups and organizations has developed standard criteria for evaluating interventions as potential EBPs (Chambless, Baker, Baucom, Beutler, & Calhoun, 1998; Hunsley, Dobson, Johnson, & Mikail, 1999; Sackett, Rosenberg, & Haynes, 1997). Although minor differences exist between groups in the criteria for determining whether a practice is supported by the evidence, there is a broad consensus on the importance of the following points: (1) transparency of the review process, (2) standardization of the intervention, (3) controlled research, (4) replication across multiple investigator teams, and (5) impact on important outcomes. A brief explanation of each of these criteria is provided below.

### Transparency

Both the criteria (e.g., how to find evidence, what qualifies as evidence, how to judge quality of evidence) and the process (e.g., who reviews the evidence) of review should be open for observation by public scrutiny. Reviews may include specific years in which they were conducted, specific publications, or specific qualifications; and they may be conducted by experts in the particular field, experts in scientific process, or mixed groups with expertise in a variety of areas. All of these decisions should be available to others in the field and to the public.

## Standardization

An intervention must be standardized so that it can be replicated elsewhere by others. Standardization typically involves a manual or book that clearly defines the practice and measures to assess if the intervention is being accurately practiced. Without a thorough description of how the intervention works, including the detailed criteria and procedures for assessment, treatment, and outcome measurement, practitioners cannot be sure they are delivering the same intervention that has been found to be effective in research studies. Intervention developers are also expected to develop a measure of therapist adherence or treatment fidelity that quantifies the accuracy with which a standardized intervention is implemented, thereby facilitating replication of the treatment (Bond et al., 2002; Mueser, Noordsy, Drake, & Fox, 2003; Teague, Bond, & Drake, 1998).

## Controlled Research

**Randomized controlled trial**

The most rigorous methodological approach to evaluating an intervention is to conduct a randomized controlled trial (RCT), in which consumers are randomly assigned (i.e., by chance) to receive one of two or more interventions (which can include "treatment as usual" or "wait-list" control groups) and are then followed up and evaluated after treatment to determine which intervention is most effective. Because the consumer in an RCT has an equal chance of being in any of the possible treatment groups, significant differences between treatment groups in outcomes are assumed to be a result of the treatment and not some other factors, such as unobserved or unknown pretreatment differences between the groups. When several RCTs consistently show that one intervention is more effective then another, the evidence supporting the effectiveness of that intervention is considered very strong.

**Quasi-experimental design**

Although RCTs represent the strongest experimental design for evaluating treatment effectiveness, they are challenging studies to conduct and present many practical difficulties in applied clinical settings. A less rigorous alternative to the RCT is the quasi-experimental design, in which consumers receiving two (or more) different treatments are compared to one another, but membership in the different groups is not randomly assigned. For example, the consumers in one mental health center receiving one treatment are compared to the consumers in another center receiving a different treatment, or the outcomes of consumers who express an interest in, and participate in, a treatment program are compared to those of consumers who decline to participate in the treatment program. Any comparison of two or more groups of consumers receiving different interventions, but not assigned to those treatments by randomization, is a quasi-experimental design. Although important information can be gleaned from quasi-experimental designs, their most significant limitation is that it is impossible to be confident that the compared groups of consumers are similar in other important ways that could lead to different outcomes unrelated to the treatment in question. For example, when comparing outcomes of different treatments at different mental health centers, we do not know whether the treatment being studied is responsible for different outcomes, or whether the consumers or centers differ in important ways that could lead to different outcomes. Even within a mental health center, differences in outcomes between consumers who choose one intervention and to those who choose another may be caused by subtle differences between the consumers, rather than the treatments themselves. Nevertheless, quasi-experimental designs can provide valuable information about the potential effectiveness of an intervention, especially if the results are used to plan an even more rigorous test of the treatment.

Most controlled research on EBPs is based on RCTs, but there are also rigorous research designs for evaluating the effects of an intervention on single case studies. There are numerous examples of single case designs that provide a strong basis for inferring that a treatment is effective (Hersen & Barlow, 1992). For example, in a multiple-base-

Single case study research

line design, a consumer's behavior, symptoms, or functioning are assessed repeatedly before an intervention is provided, and then again while the intervention is provided, as well as at follow-up. Multiple assessments before the intervention is provided can minimize the chances of spontaneous improvements being misinterpreted as the result of treatment. By combining the results over multiple rigorous single case studies, strong support for the effectiveness of an intervention can be garnered.

## Replication

Replication of research findings means that more then one study finds similar positive effects when consumers receive the intervention. The replication of research findings is fundamental to the conduct of all science, because findings due to chance are always possible, but similar results obtained across multiple studies are unlikely to be the result of chance. In addition, it is important for different investigators or research teams to replicate the same findings in order to minimize the possibility of investigator bias and to ensure that different clinicians can implement the intervention.

## Meaningful Outcomes

Effective interventions must show that they can help consumers to achieve important goals or outcomes related to impairments from a severe mental illness (SMI). What constitutes an important goal or outcome for people with SMI is a source of some debate, but the areas of greatest concern are those that reflect symptoms and their associated functional impairments. There is consensus that interventions that help consumers to improve in any of the following functional domains are valuable:

Functional outcome
domains

- Reduction in the severity of psychiatric symptoms (e.g., psychotic symptoms, negative symptoms, anxiety, depression)
- Improvements in social functioning, improvements in role functioning (e.g., school, work, parenting)

- Increased self-care skills
- Increased independent living skills
- Reduced hospitalizations (and other institutional care)
- Securing stable and independent housing in the community
- Enhanced quality of life (i.e., subjective satisfaction in different life domains, such as social relationships, housing, and finances)
- Reductions in impairments due to substance abuse
- Improvements in general medical health

There is more debate about other outcomes. For example, even though impairments in social skills are common in people with SMI and are related to impaired functioning in the community (Bellack, Morrison, Wixted, & Mueser, 1990; Bellack, Sayers, Mueser, & Bennett, 1994), it is probably not sufficient to demonstrate that social skills training can improve social skills within a treatment group; there also needs to be evidence that those improvements in social skills contribute to better functioning in the community, as indicated by such markers as improved social relationships (Heinssen, Liberman, & Kopelowicz, 2000). Similarly, although cognitive functioning has a significant impact on functional impairments (Green, 1996; Mueser, 2000), most researchers agree that it is not sufficient to show that cognitive rehabilitation simply improves cognitive functioning; there also needs to be evidence that such improvements translate to better consumer functioning in the community.

## Steps for Developing an EBP

Despite the growth in EBPs for people with SMI in recent years (Mueser, Torrey, Lynde, Singer, & Drake, 2003), there is only limited guidance available for clinical researchers on the process of developing an EBP. For example, Onken, Rounsaville, and colleagues have described a three-stage approach to the development and validation of effective clinical interventions: (1) feasibility and pilot testing, (2) RCTs of the intervention, and (3) studies to demonstrate generalizability and implementation (Onken, Blaine, & Battjes, 1997; Rounsaville, Carroll, & Onken, 2001). Interventions that have passed stage 2 of this model, and are supported by multiple RCTs, are considered EBPs, although important questions concerning the transportability of the practices to routine practice settings remain. In this section, guidelines for establishing an EBP are described, following a four-step process:

1) Articulation of the problem area
2) Identification of possible treatments
3) Pilot testing the intervention
4) Controlled evaluation of the intervention.

### Articulation of the Problem Area

All EBPs begin with a statement of a problem area for which an effective treatment does not exist. There are several considerations involved in identifying a problem area in need of more effective treatment. First, as described in the previous section, there must be widespread agreement that the problem area is meaningful, such as a defining characteristic of the psychiatric disorder or a significant associated functional impairment.

Types of reliability

Second, we must be able to measure the area of problematic functioning reliably and validly (Nunnally, 1978). *Reliability* of measurement refers to reproducibility and includes interrater reliability (i.e., different observers see the same thing), internal reliability (e.g., different items on a scale are related to one another), and test–retest reliability (i.e., showing stability of the measure over relatively brief periods of time in the absence of intervention).

Validity

*Validity* means that a measure actually reflects the identified domain of functioning. For example, validity can be demonstrated by showing that the measure is strongly related to similar measures or behavioral indices believed to measure that same domain and unrelated to measures of different areas. A valid measure must also be sensitive to change, so that it can clearly identify meaningful improvements. Without reliable and valid measures of important outcomes, limited progress can be made in developing an intervention.

Third, outcome measurement should correspond to the goals of the intervention. Some interventions have broad goals (e.g., reducing hospitalization, incarceration, and homelessness), whereas others have narrow goals (e.g., increasing competitive employment). The advantage of defining a target problem area broadly is that the intervention may have a greater impact on a wider spectrum of impaired functioning. However, defining the target area broadly may also make it more difficult to develop an intervention that will effectively address all of the problem areas. For example, homelessness and institutionalization are influenced by many factors that are outside the scope of mental health, including the availability of low-cost housing. The primary advantage of defining the target area more narrowly is that it makes the task of developing an effective intervention more manageable. The primary disadvantage is that it may not successfully address problems that are closely related but not within the narrow purview of the intervention.

| Defining goals of intervention

A final consideration in articulating the problem area is defining the population of consumers for whom the intervention is intended. Similar to determining the scope of the target problem, defining the target population broadly versus too narrowly has both advantages and disadvantages. Defining the population broadly has the advantage of maximizing the number of consumers who may potentially benefit from an intervention. On the other hand, defining the target population more narrowly can make it easier to develop an intervention that is tailored to address the very specific needs of that group of individuals. There is no right or wrong answer in how to approach this problem, and whichever decision an investigator chooses, he or she can be confident of being criticized for not making the other

| Defining the intervention population

choice. Often, the research starts narrowly and expands to more general populations. For example, an intervention may be tested initially in a university clinic with white females and subsequently be replicated in more routine treatment settings with men and with minority groups.

## Identification of Possible Treatments

Once a specific problem area has been identified and the researcher has reasonable confidence about his or her ability to measure changes in that domain, the next task is to select or develop an intervention that has promise for helping consumers to make improvements in that area of functioning. In most cases, new interventions are developed based on one (or more) of the following approaches:

1. Theories concerning the nature of functioning in the problem area (e.g., factors related to the etiology or maintenance of the problem)
2. Theories of behavior change (which may or may not be related to theories about the nature of the problem area)
3. Adapting interventions that have been successfully used to address similar problems in different populations
4. Adapting interventions that have been successfully used to address different problems in the same (or similar) populations
5. Interventions that are discovered serendipitously by clinicians, clients, or researchers

Rational frame theory | An example of the first type of treatment development is an approach to psychotherapy based on relational frame theory (Hayes, Barnes-Holmes, & Roche, 2001). This theory hypothesizes that humans' capacity for language and thought leads people to interpret and respond to their thoughts as though they represent real-world experiences rather than symbolic representations. Acceptance and commitment therapy (Hayes, Strosahl, & Wilson, 1999) was

Acceptance and commitment theory |

developed on the basis of this theory and was designed to help people articulate personal goals and values, and learn how to accept and not attempt to control unpleasant thoughts and feelings that are largely beyond their control and have limited basis in reality. One recent study showed that the application of acceptance and commitment therapy to recently hospitalized consumers with schizophrenia significantly decreased the rate of their rehospitalizations (Bach & Hayes, 2002).

Two examples of the second approach to treatment development are the application of social skills training (based on social learning theory; Bandura, 1969) to a wide range of social problems (Liberman, DeRisi, & Mueser, 1989), and the use of motivational interviewing (based on the stages of change concept; Prochaska & DiClemente, 1984) with people who have addiction disorders (Miller & Rollnick, 2002). The crux of social learning theory is that people learn from observing others' behavior, as well as from the consequences of their behavior. Social skills' training involves the systematic teaching of social behaviors through a combination of modeling skills, role playing, receiving positive and corrective feedback, and practicing skills in natural situations. The stages-of-change concept is based on the observation that changes toward healthier behavior tend to occur through a sequence of distinct stages (precontemplation, contemplation, preparation, behavior change, and maintenance), and that attention to each stage is critical in matching an intervention to a consumer's motivation level. Motivational interviewing involves helping people articulate their personal goals and explore the steps required to achieve those goals, including addressing problematic substance use that may interfere with achieving a goal, thereby enhancing the consumer's motivation to address substance abuse.

An example of an intervention that was adapted for one population based on its success in another population is the individual placement and support (IPS) model of supported employment. The IPS model was developed by

*Social skills training*

*Motivational interviewing*

*Individual placement and support*

Becker and Drake (2003) as an approach to improving vocational outcomes for consumers. Employment specialists work collaboratively with mental health treatment teams to help consumers find competitive jobs that match their preferences in integrated community settings. Employment specialists also provide services to help support consumers who are employed to achieve high performance and satisfaction. The IPS model was adapted from successful supported employment approaches for individuals with developmental disabilities (Wehman & Moon, 1988).

*Assertive community treatment*

The assertive community treatment (ACT) model (Stein & Santos, 1998) was originally developed to address the problem of frequent rehospitalizations and extremely poor psychosocial functioning for consumers with some of the most severe impairments associated with SMI. The success of this model has led to many modifications to treat different problems in persons with SMI, including homelessness (Lehman, Dixon, Kernan, & DeForge, 1997), substance abuse (Drake et al., 1998), and involvement in the criminal justice system (Gold Award, 1999).

*Serendipidous observations*

Many pharmacological interventions for mental illness have been discovered by serendipitous observation. This seems less likely to occur for complex psychosocial interventions, yet many rehabilitation interventions have their roots in the observation of practices that consumers have discovered through devising self-help programs. Regrettably, the self-help programs themselves have gone largely unevaluated.

### Pilot Testing the Intervention

*Administrating and evaluating the intervention*

The primary goal of pilot testing an intervention is to establish its feasibility and promise as an intervention. Secondary goals are to standardize the intervention and to develop a measure of fidelity to the intervention model. In general, pilot testing involves administering the intervention to a limited number of consumers and evaluating the changes in the targeted outcomes in at least one, and often several, studies. The clinical investigators typically obtain informal experience before any formal pilot testing is conducted, for example, by treating a number of consumers based on the principles of the intervention in order to make a preliminary determination of the suitability of the intervention or the need for modification. These informal clinical excursions with the intervention may or may not involve formal data collection; their primary purpose is not to gather data demonstrating the feasibility and promise of the intervention, but rather to determine whether the intervention is ready for formal data collection in a pilot study. After the basic principles and methods of the intervention have been tentatively established, a formal pilot study is conducted. A variety of different research designs are possible for the pilot study. The specific design of the pilot study is of primary relevance to establishing the promise of the intervention, as discussed below.

The primary question that needs to be addressed when establishing the feasibility of an intervention is whether it can be successfully implemented with the intended population of consumers. Two criteria are generally used to evaluate feasibility: acceptability of the intervention and retention in treatment.

The *acceptability* of an intervention refers to whether consumers (or family members, if relevant) will agree to participate in an intervention. Interventions that only a small minority of eligible consumers will agree to participate in are of limited value, because most consumers will never access the intervention. Treatment *retention* refers to whether or not an intervention is able to retain consumers in treatment for the intended treatment period. Interventions can only be effective if consumers actually receive the treatment. The most rigorous evaluation approach to analyzing outcome data, the intent-to-treat model, requires investigators to include all the follow-up data for consumers who were assigned to different treatment groups, regardless of whether or not they completed treatment. Thus, the higher the dropout rate, the more difficult it is to demonstrate that an intervention is effective

| Establishing feasibility in a pilot study

| Acceptability and rentention of an intervention

| Intent-to-treat model

using an intent-to-treat analysis. Although the opinions of experts differ, generally most consider dropout rates in the 20–30% range to be acceptable, and fewer than 20% to be very good. Dropout rates over 30% are problematic and suggest a need for additional work aimed at improving retention rates.

**Evaluating promise in a pilot study**

To warrant the time, effort, and money required for an RCT, pilot studies are first used to show that the intervention has promise for helping consumers achieve the targeted outcomes. Typically, pilot testing involves giving the intervention to a small group of consumers and conducting rigorous assessments of the problem domains before treatment, after treatment, and after some follow-up period (e.g., ranging from several months to over a year).

**Need for a control group debated**

Researchers disagree about the need for a control group during pilot testing. Investigators who use a pre–post follow-up design without a control group must interpret improvements in selected outcomes as meaningful compared to what might otherwise be expected. When functioning in targeted problem areas is relatively stable without treatment, and improvements are observed following the intervention, the investigator can argue that the improvements are due to the intervention. However, most psychiatric problems fluctuate over time, so improvements could be due to natural history or historical factors.

**Effect size versus statistical significance**

Controlled research designs that include a comparison group, such as RCTs or quasi-experimental studies, provide stronger evidence supporting the promise of an intervention. Controlled studies conducted as pilot studies often lack sufficient statistical power to detect significant differences between a new intervention and the comparison group due to the small sample size (Bartels et al., 2004). This inability can lead to a conclusion that an intervention is ineffective, unless the investigator declares from the outset that the pilot study is intended to show that some clients benefit and to estimate the likely magnitude of the change (called the effect size), not to show statistical significance.

The pilot study is usually based on an outline of the intervention program or a draft of the manual. Because valuable experience delivering the intervention is gained during the pilot study, a formal treatment manual can readily be written based on the pilot. When a draft of a manual exists prior to the pilot study, some modifications are usually made after the study is completed, based on the additional clinical experience. The specificity of manuals varies greatly from one project to another and depends partly on the nature of the intervention. Most treatment manuals include information to orient clinicians to the nature of the problem, as well as some conceptual foundations of the intervention. Specific guidelines are provided regarding the logistics of the intervention, identification of consumers for whom the intervention is designed, curriculum, teaching skills, and guidance for handling common problems. Manuals often provide clinical vignettes to illustrate treatment principles and incorporate specific instruments for assessment and monitoring clinical outcomes. The length of treatment manuals typically ranges from 20 to 200 pages.

Standardizing
a manual

The purpose of a fidelity scale is to verify that an intervention is being implemented in a manner consistent with the treatment model. Such verification is crucial to conducting a rigorous assessment of the intervention, since it must first be established that the intervention has actually been implemented in order to determine its effects. Historically, there have been two methods for evaluating treatment fidelity, mainly derived from research on psychotherapy: expert judgments, and standardized, objective, observation-based measures.

Developing a
fidelity scale

When expert judgments are used to establish fidelity, a recognized expert (e.g., the developer of the intervention or an established authority on it) obtains information regarding the implementation of the intervention (e.g., by observing therapy sessions, reviewing case notes, conducting interviews) and provides feedback regarding the degree of adherence it. When an objective measure of

Expert judgments

Objective measure

fidelity is employed, behaviorally specific anchor points for rating adherence to an intervention are established, raters are trained to use the measure, interrater reliability of ratings is obtained, and fidelity ratings are based on those ratings. The primary disadvantages of the expert approach compared to the objective approach are that it is impractical for large-scale trials and dissemination efforts (because there are only so many "experts" to go around), and it may be subject to bias (i.e., experts who are invested in seeing their intervention succeed may confound their ratings of fidelity with the clinical success, or lack thereof, of the intervention). Objective fidelity ratings avoid both of these problems and provide behaviorally based information that can be useful in addressing implementation challenges and in exploring the relationship between fidelity and outcome.

**Ingredients of fidelity scales** | Fidelity scales vary greatly in their scope, specificity, and data requirements. The most common data ingredients include some of the following: interviews with consumers, clinicians, program leaders, and family members; chart reviews; audiotaped or videotaped sessions; and management information systems (MIS) data. More information on the development of fidelity measures for mental health services is available in Bond, Evans, Salyers, Williams, and Kim (2000).

### Controlled Evaluation

Rigorous evaluation is crucial to establish the effectiveness of an intervention. As previously discussed, rigorous single case study designs, replicated over multiple persons, can provide compelling evidence for the effectiveness of an intervention. In practice, however, most rigorous evaluations of promising practices are conducted using control groups. Although it is beyond the scope of this chapter to discuss all the methodological issues relevant to planning and conducting a controlled study, several of the most crucial issues are briefly addressed here, including the experimental design, the selection of a control group, inclusion/exclusion criteria for the target population, the setting for the trial, and the choice of outcome measures.

The advantages of conducting an RCT over other designs (e.g., quasi-experimental designs) involve controlling for group equivalence. Quasi-experimental designs almost inevitably have the problem of group differences on potentially important variables. For some interventions, especially those that take place at the level of the treatment team or mental health agency, a quasi-randomized controlled trial may be an option. For this design, a number of different treatment teams or mental health centers are randomly assigned to receive the experimental intervention or the control intervention. Technically, in this kind of experimental design, the true unit of analysis is the mental health treatment team or agency, rather than the individual, and there are statistical techniques to deal with the clustering of individuals within groups. In practice, the outcomes of individual consumers treated on different teams or in different mental health centers are often compared, providing they are comparable on their fidelity to the intervention. This kind of experimental design is not considered to be a pure RCT because each consumer does not have an independent and equal chance of being in either intervention. Nevertheless, this design has advantages over many other approaches, because the agencies or mental health centers are assigned by randomization and are therefore likely to be equivalent.

In RCTs the selection of the comparison group is of crucial importance to evaluating the effects of the intervention. In general, there are three possible choices when selecting a comparison intervention: an equally intensive intervention, a less intensive intervention, and treatment as usual (TAU). No treatment (i.e., watchful waiting) or delayed treatment (i.e., waiting list) may also be options. Each comparison intervention has advantages and disadvantages, with the selection of the comparison determined largely by the questions the researchers seek to answer about their experimental intervention, as well as pragmatic aspects of the proposed research. Three group designs combining some of these comparison groups are also possible and have clear advantages, but have the primary

| Research design of the evaluation

| Quasi-randomized controlled trial

| Comparison groups in the evaluation

disadvantage of requiring significantly more subjects in order to have sufficient statistical power to detect hypothesized effects.

**Inclusion/exclusion criteria in the evaluation**

Pilot work on the intervention should serve as the primary guide in determining the inclusion and exclusion criteria for the controlled study. Inclusion criteria are used to identify the population for whom the intervention is designed, and may include factors such as diagnosis (e.g., posttraumatic stress disorder), functional impairments in specific areas (e.g., not working but interested in work), or service utilization characteristics (e.g., recent psychiatric hospitalizations). In general, it is desirable to keep exclusion criteria for participation in the study to a minimum in order to maximize the likelihood that results will be applicable to the broadest possible population. Exclusion criteria should be limited to factors that can influence ability to participate in, or benefit from, the intervention. For example, substance abuse is a common exclusion criterion for medication studies, even though it is a common co-occurring problem in persons with SMI, because it is presumed to alter responses to medications. On the other hand, clients with co-occurring substance abuse have usually not been excluded from studies of supported employment, and the intervention therefore has broader applicability, or generalizability.

**Evaluation setting**

The location of a controlled trial has implications for how well the results will transfer to other settings. Clinical trials conducted in routine mental health centers, rather than in university clinics, have the greatest potential to transfer successfully to the usual settings where most people with SMI receive treatment. The general rule is that *efficacy* studies are conducted in highly controlled settings, with specially trained clinicians, carefully selected clients, and other constrained conditions for the sake of isolating and controlling the treatment intervention, whereas *effectiveness* studies are conducted under more routine (i.e., real-world) conditions, including settings, practitioners, clients, and economic constraints. Traditionally, interventions have been tested first in efficacy trials and then in effectiveness trials. Recently, however, there has been a shift to develop and test interventions solely under effectiveness conditions to ensure generalizability.

A major concern about conducting research in typical mental health agency settings is the importance of mini-mizing the burden of the research on the day-to-day clinical activities of the center. Research requirements often include many of the following: educating all staff about the nature and purposes of the research, training staff who will provide the new intervention, screening and recruiting study participants, coordinating standardized assessments of participants, obtaining clinicians' ratings of participants' functioning, and working with agency staff to access medical records and other data. These activities can be accomplished by providing specially funded research staff to minimize the time and energy of clinical staff or by estab-lishing the research as a fundamental part of the agency's mission.

Research requirements in real-world clinical setting

The selection of measures is of critical importance to controlled research on a new practice. Measures can be divided into three broad types, that assess outcome, imple-mentation, and theory. Each type of measure is described briefly below.

Outcome measures focus on the areas that the interven-tion is primarily aimed at improving (e.g., work, quality of social relationships, symptom severity, relapses, hospitaliza-tion), which have been articulated and systematically meas-ured since the earliest stages of the process of developing an EBP. When planning a controlled evaluation, outcome measures are generally divided into two broad types: primary and secondary outcomes. *Primary outcomes* are those that the intervention is most immediately focused on changing and therefore are of greatest interest. *Secondary outcomes* are those that investigators hope or expect to change chiefly through changes in the primary outcomes. For example, a primary outcome of supported employment programs is to help consumers obtain and keep jobs; common measures of this outcome include the percentage of consumers who get work, the number of hours worked,

Outcome measures: primary versus secondary

and the wages earned. Participating in a supported employment program and working may also have beneficial effects on other areas of functioning, such as self-esteem, symptoms, and satisfaction with one's life, and therefore changes in these areas are considered secondary outcomes. Clearly identifying which outcomes are primary and which are secondary makes it easier to determine whether an intervention has been successful at addressing the most important outcomes (i.e., those designated as primary).

Implementation measures | Implementation measures provide information about whether the intervention was implemented as intended among those consumers in the different treatment groups. Implementation measures can be broadly divided into those that evaluate clinician fidelity to the treatment model, and those that record consumers' exposure to their assigned treatment. In order for interventions to be effective, consumers must be exposed to, and receive at least a minimal dose of, the intervention. Treatment exposure measures include information on the number and duration of contacts between a clinical provider and consumer and the duration of treatment.

Theory-based measures | Controlled research often provides valuable information for understanding more about how an intervention works, as well as how different theoretical constructs interact with functional outcomes and the interrelationships among different domains of functioning. Theory testing and development are important to the process of evaluating interventions, because evidence based on such theories may provide guidance for refining an intervention to make it more effective or for developing a new intervention to address a related area of functioning.

## Summary and Conclusions

EBPs are interventions that have a strong scientific basis for helping people with SMI to achieve improvements in specific areas of their lives. The process of developing and establishing an EBP is a long and arduous one, which typically takes from 2 to 10 years, and which involves a series of discrete stages: (1) articulation of the problem area, (2) identification of possible treatments, (3) pilot testing the intervention, and (4) controlled evaluation of the intervention. These same stages should be applied when modification of a previously established EBP is the goal.

## References

Bach, P., & Hayes, S. C. (2002). The use of acceptance and commitment therapy to prevent the rehospitalization of psychotic patients: A randomized controlled trial. *Journal of Consulting and Clinical Psychology, 70*, 1129–1139.

Bandura, A. (1969). *Principles of behavior modification.* New York: Holt, Rinehart & Winston.

Bartels, S. J., Forester, B., Mueser, K. T., Miles, K. M., Dums, A. R., & Pratt, S., et al. (2004). Supported rehabilitation and health care management of older persons with severe mental illness. *Community Mental Health Journal, 40*, 75–90.

Becker, D. R., & Drake, R. E. (2003). *A working life for people with severe mental illness.* New York: Oxford University Press.

Bellack, A. S., Morrison, R. L., Wixted, J. T., & Mueser, K. T. (1990). An analysis of social competence in schizophrenia. *British Journal of Psychiatry, 156*, 809–818.

Bellack, A. S., Sayers, M., Mueser, K. T., & Bennett, M. (1994). An evaluation of social problem solving in schizophrenia. *Journal of Abnormal Psychology, 103*, 371–378.

Bond, G. R., Campbell, K., Evans, L. J., Gervey, R., Pascaris, A., Tice, S., Del Bene, D., & Revell, G. (2002). A scale to measure quality of supported employment for persons with severe mental illness. *Journal of Vocational Rehabilitation, 17*, 239–250.

Bond, G. R., Evans, L., Salyers, M. P., Williams, J., & Kim, H.-W. (2000). Measurement of fidelity in psychiatric rehabilitation. *Mental Health Services Research, 2*, 75–87.

Chambless, D. L., Baker, M. J., Baucom, D. H., Beutler, L. E., & Calhoun, K. S. (1998). Update on empirically validated therapies, II. *The Clinical Psychologist, 51*, 3–16.

Deegan, P. E. (1988). Recovery: The lived experience of rehabilitation. *Psychosocial Rehabilitation Journal, 11*, 11–19.

Gold Award. (1999). Prevention of jail and hospital recidivism among persons with severe mental illness. *Psychiatric Services, 50*, 1477–1480.

Green, M. F. (1996). What are the functional consequences of neurocognitive deficits in schizophrenia? *American Journal of Psychiatry, 153*, 321–330.

Hayes, S. C., Barnes-Holmes, D., & Roche, B. (Eds.). (2001). *Relational frame theory: A post-Skinnerian account of human language and cognition.* New York: Kluwer Academic/Plenum.

Hayes, S. C., Strosahl, K. D., & Wilson, K. G. (1999). *Acceptance and commitment therapy: An experiential approach to behavior change.* New York: Guilford Press.

Heinssen, R. K., Liberman, R. P., & Kopelowicz, A. (2000). Psychosocial skills training for schizophrenia: Lessons from the laboratory. *Schizophrenia Bulletin, 26*, 21–46.

Hersen, M., & Barlow, D. H. (1992). *Single case experimental designs: Strategies for studying behavior change* (Vol. 56). New York: Pergamon.

Hunsley, J., Dobson, K. S., Johnson, C., & Mikail, S. F. (1999). Empirically supported treatments in psychology: Implications for Canadian professional psychology. *Canadian Psychologist, 40*, 289–302.

Jindal, R. K., & Thase, M. E. (2003). Integrating psychotherapy and pharmacotherapy to improve outcomes among patients with mood disorders. *Psychiatric Services, 54*, 1484–1490.

Kahnemann, D., Slovic, P., & Tversky, A. (1982). *Judgment under uncertainty: Heuristics and biases.* New York: Cambridge University Press.

 Kopelowicz, A., & Liberman, R. P. (2003). Integrating treatment with rehabilitation for persons with major mental illnesses. *Psychiatric Services, 54*, 1491–1498.

Leete, E. (1989). How I perceive and manage my illness. *Schizophrenia Bulletin, 15*, 197–200.

Lehman, A. F., Dixon, L. B., Kernan, E., & DeForge, B. (1997). A randomized trial of assertive community treatment for homeless persons with severe mental illness. *Archives of General Psychiatry, 54*, 1038–1043.

Lenroot, R., Bustillo, J. R., Lauriello, J., & Keith, S. J. (2003). Integrated treatment of schizophrenia. *Psychiatric Services, 54*, 1499–1507.

Liberman, R. P., DeRisi, W. J., & Mueser, K. T. (1989). *Social skills training for psychiatric patients.* Needham Heights, MA: Allyn & Bacon.

Miller, W. R., & Rollnick, S. (Eds.). (2002). *Motivational interviewing: Preparing people for change* (2nd ed.). New York: Guilford Press.

Mueser, K. T. (2000). Cognitive functioning, social adjustment and long-term outcome in schizophrenia. In T. Sharma & P. Harvey (Eds.), *Cognition in schizophrenia: Impairments, importance, and treatment strategies* (pp. 157–177). Oxford, UK: Oxford University Press.

Mueser, K. T., Noordsy, D. L., Drake, R. E., & Fox, L. (2003). *Integrated treatment for dual disorders: A guide to effective practice.* New York: Guilford Press.

Mueser, K. T., Torrey, W. C., Lynde, D., Singer, P., & Drake, R. E. (2003). Implementing evidence-based practices for people with severe mental illness. *Behavior Modification, 27,* 387–411.

Nathan, P., & Gorman, J. M. (Eds.). (1998). *A guide to treatments that work.* New York: Oxford University Press.

Nunnally, J. (1978). *Psychometric theory* (2nd ed.). New York: McGraw-Hill.

Onken, L. S., Blaine, J. D., & Battjes, R. (1997). Behavioral therapy research: A conceptualization of a process. In S. W. Henngler & R. Amentos (Eds.), *Innovative approaches for difficult to treat populations* (pp. 477–485). Washington, DC: American Psychiatric Press.

Prochaska, J. O., & DiClemente, C. C. (1984). *The transtheoretical approach: Crossing the traditional boundaries of therapy.* Homewood, IL: Dow-Jones/Irwin.

Rounsaville, B. J., Carroll, K. M., & Onken, L. S. (2001). A stage model of behavioral therapies research: Getting started and moving on from stage I. *Clinical Psychology: Science and Practice, 8,* 133–142.

Sackett, D. L., Rosenberg, W., & Haynes, R. B. (1997). *Evidence-based medicine.* New York: Churchill Livingstone.

Stein, L. I., & Santos, A. B. (1998). *Assertive community treatment of persons with severe mental illness.* New York: Norton.

Teague, G. B., Bond, G. R., & Drake, R. E. (1998). Program fidelity in assertive community treatment: Development and use of a measure. *American Journal of Orthopsychiatry, 68*(2), 216–232.

Wehman, P., & Moon, M. S. (1988). *Vocational rehabilitation and supported employment.* Baltimore, MD: Paul Brookes.

# ELEVEN

# Developing and Sustaining Evidence-Based Systems of Mental Health Services

*Phyllis Panzano*
*Lon Herman*

MENTAL HEALTH PRACTICES PROVEN TO BE effective by research are of little benefit unless they are readily available to persons experiencing mental illness. It would be ideal if scientific advances in mental health services transferred quickly into practice. But, as in many other segments of health care, the pace at which research-guided practices are widely adopted into practice can be described as glacial, at best. In fact, data from general medicine indicate that the lag between the discovery of new treatments and their incorporation into routine patient care can take from 15 to 20 years (Goldman et al., 2001). Similarly, although considerable evidence exists about which services help persons with serious mental illness improve their quality of life, the availability of these services is far too limited. Many state mental health systems continue to struggle to implement evidence-based mental health practices that have existed for more than 10 years (Goldman et al., 2001).

The U.S. Department of Health and Human Services (1999), the National Institute of Mental Health (NIMH), and the President's New Freedom Commission on Mental Health (2003) have increased the emphasis on the importance of implementing mental health programs that have a track record of leading to valued outcomes. Similarly, a

> Evidence-based services are far too unavailable

growing number of state mental health authorities is taking action to build and sustain systems grounded in evidence-based practice. System leaders, representing various stakeholder groups from consumers to administrators to scientists, seem to agree on at least three points: (1) Consumers with mental illness have the right to receive the most effective treatment available; (2) the quality of care provided to consumers will be improved by introducing evidence-based practices (EBPs) into systems of mental health services; and (3) developing and sustaining systems of EBP is a complex and challenging process.

## A Bird's-Eye View of the Innovation-Adoption Process

The role of organizations

Organizations do not exist in a vacuum. Instead, they are "open systems" whose activities are inescapably influenced by the environments in which they operate. In order to survive, organizations must transform resources from the environment into products and services that have value in the market place. The *availability of resources* in the environment (e.g., number of psychiatrists) and *the quality of those resources* (e.g., effectiveness of psychotropic medication) affect the quality of products produced and services offered by organizations. For example, if the treatment technologies available in the health-care field are unreliable and unproven, treatment goals valued by consumers are not likely to be achieved consistently.

EBPs as innovations

EBPs are technological resources that can be implemented by organizations to build competitive advantage by improving the value of program and service offerings. Because they are state-of-the-art practices, EBPs also can be described as innovations. An *innovation* is defined as any idea, object, or practice that is perceived as new by members of an organization (e.g., Rogers, 1995), regardless of whether it is actually new in the marketplace. Thus, EBPs are innovations that have the added benefit of proven effectiveness.

Adopting or rejecting an EBP

However, even such valuable innovations as EBPs may not succeed for a variety of reasons. They may fail to meet customer needs, or they may not be seen as superior to new or existing alternatives (Frambach & Schillewaert, 2002, p. 163), or they may not be seen as feasible to implement. Thus, in order to successfully implement EBPs, it is important to understand the factors and processes that are likely to affect organizational decisions to adopt innovative practices, and the decisions that are related to sustaining the use of those practices.

The vast literature related to the adoption, diffusion, and implementation of innovations provides a bird's-eye view of the process that is expected to apply in the case of mental health innovations such as EBPs. We discuss the role that various stakeholders, (e.g., consumers, family members, practitioners, administrators, policymakers, advocates, researchers) can play in the process of implementing and sustaining EBPs. Indeed, implementing and sustaining EBPs require the concerted efforts of many different stakeholders. Clinical research (Hanley, Stuart, & Kirz, 1994) and research in organizational behavior (Nutt, 1992) indicate that when more elements of a system are marshaled to support change and reduce resistance, the more likely it is that change will be successful.

Thousands of books and articles from the fields of health care and organizational behavior are pertinent to the topic of building and sustaining EBP, even though few have been written with that specific subject matter in mind. These publications provide the basis for our discussion. Figure 11.1 is a schematic of the innovation-adoption process as it relates to organizations adopting *externally* produced innovations such as EBPs. This figure is adapted from Rogers (1995), the guru on the topic, although many experts (e.g., National Science Foundation: Meyer & Goes, 1988; Van de Ven, Angle, & Poole, 2000) have offered similar views.

**FIGURE 11.1**

**Phases in the adoption of externally developed innovations**

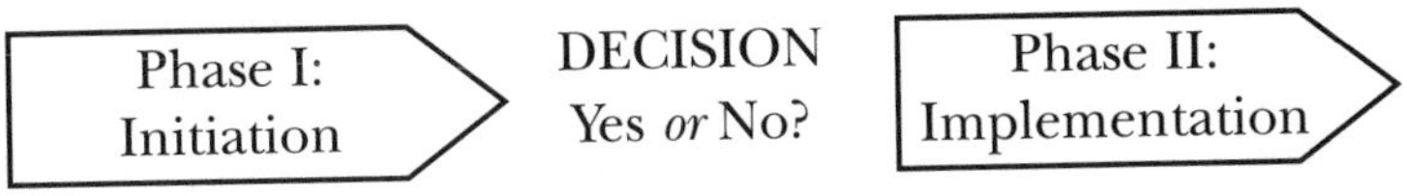

| Phase I: Initiation | DECISION Yes *or* No? | Phase II: Implementation |

**Initiation**

Initiation is the first stage. It begins with an awareness of a need, problem, or opportunity facing the organization that warrants action. This awareness stimulates a search for solutions that could include new practices such as EBPs. Potential solutions then are evaluated to determine the extent to which they are likely to suit the system's needs (e.g., solve a current or anticipated problem). These activities are at the heart of the initiation phase, a phase that is exceedingly more complex when the adopter is an organization rather than an individual (Meyer & Goes, 1988; Rogers, 1995). This added complexity is due to the potentially conflicting perspectives and interests of the many different stakeholder groups that have an influence on organizational life.

**Decision to adopt or reject innovation**

The initiation phase culminates in a decision to adopt, or not to adopt, a particular innovation. As shown in Figure 11.1, the initiation phase culminates with a decision made at a *particular point in time* that *ideally* takes into account the perspectives of a broad set of stakeholders. The decision of organizations to adopt innovative practices often is a "contingent decision process" (Frambach & Schillewaert, 2002; Rogers, 1995) because the decision is made first by organizational leadership (e.g., Hambrick & Mason, 1984; Hickson, Butler, Cray, Mallory, & Wilson, 1986), then by individuals who are expected to implement the innovation.

**Implementation**

Implementation is the second phase of the innovation-adoption process. Ideally, a plan is developed in the beginning of the implementation process to get the practice up and running. *Detailing* (e.g., Nutt, 1992) is one of several terms used to describe this activity. When the detailing process is complete, the practice can then be put into use. It is likely that adjustments may need to be made in the practice during this "clarifying" step, before the practice can be implemented on a more widespread basis. The terms *restructuring* and *reinventing* describe this aspect of the process (e.g., Rice & Rogers, 1980; Rogers, 1995). There are differences of opinion about the benefits and costs of reinvention. Box 11.1 considers this issue.

## BOX 11.1
## Fidelity versus Reinvention:
## Opposites or Complements?

The extent to which fidelity needs to be maintained or rein-vention should be allowed is a topic with important ramifi-cations when it comes to implementing EBPs. *Fidelity* refers to the strategic accuracy of the implementation process (Klein & Sorra, 1996): that is, the extent to which the inter-vention is faithfully reproduced as prescribed (Drake et al., 2001), or the extent to which the actual use of the interven-tion matches its intended use (Lewis & Siebold, 1993). In contrast, *reinvention* refers to the degree to which an innova-tion is tailored or modified by an adopting organization during the implementation process to suit local needs, an occurrence that has been widely documented in the litera-ture. Research suggests that reinvention is more likely when the intervention is complex, its uptake is irreversible, and when external consultants are less than optimal.

Some authors view reinvention as desirable (Van de Ven, Angle, & Poole, 2000); others do not, but the empirical jury is still out. For example, Leonard-Barton (1988) and Rice and Rogers (1980) contended that *customization*, defined as making judicious changes in an innovation to suit local needs, is called for and can be effective when the innovation does not specifically match an organizational structure or the particular problem. In their study of metropolitan trans-portation systems, Rice and Rogers pointed out that innova-tions are often "bundled" such that some components are adopted whereas others are excluded. They argued that careful selection of components can lead to positive outcomes. On the other hand, Carlsyn and colleagues (Carlsyn, Tornatsky, & Dittman, 1977) claimed that reinven-tion may have a "diluting effect" and may result in the failure of an intervention to achieve expected benefits. This perspective implies that measures of fidelity, alone, can be used to assess the success of implementation.

However, it is important to recognize that fidelity and reinvention are not necessarily opposite ends of a single

*Continued on following page*

---

**BOX 11.1** (*continued*)

continuum. Instead, fidelity can vary along multiple dimensions. For example, Klein and Sorra (1996) identifed at least three general dimensions along which fidelity can vary: correctness/accuracy, consistency of use, and commitment of practitioners. According to this conceptualization, fidelity is theoretically highest when implementation is carried out (1) *accurately*, (2) *consistently*, and (3) by *committed* practitioners. This framework also suggests that fidelity ratings can vary along the three dimensions, which raises the question of whether high ratings on one of these dimensions (e.g., commitment) can compensate for lower ratings on another (e.g., consistency). Finally, it is conceivable that an intervention may be rated as having high fidelity to foundational principles (e.g., integrated treatment), yet rated as having low operational fidelity (i.e., extensive reinvention to meet local constraints). Clearly, "fidelity versus reinvention?" is not a simple either/or question.

---

**Routinization**

    The optimal outcome of the implementation phase is the adoption of the practice as part of the standard operating procedures of the organization. *Routinization* (e.g., Rogers, 1995) and *assimilation* (e.g., Meyer & Goes, 1998; Yin, 1978) describe the extent to which an innovative practice has become fully embedded into daily organizational routines and is considered "business as usual."

## Barriers and Facilitators

Numerous factors, both external (e.g., funding, regulations) and internal (e.g., change in leadership) to organizations, can have important influences on each phase of the innovation-adoption process. In some cases these factors create barriers to adopting innovative practices such as EBPs; in other cases, they facilitate the process. Whether external or internal, organizational factors impact the assessment of needs, opportunities, and problems that occurs during the initiation phase.

It is useful to think about barriers and facilitators in terms of whether they are internal or external to an organization and in terms of where they are likely to fit with regard to the Figure 11.1 model. As factors are discussed in this chapter, please consider the following three questions:

1. Is the factor internal or external to the organization?
2. Which phase(s) of the innovation-adoption process (Figure 11.1) is it likely to affect?
3. Is it likely to be a barrier or facilitator?

Thinking about barriers and facilitators in this way is the first step in identifying implications for action by stakeholders at all levels within mental health systems.

For example, state, federal, county, or municipal reimbursement policies are external factors that affect every stage of the process shown in Figure 11.1. In the case of integrated dual-disorders treatment (IDDT), reimbursement for substance abuse treatment is often separate from reimbursement for mental illness treatment. Historically, and counter to the EBP model for clients with dual-diagnoses, this has led to separate rather than integrated services and often requires consumers to seek non-integrated services from two separate systems.

These external reimbursement policies create a barrier that can affect every stage of the innovation-adoption process. At initiation, agencies that are more familiar with mental health or substance abuse services may not support the need for integrated services. Even if an agency is aware of the need to provide integrated treatment for both substance use and mental illness impairments, the agency is likely to provide services that meet reimbursement regulations regardless of the research evidence about the effectiveness of integrated treatment. An agency may regard the reimbursement constraints as insurmountable and not pursue the implementation of IDDT any further.

What does this reality imply for stakeholders who are interested in implementing effective IDDT? For those in

*Reimbursement policies*

*EBP rejected for reimbursement*

*Advocacy implications for stakeholders*

administrative positions, it may imply lobbying state and federal legislators to modify reimbursement policies. Administrative leaders could undertake efforts to identify savings linked to integrated treatment that offset the costs of the programming. Front-line practitioners could gather data about the number of consumers with dual disorders and the human and economic costs of continuing to provide ineffective treatment. Consumers and family members could advocate for IDDT at all levels of the mental health system, as the most effective means to help people with dual disorders to achieve recovery. In the final analysis, removing barriers to providing EBPs is likely to involve a concerted effort by stakeholders operating at all levels within local, state, and national systems.

## Implementation Strategies

Implementing and sustaining EBPs requires the concerted effort of many different stakeholders at all levels—not only motivated clinicians, but federal, state, and local administrators, consumers, and family members—working in a coordinated fashion. A partial list of the strategies utilized at national, state, and local levels to advance the implementation of EBPs follows (Hogan & Svendsen, 2001). As you review the list, consider which phase of the innovation-adoption process (see Figure 11.1) is targeted by those strategies. For example, "amplifying the demand for evidence-based mental health services" clearly is linked to the initiation phase because it attempts to increase awareness of the need for EBPs at the system or agency level. Key strategies currently in effect include:

Key strategies in
implementation

- Amplifying the demand for evidence-based mental health services
- Creating favorable financing strategies and regulations
- Removing administrative barriers and creating incentives

- Providing expert technical assistance and advice to install EBPs
- Sustaining the effective and faithful use of these practices by assessing fidelity to the practice models
- Encouraging the use of clinical quality-improvement approaches in mental health agencies or other routine practice settings
- Promoting clinical and consumer-directed outcome measurement
- Conducting research to discover new evidence-based mental health treatments
- Documenting effective EBP implementation strategies and actions

Box 11.2 provides an overview of one state's recent strategies designed to promote the adoption and successful implementation of a targeted set of EBPs.

---

### BOX 11.2
### Putting the Pieces Together: One States' Approach to Implementing EBPs.

The Ohio Department of Mental Health (ODMH) and local mental health systems have placed a priority on promoting EBPs. As a result of strong state and local leadership, Ohio has been actively consulting with other states and localities, and has successfully pursued national research grants associated with EBP adoption. In addition, Ohio is participating in the implementing Evidence-Based Practices Project supported by SAMHSA and is funding the Innovation Adoption and Diffusion Research Project (IDARP; Panzano, Roth, & Crane-Ross, 2001) with support from the MacArthur Foundation to study the adoption and implementation of EBPs associated with four of Ohio's seven coordinating centers of excellence (CCOE; described below).

To accelerate the adoption of EBPs, Ohio has pursued a number of strategies and activities described earlier in this chapter. As a result, in the course of 3 years, 88% of Ohio's

*Continued on following page*

**BOX 11.2** (*continued*)

local mental health systems had adopted at least one of seven practices for which substantial research evidence exists, or that have been identified as priority service areas (e.g., school-based services) for which evidence is emerging. A sample of the key strategies being used in Ohio is noted below.

### Technical Assistance and Training

ODMH has supported the development of seven CCOEs, statewide institutes responsible for EBP-related teaching and training. Most of Ohio's CCOEs are linked to a research-oriented college, university, or other entity; each CCOE specializes in a particular EBP (e.g., IDDT). The CCOEs are expected to follow a research-validated model to engage and build consensus, teach and train, and then sustain the gains through assessing the faithfulness (fidelity) with which the EBP is being implemented over time.

### Performance Measurement

ODMH has developed a standardized set of consumer outcome indicators designed to contribute to improving care management at consumer and clinician levels. These indicators are also meant to improve quality and accountability at agency, local, and state mental health authority levels. Though the system is relatively new, one of its goals is to measure the effectiveness of particular evidence-based care modalities. The system has been mandated (adopted by regulation) throughout the state.

### Promotion of Quality-Improvement Techniques

The ODMH has begun to require mental health agencies throughout the state to use rigorous quality-improvement tools, either by complying with new regulatory standards or by submitting to accreditation by national authorities (e.g., as the Joint Commission on the Accreditation of Healthcare Organizations).

### Interconnection and Collaboration

Ohio's Medicaid agency exists as a cabinet-level department that is separate from ODMH. The ODMH is working collab-

*Continued on following page*

> **BOX 11.2** (*continued*)
>
> oratively with this department to come up with new financing arrangements for assertive community treatment (ACT) teams and for IDDT. The ODMH also is partnering with other cabinet-level departments. For example, ODMH is working with the department responsible for rehabilitative services to promote supported employment. Similarly, ODMH is working with the state Supreme Court and local law enforcement authorities to implement mental health courts and jail diversion programs for persons with mental illness, in an effort to place the priority on treatment rather than incarceration.

We now turn to the structures and initiatives currently existing within the mental health-care system to support the development of EBP systems of care. Governmental leaders at the federal, state, and local levels play important roles that influence mental health-care systems and are in key positions to promote the adoption of EBPs. Let us review some of the major players at each of these three levels (i.e., federal, state, and local) in mental health-care administration.

## Federal Mental Health Agencies

At the federal level, three major agencies influence mental health care: the National Institute of Mental Health (NIMH), the Substance Abuse and Mental Health Services Administration (SAMHSA), and the Centers for Medicare and Medicaid.

NIMH is the federal government's principal biomedical and behavioral research agency; it is one of 27 components of the National Institutes of Health (NIH). NIMH conducts research on mental disorders and the underlying basic science of brain and behavior, and it supports related research at universities and hospitals across the United States. The NIMH has added a research focus on methods to accelerate the adoption of evidence-based mental health practices. In 2003, several state mental health authorities

NIMH

were awarded research grants to study EBP implementation at the state and local levels, with the hope that results of these studies will guide policymakers who influence mental health-care practices.

**SAMHSA**

Located within the U.S. Department of Health and Human Services, SAMHSA focuses attention on programs and funding to improve the lives of persons with, or at risk for, mental health and substance abuse disorders (*www.SAMHSA.gov*). SAMHSA has three centers that address on mental health services, substance abuse treatment, and substance abuse prevention. The Center for Mental Health Services (CMHS) is the main center charged with improving the availability and accessibility of treatment for people with, or at risk for, mental illness and their families.

As part of its efforts to identify and promote EBPs, SAMHSA has established the Evidence-Based Practices Project. Eight state mental health authorities are involved in the project, which began in 2001. One of the goals is to develop resources and strategies to facilitate the implementation of currently identified EBPs. Information about the specific practices can be found at the project website: *www.mentalhealthpractices.org.*

SAMHSA is also responsible for administering block grants. These grants are federal funds distributed on a formulaic basis for specific service programs that address mental health services, substance abuse prevention, and addiction treatment. Many states use federal block grant funds to develop new or innovative mental health programs. In Ohio, for example, federal block grant funds are being used to support "coordinating centers of excellence," which are statewide institutes responsible for promoting EBPs (see Box 11.2).

**The centers for medicare and medicaid**

People who develop serious mental illness often find themselves impoverished and without private health insurance coverage. To meet their health-care needs, persons with serious mental illness often turn to public assistance. The Medicare and Medicaid programs are two public financing mechanisms designed to provide health-care coverage to certain persons who are aged, disabled, or impoverished. The Centers for Medicare and Medicaid set policy for each of these programs and also administer the Medicare program. Like SAMHSA, the Centers for Medicare and Medicaid are also part of the Department of Health and Human Services.

In general, Medicare provides certain levels of health-care benefits for most Americans over the age of 65, and for some Americans with disabilities. The vast majority of the costs associated with Medicare benefits are borne by the federal government. Medicare, however, provides a much smaller share of mental health financing compared to Medicaid.

| Medicare

The Medicaid program provides medical benefits to individuals and families with low incomes and resources that fit certain categories of eligibility. Unlike the federally administered Medicare program, the Medicaid program is a joint state–federal venture, with the federal government setting overall policy and each state administering its own Medicaid program. Whereas costs associated with the Medicare program are paid for with federal funds, Medicaid is a shared federal and state program, with the federal government generally paying a majority of the costs. Unlike the uniform benefits available nationwide through the Medicare program, Medicaid coverage consists of "mandatory" benefits that each state must make available, along with federally approved "optional" services that states may elect to offer.

| Medicaid

In the 1980s, Medicaid financing became a primary source of mental health reimbursement. States sought to expand their community mental health programs by using Medicaid's federal share of reimbursement to cover costs that would otherwise be borne entirely by states and local communities. For example, in 1981, Medicaid was responsible for about 13.5% of total state mental health revenues. By 2001, community mental health services will receive 42% of their support from Medicaid funding (National Association of State Mental Health Program Directors, 2003).

| Medicaid mental
| health funding

### State Mental Health Authority

At the state level of mental health administration, policies, regulations, and leadership play important roles in determining the type annd quality of mental health services and the adoption of EBPs. State administration of mental health services generally includes three primary functions: (1) regulating the mental health system by establishing standards for mental health facilities and providers; (2) financing mental health services by prioritizing the delivery of services to persons with the most severe needs or to the most impoverished members of society; and (3) providing mental health services. Some state mental health authorities are distinct departments of state government, whereas others are part of a larger agency responsible for coordinating a range of human services.

**Combined versus separate authorities**

About half of the states follow the federal SAMHSA model and have a combined mental health and substance abuse authority. The remaining states have separate mental health and substance abuse agencies. Adding to this complexity, some aspects of delivering mental health services are even controlled by other state agencies. Discord between agencies that may have different missions and goals can be a significant barrier to funding EBPs.

**National Association of State Mental Health Program Directors (NASMHPD)**

As the organization representing mental health leaders in all 50 states, NASMHPD has been actively promoting the adoption of EBPs. Within NASMHPD's Research Institute, a special Center on Evidence-Based Practices, Performance Measurement, and Quality Improvement has been developed to support the efforts of states implementing EBPs and to monitor the quality and impact of services being provided (Goldman et al., 2001). The center identifies, shares, and promotes knowledge about EBPs, supports research and quality efforts, and serves as a coordinating entity linking federal and state efforts. In a survey conducted in 2001, NASMHPD found that 47 states were involved in some type of activity leading to the implementation of EBPs in their systems.

## Local Stakeholders

Within each state, local administrations also play critical roles with regard to the promotion and installation of EBPs. Some states, such as Ohio, organized with local or regional mental health authorities, either plan, fund, or evaluate community-based mental health services within individual communities. Under these arrangements, the local mental health authorities contract with community-based mental health centers for services. These contracts can specify the types of services to be purchased—and therefore can influence the availability of EBPs. Other states, such as New York and New Hampshire, have a much more centralized approach to mental health administration, and this approach plays an equally critical role in promoting the implementation of effective services in their systems. In promoting the adoption of EBPs. states with larger and more multifaceted public mental health systems are likely to be faced with more complex challenges than smaller centralized state systems. In any state system, focused and dedicated leadership is needed to effect changes in policies and regulations that will result in the successful implementation of EBPs.

## Consumers and Families in Advocacy for EBPs

Organizations representing consumers and family members often provide critical advocacy at all levels of the mental health system. One role of advocacy is to demand access to those mental health services for which there is evidence of effectiveness in helping consumers and families achieve their goals. The National Alliance for the Mentally Ill (NAMI) has been an active and well-organized force in demanding access to effective services, such as ACT.

# The View from the Ground: Implementing and Sustaining EBPs at the Local Level

During the first part of our journey, we got a bird's-eye view of the innovation-adoption process and then reviewed some of the key structures, initiatives, and strategies available at the federal, state, and local levels for facilitating the adoption and implementation of EBPs. We now view the innovation-adoption process from the ground level.

### Phase 1: Initiation

As discussed earlier, the initiation phase sets the foundation and direction for planned organizational change. During initiation, the organization's agenda is set by identifying and prioritizing needs, problems, or opportunities facing the organization (e.g., Dutton & Duncan, 1987). For example, an important agency need, such as helping more people with mental illness to obtain competitive employment, may be identified by a number of local stakeholders. Ideally, this need is then prioritized among the other needs, to increase the agency's effectiveness in fulfilling its organizational mission. The organization then tries to identify interventions, including research-based practices, to better meet consumer and family mental health needs. If an innovation is among the potential approaches considered, the innovation-adoption process begins.

Resistance to change | Change is part and parcel of the process by which organizations continue to grow and adapt to changing environments (Huber & Glick, 1995). Organizations often engage in routine changes, such as moving to a different building or changing their name. Less often, organizations engage in nonroutine changes that result in the provision of new services such as EBPs. Whereas routine change tends to take place easily, nonroutine change is often met with resistance from stakeholders who are comfortable with the status quo and may have an investment in the way current services are provided. Stakeholders have different reactions to, and expectations about, change. Some practitioners may be excited about learning and applying new skills, whereas others may prefer their previous practice methods because they are more comfortable and familiar. It is not surprising, therefore, that forces arise both in favor of and against nonroutine change.

To ensure a successful outcome with nonroutine change it is important to seek support from organizational stakeholders. Ideally, acquiring this support should take place during the initiation phase. Stakeholders, who ultimately can affect the success of change, should be involved in initiation-phase activities (i.e., data gathering, conceptualizing, and planning). The early involvement of stakeholders in planning and implementing change provides a greater opportunity for them to develop a sense of ownership and commitment to the change process. Many agencies that have implemented EBPs have established implementation steering teams specifically to involve representatives from a variety of stakeholder groups (e.g., administrators, managers, practitioners, consumers, family members). These teams provide both a structure for addressing concerns early in the change process and for monitoring the change over time. In this manner, stakeholders establish ownership of the planned change effort from the outset.

*Early stakeholder involvement*

Evidence suggests that investment of time during the initiation phase, to build support among stakeholders, is likely to result in fewer barriers to moving forward with implementation. For example, McFarlane and colleagues (2001) found that "consensus building . . . appeared to be critical to successful outcomes" (2001, p. 935) when implementing family psychoeducation services in Maine and Illinois. By contrast, Ohio's development of CCOEs (see Box 11.2) as a mechanism to promote EBPs statewide met with barriers due to limited consensus building on some important topics (e.g., which EBPs to promote and whether CCOEs offered the best vehicle for promoting EBPs). In retrospect, an early investment in additional consensus-building activities regarding the CCOE strategy might have minimized early resistance.

*Consensus building among stakeholders*

Consensus building at all levels is also important because it is likely to lead to consistent communications by influential opinion leaders. As described earlier, the federal, state, and local mental health systems are complex; therefore, gaining alignment in views among key stakeholders at each level is critical to effective implementation.

## Phase 2: Decision Making

In order to build evidence-based systems of treatment, organizations first must decide to adopt services based on outcomes demonstrated to be effective. It is important, therefore, to understand the factors that are likely to affect this decision as it relates to a particular EBP within organizations.

An extensive body of research exists on the factors that influence the decisions of individuals to adopt innovations (e.g., purchase new products). By contrast, the body of literature about factors that influence organizations' decisions to adopt innovations is small but growing. Even so, factors at many levels—from characteristics of the innovation itself to features of the environment—appear to impact the decisions of both individuals and organizations to adopt innovations such as EBPs.

Objective versus perceived features

Innovation-level factors are features of the specific innovation such as complexity and cost. Although early research focused on the link between objective features of innovations, such as cost and the decision to adopt, interest in recent years has shifted to the perceived characteristics of innovations (Wolfe, 1994). This shift occurred with the recognition that perceptions, even if they depart from objective reality, tend to impact decisions and change actions (Daft & Weick, 1984).

Specific pro and con factors: economic considerations

A number of innovation-level factors has consistently been positively linked to the decision to adopt innovations (e.g., Rogers, 1995). For example, the extent to which the practice is seen by key decision makers to (1) involve more benefits than costs, (2) be compatible with other organizational practices, (3) allow for trial use (i.e., reversible), (4) be easy to use, (5) be backed by scientific evidence, (6) have perceived utility, and (7) lead to observable impacts has consistently been found to be positively related to the decision to adopt innovative practices. Conversely, the extent to which decision makers see innovations as complex, costly, and having uncertain effects appears to be negatively related to the decision to adopt (e.g., Frambach & Schillewaert, 2002; Meyer & Goes, 1988; Rogers, 1995; Zaltman, Duncan, & Holbek, 1973). In short, findings suggest that economic considerations are likely to play a significant role in the decision-making process (e.g., Panzano, Roth, & Crane-Ross, 2001).

However, considerations beyond economics also are likely to play a part in organizational decisions to adopt innovations. For example, in their examination of the uptake of health-care innovations in Canada, Denis, Hebert, Langley, Lozeau, and Trottier (2001) observed that factors such as stakeholder power and influence in addition to financial incentives resulted in the more rapid adoption and diffusion of innovations that were "lagging" in evidence, as compared to innovations backed by "leading" evidence (e.g., ACT).

*Stakeholder power and influence*

In summary, many of the innovation-level factors examined in prior research are consistent with an "efficient choice" perspective because they suggest a concern with feasibility, risk, and cost–benefit. In addition, because perceived factors have consistently been linked to the adoption decision, developers and promoters of EBPs need to assess and respond to the perceptions of innovations that are held by key organizational stakeholders.

*"Efficient choice" perspective*

Studies investigating the diffusion of innovations highlight the importance of the content and intensity of communication between current users and potential users of innovations (e.g., Majahan & Peters, 1985) on the uptake of innovations. This research emphasizes that the expressed experience of early adopters of innovations such as EBPs can have a sweeping impact on the decisions of potential adopter organizations. Positive experience of early adopters is likely to accelerate the rate of adoption among future adopters, whereas negative experience is likely to slow the rate of adoption (e.g., Majahan & Peterson, 1985). Furthermore, the intensity or extent of communication

*Communications with other organizations*

between early and potential adopters is expected to magnify these effects (Frambach & Schillewaert, 2002).

Due to the influence of the messages sent by early adopters on the behavior of potential adopters, it would seem prudent to conduct extensive field testing of complex innovations prior to promoting their adoption. Controlled field testing with a small set of organizations would permit implementation challenges to be addressed.

An organization's environment consists of outside influences that have the potential to affect an organization's performance. For example, the cost of atypical antipsychotic medications is an environmental factor that is likely to impact the performance of behavioral health-care firms, as measured in terms of client-level outcomes, such symptom distress.

Not surprisingly, environmental factors also can exert a major influence on organizational decisions to adopt innovations such as EBPS. For example, professional norms about treatment can have powerful effects on the adoption of new practices (e.g., Abrahamson, 1991; Rogers, 1995; Wolfe, 1994). Similarly, organizations are more likely to adopt an innovation if it is likely to facilitate interactions with other organizations that have already adopted the practice (Frambach & Schillewaert, 2002). Opinion leaders within an industry (e.g., the Surgeon General, National Alliance for the Mentally Ill) also function as environmental forces that can impact the likelihood of an organizations adopting certain practices by creating awareness of needs and by making preferred solutions salient and accessible to practitioners (Rogers, 1995).

Legal/regulatory and technological developments within specific environmental sectors are widely recognized as impacting the performance of organizations and also may partly account for organizational decisions to adopt innovations. For example, mandates may be issued by regulatory agencies that require the adoption of a particular practice. Failure to adopt might result in undesired outcomes such as less funding, loss of funding, or loss of an

---

*Controlled field testing*

*The role of the environment*

*Cost factors*

*Professional norms and opinion leaders*

*Mandated services*

agency license to provide services. Although consensus-building efforts are preferable before edicts are issued, some situations, such as ongoing consumer suffering without access to effective services, may warrant the mandated adoption of selected practices by organizations. Of course, it is preferable that organizations adopt mandated practices not simply because they are required but also because increased access to effective services has been identified as an organizational priority.

There is an extensive body of research that suggests that many factors at many levels, such as perceived features of innovations (e.g., complexity), are likely to impact organizational decisions to adopt innovations such as EBPs. This information is likely to have implications for action stakeholders involved in building EBP service systems. For example, research suggests that organizations with successful track records in innovation might be recruited as early sites for implementing EBPs prior to promoting them on a systemwide basis. In this manner, the influential messages of early adopter organizations to potential adopter organizations are more likely to facilitate adoption. Similarly, findings related to the role of environmental factors suggest that timing or selective promotion of EBPs may be important to consider. That is, it may be more cost-effective to promote EBPS first in locales that have fewer barriers, while working with stakeholders to reduce barriers in other systems. Promotion efforts might also be directed first toward practices that have lower barriers in an effort to build the perception that EBPs are accepted practices (DiMaggio & Powell, 1983) within the industry. Clearly, research related to factors that impact adoption decisions has implication for the actions of stakeholders at many levels within systems.

*Facilitating adoption*

### Phase 3: Implementation
One important premise underlying this chapter is that EBPs must be seen by organizations as (1) leading to desired outcomes, and (2) feasible to implement and

sustain in routine mental health services. Consequently, it is important to consider the elements of implementation success and to review the factors that are expected to impact success.

Remarkably, there have been few attempts to study what happens after organizations decide to adopt innovative practices. The decision itself is often the endpoint of research. When follow-up does occur, in-depth case studies that focus on one innovation are most common. Studies that are longitudinal, involve many organizations, and consider several innovations (e.g., Meyer & Goes, 1988) are rare. EBP studies of this type (Drake et al., 2001; Roth, Panzano, Crane-Ross, & Seffrin, 2003) are also uncommon but are sorely needed in order to fully understand the factors that contribute to implementation success.

**Defining implementation success**

Using the decision to adopt an innovation as the indicator of success may be justified when the primary interest is to increase the number of first-time purchasers of new products. It makes little sense, however, to define success in this way when it comes to building systems based on the accurate, committed, and ongoing use of innovative services such as EBPs.

Fortunately, the definition of implementation success for complex innovations such as EBPs has come to include what happens during, and as a result of, implementation. Two classes of success measures have been identified as important to include in implementation research: measures of implementation effectiveness, and measures of innovation effectiveness (Klein & Sorra, 1996; Wolfe, 1994).

**Implementation effectiveness**

*Implementation effectiveness* is defined as the accurate, committed, and consistent use of a practice by targeted employees (i.e., staff directly involved in implementation or serving in support roles; Klein & Sorra, 1996). The fidelity of implementation and the extent to which the practice has been assimilated into daily operations, also known as penetration, are two examples of measures of implementation

**Innovation effectiveness**

effectiveness. *Innovation effectiveness* is defined as the benefits that accrue to organizational stakeholders as a function of implementing a practice. For example, an increase in the number of consumers achieving recovery from dual disorders or obtaining competitive employment are two measures of innovation effectiveness. Thus, measures of implementation effectiveness focus on the extent to which an innovation is implemented correctly and consistently, whereas measures of innovation effectiveness focus on outcomes for consumers and other system stakeholders.

The emphasis on evaluating the success of EBPs in field settings sometimes focuses on implementation effectiveness, as evidenced by evaluating the fidelity of implementation. There is some justification for this focus because, by definition, practices classified as "evidence-based" are supported by research that demonstrates a direct positive relationship between high-fidelity practices and outcomes (e.g., Drake et al., 2001). Even so, as EBPs become more widely adopted in the field, it is important to track both types of implementation success measures in order to better understand the conditions under which these linkages do or do not hold up (e.g., Bond, Becker, Drake, & Vogler, 1997).

A simple formula, rooted in psychology, provides a way of thinking about factors that contribute to the success of implementation efforts: implementation success (i.e., performance) is a function of know-how, motivation, and the opportunity to perform:

**Implementation Success = $f$ [know-how × motivation × opportunity to perform]**

Few would argue that staff members need to have the knowledge, skills, and abilities to administer the practice accurately. Agency staff must be educated and trained in how to implement the innovation, develop and maintain a level of competence, and have access to technical assistance or support when questions arise (e.g., Davis, Bagozzi, & Warshaw, 1989; Mathieson, 1991; Meyer & Goes, 1988; Roth, Panzano, Crane-Ross, & Seffrin, 2003). Practice guidelines represent a traditional health-care system

Know-how

approach to increasing the know-how of practitioners. They generally focus on the content of services—that is, how to do something new, different, or better. In recent years, practice guidelines have been developed for EBPs and disseminated by a variety of entities such as the American Psychiatric Association (Torrey et al., 2001). Yet, practice guidelines alone have not been found to be sufficient to change clinical practices or to produce widespread adoption of EBPs. This should not be surprising, given that know-how is only one of three critical ingredients to implementation success.

**Motivation to implement**

Although know-how is a necessary ingredient, it is not sufficient without the motivation or drive to implement a given practice. Targeted employees need intrinsic or extrinsic sources of motivation in order for implementation to be successful.

**Intrinsic motivation**

Two frameworks have recently been examined that touch upon intrinsic motivations for implementing innovations. Both the technology acceptance model (e.g., Mathieson, 1991) and the theory of planned behavior (Fishbein & Ajzen, 1975) suggest that attitudes, intrinsic motivational factors, can impact the intended or actual use of innovations. Research related to these frameworks suggests that the more positive the attitude of an agency's staff toward the practice, the more likely the staff will be to use an innovation. Furthermore, this research revealed that user attitudes are linked to perceptions about innovations (e.g., perceived usefulness; Mathieson), which implies that attitudes toward, and beliefs about, innovations are interrelated and that beliefs may change along with attitudes, or vice versa (Zajonc, 1984)

**Extrinsic motivation**

Recent research also points to several extrinsically motivating factors with likely links to implementation success. Most of these factors have been identified as elements of the climate of an organization for implementation (e.g., Klein & Sorra, 1996; Van de Ven et al., 2000; Linton, 2002; Mathieson, 1991). These factors include (1) organizational or social norms for adoption, (2) perceived management support for the innovation, (3) perceived authority messages urging use, (4) clear understanding of the goals of implementation, (5) performance monitoring of implementation processes and outcomes, (6) rewards and sanctions related to use/non-use or actual rewards/sanctions, and (7) freedom-to-express doubt about the innovation. In addition, organizational cultures that embrace risk taking, encourage learning, and view change in a positive way also are likely to serve as additional external sources of motivation for staff engaged in the implementation of innovations (e.g., Van de Ven et al., 2000).

In addition to having the know-how and the motivation to implement innovations such as EBPs, community mental health center staff must also be given adequate opportunity to perform. This means that organizations must be prepared to remove or minimize barriers that interfere with implementation. For example, if illness management and recovery practitioners are expected to prepare and review practice modules before working with consumers, then it is incumbent upon the agency to provide for this time without creating an additional burden or strain on the staff person. Some factors that are likely to facilitate the opportunity to perform include (1) the presence of an innovation champion (e.g., Rogers, 1995), (2) an implementation project manager who has clout or authority (e.g., Meyer & Goes, 1988; Nutt, 1992), (3) the availability of dedicated resources to facilitate implementation and deal with barriers as they arise (e.g., staff, money, equipment; e.g., Klein, Conn, & Sorra, 2001), (4) ongoing access to user support, and (5) the existence of an in-house support function (e.g., Davis et al., 1989; Igharia, Parasuraman, & Barudi, 1996).

In summary, there are two key elements of implementation success: implementation effectiveness and innovation effectiveness. It is important to pay attention to both types of success measures when one is engaged in implementing or studying the implementation of innovations such as EBPs. Success can be impacted by a multitude of factors that relate to know-how, motivation, and the opportunity to

> Opportunity to perform

perform. Organization and system leaders (see Box 11.3 must attend to all three elements of the success equation in order to build and sustain systems of evidence-based care.

---

**BOX 11.3**
**The Managerial Roles of Leadership**

There are literally thousands of published articles on leadership and many leadership theories, so the statement "leadership is critical to the innovation-adoption process" is likely to mean different things to different people. Regardless of the particular theory of leadership, the role of leader is considered to be only one of many important roles that top managers play during the innovation-implementation process. In fact, leader is seen as 1 of 10 managerial roles that fall within three broader role sets: interpersonal roles (i.e., figurehead, leader, liaison), informational roles (i.e., monitor, disseminator, spokesperson), and decisional roles (i.e., entrepreneur, disturbance handler, resource allocator, and negotiator; Mintzberg, 1975). In performing this multitude of roles during the innovation-adoption process, effective managers must be able to make things happen by motivating others. More specifically, managers must be prepared to (1) communicate a vision and guide the organization and its stakeholders through a thorough and thoughtful decision process; (2) articulate goals; (3) support the development of an effective operational plan for achieving goals and see that progress toward goal achievement is monitored; (4) implement appropriate education and training programs and ongoing technical support functions so that targeted implementers will have the know-how to move forward with the business of implementation as prescribed; (5) establish reward structures that keep staff motivation high once implementation has gotten underway; and (6) remove obstacles and other barriers that might arise during day-to-day implementation, so that implementers have the opportunity to perform. In other words, in the course of guiding the innovation-adoption process, effective leaders are likely to be engaged in many different managerial roles.

## References

Abrahamson, E. (1991). Managerial fads and fashions: The diffusion and rejection of innovations. *Academy of Management Review*, 16, 586–612.

Bond, G. R., Becker, D. R., Drake, R. E., & Vogler, K. M. (1997). A fidelity scale for the individual placement and support model of supported employment. *Rehabilitation Counseling Bulletin, 40*, 265–284.

Carlsyn, R., Tornatsky, L. G., & Dittman, S. (1977). Incomplete adoption of an innovation: The case of goal attainment scaling. *Evaluation, 4*, 128–130.

Daft, R., & Weick, K. (1984). Toward a model of organizations as interpretation systems. *Academy of Management Review, 9*, 284–296.

Davis, F. D., Bagozzi, R. P., & Warshaw, P. R. (1989). User acceptance of computer technology: A comparison of two theoretical models. *Management Science, 35*, 982–1003.

Denis, J.-L., Hebert, Y., Langley, A., Lozeau, D., & Trottier, L.-H. (2001, August). *Explaining diffusion patterns for complex health care innovations.* Paper presented at the annual conference of the Academy of Management, Washington, DC.

DiMaggio, P. J., & Powell, W. W. (1983). The iron cage revisited: Institutional isomorphism and collective rationality in organizational fields. *American Sociological Review, 48*, 147–160.

Drake, R. E., Goldman, H. H., Leff, H. S., Lehman, A. F., Dixon, L., & Mueser, K. T., et al. (2001). Implementing evidence-based practices in routine mental health settings. *Psychiatric Services 52*, 418–411.

Dutton, J. E., & Duncan, R. B. (1987). The creation of momentum for change through the process of strategic issue diagnosis. *Strategic Management Journal, 8*, 279–295.

Fishbein, M., & Ajzen I. (1975). *Belief, attitude, intention and behavior: An introduction to theory and research.* Reading, MA: Addison-Wesley.

Frambach, R. T., & Schillewaert, N. (2002). Organizational innovation adoption: A multi-level framework of determinants and opportunities for future research. *Journal of Business Research, 5*, 163–176.

Goldman, H. H., Ganju, V., Drake, R. E., Gorman, P., Hogan, M. F., & Hyde, P. S. (2001). Policy implications for implementing evidence-based practices. *Psychiatric Services, 52,* 1591–1597.

Hambrick, D. C., & Mason, P. A. (1984). Upper echelons: The organization as a reflection of its top managers. *Academy of Management Review, 9,* 193–206.

Hanley, M. R., Stuart, M. E., & Kirz, H. L. (1994). An evidence-based approach to evaluating and improving clinical practice. *Practice Guidelines: HMO Practice, 8,* 75–83.

Hickson, D. J., Butler, R. J., Cray, D., Mallory, G. R., & Wilson, D. C. (1986). *Top decisions: Strategic decision making in organizations.* San Francisco: Jossey-Bass.

Huber, G. P., & Glick, W. H. (Eds.). (1995). *Organizational change and redesign: Ideas and insights for improving performance.* New York: Oxford University Press.

Igbaria, M., Parasuraman, M., & Barudi, J. (1996). A motivational model of microcomputer usage. *Journal of Management Information Systems, 13,* 127–143.

Klein, K., & Sorre, J. S. (1996). The challenge of innovation implementation. *Academy of Management Review, 21,* 1055–1080.

Klein, K. J., Conn, A. B., & Sorra, J. S. (2001). Implementing computerized technology: An organizational analysis. *Journal of Applied Psychology, 86,* 811–825.

Leonard-Barton, D. (1988). Implementation characteristics of organizational innovations: Limits and opportunities for management strategies [Special Issue]. *Innovative Research on Innovations and Organizations, 15,* 603–631.

Lewis, L. K., & Siebold, D. R. (1993). Innovation modification during intraorganizational adoption, *Academy of Management Review, 18,* 322–354.

Linton, J. D. (2002). Implementation research: State of the art and future directions. *Technovation, 22,* 65–79.

Majahan, V., & Peterson, R. A. (1985). *Models for innovation diffusion.* Newbury Park, CA: Sage.

Mathieson, K. (1991). Predicting user intentions: Comparing the technology acceptance model with the theory of planned behavior. *Information Systems Research, 2,* 173–191.

McFarlane, W. R., McNary, S., Dixon, L., Hornby, M. A., & Cimett, E. (2001). Predictors of dissemination of family psychoeducation in community mental health centers in Maine and Illinois. *Psychiatric Services, 52,* 935–942.

Meyer, A. D., & Goes, J. B. (1988). Organizational assimilation of innovations: A multilevel contextual analysis. *Academy of Management Journal, 31*, 897–923.

Mintzberg, H. (1975). The manager's job: Folklore and fact. *Harvard Business Review, 53*, 49–61.

National Association of State Mental Health Program Directors (NASMHPD) (2003, May). *Funding sources and expenditures of state mental health agencies for fiscal year 2001: Final report.* Alexandria, VA: Author.

National Association of State Mental Health Program Directors Research Institute. (2002a, June). Implementation of evidence-based services by state mental health agencies, 2001. *State Profile Highlights*, No. 02-02.

Nutt, P. C. (1992). *Planning methods for healthcare organizations* (2nd ed). New York: Wiley.

Panzano, P. C., Roth, D., & Crane-Ross, D. (2001). The innovation diffusion and adoption research project (IDARP): Moving from the diffusion of research results to promoting the adoption of evidence-based innovations in the Ohio mental health system. *New Research in Mental Health, 15*. (Available from the Ohio Department of Mental Health, Office of Program Evaluation and Research.)

President's New Freedom Commission on Mental Health. (2003). *Achieving the promise: Transforming mental health care in America.* SDHHS Publication No. SMA- 03-3832, Rockville, MD.

Rice, R. E., & Rogers, E. M. (1980). Re-invention in the innovation process. *Knowledge, 1*, 499–514.

Rogers, E. M. (1995). *Diffusion of innovations* (4th ed.). New York: Free Press.

Roth, D., Panzano, P., Crane-Ross, D., & Seffrin, B. (2003, February). *Factors associated with the adoption and successful assimilation of evidence-based practices.* National Association of State Mental Health Program Directors, National Research Institute, Baltimore, MD.

Torrey, W. C., Drake, R. E., Dixon, L., Burns, B. J., Rush, A. J., Clark, R. E., & Klatzker, D. (2001). Implementing evidence-based practices for persons with severe mental illnesses. *Psychiatric Services, 52*(1), 45–50.

U.S. Department of Health and Human Services (DHHS). (1999). *Mental health: A report of the Surgeon General.* Washington, DC: Author.

Van de Ven, A. H., Angle, H. L., & Poole, S. (Eds.). (2000). *Research on the management of innovation: The Minnesota studies.* New York: Oxford University.

Wolfe, R. A. (1994). Organization innovation: Review, critique, and suggested research directions. *Journal of Management Studies, 31,* 405–430.

Yin, R. K. (1978). *Changing urban bureaucracies: How new practices become routinized.* Santa Monica, CA: Rand.

Zajonc, R. B. (1984). On the primacy of affect. *American Psychologist, 39,* 117–123.

Zaltman, G., Duncan, R., & Holbeck, J. (1973). *Innovation and Organizations.* New York: Wiley.

TWELVE

# The Interface of Cultural Competency and Evidence-Based Practices

*Carole Siegel*
*Gary Haugland*
*Robert Schore*

MAJOR DEMOGRAPHIC SHIFTS MAY RESULT in a greater likelihood that people with severe mental illness may be from diverse cultural groups. It is a challenge for mental health providers to find ways to ameliorate the differences in services provided to culturally diverse groups. The consensus of stakeholders of the mental health system is that the promotion of cultural competency (CC) in mental health services will ameliorate problems related to disparities in access to, receipt of, and outcomes of mental health services (Brach & Fraser, 2000). Both the 2001 Surgeon General's supplement on minorities (U.S. Department of Health and Human Services), and the 2003 President's New Freedom Commission on Mental Health recognize that improved access for cultural groups to quality care that is culturally competent is required.

There are several definitions of CC, each representing the consensus of different national groups who strive to improve treatment services for cultural groups. One such definition, formulated by Siegel, Chambers, and colleagues is: "The attribute of a behavioral health care organization that describes the set of congruent behaviors, attitudes and

Definition of cultural competency

skills, policies and procedures that enable its caregivers to work effectively and efficiently in cross/multicultural situations at all of its organizational levels" (2000, p. 92). Concrete standards and performance measures have been developed in response to this definition. The premise is that if a person's cultural characteristics and values are understood, respected, and reflected in the treatment engagement and delivery processes, then the person will be more responsive to, and satisfied with, the services provided and therefore experience greater benefits. The acceptance of this premise has led to efforts on the part of federal, state, and cultural groups to incorporate principles of CC into mental health delivery systems, to introduce procedures to monitor how well mental health systems follow these principles, and to develop tools to monitor progress.

**EBPs and CC**

One method of improving treatment is through the implementation of evidence-based practices (EBPs). In the national EBP project, CC has been taken into consideration in the promotion of these services. All stakeholder groups have reviewed the EBP toolkits for how language applies to culture and to determine whether the vignettes used reflect cultural diversity. Scientific evidence, however, is limited for cultures other than the major culture.

This dearth of evidence raises several questions that will need to be answered as EBPs are implemented nationwide. Can an EBP that has not been tested on a cultural group be considered an EBP for that group? Or, if the EBP is tailored to the culture by an organization, can the adapted EBP still be considered a scientifically supported EBP? How is the fidelity measurement impacted by cultural applications? This chapter discusses several of these issues. First, we describe the service problems of minority cultures and efforts that have been made to improve service delivery. We then describe the construct of CC and tools for its measurement. Lastly, we discuss the salient role of CC in the adaptation and implementation of EBPs when an agency provides mental health treatment services to people from diverse cultures.

## Problems Experienced by Culturally Diverse Groups in Mental Health Treatment

In studies of health outcomes, people from minority groups show higher prevalence rates for physical and mental illnesses than the dominant population group. These findings are attributed, in part, to the lower socioeconomic status of many cultural minority groups who have less access to health care and less favorable outcomes. Contributing conditions include housing segregation, substandard education, unsafe working conditions, and increased at-risk social behaviors (George Washington University, 1997).

In a report by the U.S. Surgeon General, it was noted that "even more than other areas of health and medicine, the mental health field is plagued by disparities in the availability and access to its services" (1999, p. iv). People from multicultural ethnic groups bear the heaviest burden of unmet mental health needs and reduced productivity (U.S. Department of Health and Human Services, 1999, 2001). Barriers to accessing services include financial deterrents, lack of insurance, lack of primary care physicians to expedite referrals, and failure of programs to locate close to the population base of minority consumers, or provide service delivery schedules that would accommodate employed individuals or parents with child-care responsibilities, or provide services in the languages of the population being served (U.S. Department of Health and Human Services, SAMHSA, 1997). Where insurance is available, managed care may compound problems. Many managed care organizations have rules and regulations that are not written in the language of the minority cultures served and, therefore, cannot be understood by consumers and their families. Cultural group members often lack the know-how to negotiate the managed care plan. Some plans offer lower levels of reimbursement for treating the very disorders that occur more frequently among minorities, including alcoholism, chemical dependency, and posttraumatic stress disorders (Sanchez et al., 1997b). Often, decisions that affect

Barriers to treatment

consumer care are made by managed care planning administrators who are away from treatment locations and who lack knowledge of the specific cultures served and their unique needs (Dana, 1998). The President's New Freedom Commission on Mental Health (2003) cited barriers to adequate care that result in

- Racial and ethnic minorities' hesitancy to seek treatment in the current system
- Stigma that surrounds mental illnesses
- Unfair treatment limitations and financial requirements placed on mental health benefits in private health insurance
- The fragmented mental health service delivery system

**Social stigma and lack of information**

Problems are further compounded by the failure of existing mental health programs to accommodate needs idiosyncratic to particular cultures. Consumers from cultural groups experience strong feelings of social stigma and a lack of information about health services that often result in delayed treatment. Treatment, therefore, is sought only when symptoms have become severe and difficult to treat and community and family support systems have been exhausted (Munoz & Sanchez, n.d.; Rogler, Cortes, & Malgady, 1991; U.S. Department of Health and Human Services, SAMHSA 1997). Among cultural groups, family members and alternative health healers are more likely to be relied on in the early phases of mental illness than the formal mental health system. Others turn to primary care physicians, rather than the mental health system, for help

**Latinos**

with problems of mental illness. The traditional approach to treating the mental health needs of Latinos often overlooks their cultural framework, which values family support and involvement (Tirado, 1996). Asian/Pacific Islander

**Asian-Pacific Islanders**

consumers find few agencies with personnel who speak their languages or who are knowledgeable about their culture and as a result, they often seek help from alternative, traditional healers (U.S. Department of Health and

Human Services, Asian and Pacific Islander American Task Force, 1997). Native Americans face obstacles to obtaining services because of an archaic structure of federal and tribal agencies that are underfunded and poorly coordinated. A history of oppression, forced relocations, and weakening of tribal structures contributes to the emotional problems faced by Native Americans (Sanchez et al., 1997a). The experience of African American consumers is that clinical issues often "are not examined from an ethnic or racial perspective because such views do not fit the dominant cultural perspective," and the dominant culture does not take into account discrimination, community, family, and spirituality in addressing critical life experiences (Davis, n.d.).

Native Americans

African Americans

The failure to accommodate cultural groups results in a lower utilization of community services by members of cultural minorities, compared to the dominant population. By the time help is sought, emotional problems have become severe and minority group members are likely to require hospitalization, often on an involuntary basis, at rates three times greater than the general population (Munoz & Sanchez, n.d.; Sanchez et al., 1997a; Snowden & Clancy, 1990; Ying & Hu, 1994). Language barriers and difficulties in communication at points of admission, assessment, and treatment can lead to inappropriate treatment, misdiagnosis, ineffective case management, and inadequate referrals for needed services (Lopez & Hernandez, 1986; New York State Office of Mental Health [NYSOMH], 1997; Sue, Fujino, Hu, Takeuchi, & Zane, 1991). Individuals with lower socioeconomic status tend to receive more severe diagnoses (Munoz & Sanchez, n.d.), and misdiagnosis contributes to inappropriate hospital admissions. Cultural misunderstandings by clinicians are also a factor leading to incomplete assessments, improper diagnoses or treatment, and failed treatment alliances (Kirmayer, Groleua, Guzder, Bla, & Jarvis, 2003). As a further result, many people with severe mental illness who seek services feel alienated and leave treatment prema-

Ramifications of failure to accommodate cultural groups

turely (Proctor & Davis, 1994; Snowden, 1996, 2001). Delays in entering service and early terminations create a cyclical reliance on more costly services (Munoz & Sanchez, n.d.).

## Efforts to Improve Cultural Competency

A primary focus has been to remove language barriers that hinder access to both general and mental health care for minority populations (Baker, Parker, Williams, Coates, & Pitkin, 1998; Knisley, 1991; Tirado, 1996). A Presidential Executive Order mandated that language assistance be provided to individuals with limited English proficiency (LEP), whenever health services are delivered in programs receiving federal dollars (Federal Register, 2000). The U.S. Department of Health and Human Services, Office of Civil Rights (2000), published written guidelines and allowed for flexible implementation depending on the circumstances of individual facilities and the size of the user populations with LEP.

Insufficient evidence for multicultural groups

Studies have begun to examine the advantages gained when bilingual professionals are employed in mental health agencies (Manoleas, Organista, Negron-Velasquez, & McCormick, 2000; Tobin, Chen, Edwards, & Chan, 2000). Several studies also pointed to the need for interventions that go beyond language factors (Brach & Fraser, 2000; Flaskerud, 1986; Heinrich, Corbine, & Thomas, 1990; Manoleas et al., 2000; Snowden & Clancy, 1990; Sue et al., 1991) and that increase cultural sensitivity (Herrick & Brown, 1998; Resnicow, Baranowski, Ahluwalia, & Braithwaite, 1999). Overall, however, evidence is lacking about mental health techniques that would effectively meet the needs of multicultural groups (Brach & Fraser, 2000; Johnson & Cameron, 2001; Leong & Lau, 2001; Phillips, Mayer, & Aday; 2000; Saha, Taggart, Komaromy, & Bindman; 2000; Snowden, 2001; Vega & Lopez, 2001).

Definition of cultural group

The implementation and sustenance of CC in behavioral health-care organizations are thought to be the most effective strategies for improving mental health services for cultural groups. In its broadest sense, a cultural group might be defined by commonality in thinking, acting, feeling, values, beliefs, customs, and perceiving the world. Most groups working on CC have received input about the concerns of the four major cultural groups named in the Surgeon General's Report. These groups, defined by race, ethnicity, and language needs, are African American, Asian/Pacific Islander, Latino, and Native American/ Alaskan Native. However, work on CC takes into account that within these groups there are many subgroups that can differ substantially from each other and from the dominant cultural base. A multicultural situation is one in which one or more of these cultural groups are part of the population served by the organization. From the broader perspective, however, a cultural group may be identified as a group that requires special considerations, including, for example, people with hearing impairments or rural farmers.

Although the definition of CC may be clear, it does not specify the desirable behaviors, attitudes, skills, polices, and procedures that comprise and facilitate it. Many groups have worked to provide the details and building blocks of CC through the specification of standards. Outstanding among these efforts are the Culturally and Linguistically Appropriate Services (CLAS) standards endorsed for mental health and substance abuse by SAMHSA (U.S. Department of Health and Human Services, Office of Minority Health, 2001a, 2001b). The standards (see Table 12.1) address staff attitudes, staff training, and both written and oral language capacity for communication, planning, community partnerships, data needs and information sharing.

| Standards of culturally and linguistically appropriate services

The President's New Freedom Commission Report on Mental Health (2003) emphasizes certain organizational behaviors and policies regarding services and staff deemed essential to CC:

| New Freedom Commission Report

1. Tailoring or developing services for culturally diverse populations.

2. Having a mental health service provider workforce that includes members of ethnic, cultural, and linguistic minorities as well as individuals who share and respect the beliefs, norms, values, and communication patterns of culturally diverse populations.

3. Conducting research and training to aid clinicians in how to appropriately tailor interventions to the needs of consumers, recognizing such factors as race, culture, ethnicity, and locale.

---

**TABLE 12.1**

**National Standards on Culturally and Linguistically Appropriate Services (CLAS)**

---

The organization:

1. Should ensure that patients/consumers receive effective, understandable, and respectful care from all staff members that is provided in a manner compatible with their cultural health beliefs and practices and preferred language.

2. Should implement strategies to recruit, retain, and promote a diverse staff and leadership at all levels of the organization that are representative of the demographic characteristics of the service area.

3. Should ensure that staff at all levels and across all disciplines receive ongoing education and training in culturally and linguistically appropriate service delivery.

4. Must offer and provide language assistance services, including bilingual staff and interpreter services, at no cost to each patient/consumer with limited English proficiency, at all points of contact and in a timely manner during all hours of operation.

5. Must provide patients/consumers with both verbal offers and written notices, in their preferred language, informing them of their right to receive language assistance services.

6. Must assure the competence of language assistance provided by interpreters and bilingual staff to patients/consumers with limited English proficiency. Family and friends should not be used to provide interpretation services (except on request by the patient/consumer).

*Continued on following page*

**TABLE 12.1** (*continued*)

7. Must make available easily understood patient-related materials and post signage in the languages of the commonly encountered groups and/or groups represented in the service area.

8. Should develope, implement, and promote a written strategic plan that outlines clear goals, policies, operational plans, and management accountability/oversight mechanisms to provide culturally and linguistically appropriate services.

9. Should conduct initial and ongoing organizational self-assessments of CLAS-related activities, and are encouraged to integrate cultural and linguistic competence-related measures into their internal audits, performance improvement programs, patient satisfaction assessments, and outcome-based evaluations.

10. Should ensure that data on the individual patient's/comsumer's race, ethnicity, and spoken and written language are collected in health records, integrated into the organization's management information systems, and periodically updated.

11. Should maintain a current demographic, cultural, ad epidemiological profile of the community as well as a needs assessment to accurately plan for and implemeny services that respond to the cultural and linguistic characteristics of the service area.

12. Should develop participatory, collaborative partnerships with communities and utilize a variety of formal and informal mechanisms to facilitate community and patient/consumer involvement in designing and implementing CLAS-related activities.

13. Should ensure that conflict and grievance resolution processes are culturally and linguistically sensitive and capable of identifying, preventing, and resolving cross-cultural conflicts or complaints by patients/consumers.

14. Are encouraged to regularly make available to the public information about their progress and successful innovations in implementing the CLAS standards and to provide public notice in their communities about the availability of this information.

---

The Substance Abuse and Mental Health Services Administration (SAMHSA) has been at the forefront in promoting CC in mental health systems and organizations. It has identified specific areas within mental health | SAMHSA promotes cultural competency

programs where CC issues arise (Tirado, 1996). Measures of
CC have been added to a consumer-oriented "report card"
on mental health programs that assesses the quality and
cost of services (SAMHSA, 1996). It has developed principles and standards regarding policies, perspectives, and
attitudes, knowledge and experience, practices and skills,
and evaluation and accountability (Munoz &Sanchez, n.d.;
WICHE, 1998, 1999). As the primary sponsor of the EBP
Project, SAMHSA has required integration of CC information into the implementation resource kits. Most recently,
SAMHSA has funded projects to develop CC performance
measures and their benchmarks (Siegel, Haugland, &
Chambers, 2000, 2003). This project is described below.

**States promote cultural competency**

A number of states has developed standards for culturally competent mental health treatment, including
*California* (California Health Ethnic Service Managers,
1995; Pettigrew, 1997; Tirado, 1996), *New York* (Aponte &
Mason, 1996; New York State Office of Mental Health,
1997), *Arizona* (Dillenberg & Carbone, 1995), and *Texas*
(Saldana, Mosty, Rodriquez, Luna, & Gilbert, 1997; Saldana
& McRoy, 1995). Some of these states have developed
specific assessment tools (Chambers et al., 1998; Marti,
2001; Weiss & Minsky, 1996). There remains, however,
broad variation in how each state promotes CC within
mental health programs under this aegis (Stork et al.,
2001).

**Professional groups promote cultural competency**

In addition to governmental activities, professional disciplines also have addressed CC issues by providing guidelines and tools for promoting culturally competent
practices among their members. For example:

*Social workers:* National Association of Social Workers,
National Committee on Racial and Ethnic Diversity,
2001
*Nurses:* Campinha-Bacote, 1994
*Psychiatrists:* Group for the Advancement of Psychiatry,
Committee on Cultural Psychiatry, 2002; Mezzich et al.,
1996

*Psychologists*: American Psychological Association (2002) Guidelines for Providers of Psychological Services to Ethnic, Linguistic, and Culturally Diverse Populations, 2002 (*http:// www.apa.org*)
*Counselors*: Sue, Arredondo, & McDavis, 1992

Similar efforts to develop a culturally competent psychotherapy approach have been reported in Canada (Lo & Fung, 2003).

At the grass-roots level, cultural groups have developed their own organizations to promote CC in mental health services. These include the National Leadership Council on African American Mental Health, the National Alliance for Hispanic Health (SAMHSA, 2001), and the Gathering of Native Americans (U.S. Department of Health and Human Services, Center for Substance Abuse Prevention, 1999). Outlines, standards, and training manuals are being produced. | Cultural groups promote cultural competency

Performance measures assess how well CC standards are being met by an organization. The Lewin Group (2001) has conducted an extensive literature review for the Human Resources Service Administration on measuring CC (see *http://www.hrsa.gov/OMH/*). Based on this review, they published a list of potential indicators of CC for health-care organizations. | Measuring cultural competency

Several CC assessment scales have been developed, but none has yet been psychometrically tested. Most are self-assessment scales intended to assess clinicians' or administrators' level of CC. For example: | Existing CC scales for clinicians

Inventory for Assessing the Process of Cultural Competence among Health Care Professionals, Campinha-Bacote, 1998
Cultural Competence Self-Assessment Instrument, Child Welfare League of America, 1993
Cultural Competence Self-Assessment Questionnaire, Mason, 1995
Self-Assessment of Cultural Competence

Program Self-Assessment Survey for Cultural Competence, New Jersey Division of Mental Health Services 1996

Self-Assessment Checklist for Personnel Providing Services and Supports to Children with Special Health Needs and their Families, Goode & Tawara, 2002

**Existing CC scales for organizations**

A few organizational-level scales have been developed (e.g., Dana, et al, 1992; Roizer, 1996). The Vancouver region of the Ministry for Children and Families has an organizational level instrument on its website (*http://www.mcf.gov.bc.ca/publications/*) designed to assist community agencies in acquiring CC. The Cultural Competency Assessment Scale, described below, is one of the few scales to assess CC on an organizational level by examining the organization's procedures and policies.

**New measurement approaches**

Performance measures of CC, along with their benchmarks, were recently selected in a SAMHSA-funded project. An expert panel of multicultural mental health stakeholders, comprised of planners, providers, consumers, family members, and persons who have conducted activities to increase CC in health-care organizations, guided the work of the project. In addition, consumer focus group reviews were held in several states. Extant definitions of CC in health-care organizations were made specific to the activities, procedures, and behaviors that would need to be in place for an organization to be assessed as culturally competent. An extensive review of existing literature regarding CC in health and mental health systems was conducted.

**CC assessment domains**

Using this material, six domains were identified: (1) needs assessment, (2) information exchange, (3) services, (4) human resources, (5) policies and planning, all of which are linked to (6) outcomes. The project also identified the levels of an organization that need to be involved in the delivery of culturally competent services: At the administrative level, a public mental health authority or a managed care entity; at the service delivery level, direct providers of service in the community; at the individual

level, persons involved directly or indirectly with the
delivery of care. Performance measures were defined for
each of these domains to determine whether or not a CC
activity takes place (New York State Office of Mental
Health, 1998; Siegel et al, 2000)

Subsequently, the selected set of measures were further
reduced in number and benchmarks for these were identified. To assist in the benchmarking task, panelists identified
21 "good-practice" sites. Key informants at the sites participated in a telephone survey interview. Data were collected
on whether and how a set of delineated activities actually
occurred at each site. The project team used this information to develop a set of CC benchmarks for the reduced set
of measures.

Criteria for benchmarks formulated in terms of (1) an
activity that should take place, and (2) details on specific
features of that activity. For example, for the indicator "an
agency should have a CC committee," the benchmark was:
(1) "There is a CC committee if there are prevalent
(threshold level) cultural groups in the agency's target
community," and (2) "details on the composition of the
committee" (New York State Office of Mental Health, 2002;
Siegel et al., 2003).

| Benchmarking task

## The Cultural Competency Assessment Scale

In the process of implementing an EBP, a scale that measures CC for an organization would provide useful information about how to enhance the effectiveness of that practice
in order to achieve maximum benefit for consumers and
family members. Presumably, sites that have greater levels
of CC might have greater ease in implementing/adapting
EBPs.

The performance measures and their benchmarks were
used to develop the Cultural Competency Assessment Scale
(CCAS), designed as an organizational-level instrument for
behavioral health-care service settings that serve multicultural groups and intended to be used as an organizational

| Organizational self-
assessment tool

self-assessment tool. The scale items describe concrete activities believed to be essential for establishing or improving CC. The specificity of the items makes the CCAS substantially different from other scales.

**Pilot tested** | The design of the scale is consistent with the fidelity instruments for EBPs; that is, for each criterion, there is a graduated 5-point scoring system. In consultation with expert panel members, 11 key CC areas were chosen along with the items for each of the levels on a 5-point scale. The CCAS has already been pilot tested for content relevance, scale-item ordering, clarity of terms, and feasibility of administration. Its reliability and validity will be tested in the near future. The 11 areas and the activities covered within each of their 5-point scales are:

1. Organizational commitment to CC—having a responsible staff person, an identifiable budget, and a comprehensive plan to address cultural issues.
2. Assessment of service needs—having data on the number of persons by race, ethnicity, country of origin, preferred language for persons currently being served and for persons in the target community, and identification of prevalent cultural groups.
3. Cultural input into agency activities—indication of active participation of persons from prevalent cultural groups in directing CC activities through a participatory mechanism such as an advisory committee.
4. Integration of CC committee/group within organization—having a service review function as part of the CC advisory committee (or other group) and CC activities integrated within the organization.
5. CC staff training—having requirements for staff training/education.
6. Recruitment, hiring, and retention of CC staff—having hiring and retention strategies aimed at increasing prevalent cultural group representation among staff.

7. Language capacity/interpreters—providing interpreters, when needed, at point of first access and at service encounters for prevalent cultural groups.

8. Language capacity/ bilingual staff—having bilingual staff members to provide service to user cultural groups with significant numbers in need of language assistance.

9. Language capacity/translation of key forms—having key forms available in languages of prevalent cultural groups.

10. Language capacity/service descriptions and educational materials—having educational materials about behavioral health problems and treatment options available in languages and formats understood by prevalent cultural groups of the target community.

11. Assessment/adaptation and introduction of services—reviewing services and adapting existing services or introduction of services to address unique cultural needs of prevalent cultural groups of service users.

## Salient Role of CC in the Implementation and Adaptation of EBPs

Both national and state mental health agencies are promoting the dissemination and implementation of EBPs into the service delivery community. The goal is to help consumers in the most effective manner possible. Practices will help consumers most effectively when the agency addresses the diverse cultural issues related to the people they serve at every level of the organization.

Culturally competent agencies that are implementing EBPs are likely to examine whether the EBP needs adaptations to meet the needs of their clients. In some cases, this may be easy to determine and no adaptation is required. Drake and colleagues stated: "Because supported employment improves outcomes for whites, African-Americans,

Cultural adaptation and EBP fidelity

and Hispanics, offering it to other cultural minorities would be a logical decision unless there are obvious cultural differences in the meaning of work" (2001, p. 182). On the other hand, although medication algorithms could be endorsed as an EBP, specific racial and ethnic groups may need specific guidelines (U.S. Department of Health and Human Services, 1999, 2001). If adaptation of the EBPs for cultures is required, the limits of change need to be determined for it to still be considered an EBP. Furthermore, it is crucial to consider the extent to which cultural adaptations may influence an agency's fidelity for a specific EBP, especially if fidelity assessments are tied to funding or other regulations. But even if the EBP is judged suitable for the cultural group, it still is necessary that an organization be CC in terms of the language and other specific cultural needs of the population who are receiving services from the agency staff.

**Cultural-specific outcomes**

In evaluating the success of an EBP for consumers and families from diverse cultural groups, the results need to be judged in terms of culture-specific outcomes as well as usual outcomes. For example, if family participation is culturally desirable, a measure of this behavior should be included. Ascertaining consumer satisfaction with EBPs requires repeated assessment, evaluation, and feedback in an ongoing quality improvement process. In terms of outcomes, if the EBP is used both by the cultural group and a predominant majority group, outcomes of the two groups should be compared, controlling for factors that might impact the outcomes. The six As of CC and EBPs are presented in Table 12.2.

**Quality improvement process**

**EBPs will require adaptation for cultural groups**

As with most research on mental health interventions, the evidence base is strongest for members of the majority culture. The best approach for endorsement of an EBP for a cultural group would be through research on that group. Because there are many groups to consider, developing acceptable principles of adaptation may be more pragmatic. There are features of ACT specified in the Dartmouth Assertive Community Treatment Scale

(DACTS) that might be amenable to adaptation. The areas in which CC could be addressed include program staffing, the types of services provided, the nature of engagement mechanisms, and connections to informal support systems.

---

**TABLE 12.2**
**The Six A's of Cultural Competency and Evidence-Based Practices**

---

1. **A**nalysis: There should be scientific evidence that the EBP works for the cultures of an organization. If there is no evidence, there should be a consensus opinion that lack of evidence should not matter.
2. **A**ccommodation: An organization should have in place elements of CC that would facilitate the introduction and implementation of an EBP.
   *Example*: If language capacity has already been addressed, this will facilitate the introduction and use of an EBP.
3. **A**ssessment: An organization should examine the EBP for its suitability to the cultures it is intended to serve. Features of an EBP may make it unsuitable for a culture.
   *Example*: Family involvement may not be acceptable to people from certain cultures.
4. **A**daptation: An entity needs to be in place (or be identified) that can adapt the practice, if appropriate, to cultural groups.
   *Example*: If a small independent organization serves Asian groups, a university affiliate might be approached to develop appropriate medication guidelines.
5. **A**ppraisal of fidelity: Fidelity scales should be adjusted to reflect cultural adaptations or cultural requisites, especially if reimbursement is tied to its scores
6. **A**ppraisal of outcomes: The terms of client outcome measurement should be relevant to a culture and should include consumer satisfaction with the service. If the service is also used by majority groups, minority comparisons with majority groups on clinical and functional outcomes should be examined.

---

DACTS has specific staffing requirements, but these do not address the CC of staff. It is well recognized that workforce diversity is a desirable goal (President's New Freedom Commission on Mental Health, 2003), and CC requires that

DACTS requirements and CC

an organization recruit, hire, and retain staff members who have experience with, or are from, the prevalent nonmajority cultural groups it serves. In addition, training in CC for direct service staff and for staff at other levels of the organization must become an integral part of the ongoing educational and training activities of the agency. Furthermore, the provision of language assistance is required for those cultural groups who have members with LEP. It is often best to hire bilingual staff. This is also a lower-cost option than utilizing interpreter services when there is a high number of persons requiring language assistance. Treatment teams that serve persons with LEP would benefit from bilingual members.

The DACTS measures the extent to which the program provides a broad array of services. CC requires that these services be reviewed to ensure that cultural issues are adequately addressed and that alternative services are made available when existing services are not suitable for the prevalent cultural groups. Information about services provided by the organization needs to be understood not only by persons with LEP but also by persons with limited reading skills. Service descriptions must be available in prevalent languages of the community and in formats that are understandable at a basic literacy level.

DACT specifies assertive engagement strategies that need to be considered from a cultural perspective. For example, in urban areas where there may be undocumented immigrants in the families of persons in ACT programs, it may be hard to work with the family if these members choose to remain hidden. The relationship between the ACT team and the consumer may be at risk if the family feels threatened by team member contacts with parole officers, landlords, and employers. The role of family members in treatment can best be learned from members of the culture in the community. This information is also critical to developing effective strategies in working with a consumer's informal support group.

The implementation of all of the EBPs will benefit, by helping consumers to achieve their goals most effectively, from a CC review in every community mental health center. Here we briefly summarize some issues of CC that might need to be addressed for EBPs.

For integrated dual-disorders treatment, CC would ensure that staff receive education about the cultures served, and that, when available, screening tools and assessments that have been validated for different cultural groups would be used and translated into appropriate languages.

Integrated dual-disorders treatment and CC

Organizations that offer supported employment services benefit from knowledge of cultural aspects of work and employment, poverty, and supports for persons who do not work and for those trying to enter competitive employment. Language is often a key component of successful employment.

Supported employment and CC

Illness management and recovery and family psychoeducation are most effective when the treatment providers understand the variance of sanctions and supports from a consumer's support group that are based on cultural diversity. The cultural dynamics within families influence the acceptance of information about mental illness as well as substance use and abuse. These elements are critical when engaging consumers and family members in the treatment process. Issues surrounding LEP and level of educational attainment contribute to the successful implementation of illness management. Additional issues concern culture-bound behaviors, such as deference based on age and gender, respect for authority figures, and commitment to a Western-medicine-based treatment plan.

Illness management and recovery, family psychoeducation, and CC

There is a large and growing body of research evidence about gender and age differences in medication dosage ranges, side effects, and overall effectiveness that is relevant to medication management. Evidence about racial and cultural differences is not as well established. NIH/NIMH and other federal agencies have embarked on research programs to expand this knowledge base. Medication efficacy may have a strong cultural component. The relation-

Medication management and CC

ships between professional caregivers and informal (e.g., family) support groups may strongly influence the acceptability and use of "Western" medications. In addition, factors associated with the effectiveness of medication treatments may also have cultural underpinnings. For these reasons, it is important that the cultural aspects of medication management are not only explored in scientific research but also be made part of staff education and training in agencies that serve culturally diverse populations. Knowledge of the cultures will also enable clinicians to understand the complementary role that non-western interventions (e.g., acupuncture, herbal remedies) play in the overall treatment of a person with strong ties to traditional culture. Respect for other values, beliefs, and health practices can help to ensure effectiveness of medication management and continued engagement in the therapeutic process.

**Development of a CC evidence base**

As a final note, CC itself is an organizational practice that would benefit from an evidence base. The adoption of CC practices, policies, and behaviors by an organization will be more likely to happen when there is scientific evidence that such practices reduce disparities in the ways that consumers and family members from diverse cultures engage in, and benefit from, mental health treatment services. Additionally, effective and earlier engagement offers the opportunity not only to reduce costs, but also to reduce poor outcomes associated with delays in receiving effective treatments. With the gathering of evidence for cost-effectiveness and better outcomes, CC will itself become an EBP.

## References

American Psychological Association (APA). (2002). APA guidelines for providers of psychological services to ethnic, linguistic and culturally diverse populations. Retrieved September 1, 2004, from *http://www.apa.org.*

Aponte, C., & Mason, J. (1996). A demonstration project of cultural competence self-assessment of 26 agencies. In M. Roizner (Ed.), *A practical guide for the assessment of cultural competence in children's mental health organizations* (pp. 72–73). Boston: Judge Baker Children's Center.

Baker, D. W., Parker, R. M., Williams, M. V., Coates, W. C., & Pitkin, K. (1998). Use and effectiveness of interpreters in an emergency department. *Journal of the American Medical Association, 275*, 738–788.

Brach, C., & Fraser I. (2000). Can cultural competency reduce racial and ethnic health disparities? A review and conceptual model. *Medical Care Research Review, 57*(Suppl. 1), 181–217.

California Mental Health Ethnic Services Managers. (1995). *Cultural competency goals, strategies and standards for mental health care to ethnic clients* Sacramento, CA: Author, with Managed Care Committee, California Mental Health Directors Association.

Campinha-Bacote, J. (1994). Cultural competence in psychiatric mental health nursing: A conceptual model. *Nursing Clinical North America, 29*, 1–8.

Campinha-Bacote, J. (1998). *Inventory for Assessing the Process of Cultural Competence (IAPCC) among health care professionals.* Cincinnati, OH: Transcultural C.A.R.E. Associates.

Chambers, E. D., Siegel, C., Haugland, G., Aponte, C., Bank, R., & Blackshear, R. (1998). *A framework for the development of performance measures of cultural competency in managed care and other mental health organizations.* Albany: New York State Office of Mental Health.

Dana, R. H. (1998). Problems with managed mental health care for multicultural populations. *Psychological Reports, 83*, 283–294.

Davis, K. (1997). *Consumer driven standards and guidelines in managed mental health for populations of African descent: Final report on cultural competence.* Rockville, MD: Center for Mental Health Services.

Dillenberg, J., & Carbone, C. P. (1995). *Cultural competency in the administration and delivery of behavioral health services.* Phoeniz AZ: Arizona Department of Health Services.

Drake, R. E., Goldman, H. H., Leff, H. S., Lehman, A. F., Dixon, L., & Mueser, K. T. (2001). Implementing evidence-bBased practices in routine mental health service settings. *Psychiatric Services, 52*, 179–182

Federal Register Executive Order 13166. (2000). *Federal Register, 68*, 159.

Flaskerud, J. H. (1986). The effects of culture-compatible intervention on the untilization of mental health services by minority clients. *Community Mental Health Journal, 22*, 127–141.

George Washington University. (1997). *Cross-cultural competency in a managed care environment* (Issue Brief No. 705). Washington, DC: National Health Policy Forum.

Goode, T. D., & Tawara, D. (2002). *Self-assessment checklist for personnel providing services and supports to children with special needs and their families.* Washington, DC: Georgetown University Center for Child and Human Development.

Group for the Advancement of Psychiatry (GAP), Committee on Cultural Psychiatry. (2002). *Cultural assessment in clinical psychiatry* (Report 145). Washington, DC: American Psychiatric Associations.

Heinrich, R. K., Corbine, J. L., & Thomas, K. R. (1990). Counseling Native Americans. *Journal of Counseling and Development, 69*, 128–133.

Herrick, C. A., & Brown, H. N. (1998). Underutilization of mental health services by Asian-Americans residing in the United States. *Issues in Mental Health Nursing, 19*, 225–240.

Johnson, J. L., & Cameron, M. C. (2001). Barriers to providing effective mental health services to American Indians. *Mental Health Services Research, 3*, 181–187.

Kirmayer, L. J., Groleau, D., Guzder, J., Bla, C., & Jarvis, E. (2003). Cultural consultation: A model of mental health service for multicultural societies. *Canadian Journal of Psychiatry, 48*, 145–153.

Knisley, M. B. (1991). *Culturally sensitive language community certification standards.* Columbus, OH: Ohio Department of Mental Health.

Leong, F. T., & Lau, A. S. L. (2001). Barriers to effective mental health services to Asian Americans. *Mental Health Services Research, 3*, 215–223.

Lewin Group. (2001). *Health resources and services administration study on measuring cultural competence in health care delivery settings: A review of the literature.* Washington, DC: U.S. Department of Health and Human Services, Health Resources and Services Administration.

Lo, H., & Fung, K. (2003). Culturally competent psychotherapy. *Canadian Journal of Psychiatry, 48*, 161–170.

Lopez, S., & Hernandez, P. (1986). How culture is considered in evaluations of psychopathology. *Journal of Nervous and Mental Disease, 176*, 598–606.

Manoleas, P., Organista, K., Negron-Velasquez, G., & McCormick, K. (2000). Characteristics of Latino mental health clinicians: A preliminary examination. *Journal of Community Mental Health, 36*, 383–394.

Marti, S. (2001). Development of a culturally competent and recovery oriented system of care. *Mental Health American, Fall*, unpaginated newsletter.

Mason, J. L. (1995). *The cultural competence self-assessment questionnaire: A manual for users.* Portland, OR: Portland State University, Research and Training Center on Family Support and Children's Mental Health, Graduate School of Social Work.

Mezzich, J., Kleinman, A., Fabrega, H., & Parrow, D. L. (1996). *Culture and psychiatric diagnosis. A DSM-IV perspective.* Washington, DC: American Psychiatric Association.

Munoz, R. H., & Sanchez, A. M. (n.d.). *Developing culturally competent systems of care for state mental health services.* Boulder, CO: Western Interstate Commission for Higher Education.

National Association of Social Workers (NASW), National Committee on Racial and Ethnic Diversity. (2001). *Standards for cultural competence in social work.* Retrieved November 11, 2004, from *http://www.naswdc.org/pubs/standards/cultural.htm*

New Jersey Division of Mental Health Services (DMHS). (1996). *Program self-assessment survey for cultural competence.* Trenton, NJ: Author, Multicultural Services Advisory Committee.

New York State Office of Mental Health (OMH). (1997). *Cultural and linguistic competence standards.* Albany, NY: Author.

New York State Office of Mental Health (OMH). (1998). *Cultural competence performance measures for managed behavioral healthcare programs.* Albany, NY: Author.

New York State Office of Mental Health (OMH). (2002). *Cultural competency in mental health systems of care: Selection and benchmarking of performance measures.* Albany, NY: Author, Nathan Kline Institute for Psychiatric Research, Center for the Study of Issues in Public Mental Health.

Pettigrew, G. M. (1997). *Plan for culturally competent specialty mental health services.* Sacramento, CA: California Mental Health Planning Council.

Phillips, K. A., Mayer, M. L., & Aday, L. A. (2000). Barriers to care among racial/ethnic groups under managed care. *Health Affairs, 19,* 65–75.

President's New Freedom Commission on Mental Health. (2003). *Achieving the promise: Transforming mental health care in America.* DHHS Publication No. SMA-03-3832, Rockville, MD.

Proctor, E. K., & Davis L. E., (1994). The challenge of racial differences: Skills for clinical practice. *Social Work, 39,* 314–323.

Resnicow, K., Baranowski, T., Ahluwalia, J. S., & Braithwaite, R. (1999). Cultural sensitivity in public health: Defined and demystified. *Ethnicity and Disease, 9,* 10–21.

Rogler, L. H., Cortes, E. E., & Malgady, R. G. (1991). Acculturation and mental health status among Hispanics. *American Psychologist, 46,* 585–597.

Saha, S., Taggart, S. H., Komaromy, M., & Bindman, A. B. (2000). Do patients choose physicians of their own race? *Health Affairs, 19*(4), 76–83.

Saldana, D. H., & McRoy, R. G. (1995). *Conducting culturally sensitive and competent research.* Workshop presented at the national conference on State Mental Health Agency Services Research and Program Evaluation, San Antonio, TX.

Saldana, D. H., Mosty, M., Rodriquez, T., Luna, D., & Gilbert, D. (1997). *Development of a cultural competency score card/cultural assessment facility profile: General scoring guide.* Paper presented at national conference on State Mental Health Agency Services Research and Program Evaluation, Washington, DC.

Sanchez, A. M., et al. (1997a). *Cultural competence standards in mental health managed care for four underserved/underrepresented racial/ethnic groups.* Washington, DC: U.S. Department of Health and Human Services, Western Interstate Commission for Higher Education.

Sanchez, A. M. et al. (1997b). *Cultural competence guidelines for Native American populations.* Washington, DC: U.S. Department of Health and Human Services, Western Interstate Commission for Higher Education.

Siegel, C., Chambers, E. D., Haugland, G., Bank, R., Aponte, C., & McCombs, H. (2000). Performance measures of cultural competency in mental health organizations. *Administration and Policy in Mental Health, 28,* 91–106.

Siegel, C., Haugland, G., & Chambers, E. D. (2002). *Cultural competency methodological and data strategies to assess the quality of services in mental health systems of care.* Final report to SAMHSA/CMHS. Albany, NY: New York State Office of Mental Health, Center for the Study of Issues in Public Mental Health.

Siegel, C., Haugland, G., & Chambers, E. D. (2003). Performance measures and their benchmarks for assessing organizational cultural competency in behavioral health care service delivery. *Administration and Policy in Mental Health, 31*(2), 141–170.

Snowden, L. R. (1996). Ethnic minority populations and mental health outcomes. *New Directions for Mental Health Services, 71,* 79–87.

Snowden, L. R. (2001). Barriers to effective mental health services for African Americans. *Mental Health Services Research, 3*(4), 181–187.

Snowden, L. R., & Clancy, T. (1990). Service intensity and client improvement in a predominantly black community mental health center. *Evaluation and Program Planning, 13,* 205–210.

Stork, E., Scholle, S., Greeno, C., Copeland, V. C., Kehheher, K. (2001). Monitoring and enforcing cultrual competence in Medicaid managed behavioral health care. *Mental Health Services Research, 3*(3): 169–177.

Substance Abuse and Mental Health Services Administration (SAMHSA). (1996). *Consumer oriented mental health report card.* Rockville, MD.

Sue, D. W., Arredondo, P., & McDavis, R. J. (1992). Multicultural counseling competencies and standards: A call to the profession. *Journal of Counseling and Development, 70,* 477-483.

Sue, S., Fujino, D. C., Hu, L., Takeuchi, D. T., & Zane, N. W. S. (1991). Community mental health services for ethnic minority groups: A test of the cultural responsiveness hypothesis. *Journal of Consulting and Clinical Psychology, 59,* 533–540.

Tirado, M. D. (1996). *Tools for monitoring cultural competence in health care.* Final Project Report, Office of Planning and Evaluation, Health Resources and Services Administration, DHHS. San Francisco, CA: Latino Coalition for a Healthy California.

Tobin, M., Chen, L., Edwards, J. L., & Chan, S. (2000). Improving the utilisation of bilingual counsellors within a public sector mental health service. *Australian Health Review, 23,* 190–196.

United States Public Health Service Office of the Surgeon General (OSG). (2001). *Mental Health: Culture, Race, and Ethnicity: A supplement to mental health: A report of the Surgeon General.* Rockville, MD: Department of Health and Human Services, U.S. Public Health Service.

United States Public Health Service Office of the Surgeon General (OSG). (1999). *Mental Health: A report of the Surgeon General.* Rockville, MD: Department of Health and Human Services, U.S. Public health Service

U.S. Department of Health and Human Services (DHHS), Asian and Pacific Islander Task Force, SAMHSA. (1997). *Cultural competence guidelines in mental health managed care for Asian and Pacific Islanders.* Washington, DC: Author, Western Interstate Commission for Higher Education.

U.S. Department of Health and Human Services (DHHS), Center for Substance Abuse Prevention, SAMHSA. Indian Health Service (1999). *Gathering of Native Americans (GONA) facilitator guide.* Washington DC: Author.

U.S. Department of Health and Human Services (DHHS), National Alliance for Hispanic Health, SAMHSA. (2001). *Quality health services for Hispanics: The cultural competency component.* Washington, DC: Author.

U.S. Department of Health and Human Services (DHHS), Office of Civil Rights (OCR). (2000). *Policy guidance on the Title VI prohibition against national origin discrimination as it affects persons with limited English proficiency.* Washinbgton, DC: Author.

U.S. Department of Health and Human Services (DHHS), Office of Minority Health (OMH). (2001a). Office of Civil Rights focuses on Title VI policy, provides guidance for ensuring linguistic access. *Closing the Gap* (newsletter), Feb./March.

U.S. Department of Health and Human Services (DHHS), Office of Minority Health (OMH). (2001b). Revised CLAS standards from the Office of Minority Health. *Closing the Gap* (newsletter), Feb./March.

U.S. Department of Health and Human Services (DHHS), SAMHSA. (1997). *Cultural competence performance measures for managed behavioral health care programs.* Rockville, MD: Author.

Vega, W. A., & Lopez, S. R. (2001). Priority issues in Latino mental health services research. *Mental Health Services Research,* *3*(4), 189–200.

Weiss, C. I., & Minsky, S. (1996). *Program self-assessment survey for cultural competence: A manual.* Trenton: New Jersey Division of Mental Health Services.

Western Interstate Commission for Higher Education (WICHE) Mental Health Program, CMHS. (1998). *Cultural competence standards in managed mental health care for four underserved/underrepresented racial/ethnic groups.* Boulder, CO: Author.

Western Interstate Commission for Higher Education (WICHE) Mental Health Program, CMHS. (1999). *Pilot study on validating core cultural competence standards in managed mental health services: Final report.* Boulder, CO: Author.

Ying, Y. W., & Hu, L. (1994). Public outpatient mental health service use and outcome among Asian Americans. *American Journal of Orthopsychiatry, 64,* 448–455.

# THIRTEEN

# Recovery Perspectives in Evidence-Based Practice

*Gretchen Grappone*
*Melinda Fox*

GRETCHEN GRAPPONE AND LINDY FOX SHARE many things in common. They both live with mental illness, and they both have been recipients of "traditional" mental health services. After and overview of mental health practices, Gretchen and Lindy describe their perspectives on recovery, mental illness, and evidence-based practices both as consumers and advocates.

## Overview of Mental Health Care

Throughout the history of mental health care in the United States there have been as many different concepts about recovery as there have been treatment models or ideas. In colonial America, treatment consisted of isolating people with severe mental illness from their communities and their families, especially by physical means. Many people with mental illness were left in remote sheds, or attics, sometimes restrained by chains. For decades, the idea of treatment was entangled with the idea of seclusion, restraint, and removal. The concept of recovery did not even have a place in that world. Treatment options ranged from being bound and secluded to ice water baths and spiritual interventions. It was hard to believe that there was much hope of providing those people with mental illness any choices about treatment, or life goals, or even the hope of health.

**Moral treatment movement**

The moral treatment movement attempted to infuse some sense of humanism into the dismal life conditions that were pervasive for people with mental illness, especially in large institutions where isolation and containment were the currency of the day. This movement advocated some progressive ideas, including the use of manual labor, recreational activities, and social interactions. Although these concepts were a welcome improvement, they were provided within the context of large institutions, leaving little choice to patients, and sparking little belief or hope that these meaningful roles or activities would ever be put to use in the community.

**Pharmacological interventions**

Ironically, the progress of pharmacological interventions stimulated the first movement toward recovery for people with mental illness. Although many horrid accounts exist regarding the misuse of medications and psychosurgery for people with mental illness, pharmacological advances began a new era focused on the management of symptoms rather than people. The roots of recovery first emerged in this environment.

**Hospital treatment**

For decades, society has provided hospital-based treatment for people with devastating illnesses, with the expectation that patients would return to their homes, their families and in their lives in the community. This type of vision in mental health lagged sorely behind other parts of the health-care field. Even today, we have significantly different expectations of, and reactions to, the news that a person has a mental illness compared to other illnesses. Imagine two different but parallel stories, both about a young woman diagnosed with medical illnesses, both illnesses serious, both illnesses requiring inpatient and outpatient treatments for extended times: One young woman is diagnosed with cancer, and one young woman is diagnosed with a bipolar disorder. Which woman would most likely receive cards of support and encouragement from her friends and coworkers? Which woman would most likely receive flowers and offers of help with anything she

**Societal reactions: mental versus physical health care**

might need? Which woman would frequently hear questions such as, "Have you heard any news about how long before you will be back at work?" Or, "How long before you will be better?" Or, perhaps most poignantly, "How long before this illness will be in remission, or you will be in recovery?" Are these two different sets of responses and expectations caused by stigma or a general belief or even basic value about recovery from mental illness?

The past few decades have produced a significant shift in perspective regarding what mental health services could and should be. At one point, the idea of simply maintaining a person free from extended hospitalizations was the goal. When consumers began to unite and seek more of a life, the focus began to change. The idea of empowerment took hold. Consumers began to demand information and input regarding treatment decisions, options, and goals. Many rallied around the cry of "Nothing about us without us!" Some mental health service systems adjusted to this shift and began to redesign themselves; others stayed the same and changed their language but not their services.

*Consumer advocacy*

All of us in the world of mental health, from consumers, to family members, to providers, should take the time to contemplate recovery and our personal or professional reactions to it. We should also look carefully at mental health practices and mental health research to understand what is helpful to a person's recovery process and what hinders it. Hundreds of personal accounts regarding recovery from mental illness point to a few key themes. Among them is the idea that recovery is a personal process that is defined by the person with mental illness. Another is the importance of hope and inspiration. Progress toward recovery is not simply about reducing the symptoms of a mental illness, but also about regaining or attaining meaningful roles, relationships, and activities. In the following personal recovery accounts, we each describe what was hopeful and helpful to us and, in retrospect, some of the differences that access to evidence-based practices might have made for each us.

*Reactions to recovery*

**Gretchen Grappone**

Recovery in mental health

For me, the concept of recovery in the world of mental health appears to be constantly evolving. At one time my definition of recovery was simple: getting to the point where I didn't want to die. After finding a treatment that decreased my symptoms of severe depression, my characterization of recovery has changed. I now view recovery as feeling healthy enough to find and keep meaningful employment, and being able to develop important relationships.

Illness management and recovery

I was first introduced to the concept of evidence-based practices for mental illness when a colleague asked me to participate in an illness management and recovery (IMR) training. I was invited to take part to add a consumer's perspective at the training. During this training I was impressed by several aspects of the practice. Unlike any treatment I had ever received, IMR focuses on the concept of recovery from mental illness and stresses the role of hope and respect in the working relationship between the consumer and the IMR practitioner. IMR also incorporates the value of consumers benefiting from education about mental illness and the benefit of involving family and friends. IMR also addresses the stigma associated with mental illness by providing support and understanding.

Since my participation in that initial IMR training, I have been involved with IMR and family psychoeducation (FPE) as a monitor and a researcher in a major implementation project. Both experiences have taken me back to my own recovery process, especially my teenage and young-adult years. After attending the IMR training, I began to wonder if having access to IMR as a teenager would have made a difference in the course, duration, or outcome of my own illness. Now that I have seen IMR implemented in mental health settings and witnessed the positive experience of many IMR recipients, I believe that had I received IMR when I was first involved with the mental health system as a teenager, I might have had a much different course in my own recovery process.

The <u>expectation of recovery is an essential aspect of</u> <u>evidence-based practice</u>. To be effective a <u>practitioner must</u> <u>truly believe that it is just as possible for a person with a</u> <u>serious mental illness to realize his or her own goals as it is</u> <u>for a person without a mental illness.</u> Although this appears to be a simple concept, I have learned that it is more the exception for practitioners to have this view. As a young adult, I did not encounter any service providers who gave me information about recovery or asked me what would be important to me in my recovery process. I was left struggling to understand if and how mental illness would forever change my view of my future and myself. In viewing my past and my present circumstances, I understand the power of expectations regarding one's own illness and the course of treatment and recovery.

**Hope and expectation**

I recently obtained my medical records from the hospital where I received treatment for my depression. Reading through my chart, I was particularly struck by something my psychiatrist had written about me. On one of my progress notes, he wrote that I was an intelligent woman but that I wanted too much involvement in the choice of treatment for my depression. Even before I read my record, I had long wondered how that doctor perceived me as a patient. I had felt his disapproval and frustration with me from the moment I became his patient. Could an EBP have improved the doctor–patient relationship in this particular case? I think so. Had this doctor been trained to regard me as a person, with the rights and values to be involved in her own treatment, the treatment I received might have been better and I might have felt the respect of this professional in ways that could have aided my recovery process. The idea of this practitioner discussing my view of my own recovery with me would have changed my whole perspective on treatment.

**Practitioner degradation**

When I was first informed about my diagnosis, like many others with mental illness, I was simply told that I suffered from depression. Having depressed moods, feelings, and thoughts was not new to me, but I knew little about depres-

**Informed collaboration**

sion. None of my treatment providers gave me any information about what depression meant in terms of symptoms, illness course, or effective treatment options. Instead, I was instructed to take medications that were prescribed for me and to see a therapist that was assigned to me. The idea of anyone actually presenting me with information about the evidence of effectiveness for any treatment was foreign to me at that point. Unlike consumers who receive information and support to discuss and explore a mental illness in IMR services, I was alone in my quest for what a diagnosis of depression really meant for my life and myself. Fortunately, I had the motivation, the drive, and the resources to begin my own journey in pursuit of information about, and an understanding of, depression.

Limiting of goal setting | My desire to learn about depression stirred an even bigger thirst in me, a thirst to get more information about mental illness, in general, and to work in the field of mental health. I decided to pursue a degree in social work at a local university. During the course of my college work, the symptoms of my depression worsened. I tried to develop some type of effective communication between my treatment providers and the faculty at the university, because I needed the faculty to understand that the presence of depression in my life was not going to prevent me from succeeding in the social work program. I also needed my treatment providers to explain that my current impairments were of a medical origin and that, in time, I would be able to do all that was expected of me as a college student. Had my practitioners and I been working within an IMR perspective, this would have been successful. Instead, I was unsuccessful in my attempts to be understood as a capable student with a mental illness that would, at times, make it more difficult for me to do what was required.

I remember being at a dental appointment several years after I had dropped out of college and telling my dentist about my plans to return to school to finish my social work degree. He knew that I had dropped out several years before due to my mental illness. When I told him that I planned to return as a full-time student, he grew concerned and told me that I would be better off to start with just one or two classes, and then, if that went well, I could return to college with a more rigorous schedule. My dentist became another voice in the chorus of people from both professional and personal relationships who were convinced that I should adjust my life goals and desires to something more appropriate for a person with a mental illness.

Looking back on those early years in learning to live with depression and struggling to understand all the problems that *others* foresaw for me, I wonder about the huge benefit that FPE could have provided, not only for me, but also for my family. The symptoms of my depression caused me to require inpatient treatment at a local hospital during my high school years. If the hospital staff had been trained in FPE, they would have been able to use this family crisis as an ideal opportunity to teach my family members about depression, including the symptoms and effective treatment strategies. FPE would have also provided us with incredibly valuable tools, including problem-solving strategies and ways to develop my own coping mechanisms.

The opportunity for my family members to meet other families, whose lives were also complicated by mental illness, would have been incredibly valuable to all of us. As I struggled to make sense of my own depression, I felt isolated and different and I watched my family members wrestle with their own doubts and struggles. Spending time listening and being listened to by other families would have helped my family to feel more normal and accepted. The stress and confusion of my psychiatric hospitalization would have been more manageable for all of us.

My twin sister often reminds me of the desperation she felt as she and the rest of my family left me that first day as an inpatient at a psychiatric hospital. My sister described her emotional and physical pain as I was led away. Searching for some kind of solace, my twin was left hanging with 10 words from the nurse who led my family from the ward: "I'm a twin, too. We'll take good care of her." Those

**Family psychoeducation**

words, spoken in an offhand manner, as my family was halfway to the parking lot, were hardly enough. What if that nurse had been available to speak with my sister for 15 minutes or half an hour? What if the nurse had provided information to both of my sisters, explaining what it might feel like to have a sibling enter a psychiatric hospital? And for my parents, how critical and helpful it would have been for them to have been given accurate information about depression and its effect on a person. What a radical idea if that hospital had facilitated, as family psychoeducation does, conversations about how my parents could help me in my recovery process. I am sure my parents would have soaked up the idea of helping me to move forward, rather than feeling lost in the despair about what the future might bring.

I can see endless opportunities for people with mental illness to benefit from specific evidence-based practices and from the foundation underlying these practices. Simply put, people who experience mental illness deserve information about, and access to, treatments that actually have demonstrated effectiveness in facilitating recovery. I certainly don't profess to speak for everyone who experiences a major depressive disorder, nor do I speak for the "consumer perspective." In fact, it is worrisome for people to believe that a single consumer perspective exists. I do, however, subscribe to the notion that there exists a group of key values and principles that is important, in general, to many consumers. In the course of my own struggles with depression and its different treatments, and in my work on the evidence-based practices project, I have experienced and observed the power of these principles.

**Self-determination**

Self-determination is one of those principles. I have learned that many well-meaning people, including some practitioners, equate having a mental illness with an inability to determine what the affected person prefers to do with his or her own life. One of the keys to evidence-based practices is that they should be used to support a consumer's own individual goals and preferences. The idea of providing a proven way to help a consumer to achieve personal goals provides hope and support for self-determination. Practitioners often face the task of helping consumers make progress in their recovery process without any effective tools or strategies. Observing the process of practitioners develop a sense of hope with a practice model such as IMR or FPE changes all of that.

People with mental illness are often stigmatized, and many are confronted, subtly and sometimes openly, with discrimination. I have learned this personally through repeated experiences with people, agencies, and organizations in many different places. Helping consumers to understand and be prepared to experience, confront, and challenge stigma is incredibly useful. I recall a significant amount of chatter about my own desire to work. "She is setting herself up for failure." "She is not ready for work." Programs such as supported employment (SE) confront and challenge the stigma of mental illness, by providing services for consumers who want to work at real jobs. Other evidence-based practices, such as IMR, help people to prepare for this unfortunate and potentially lifelong battle. For many of us, stigma rears its ugly head not only where we expect it, but also where we least expect it. | Stigma

The idea of recovery, a concept that I first learned about through reading, is a crucial principle. My belief and understanding of my personal recovery have been supported by receiving effective treatment for depression, through my own work, and through the support of my friends and family. I have watched the effect that working from a recovery perspective has on consumers and, interestingly, on practitioners. Working with a consumer using a recovery focus challenges practitioners to examine and confront their own beliefs and attitudes about recovery and mental illness. I frequently have the opportunity to present my ideas about mental illness, and especially depression, to many different audiences. For a number of years I have suggested to people with mental illnesses and their families that it is important to develop their own information about | Recovery effective treatments that help support recovery. Now, with the beginning of the evidence-based practices movement for mental health, access to that information—and, hopefully, to effective services—will become easier.

### Lindy Fox

Recovery as a process

I have bipolar disorder and am a recovering alcoholic. I am now in recovery from these illnesses. I haven't always been in recovery. I believe that recovery is a process that each person defines for him- or herself. For me it means stability in my mental illness and abstinence from alcohol and other substances. Recovery is not a finite, one-time occurrence; it is ongoing, something I am always working on.

Early treatment

I did not have the benefit of evidence-based practices in my recovery process. I believe there were times when they would have made a big difference and been very helpful. I was 17 years old when I had my first episode of major depression. Seventeen was also the age at which I started to drink alcohol. My early treatment providers had no information about co-occurring disorders, to say nothing of integrated dual-disorders treatment (IDDT). Therefore, the existence of my dual disorder went undetected for many years, despite the presence of symptoms. I was drinking heavily in college. I met my husband in a bar the winter of my freshman year and we married that summer. My drinking decreased but I became very depressed. At some level I knew I needed help, but I didn't know where to go. I had no information about what types of treatment were available, and, of course, no information about which treatments were effective.

I managed to graduate from college. My husband and I moved back to my hometown, where we both had found jobs. To fill the terrible hole I felt in my life, I joined a church and began to have children. I had four daughters, born very close together. I suffered very severe postpartum depressions. When I was pregnant with my fourth daughter, I was still suffering from the depression after the birth of my third daughter. The depression was so severe that, for the first time, it was apparent to everyone around me that something was very wrong. I got into treatment with a psychologist. This psychologist worked with me to get through the pregnancy while I was severely depressed. He viewed my marriage and other three small children as stressors. After the birth of my daughter, I was hospitalized for depression and diagnosed with bipolar disorder. Upon discharge from the hospital, I returned home, got into a fight with my husband, and attempted suicide. I was rehospitalized.

All my caregivers viewed my marriage and my children as stressors. My treatment providers were not trained in illness management and recovery, and other evidence-based practices, to develop consumer-centered goals and preferences. They failed to recognize that my family provided me with meaning and a reason to live, as well as a source of social support. The opportunity to receive a family-centered practice, such as FPE, would have made an incredible difference. No services were provided to us as a family to help us solve some of our problems and to develop better family coping skills to reduce the stress of a mental illness. FPE might have helped my family and me to experience a different course of the illness and to reduce the impact on all of us. Instead, the result was separation and divorce, with my husband gaining physical custody of the children.

*Absence of family psychoeducation*

From the beginning I could have benefited from IDDT. The next 4 years of my life were very unstable. During the years when I was having children, I didn't drink, but after the birth of my last child I began to drink heavily. My bipolar disorder and my drinking soon got out of control and led to a cycle of inpatient admissions for treatment. It was only after 2 years and more than 15 hospitalizations that a provider asked me about my substance use. If any of the providers I had been working with had offered an integrated assessment of substance abuse and mental illness, it is likely that I would not have experienced so many hospitalizations. Finally, the psychiatrist I was seeing realized I was drinking.

*The need for integrated dual-disorder treatment*

Once the presence of dual disorders was identified, I still did not have access to treatment that addressed both a bipolar disorder and a substance use disorder. Instead, I was referred to a substance abuse counselor for my drinking problem, while my psychiatrist managed my bipolar disorder. There was no integration of these separate treatments.

With this fragmented treatment, albeit from two well-intentioned professionals, it took me 2 years to get sober. I sporadically attended Alcoholics Anonymous groups, but I continued to drink and continued to go in and out of the hospital. Finally, my psychiatrist referred me to the psychiatric unit at Dartmouth Hitchcock Medical Center to receive electroconvulsive therapy (ECT). When I was admitted, a doctor felt that I needed treatment for my alcoholism before I received ECT treatments. I was referred to a residential alcohol and drug treatment program. My work in that program was a real turning point, but not for the usual reasons. My ex-husband brought my four daughters to visit me there, and that visit had a huge impact on me. I decided that I didn't want my children to visit me in a drug and alcohol treatment program. I had finally found my motivation to stop drinking. Had I received motivational counseling, such as that offered in IDDT, I might have found my motivation in a timelier and less costly manner. I really wanted to stop drinking, and I did. That was 17 years ago.

An amazing thing happened when I stopped drinking. I also stopped going in and out of the hospital. Over the 4 years I had been drinking heavily, I had over 30 hospitalizations. Over the last 17 years, I have had four hospitalizations. My bipolar disorder has not gone away, but it has become more stable. I now recognize early warning signs of relapse and check in with my psychiatrist before I have a full-blown relapse.

**Work benefits**

Like many people who experience a mental illness, or dual disorders, work has been an important part of my recovery process. I work for an employer who understands my mental illness and supports me through difficult times.

Work has given me a sense of purpose, a structure to my day, a sense of self-worth, the feeling that I am contributing to others, and a way to support myself. I was fortunate that during the first 4 years, when my illness was the worst, I was able to maintain employment. It is now clear to me that I would have received substantial benefit from the employment supports that are part of the EBP of supported employment. It would have been beneficial for me to have an employment specialist talk with my employers about my illness and any work accommodations that might have been helpful.

Today, in my recovery, I am fortunate to have a family that is educated about my mental illness. I hope that more family members will benefit from this information, especially early on, either through FPE or the family component of IDDT. I have benefited from integrated treatment for my dual disorder, and I also have supportive employers. Evidence-based practices provide opportunities for consumers and their families to access effective treatments. It is my hope that the barriers to implementing evidence-based practices will be overcome so that we, as consumers, and our families will have the opportunity to benefit from the most effective treatments available. As we move toward an evidence-based system of treatment, it is critical that we continue to assure the presence of true consumer choice and self-determination in the recovery process for each person.

True consumer choice and self-determination

*Part IV*
The Practices

FOURTEEN

# Assertive Community Treatment

*Gary Morse*
*Mike McKasson*

ASSERTIVE COMMUNITY TREATMENT (ACT) is a comprehensive and cost-effective approach for providing community-based treatment to people with severe mental illness. It entails a complex set of interventions, that is difficult to describe in a few words. Some proponents of ACT have attempted to convey the nature of the program through an analogy, referring to it as the "hospital without walls" (see U.S. Department of Health and Human Services, 1999). This term, which reflects the early origins of the program, appropriately conveys some aspects of the service. As in a hospital, ACT provides intensive and comprehensive services to a designated set of consumers; as well, ACT and hospital programs both use teams of highly trained professionals, including a part-time psychiatrist, nurses, social workers, counselors, and other specialists. But the "hospital without walls" analogy may also lead to some misconceptions. For example, ACT is focused on community—not institutional—interventions. Furthermore, unlike the traditional inpatient setting with its typical emphasis on stabilizing psychiatric symptoms, ACT supports a broad range of long-term individualized consumer goals that are recovery oriented. Whether "hospital without walls" is the best analogy remains debatable, but this much is clear: ACT is a

Hospitals without walls

highly effective service for assisting designated people with severe mental illness to live healthy, satisfied lives in the community.

## History and Development

Origins | ACT, (sometimes called PACT, for Program for Assertive Community Treatment), had its origins in the late 1960s in the inpatient psychiatric research unit at Mendota State Hospital (Madison, WI; Allness & Knoedler, 1998). A team of mental health researchers and clinicians, including Arnold Marx, Leonard Stein, and Mary Ann Test, designed interventions that assisted people with major mental illness to improve to the point that they could be discharged from the hospital. They found, however, that the gains consumers made (e.g., in symptom management and skills acquisition) while in the hospital did not transfer to the community; the consumers were frequently readmitted to the hospital, often within a short span of time. The researchers also observed that these consumers often failed to receive the services they needed to live successfully in the

Commitment to research | community. Based on their observations and hypotheses, they designed a comprehensive, intensive set of services to provide treatment for consumers in their community. One hallmark of the developers of ACT has been their commitment to rigorous research. Using scientific methods, Stein and Test showed that ACT is an effective approach for helping people with severe and persistent mental illnesses to live outside of the hospital, to experience fewer mental health symptoms, and to function at higher levels (Stein &

ACT outcomes | Test, 1980). The success of the program has attracted the attention of many individuals, including consumers, family members, policymakers, service providers, and other researchers. The program has been widely replicated in a number of different states and a few foreign countries. One survey found that over 300 ACT programs were reported to exist in the United States by 1992 (Deci, Santos, Hiott,

Schoenwald, & Dias, 1995). Research findings have consistently replicated the results from Stein and Test; ACT, as compared to standard community services, consistently leads to better outcomes for consumers (Bond, Drake, Mueser, & Latimer, 2001.

Although ACT has grown rapidly, other research has indicated that relatively few people with severe and persistent mental illnesses actually receive the service (see Lehman, Steinwachs, & co-investigators, 1998). This finding, along with the extensive body of research that demonstrates the effectiveness of ACT, has sparked increased interest in disseminating the program. In 1998, the National Alliances for the Mentally Ill (NAMI), a national advocacy organization initiated by family members of consumers, began a campaign to increase the availability of ACT services. This effort included not only educational and advocacy activities, but also the development of a well-documented manual on starting and operating an ACT team, written by contemporary leaders of the Madison PACT program (Allness & Knoedler, 1998). One year later, the Surgeon General's Report on Mental Health (U.S. Department of Health and Human Services,1999) highlighted ACT as an effective service for people with severe and persistent mental illness. The same year, the federal Health Care Financing Administration issued an advisory letter to state governments that clarified, and thereby encouraged, the use of Medicaid to fund ACT services. More recently, the Substance Abuse and Mental Health Services Administration (SAMHSA), the agency primarily responsible for federal mental health services funding, determined that the presence of ACT services is one of three indicators of the quality of a state's mental health system (Substance Abuse and Mental Health Services Administration, 2002). In collaboration with the Robert Wood Johnson Foundation, SAMHSA is also supporting the Evidence-Based Practices Project and the dissemination of ACT as one of the six evidence-based practices (EBP) services.

> Current advocacy

> Policy initiatives

> Availability of services

This chapter focuses on:

- Identifying and discussing the principles underlying ACT
- Discussing how ACT teams conduct consumer assessments and treatment planning
- Elaborating on the type of services that ACT teams provide to consumers
- Illustrating ACT in practice, by describing a typical day of services
- Reviewing the research supporting ACT as an EBP
- Highlighting contemporary issues and future directions concerning ACT

## Principles of Assertive Community Treatment

ACT is characterized by 10 core principles, plus 3 emerging one, described below and summarized in Table 14.1. (Note that practitioners and researchers sometimes identify a slightly different number of ACT principles, which are also referred to as characteristics or basic elements—see, for example, Allness & Knoedler, 1998; Phillips et al., 2001; these differences are more a function of categorization and labeling than controversy about the essential nature of the program.) These principles reflect the ACT philosophy, and the inherent values guide how staff relate with consumers and provide operating specifications regarding team organization and service delivery.

*Share the responsibility*

1. A team of professionals *shares the responsibility* for providing services to the consumers in the program. Unlike most community mental health programs, ACT staff members do not carry individual caseloads. Rather, the team together shares the responsibility for treating and supporting the consumers admitted to the program. The shared responsibility makes it critical that members communicate in structured, regular, and efficient ways.

*Specify target group*

2. Services are provided to a *specific target group* of consumers. ACT teams enroll consumers in the program in

**TABLE 14.1**
**Service Principles**

1. Shared caseload
2. Specific admission criteria: targeted clients
3. Transdisciplinary team
4. Primary service responsibility
5. Comprehensive care
6. Intensive services
7. In-vivo services
8. Individualized service
9. Assertiveness and flexibility
10. Open-ended service
11. Consumer centered
12. Family focused
13. Recovery orientation

accordance with specific admission criteria. These criteria may be broadly defined, such as any person with severe and persistent mental illness who can benefit from the service. More typically, however, admission criteria are developed for consumers with especially high levels of need for service, for example, consumers with one or more of the following characteristics: (1) people who are at high risk of hospitalization (e.g., those with long or frequent recent histories of inpatient treatment); (2) people who are frequently in crisis and requiring emergency interventions; (3) individuals with especially severe and disabling symptoms, especially those who have not benefited from traditional outpatient programs; (4) people who are also homeless; (5) those with co-occurring substance abuse disorders; or (6) those who are at risk of involvement with the criminal justice systems (see Allness & Knoedler, 1998).

3. The ACT team is staffed by professionals from varying disciplines who work closely together in a *transdisciplinary* manner. A fully staffed team typically employs 10–12 professionals, including specialists such as a psychiatrist, nurses, psychologists, social workers, occupational therapists, and supported employment (vocational rehabilitation)

Transdisciplinary
approach

personnel. Given the prevalence of co-occurring substance use disorders among people with severe mental illnesses, many programs have added one or more substance abuse counselors to the team. Some policymakers and providers have also recognized the value and benefit of integrating a consumer specialist as part of the team. What is important within ACT is not only the composition of the staff, but also *how* staff members interact. Rather than operating as a disparate collection of professionals, ACT team members follow a transdisciplinary model of care (Substance Abuse and Mental health Services Administration, 2002). In this model each specialist assesses the needs and strengths of each individual consumer, and the information is shared in a highly collaborative manner as the team and the consumer jointly develop a treatment plan addressing his or her problems, needs, dreams, hopes, and goals. Furthermore, all team members receive cross-training in each specialty area, allowing each team member to better understand, assess, and support the interventions provided by every specialist. In this way, the team is able to provide integrated, rather than fragmented, treatment to each consumer.

ACT is the primary provider

4. The ACT team assumes the responsibility for being the *primary provider* of mental health and related support services for each consumer admitted to the program. Too often in the history of deinstitutionalization, people with severe mental illnesses have fallen into the cracks of the service systems. In the past consumers—and their family members—have felt that some practitioners transferred responsibility to someone else rather than providing needed services (see, e.g., Allness & Knoedler, 1998). ACT circumvents this problem by assuming the primary service responsibility for all consumers served by the team. Rather than referring consumers elsewhere for needed services, the team directly provides treatment, rehabilitation, and support. Exceptions to this direct service policy are made when consumers require hospitalization or specialty care in other areas, such as primary health care. Even in these areas, however, the team assumes the responsibility for

ensuring that consumers get the service they need by providing professional consultations, monitoring the service, and offering the consumer emotional support and necessary concrete assistance (e.g., transportation).

5. Flowing naturally from the principle of primary service responsibility, ACT teams provide *comprehensive care*. *Comprehensiveness* refers, in part, to the range of available ACT services. ACT teams conduct a broad assessment to determine the full range of each consumer's human service needs. Specifically, the assessment covers such areas as mental health, nursing and general health, substance abuse, employment, housing, daily living skills, social skills, family and social supports, recreation and leisure, need for income assistance, and other benefits. Moreover, the team offers a variety of services to assist with consumers' needs in these areas.

Comprehensive care

Another aspect of ACT comprehensiveness relates to the hours when services are available. Most mental health programs operate from 8:30 A.M. to 5 P.M., Monday through Friday. Yet consumers often need assistance and support during the evening and on weekends. Indeed, weekends and nights are sometimes the most difficult times for consumers, the periods when crises are most likely to occur. ACT addresses this need by providing services into the evening and on weekends. In the well-developed ACT program, services are offered 12 hours a day and at least 8 hours on each day of the weekend. Furthermore, the team operates an on-call service that responds to urgent and crisis situations 24 hours a day, 365 days a year. Under this on-call system, team members may respond either over the telephone or in person, depending on the consumer's need.

24-7 services

6. Another key feature of ACT is intensity. Consumers in well-functioning ACT teams receive about four face-to-face service contacts per week, with about 2 or more hours of individual contact. This figure is an average; the frequency of services is adjusted according the needs of each consumer. Individuals who are advancing in their recovery

Services are intensive

may need less than four contacts each week. Other consumers may require multiple contacts each day, because of the severity of their impairments, the phase of their illness, and other situational factors. More frequent contact is not always associated with problems; sometimes consumers require extra support during periods of change and growth in their recovery. Trisha, a 29-year-old female, who has schizophrenia, had been living on the streets and in shelters for about 7 years. She achieved her goal, with assistance from the ACT team, of obtaining her own apartment. During this transition time, Trisha experienced an increased level of stress and increased symptoms of her thought disorder, such as more paranoid thoughts. These added challenges required more frequent and intense services in the community. As Trisha adjusted to her new living arrangement, and the intensity of her symptoms abated, the services she received were tapered back to the previous level. Similarly, many consumers need extra support when adjusting to the initial stress of working, even though employment is often an important personal goal. Consumer-to-staff ratios are kept low, at about 10:1, in order to provide frequent and intensive services based on changing consumer needs and circumstances.

Services are conducted in the community

7. ACT provides consumers with *services in the community settings* where they need support, assistance, and treatment. Traditional community mental health services for people with severe mental illnesses often occur, not in the diverse environments in which consumers live, work, and recreate, but in the offices and buildings of the providers. This context creates a barrier, however, because many people with severe mental illness are unable or unwilling to come to office settings. More importantly, consumers (like everyone else, but to a greater extent because of their mental illness) are more likely to use new skills if they are learned in the actual situation where they are needed, instead of attempting to generalize skills from an office or classroom setting. For example, an ACT team member may teach the consumer how to stretch a tight budget by doing

comparative shopping with the consumer, in the consumer's neighborhood grocery store, rather than lecturing the person in a classroom. Another consumer who has obtained his first apartment is taught how to cook his dinner using his own kitchen, in his home, rather than preparing a meal for 30 people in an institutional kitchen. The examples are nearly endless, but the principle consistent: ACT helps consumers to learn and practice a variety of needed skills *in vivo*, that is, in their own communities, including their homes, places of employment, recreation sites, and other locations where consumers live, work, and socialize. Not surprisingly, the vast majority (about 80%) of services provided by well-functioning ACT teams take place in community locations, not the program's office.

8. As implied by several other principles, ACT provides *highly individualized* services to each consumer (Allness & Knoedler, 1998). ACT teams do not provide every consumer with the same set of services. Instead, the team spends considerable time understanding each consumer's unique goals, dreams, strengths, needs, preferences, and problems. Services are then individually tailored for each person. Additionally, each individual's service plan is monitored on a daily basis, and adjustments are made based on the person's progress, problems, and changing circumstances.

> Services are highly individualized

9. ACT practices an *assertive yet flexible approach* to serving consumers. In traditional mental health programs, many people with severe and persistent mental illness drop out from treatment. This occurs for a variety of reasons, many of which are directly associated with the impairments of a mental illness, including a failure to keep scheduled appointments, mistrust of service providers, or dissatisfaction with services or program requirements. In contrast, ACT staff bear the responsibility for outreach and for engaging consumers, earning their trust, and developing a positive working alliance to collaboratively pursue each individual's goals. Staff members are assertive, in that they bring needed services to the person on the street, in the

> Services are assertive and flexible

home, or wherever needed. Staff members are persistent in their attempts to serve consumers and do not give up because of missed contacts or other difficulties that might arise and otherwise interfere with needed services.

Additionally, ACT staff members are called upon to be flexible by accommodating the needs of consumers rather than maintaining policies or practices that might function as barriers to service. Allness and Knoedler summarized this principle succinctly: the "team works to adapt the environment and themselves to meet the client's needs rather than requiring the client to adapt to or follow the rules of a treatment program" (1998, p. 3). ACT flexibility influences staff roles and activities as well as program policies. A common staff axiom is that the ACT team "does whatever needs to be done" to assist consumers with their individual service needs and goals (see also Allness & Knoedler, 1998, p. 3). Within a single day, this may mean undertaking such varied activities as administering an injection of psychotropic medication, planning a monthly budget with a consumer, counseling an individual on how to cope with stress-induced symptoms, advocating on behalf of a person for entitlement benefits, and assisting a consumer with cleaning her bathroom.

**Services are open-ended**

10. ACT is provided to consumers on an *open-ended* rather than time-limited basis. Just as severe and persistent mental illness is long-term by the nature of the condition, so too service provision needs to be offered on a longitudinal basis. Rather than terminating or transferring treatment because of an arbitrary administrative time requirement, ACT is offered continuously depending on the consumer's treatment needs and desires. This does not mean that services are static, however. Services to each consumer are adjusted and titrated, and goals change as the individual progresses (or relapses) in the course of his or her recovery from severe mental illness.

In addition to these 10 core service principles, three more principles concerning ACT are emerging in the literature and practice. Perhaps the principles are long-

standing, and only seem new, because they are being articulated more clearly; indeed, much of the entire field of
community mental health is becoming aware of the same
concepts.

11. ACT is *consumer centered*; service efforts are focused
on the goals, dreams, strengths, and aspirations of
consumers. Interventions consider and build upon
consumers' strengths as well as their needs. Most importantly, perhaps, ACT staff members value each consumer as
a person of worth, dignity, and potential. Team members
convey this respect by providing services in a caring and
empathic way.

| Services are
| consumer centered

12. ACT teams also *focus on family members*. When it is
helpful, family members (and other, important, nonrelated
providers of social support) are regarded as valuable partners. The team conveys respect for the family and listens
attentively to the wealth of information that members may
provide as part of the assessment and treatment planning
process. With the consumer's consent, team members may
also collaborate with family members on an ongoing basis
and provide support and assistance to the family, as needed.

| Services are family
| focused

13. ACT emphasizes *recovery as the goal* of services. The
primary goal of many mental health services remains
focused either on reducing problems (e.g., symptoms,
hospitalizations) or on maintaining stability. Although
these may be important objectives in some treatment plans,
ACT is oriented toward a larger, overarching goal: recovery.
Various definitions of recovery exist (e.g., Anthony, 1993;
Deegan, 1988). A common theme is that consumers can
grow and establish lives and identities beyond their
illnesses. Frequently, when provided with effective services,
consumers are able to live fulfilling lives, even when some
symptoms persist. Recovery from severe mental illness is
associated with a number of positive developments (Morse,
2000): (1) increased awareness of one's condition,
(2) increased hope, (3) greater self-control over both symptoms and the direction of one's life, (4) a greater sense of
meaning and purpose, (5) a more positive self-image, and

| Emphasis on recovery
| as the goal

(6) a greater sense of well-being. ACT strives to assist and support consumers in their journey for this larger and more positive vision of their life.

## Assessment and Treatment Planning

Flexible and individual approach to treatment

The comprehensive assessment and treatment plan drives service delivery. In ACT, the team engages each consumer in the assessment and treatment planning process by understanding and assisting a consumer with his or her goals—not dictating goals that are based on program requirements. For example, Paul, a 33-year-old man who has a long history of bipolar illness begins services with an ACT team. In his early meetings, Paul states that he is interested in working and "wants a job now." In ACT, the team responds to Paul's goals immediately. A member of the ACT team begins the process of gathering information about what types of work interest Paul, what things he enjoys doing, and what work, if any, Paul has done in the past. This is the beginning of the employment process for Paul with the support and collaboration of the ACT team. One early activity might be that Paul and the ACT team explore available jobs near his residence. This example reflects the flexibility and individual approach to treatment of ACT. The same client making the same statement in a Day Treatment program might get a different response, following this scenario: "I hear that you want a job, but first you will need to complete 3 months of day treatment, and then your case will be reviewed by your doctor and therapist. They will decide if you are ready for a referral to vocational rehabilitation for an assessment and referral to a jobs program." The bottom line is that for treatment to work, it must be based on the consumer's desired goals, not the program's goals.

An ACT team conducts a comprehensive assessment by gathering information while working on the immediate needs of the client. For example, a nurse taking a client to a doctor's appointment may discover a large number of empty beer cans in the client's home. This discovery would stimulate her to ask some questions about substance use and to report back to the team her findings to determine if there is need for further assessment by the addiction specialist. Observing a consumer in her own environment while performing a task (e.g., going to a grocery store) results in a better understanding of how the individual's mental illness affects functioning in daily life; there is also an opportunity to discover the individual's strengths and talents, which can be drawn upon to accomplish his or her goals.

The individual treatment team, or ITT, completes the comprehensive assessment and develops the treatment plan with the consumer. This smaller, transdisciplinary team may be comprised of a nurse, psychiatrist, addiction specialist, and case manager. The written ACT comprehensive assessment typically covers, at a minimum, the following elements: psychiatric history, mental status, and diagnosis; physical health; use of drugs or alcohol; education and employment; social development and functioning; activities of daily living; and family structure and relationships.

| The role of ITT

After the ITT has completed the comprehensive assessment (within 30 days), they meet with the consumer and family member(s) to develop the treatment plan. The tasks identified in the treatment plan are then used to construct a weekly consumer schedule of specified service activities. This schedule is used daily by the team to organize their service contacts with the consumer.

## ACT Services

ACT offers a wide array of services to meet the needs and goals of consumers. ACT teams provide services in 11 areas (or domains) that are commonly needed by people with severe mental illness. As shown in Table 14.2, ACT teams assist consumers through a variety of activities in areas ranging from mental health to grocery shopping to employment and recreation. Table 14.2 also indicates some of the specific types of assistance needed by consumers (modified from Allness and Knoedler, 1998; Phillips et al., 2001).

---

**TABLE 14.2**
**ACT Service Domains and Types of Assistance**

---

1. Mental health
   - Medication evaluation and management
   - Effective use of medications
   - Individual therapy
   - Crisis intervention
   - Hospitalization assistance
2. Activities of daily living
   - Shopping
   - Nutrition
   - Cooking
   - Housekeeping
   - Use of transportation
3. Housing
   - Locating desired housing
   - Obtaining subsidies
   - Negotiating leasing contracts
   - Communicating with landlords and neighbors
4. Entitlements
   - Applying for benefits
   - Obtaining supporting documentation
   - Transportation assistance
5. Social relationships
   - Social skills
   - Repairing and expanding social networks
6. Family support
   - Involving family members
   - Providing education and counseling
   - Assisting with parenting
   - Coordinating with child services
7. Employment and meaningful activity
   - Structuring time
   - Motivational enhancement
   - Locating jobs
   - Supported employment

8. Finances
   - Budgeting
   - Paying bills
9. Health
   - Screening and assessment
   - Basic nursing assistance
   - Coordination of services
   - Safe sex education
   - Reproductive counseling
10. Alcohol and drug use
   - Integrated treatment
11. Recreation and leisure
   - Planning
   - Skills training
   - Practical assistance

Table 14.2 lists the content areas in which services are provided. Another way to understand ACT services is to consider the types of services. ACT interventions can be conceptualized as falling into three primary types of services: treatment, rehabilitation, and support and direct assistance (Allness & Knoedler, 1998; see Table 14.3).

---

**TABLE 14.3**
**ACT Service Activities**

---

1. Treatments
   - Engagement and relationship development
   - Medication management
   - Individual counseling
   - Crisis intervention
   - Integrated treatment
2. Rehabilitation services
   - Teaching and reinforcing skills for:
     - activities of daily living
     - social relations
     - use of leisure time
     - employment

*Continued on following page*

**TABLE 14.3** (continued)

3. Support and direct assistance
   - Medication adherence
   - Casework assistance
   - Advocacy
   - Transportation
   - Consultation for hospitalizations

---

*Treatment*

Engagement

Treatment interventions begin with engaging new consumers admitted to ACT teams. Engagement is a clinical activity that requires a thoughtful and sometimes intensive approach to developing a trusting, positive relationship between the consumer and ACT staff. Engagement is enhanced by a variety of strategies, including careful attention to consumer goals and preferences and active assistance to address the consumer's priority needs (see Morse, Calysn, Rosenberg, Gilliland & West, 1996).

Medication evaluation and management

Medication evaluation and management are other important treatment interventions. A thorough assessment allows the team psychiatrist to determine the initial medication regimen with each consumer. Because of the low consumer-to-staff ratio, the ACT psychiatrist can meet with each consumer on a frequent basis and incorporate the observations of other team members. In collaboration with the consumer, the psychiatrist is able to adjust medications rapidly to effectively address symptom exacerbations, crisis situations, or problems with medication-related side effects.

Counseling

Counseling is another treatment intervention to help consumers improve their symptom management and improve functioning. In ACT, the approach to counseling is multifaceted. It is grounded in a supportive relationship between the consumer and a team member and focused on assisting the consumer to find positive solutions to problems that arise in community living. The counseling approach also focuses on helping consumers to better manage their illnesses. Specifically, counseling may include providing psychoeducational information concerning the person's mental disorder, teaching cognitive and behavioral strategies that reduce psychiatric symptoms, and helping the consumer to devise plans that prevent psychiatric relapses and promote recovery (see Chapter 17; Copeland, 1997; Curtis, 1993; Morse, 2000).

ACT teams have adapted to the high prevalence of co-occurring substance use disorders by providing substance abuse treatment services. Typically, ACT teams provide a model of substance abuse treatment termed "integrated treatment" (see Chapter 15). Abstinence is not a prerequisite for substance abuse treatment in the integrated treatment approach; instead, the team begins with the client's current stage of recovery, accommodating a longitudinal approach to abstinence, while assertively providing interventions that are appropriate to the person's current needs. In particular, ACT team members are trained to assess the person's substance use and provide motivational counseling, which facilitates the person's willingness to stop using substances over time. As a consumer becomes more aware and committed to change, the team provides intensive substance abuse counseling; once abstinence is achieved, the team assists the person to develop relapse prevention plans.

In addition to the regular, one-to-one counseling times with an ACT staff person, the team also provides crisis intervention services 24 hours a day, as previously described.

*Integrated treatment*

*Crisis intervention*

### Rehabilitation

ACT provides rehabilitation services in addition to clinical treatments. Rehabilitation services are focused on helping consumers learn and use skills that are beneficial for their independent community living, especially in areas related to activities of daily living, social relations, work, and leisure activities. Many consumers served by ACT teams may be living independently in an apartment for the first time. They may benefit from skills training in relation to shopping, cooking, and cleaning. Other consumers may need to learn social skills, such as how to start and continue conversations, in order to expand their network of friends. ACT teams also incorporate supported employment, which is a rehabilitation approach to assisting consumers to learn and practice skills to obtain and maintain jobs in the competitive market (Becker & Drake, 2003; see Chapter 16).

### Support and Direct Assistance

Although an objective of ACT is to help consumers learn and practice needed skills to support their goal of independent living, many people with severe mental illness also need help and direct assistance. ACT provides needed support to consumers in a number of areas. For example, ACT team members deliver psychiatric medications to some consumers' homes one or more times a day to help them achieve maximum benefit from the medications. Other consumers may need support from ACT for budgeting and money management; the team may help manage some of a consumer's income to ensure that the person's rent and utility bills are paid. ACT also provides direct assistance to consumers in finding housing, applying for entitlements, and obtaining primary health care. The direct assistance takes many shapes; it may include providing transportation, conducting casework assistance, locating resources, assistance with forms, and advocating on behalf of a consumer. ACT teams practice the philosophy of doing "whatever it takes" to assist a consumer in achieving successful community living.

Although ACT teams generally seek to help consumers successfully resolve crises in the community, it is sometimes necessary for consumers to be admitted to the hospital for psychiatric stabilization or safety reasons. The ACT team takes an active support role during such stressful periods by providing support to the consumer during the hospitalization and consulting with the consumer and hospital staff to facilitate admission, inpatient treatment, and discharge.

## ACT in Practice

Daily team meeting

Operating an ACT team is a complex process. Using the shared caseload approach, the team may serve up to 120 consumers with as many as 12 staff members. Communication and coordination are essential. The *daily team meeting*, which often occurs in the morning, is a key means of providing services smoothly and efficiently.

The team meeting, which lasts about 1 hour, is designed to review all contact with consumers who received services in the past 24 hours. Each consumer contact is reviewed in a brief report, including the consumer's status and current needs. This information is then recorded in the daily log, which is used as a quick reference for all team members.

One staff person serves, on a rotating basis, as the *shift manager* for the day. The shift manager is responsible for constructing a schedule of staff activities for the day, created from the reports given during the meeting about the needs and status of each consumer, and by incorporating the services specified on each person's Weekly Consumer Schedule (as previously discussed, this form lists the services needed each day of the week to assist each individual to achieve his or her treatment goals). The shift manager also assigns specific team members to provide each of the services that is necessary for the day. At the end of the meeting, the team reviews the daily schedule.

| Shift manager

## A Day in the life of an ACT Team Member
Given the complexity of the ACT operations, it may be useful to illustrate services by describing the activities of one team member for a given day.

DARLENE, A NURSE ON AN ACT TEAM, begins her workday by stopping at a consumer's apartment at 7:45 A.M., where she provides Gail with her week's supply of medication and also inquires about her progress with her job, which the team helped her obtain 3 weeks earlier. Gail reports that she is pleased with the new job and has just received her first paycheck. Darlene then goes to the office to attend the daily team meeting, from 8:30 to 9:30 A.M. After the team meeting, Darlene reviews and prepares medications that the team will deliver to consumers in the afternoon and evening. She then leaves to meet a consumer recently referred to the ACT team. Darlene visits Charlie at his

apartment in the community to gather assessment information about his daily living skills. During this visit, she asks
Charlie about how he does his shopping, prepares meals,
and if he has any questions or concerns about his cooking
skills and his nutrition. By visiting Charlie in his environment, she will be able to observe what kinds of food he has
on hand and what resources he has for food preparation.

During this visit, Darlene learns that Charlie has some
food stamps but no food on hand, except for some bread
and milk. She asks Charlie if he is willing to go shopping in
his neighborhood grocery store, and he agrees. They
discuss food selection and basic meal planning. This is
especially important because Charlie has diabetes and
needs to follow a diet prescribed by his primary care physician. Upon returning to Charlie's apartment, they share in
the meal preparation. In one visit, Darlene completes her
task of assessing Charlie's skills, helps him better understand his diabetes, and strengthens their therapeutic relationship. After lunch, Darlene drives Charlie to meet with
the team's addiction specialist for individual substance
abuse counseling.

Next, Darlene drives to the apartment of Lee, another
consumer. She helps him gather information to complete
his application for Social Security Disability Insurance
(SSDI) benefits. After completing the form, she drives Lee
back to the office, where he is scheduled to meet with the
team psychiatrist who will complete his psychiatric evaluation, which is a required part of Lee's SSDI application.
Darlene briefly updates the team psychiatrist on Lee's
current status, including the information that Lee reports
he is sleeping better with a recent medication change, and
that he appears more organized in his thoughts. She checks
with Lee to see if he has any questions or concerns about his
medications before they leave the psychiatrist. She then
drives Lee back to his apartment.

After dropping Lee off, at his home, Darlene heads for
another home visit, this time to see Evelyn. At the morning
meeting, another team member expressed concern that
Evelyn was having increasing and pronounced difficulties

in managing her hygiene and appearance. Darlene talks with Evelyn in her apartment, and Evelyn states that she has been having difficulty sleeping at night. Darlene remembers that Evelyn sometimes experiences increased auditory hallucinations when her sleep is disturbed and asks Evelyn about that in a calm manner. Hesitantly, Evelyn acknowledges that she has been hearing voices more frequently. Darlene and Evelyn agree that in the past, these early warning signs became so troubling and difficult to manage that Evelyn ended up hospitalized. To address this concern as soon as possible, Darlene suggests that Evelyn come to the office to discuss these concerns with the team psychiatrist. Evelyn agrees to come into the office, but only if Darlene will help her discuss what is happening with the psychiatrist. The psychiatrist, Darlene, and Evelyn discuss her condition and review some ideas that may help Evelyn sleep better and reduce the voices she is hearing. Evelyn agrees to reduce her caffeine intake (especially at nighttime, because this is probably making it more difficult for her to sleep) to use relaxation exercises she has used before to aid her in sleeping, and to call during the night if she has difficulties. The psychiatrist and Evelyn also agree to a change in medication. Darlene drives Evelyn to the pharmacy to pick up her new medication. On the way home, they review the plan to manage her symptoms. Together they practice the relaxation exercise that Evelyn will use to help her fall asleep at night.

Darlene makes two more home visits to consumers. During these visits, she checks on their current status, reviews how things are going at their apartments, drops off evening medications, and provides emotional support to one consumer who recently started a part-time job. After completing these shorter home visits, Darlene returns to the office to write her notes for the day.

## Research Findings

As noted earlier, ACT has a strong foundation in research. The first major study of ACT showed that the consumers

Strong emphasis on research

who were served by ACT were far less likely than consumers in the control condition to be hospitalized. Furthermore, consumers in the ACT program had fewer psychiatric symptoms, spent more time in independent living situations, earned more income from competitive employment, and experienced more positive social relationships and greater life satisfaction (Stein & Test, 1980). Many other research studies have also found that ACT leads to better outcomes for consumers, as compared to standard community mental health services. Several major articles have reviewed the extensive literature (more than 40 empirical studies have been conducted—see Drake, 1998) on the effectiveness of ACT (Bond et al., 2001; Burns & Santos, 1995; Mueser, Bond, Drake, & Resnick, 1998; Olfson, 1990). Several key findings are consistent across a majority of the research studies (see Table 14.4): ACT leads to better consumer outcomes in terms of decreasing the amount of time spent in hospitals and also in improving the time spent in stable housing in the community. Furthermore, consumers consistently experience more positive satisfaction with ACT services than comparison services, as do family members.

---

**TABLE 14.4**
**Outcomes**

---

Consistent findings demonstrate superior results for:
- Decreasing hospitalizations
- Improving stable housing
- Producing positive consumer satisfaction
- Facilitating positive family satisfaction
- Cost effectiveness

There are often (though less consistently) positive findings for:
- Decreasing psychiatric symptoms
- Improving social functioning
- Improving vocational functioning
- Improving quality of life
- Taking medications as prescribed

---

The research literature also indicates that ACT leads to other consumer outcomes that are often, but not always, superior to control services. Specifically, consumers served by ACT sometimes experience a decrease in psychiatric symptoms, improved social functioning, improved vocational functioning, and an improvement in quality of life; in some studies, there were similar rather than significant differences between ACT and comparison services in these areas. It is not clear why ACT helps consumers to achieve better outcomes in these areas in some, but not all, studies. The failure to find more consistent positive outcomes in these areas may relate to two factors. The first factor is the degree to which the ACT program adheres to the ideal ACT principles, services, and operations (i.e., fidelity); some ACT teams are not exceptionally strong in all areas, which leads to weaker outcomes (see Teague, Bond, & Drake, 1998). Second, usual treatment, or comparison services, has improved, often offering interventions, such as intensive case management, which approximate some of the key features of ACT (see Burns & Santos, 1995; Drake, 1998). Additional research is needed to clarify the issue, but it can still be concluded that ACT produces outcomes that are at least equal to, and often better than usual treatment in these areas of symptoms, social functioning, and employment, in addition to the clearly superior outcomes for hospitalization, housing, and consumer and family satisfaction.

| Consumer outcomes

Another noteworthy trend is that many of the ACT studies conducted in the last decade served especially high-need subpopulations of people with severe mental illness: (1) people who are homeless (Lehman, Dixon, Kernan, DeForge, & Postrado, 1997; Morse, Calsyn, Allen, Tempelhoff, & Smith, 1992; Morse et al., 1997), (2) individuals with co-occurring substance use disorders (see Phillips et al., 2001), and (3) veterans with multiple problems (see Phillips et al., 2001). Although additional studies are needed, a growing body of research indicates that ACT is successful in helping high-need consumers to achieve positive outcomes.

| ACT and
| subpopulations

ACT is cost effective

One other major finding emerges from the literature: ACT is cost effective. Studies have generally found that ACT is no more costly than the services that are provided to consumers not receiving ACT services. Because of superior outcomes, ACT is actually more cost effective (see Allness & Knoedler, 1998; Phillips et al., 2001; Weisbrod, Test, & Stein, 1980; Wolff et al., 1997).

## Contemporary Issues and Future Directions

The core principles and practices of ACT have changed relatively little since its inception over 30 years ago. There are, however, at least four important issues that will impact the role of ACT in the mental health systems of the future. These issues revolve around matters of implementation, further service development, and policy. The issues can be framed in terms of four questions:

1. How can the quality (or fidelity) of ACT be ensured?
2. How can ACT effectiveness be further enhanced?
3. How can ACT best facilitate recovery?
4. How can ACT efficiency be improved and system resources maximized?

Treatment fidelity

A disturbingly large number of programs that were intended to provide ACT—or which call themselves ACT—end up being something significantly different. Deci and colleagues (1995) found that only one-third of over 300 programs that identified themselves as ACT teams actually met core criteria defining valid ACT programs. Most of the other programs had failed to implement the basic, key principles and operations of ACT or had drifted away from the core principles of the model over time. This is an especially disconcerting finding, given a strong positive relationship between the fidelity of a program to ACT criteria and good consumer outcomes (Teague et al., 1998). Programs with higher fidelity (i.e., those that follow ACT principles and practices more closely) facilitate better outcomes for consumers, whereas those with lower fidelity lead to poorer consumer outcomes.

These research findings suggest that it is crucial for agencies and programs to achieve and maintain a high degree of fidelity to the ACT model in order to provide the most effective services to consumers. Three complementary methods are most helpful to program administrators for ensuring the quality of ACT services. One, agencies seeking to develop and operate ACT teams should avail themselves of recently developed resource materials to guide their efforts. Allness and Knoedler's PACT manual (1998) is one important resource for starting ACT teams. Other helpful resource materials can be found in the implementation resource kit for ACT, developed as part of the EBP project (Substance Abuse and Mental Health Services Administration, 2002). Two, agencies developing ACT teams can also benefit from training with, and receiving consultation from, outside experts. Mental health systems that are planning a widespread development of ACT teams might consider developing state technical assistance centers to facilitate this effort. Third, mental health system administrators and funders should monitor the fidelity of ACT programs and the consumer outcomes. Teague and his colleagues (1998) have developed an instrument to measure the fidelity of ACT teams. This instrument should be used on a regular basis (e.g., every 6 months) to assess the quality of the program. Data should also be collected at a regular interval to monitor and ensure that consumers are receiving ACT services that help them with their recovery process in the most effective manner. Both consumer outcome data and fidelity assessment data can be used to direct ongoing quality improvement.

ACT is an extremely effective approach for providing treatment services to a defined group of people with severe mental illness. Still, a challenge remains: How can we further enhance the effectiveness of ACT? The question is important, in part, because of the changing needs of consumers, which are perhaps more complex and severe than ever before. Maintaining a high level of fidelity, as

| Methods of ensuring fidelity

| Enhancing effectiveness

previously discussed, is one strategy. Additionally, there is the possibility of further enhancing outcomes in specialized areas of need by incorporating stronger and more specific interventions. Specifically, consumer outcomes will be enhanced as ACT teams incorporate very specific treatments—such as integrated dual-disorders treatment, family psychoeducation (McFarlane, 1997), supported employment, and illness management—into daily practice. Each of these other EBPs is compatible with ACT. Indeed, the general approaches of these other interventions are included in the ACT model of services. Furthermore, research studies have demonstrated that specifically combining ACT with well-developed interventions of family psychoeducation (McFarlane, 1997), integrated dual-disorders treatment (Drake et al., 1998), and supported employment (Drake, McHugo, Becker, Anthony & Clark, 1996) leads to superior consumer outcomes in the respective areas of hospital recidivism, substance abuse, and employment. In typical practice, however, many ACT teams are not currently implementing these interventions with the same level of intensity and sophistication as occurs in demonstration research projects. Consumer outcomes will improve as administrators ensure that ACT teams strengthen their knowledge and skills in these specialized areas. To do so, however, will require a greater commitment to consultation, training, and skill development for ACT team members.

In addition to incorporating other EBPs, ACT (and the mental health field, in general) should make it a priority to collect information about common areas of unmet consumer needs. Many consumers, for example, suffer from poor general health, with a high prevalence of infectious diseases such as hepatitis B and C, HIV (Klinkenberg et al., 2003), and other chronic health conditions (e.g., diabetes, hypertension, coronary diseases). Outcomes will be improved when practitioners, researchers, and consumers design more specialized interventions for these common problems.

The treatment philosophy of ACT embraces the vision of recovery for consumers. For ACT, like most of the field, however, the relevant question concerns how best to support and facilitate consumer recovery. Greater attention needs to be paid to this issue. It seems that ACT team members can (and often do) begin facilitating recovery from their very first encounters with consumers. Understanding and respecting consumers as individuals of worth and potential and working with them in a hopeful and collaborative manner are two important ingredients. The assessment and treatment planning process further supports recovery by paying special attention to eliciting and fostering the consumer's dreams, strengths, goals, and preferences. A number of other service activities appears promising for facilitating recovery (Morse, 2000). These include methods for helping consumers gain a sense of hope, visualize and plan for recovery, foster a more positive sense of self, self-manage symptoms, develop alternative social roles (e.g., as employee), and discover meaning in their lives beyond illness. Illness management techniques (see Chapter 18) offer compatible methods for supporting recovery.

*Facilitating recovery*

Depending on how "costs" are counted, ACT is considered a high-cost service (e.g., Drake, 1998). The annual cost of providing ACT services has been estimated to range from $8,000 to $12,000 per consumer (NAMI, n.d.). Not surprisingly, policymakers are interested in how to best manage scarce resources and how to increase the efficiency of ACT. One common approach has been to limit ACT to those consumers who have the greatest level of need. ACT services are sometimes limited to those consumers who would be expected—without ACT—to generate substantial costs from high rates of hospitalization.

*Improving efficiency and maximizing resources*

Another suggested approach has been to limit the length of stay in ACT for each consumer and then to transition the person to a less intensive service. This strategy, depending on how it is operationalized, can run counter to the traditional ACT principle of providing consumers with

*Transitioning consumers*

continuous services, without arbitrary time limits. Early research found that the positive outcomes from ACT quickly disappeared if services were discontinued (Stein & Test, 1980). One more recent study, however, found no ill effects of transitioning consumers, based on their changing needs, from ACT to a less intensive program (Salyers, Masterton, Fekete, Picone, & Bond, 1998). It is safe to conclude that at present, there is too little research on the topic of whether—and, if so, how—consumers could be successfully transitioned in a timely way from ACT to less intensive services. Any attempts to do so will probably be more successful when transitions are individualized and tied to each consumer's particular progress and needs, and not mandated by an arbitrary, administrative time limit.

An alternative approach would be to experiment with increasing the efficiency of ACT by adding new consumers to an ACT program after other consumers have progressed with their recovery and require less intensive services. If greater attention is paid to facilitating recovery and community integration, consumers may need less intensive services over time, which will increase staff time to see new consumers. Interventions that gradually help consumers develop other social roles and sources of support may facilitate independence and lessen the need for ACT services. Supported employment, peer-support programs, and social network interventions (which assist consumers with expanding their support from family and other community members) appear to be particularly promising in this regard.

**Expanding roles and sources of support**

**Make ACT more widely available to consumers**

Finally, the flip side of the resource issue also needs to be examined. Specifically, some researchers estimate that 15–20% of people with severe mental illness are in need of ACT (Drake, 1998). Advocates within NAMI have put the figure even higher, estimating that 20–40% of people with severe mental illness could benefit. In either case, the number of people with severe mental illness who could benefit from ACT is far in excess of the number actually receiving services—which may be only about 2% or less (see Lehman et al., 1998). The relevant question, therefore, should not be limited to finding ways to reduce the need for ACT. Instead, given that that the program is clearly both effective and cost effective, there should be greater attention and advocacy for providing the resources needed to bring ACT to more consumers.

## References

Allness, D. J., & Knoedler, W. H. (1998). *The PACT model of community-based treatment for persons with severe and persistent mental illness: A manual for PACT start-up.* Arlington, VA: NAMI.

Anthony, W. A. (1993). Recovery from mental illness: The guiding vision of the mental health service system in the 1990's. *Psychosocial Rehabilitation Journal, 16,* 11–24.

Becker, D.R., & Drake, R.E. (2003). *A working life for people with severe mental illness.* Oxford UK: Oxford University Press.

Bond, G.R., Drake, R.E., Mueser, K.T., & Latimer, E. (2001). ACT for people with severe mental illness. *Disease Management and Health Outcomes, 9,* 141–159.

Burns, B.J., & Santos, A.B. (1995). ACT: An update of randomized trials. *Psychiatric Services, 46,* 669–675.

Copeland, M. E. (1997, May). *Wellness recovery action plan.* Brattleboro, VT: Peach Press.

Curtis, L. (1993). Crisis prevention: The cornerstone of crisis response. *In Community* (Newsletter published by the Center for Community Change, Trinity College of Vermont), 6–7.

Deci, P. A., Santos, A. B., Hiott, D. W., Schoenwald, S., & Dias, J. K. (1995). Dissemination of ACT programs. *Psychiatric Services, 46,* 676–678.

Deegan, P. E. (1988). Recovery: The lived experience of rehabilitation. *Psychosocial Rehabilitation Journal, 11,* 11–19.

Drake, R. E. (1998). Brief history, current status, and future place of ACT. *American Journal of Orthopsychiatry, 68,* 172–175.

Drake, R. E., McHugo, G. J., Becker, D. R., Anthony, W. A., & Clark, R. E. (1996). The New Hampshire study of supported employment for people with severe mental illness. *Journal of Consulting and Clinical Psychology, 64,* 391–399.

Drake, R. E., McHugo, G. J., Clark, R. E., Teague, G. B., Xie, H., Miles, K., et al. (1998). ACT for persons with co-occurring severe mental illness and substance abuse disorder: A clinical trial. *American Journal of Orthopsychiatry, 68,* 201–215.

Klinkenberg, W. D., Calsyn, R. J., Morse, G. A., Yonker, R. D., McCudden, S., Ketema, F., et al. (2003). Prevalence of HIV, hepatitis B, and hepatitis C among homeless persons with co-occurring severe mental illness and substance use disorders. *Comprehensive Psychiatry, 44,* 293–302.

Lehman, A. F., Dixon, L., Kernan, E., DeForge, B. R., & Postrado, L. T. (1997). A randomized trial of ACT for homeless persons with severe mental illness. *Archives of General Psychiatry, 54,* 1038–1043.

Lehman, A. F., Steinwachs, D. M., & co-investigators. (1998). Patterns of usual care for schizophrenia: Initial results from the schizophrenia patient outcomes research team (PORT) client survey. *Schizophrenia Bulletin, 24,* 11–32.

McFarlane, W. R. (1997). Fact: Integrating family psychoeducation and Assertive Community Treatment. *Administration and Policy in Mental Health, 25,* 191–198.

Morse, G. A. (2000). On being homeless and mentally ill: A multitude of losses and the possibility of recovery. In J. H. Harvey & E. D. Miller (Eds.), *Loss and trauma: General and close relationship perspectives* (pp. 249–264). Philadelphia: Brunel/Mazel.

Morse, G. A., Calsyn, R. J., Allen, G., Templehoff, B., & Smith, R. (1992). Experimental comparison of the effects of three treatment programs for homeless mentally ill people. *Hospital Community Psychiatry, 43,* 1005–1010.

Morse, G. A., Calsyn, R. J., Klinkenberg, W. D., Trusty, M. J., Gerber, F., & Smith, R., et al. (1997). An experimental comparison of three types of case management for homeless mentally ill persons. *Psychiatric Services, 48,* 497–503.

Morse, G. A., Calsyn, R. J., Ronsenberg, P., Gilliland, J., & West, L. (1996). Outreach to homeless mentally ill people: Conceptual and clinical considerations. *Community Mental Health Journal, 32,* 261–274.

Mueser, K. T., Bond, G. R., Drake, R. E., & Resnick, S. G. (1998). Models of community care for severe mental illness: A review of research on case management. *Schizophrenia Bulletin, 24,* 37–74.

National Alliance for the Mentally Ill (NAMI). (n.d.). *The PACT advocacy guide* [brochure]. Waldorf, MD: Author.

Olfson, M. (1990). ACT: An evaluation of the experimental evidence. *Hospital and Community Psychiatry, 41,* 634–641.

Phillips, S. D., Burns, B. J., Edgar, E. R., Mueser, K. T., Linkins, K.W., & Rosenheck, R.A. (2001). Moving ACT into standard practice. *Psychiatric Services, 52,* 771-779.

Salyers, M. P., Masterton, T. W., Fekete, D. M., Picone, J. J., & Bond, G. R. (1998). Transferring clients from intensive case management: Impact on client functioning. *American Orthopsychiatric Association, 68,* 233–245.

Stein, L. I., & Test, M. A. (1980). Alternative to mental hospital treatment, I: Conceptual model, treatment program and clinical evaluation. *Archives of General Psychiatry, 37,* 392–397.

Substance Abuse and Mental Health Services Administration (SAMHSA). (2002). *Assertive community treatment: Implementation resource kit, draft version 1.* Rockville, MD: Author.

Teague, G. B., Bond, G. R., & Drake, R. E. (1998). Program fidelity in ACT: Development and use of a measure. *American Journal of Orthopsychiatry, 68,* 216–232.

U.S. Department of Health and Human Services (DHHS). (1999). *Mental health: A report of the Surgeon General.* Rockville, MD: Author, Substance Abuse and Mental Health Services Administration.

Weisbrod, B. A., Test, M. A., & Stein, L. I. (1980). Alternative to mental hospital treatment, III: Economic benefit cost analysis. *Archives of General Psychiatry, 37,* 400–405.

Wolff, N., Helminiak, T. W., Morse, G. A., Calsyn, R. J., Klinkenberg, W. D., & Trusty, M.L. (1997). Cost-effectiveness evaluation of three approaches to case management for homeless mentally ill clients. *American Journal of Psychiatry, 154,* 341–348.

# FIFTEEN

# | Integrated Dual-Disorder Treatment

*Patrick Boyle*
*Christina M. Delos Reyes*
*Richard A. Kruszynski*

ROUGHLY HALF THE PEOPLE WHO EXPERIENCE severe mental illness develops substance use problems at some point in their lives, and half of this latter group has substance use problems currently, a frequent complicating factor that has increased since the 1960s. Substance use in this vulnerable population is associated with greater risk for poor outcomes, including higher suicide rates, worsening psychiatric symptoms, behavioral problems, hostility and physical assault, poor self-care, homelessness, increased impairments in social functioning, and a greater risk for HIV and other infections (Mercer-McFadden et al., 1998).

Mental illness and substance use problems

Community-based treatments for people with severe mental illness and co-occurring substance use disorders were spawned during the late 1960s and early 1970s but proceeded along parallel tracks. People with mental illness were provided services within the mental health system and people with alcohol or drug abuse were provided services within a separate system of services. Linkages between these services systems were minimal. At the same time thousands of people with severe mental illness were being released into the community from state hospitals, and state mental health authorities struggled to establish effective services to help these people manage the challenges of living in their

Traditional treatment

communities. The mental health service system during this era continued the process of segregation and fostering dependence, rather than helping people to develop meaningful lives (Anthony, 1993; Becker, & Drake, 2003).

In the traditional mental health system, substance abuse problems were usually not detected. When substance abuse was identified, consumers were referred to the alcohol and drug abuse treatment system, which was unprepared to deal with the problems associated with mental illness. The bouncing back and forth between nonintegrated treatment systems did not help consumers in their attempts at recovery. Family members and treatment professionals shared the consumers' frustrations.

**Self-help programs**

Although self-help interventions and supports showed evidence of being helpful to people with substance abuse when it was not complicated by the presence of mental illness, self-help programs were not receptive to people with dual disorders. These consumers were confused and overwhelmed by seemingly contradictory messages regarding the use of medications and the causes of the symptoms they experienced.

**Prevalence of substance abuse**

Substance use disorders (abuse or dependence) should be diagnosed if a consumer's use of alcohol or another mood-altering drug produces persistent negative effects on his or her life, as defined by the *DSM-IV* (American Psychiatric Association, 1994). Prevalence (i.e., the number of diagnosed cases in a population) rates of substance abuse in persons with mental illness vary across studies, largely due to differences in assessment methods, diagnostic criteria, sample sites, and demographic characteristics of the sample. Most surveys of recent substance abuse in the population with mental illness (i.e., within the past 6 months) are between 25–35% (Graham et al., 2001; Mueser et al., 1990; Rosenberg et al., 1998). The most extensive study to examine the prevalence of dual disorders was the epidemiological catchment area (ECA) study (Regier et al., 1990), which conducted structured interviews with over 20,000 people randomly selected throughout the United States. Lifetime rates of substance use disorders for people with some severe mental illnesses such as schizophrenia and bipolar disorder were found to be three to five times higher than the general population. A recently published comprehensive guide to dual-disorder practice (Mueser, Noordsy, Drake, & Fox, 2003) provides in-depth information on this topic.

Traditional approaches to treating the dual problems of mental illness and substance abuse have been fragmented; two different treatment systems have directed separate services for the disorders, resulting in either sequential or parallel treatment experiences. One approach is to treat the substance abuse problem before the symptoms of mental illness. For a person with dual disorders, the result is exclusion from the mental health treatment setting until the substance use disorder has been successfully stabilized. In the opposite scenario, people are required to stabilize or stop treatment for the symptoms of a mental illness before receiving substance use services. Our separate mental health and substance abuse treatment systems often provide staff with insufficient education to address both disorders, lack of cross-training opportunities, and segregated credentialing. This pattern has reinforced the separation of services, to the detriment of consumers with dual disorders. Services provided through different treatment professionals working for different departments or separate agencies are ineffective and place the burden of integration and coordination on the consumer's shoulders during a vulnerable time.

| Poor outcomes of traditional treatments

The poor outcomes for people with mental illness and substance use disorders began to draw the attention of practitioners, administrators, researchers, and policymakers from all systems of care. It became clear that ineffective services resulted in shunting people with co-occurring disorders to hospitals, jails, and prisons.

## The Development of Integrated Dual-Disorder Treatment

As discussed in earlier chapters, *deinstitutionalization* refers to the shifting of mental health services from large state psychiatric hospitals to community mental health centers. Some 40 years after the deinstitutionalization movement of the 1960s, the collaborative work of several leading researchers across the country converged in a coordinated effort at the New Hampshire–Dartmouth Psychiatric Research Center to develop an integrated model of treatment. This model specified that the same treatment teams, with one consistent philosophy, technology, and treatment plan, should provide mental health and substance abuse treatments simultaneously.

**Shared decision making**

Integrated dual-disorder treatment (IDDT) is the result of dozens of experimental clinical trials that began in the late 1980s (Mercer-McFadden, Drake, Clark, Verven, Noordsy, & Fox, 1998) and continue today. Numerous demonstration and research projects, funded by the National Institute on Alcohol Abuse and Alcoholism (NIAAA), the National Institute of Mental Health (NIMH), the National Institute on Drug Abuse (NIDA), and the Substance Abuse and Mental Health Services Administration (SAMHSA), have led to this evolving approach known as IDDT (Mueser et al., 2003). IDDT has emerged as an evidence-based practice with identified core characteristics, values, and principles.

IDDT emphasizes the treatment of both mental illness and substance use disorders by the same team of clinicians in the same location at the same time. Programs that use this treatment model share the common value of shared decision making, embracing the view that clients with dual disorders are capable of making decisions about their own goals and the management of their illness in the recovery process. This process fosters greater knowledge, offers more choices regarding treatment, and expects increased responsibility for self-management by clients and their families.

**Organizational factors in IDDT**

Characteristics of the IDDT model can be divided into two major categories: organizational factors and treatment factors. Organizational factors refer to those elements at the administrative level that are necessary for the implementation, ongoing management, and sustaining of effective dual-disorder programs. Treatment factors refer to the specific interventions, at the service delivery level, that are necessary for integrated treatment. One key aspect of the model, consistent with all EBPs, is that a program regularly evaluates its fidelity to the principles of the model through the use of a fidelity scale, which is divided into both organizational and treatment factors. Regular fidelity assessments, within the context of an ongoing quality-improvement process, provide a mechanism for the program to improve by using data to increase strengths and identify areas needing improvement. Table 15.1 presents a list of criteria for the IDDT practice and fidelity. Reviewing this table provides a summary of IDDT.

Fidelity assessments

---

**TABLE 15.1**
## Characteristics of Integrated Dual-Disorder Treatment

---

**Multidisciplinary Team**: Case managers, counselors, psychiatrist, nurses, team leader, residential staff, and vocational specialists work collaboratively on the mental health treatment team.

**Integrated Substance Abuse Specialist**: The substance abuse specialist works collaboratively with the treatment team, modeling IDDT skills and training other staff in substance use disorder techniques.

**Stage-Wise Interventions**: Treatment consistent with each client's stage of recovery (i.e., engagement, persuasion, action, relapse prevention).

**IDDT Clients' access to Comprehensive Services**
- Residential services
- Supported employment
- Family psychoeducation
- Illness management
- ACT or intensive case management

**Time-Unlimited Services**
- Substance abuse counseling
- Residential services
- Supported employment
- Family psychoeducation

*Continued on following page*

**TABLE 15.1** (*continued*)

**Outreach**: Program demonstrates consistently well-thought-out strategies and uses outreach in community whenever appropriate:
- Housing assistance
- Medical care
- Crisis management
- Legal aid

**Motivational Interventions**: Clinicians who treat IDDT clients use strategies such as:
- Expressing empathy
- Developing discrepancy between goals and continued use
- Avoiding argumentation
- Rolling with resistance
- Instilling self-efficacy and hope

**Substance Abuse Counseling**: Clients who are in the *action* or *relapse prevention* stage receive substance abuse counseling that include:
- Teaching how to manage cues to use and consequences of use
- Teaching relapse prevention strategies
- Training in drug and alcohol refusal skills
- Training in problem-solving skills training to avoid high-risk situations
- Challenging clients' beliefs about substance abuse
- Training in coping skills and social skills

**Group DD Treatment**: Clients are offered group treatment specifically designed to address both mental health and substance use disorders.

**Family Psychoeducation on DD**: Clinicians provide family members (or significant others):
- Education about dual disorders
- Coping skills training
- Collaboration with the treatment team
- Support

**Participation in Alcohol and Drug Self-Help Groups**: Clients in the action or relapse prevention stage attend self-help programs in the community.

*Continued on following page*

**TABLE 15.1** (*continued*)

**Pharmacological Treatment**
Prescribers for IDDT clients:
1. Prescribe psychiatric medications despite active substance use
2. Work closely with team/client
3. Focus on increasing adherence
4. Avoid benzodiazepines and other addictive substances
5. Use clozapine, naltrexone, disulfiram

**Interventions to Reduce Negative Consequences**
Examples include:
- Teaching how to avoid contracting infectious diseases
- Supporting attempts to reduce substance abuse
- Helping clients avoid high-risk situations and victimization
- Securing safe housing
- Encouraging clients to pursue work, medical care, diet, and exercise

**Secondary Interventions for Substance Abuse Treatment Nonresponders**
The program has a protocol for identifying substance abuse treatment nonresponders and offers individualized secondary interventions, such as:
- Representative payeeships
- Inpatient or outpatient civil commitment
- Coordination with probation or parole departments

---

Persons with mental illness and co-occurring substance disorders usually receive the majority of their services from mental health systems. Therefore, the most common way to implement the IDDT model is to integrate substance abuse treatment into the already existing mental health system. An alternate method is to develop new service structures that include blended teams of mental health and substance abuse professionals; in practice, however, creating a completely new system is fraught with problems.

| Implementation of the IDDT model

The implementation—putting into practice an IDDT program—requires several critical organizational factors. The program must have a clearly articulated and written philosophy that embodies the principles of integrated treatment with the mission of the agency. Other factors include:

| Critical organizational factors

- Committed multilevel leadership
- An infrastructure that supports IDDT
- Specific training and consultation
- Coordination of levels of care
- Integration of expertise into all programs
- Linkage with the self-help system

The agency needs to provide comprehensive assessments of clients in order to identify those most appropriate for treatment in the integrated model. The agency must also thoughtfully review and consistently monitor clinical reviews, program data, policies and procedures, documentation, and financial mechanisms to be sure they facilitate and sustain the adoption of the practice. The agency must assure that each consumer has a specific and regularly updated treatment plan that is consistent with his or her identified goals and assessed needs. The development of a clear and structured system of supervision, training, and quality assurance that monitors each of these organizational factors and has self-correcting feedback mechanisms is crucial to improving consumer outcomes in IDDT.

## IDDT Treatment Factors

The IDDT model is based on several guiding principles or core components (Mercer-McFadden et al., 1998). These core components comprise the treatment factors in the IDDT model:

- Integration of services
- Comprehensiveness
- Assertive outreach
- Reduction of negative consequences
- Secondary interventions for treatment nonresponders
- Time-unlimited services (long-term perspective)
- Stage-wise treatment
- Use of multiple psychotherapeutic modalities
- Hope

Each of these components is described, followed by a discussion of how the components work together.

## Integration of Services

In this model integration occurs on different levels. The same clinicians, or team of clinicians provide treatments for symptoms of mental illness and substance use disorders at the same time. The burden of integration is on the treatment providers. Integration is evident in clinical services of assessment, treatment planning, and crisis planning. An integrated assessment identifies how substance use disorders and mental illnesses interact with each other and leads naturally to an integrated treatment plan, which specifically addresses the interactions between the two disorders. For example, a person with a bipolar disorder may be particularly prone to relapse on alcohol and other drugs during the manic phase of the illness; this vulnerability is addressed as part of the treatment plan. For this same person, it may also be true that relapse on drugs and alcohol results in not using medications effectively and a corresponding increase in depressive symptoms. Likewise, this vulnerability is identified and addressed in an integrated treatment plan.

Because clients with dual disorders are at increased risk for experiencing crises, a crisis plan must be developed that addresses both disorders. A crisis plan identifies the signs and symptoms of an emerging crisis and the steps a client can take to manage the crisis, including seeking help. This plan also includes signs that clients perceive themselves as being at increasing risk for use or relapse of substances. Individual crisis plans are collaboratively developed and updated regularly; a copy is given to the client and is kept in the client's chart.

## Comprehensiveness

Mental illnesses and substance use disorders affect almost all areas of a person's life and functioning. A treatment program, therefore, needs to be comprehensive in nature. Comprehensive programs include several types of services, such as case management services that provide assertive

> Integrated assessment and treatment plan

> Integrated crisis plan

outreach and a broad spectrum of community based services, residential services, employment services, family psychoeducation, social skills training, illness management training, and pharmacological treatment. Assertive community treatment (ACT) is an evidence-based model of comprehensive case management services discussed in detail in Chapter 14. Many agencies that provide residential services exclude consumers with substance use or expel consumers for substance use. Given the nature of frequent relapses, such policies and procedures run contrary to the IDDT model. Residential services may range from short-term crisis stabilization units, where clients can stay for up to 2 weeks, to long-term, supported housing options, where clients can live permanently. Residential treatment programs are critical for clients who do not respond to an outpatient approach. In general, long-term residential treatment tends to produce better substance abuse outcomes than short-term programs. Staff members from residential treatment programs are regularly invited to share information regarding clients or to be a part of the IDDT treatment team.

Supported employment is an evidence-based model of employment services that is discussed in detail in Chapter 16. Family psychoeducation is a method of providing information about mental illness, dual disorders, and problem-solving techniques to clients and their support systems, including families. Family psychoeducation (FPE) is an evidence-based model discussed in detail in Chapter 18. Interventions aimed at family members have been shown to improve outcomes in both mental illness and substance use disorders (Mueser et al., 2003).

Social skills training helps consumers to develop or improve interpersonal skills through role playing, modeling, positive feedback, and homework. These skills are important for clients because problems associated with social relationships play a major role in substance use and recovery from dual disorders. Examples of particularly useful skills include how to refuse offers to use drugs, how to get basic needs met, and how to develop positive, healthy relationships. Improved social functioning increases the likelihood that a client will achieve sobriety while developing more satisfying relationships (Mueser et al., 2003).

Illness management training uses a variety of methods to help clients improve their knowledge about mental illness, the effective use of medications, and identify ways to manage symptoms and relapses more effectively. illness management and recovery (IMR) is an evidence-based model discussed in detail in Chapter 17. One of the significant challenges in providing integrated treatment is to ensure that clients with dual disorders are not excluded from the benefits of effective medications to help manage the symptoms of mental illness. IDDT embraces the idea that useful pharmacological treatments should be available to all dually diagnosed clients, even those who may be actively using substances. Medications such as antidepressants, antipsychotics, and mood stabilizers have demonstrated usefulness in the treatment of mental illness symptoms. Medications such as disulfiram and naltrexone have been shown to be helpful in decreasing substance use (Mueser et al., 2003).

| Illness management

### Assertive Outreach
Practitioners who work in an IDDT program actively engage clients with dual disorders through a continuous process of assertive outreach. This approach requires staff to leave the mental health center and meet with clients where they live, spending clinical time in the community. Practitioners should provide skills and practical assistance for consumers to help with consumer-identified goals in the community. This process engenders a sense of trust and a genuine working alliance between clients and staff. Practical assistance may include helping clients with housing needs, basic living skills, or securing available entitlements or benefits.

### Reduction of Negative Consequences
Recovery from substance use disorders is often a long-term process for clients whose lives are further complicated by mental illness. This model promotes the value of helping

clients reduce the profoundly negative consequences of substance abuse while they are developing the motivation to reduce or eliminate their own use of substances. The reduction of negative consequences can be accomplished through a combination of education and services, such as information about safe sex, education about prevention of infectious diseases, obtaining medical screening and assessments, and access to public health services.

### Secondary Interventions for Treatment Nonresponders

Some of the most impaired consumers with co-occurring disorders may benefit from the use of involuntary interventions to engage them in treatment; for example, involuntary hospitalizations, civil commitments, outpatient commitments, and representative payeeships (i.e., management of financial entitlements for benefits, such as Social Security Disability Income). In the case of consumers who have outstanding legal or court commitments, this intervention may also include active coordination with parole or probation departments. A civil commitment involves the process of legally requiring that a client be placed in an inpatient hospital or outpatient treatment program. This procedure is based on a court ruling that the person is at significant risk and is so impaired by the symptoms of a mental illness that he or she is not competent to make treatment and other decisions in his or her own benefit.

### Time-Unlimited Services

In the IDDT model, services are provided based on the needs of the client. Artificial time limits are not used; rather, services are provided on a time-unlimited basis. Clients usually improve gradually, over time. The research suggests that approximately 10–20% clients achieve stable remission of their substance use disorders per year and that after 3 years in integrated treatment, 40–50% achieve durable abstinence (Drake, McHugo, & Noordsy, 1993).

Having a long-term perspective built into the model serves to give clients time to recover at their own pace. The recovery process for people with dual disorders is measured in months and years rather than in days and weeks.

## Stage-Wise Treatment

Adapting treatment interventions to the client's motivation for change is a central concept of IDDT. This framework allows clinicians to select interventions that are most likely to be helpful for each client, based upon his or her particular stage of treatment. Prochaska, DiClemente, and Norcross (1992) observed that behavior change occurs in a series of overlapping motivational stages: precontemplation, contemplation, preparation, action, and maintenance. Although this concept is primarily used in relationship to substance use behaviors, the stages of change are also useful in understanding how clients take action regarding the management of the symptoms of mental illness.

Osher and Kofoed (1989) were the first to connect the client's stage of readiness for change to a specific stage of treatment. The Substance Abuse Treatment Scale identifies eight behaviorally focused stages of treatment: pre-engagement, engagement, early persuasion, late persuasion, early active treatment, late active treatment, relapse prevention, and remission/recovery. Each stage of treatment is related to specific clinical interventions and strategies that match the client's stage of change. Thus, a client in the precontemplation stage of change would be in the engagement stage of treatment, whereas a client in the contemplation and preparation stages of change would be in the persuasion stage of treatment. A client in the action stage of change would be in the active treatment stage of treatment, and a client in the maintenance stage would be in the relapse prevention stage of treatment. A summary of parallel models is presented in Table 15.2.

Substance abuse
treatment scale

| TABLE 15.2 |  |
| --- | --- |
| Stages of Treatment and Change |  |
| **Stages of treatment** | **Stages of change** |
| Engagement | Precontemplation |
| Persuasion | Contemplation |
|  | Preparation |
| Active treatment | Action |
| Relapse Prevention | Maintenance |

ROSA IS A 40-YEAR-OLD WOMAN who has been diagnosed with schizophrenia and alcohol dependence. She lives in a temporary shelter in an economically depressed area of the city that is known for its high crime rate and high incidence of drug and alcohol abuse. She knows that she will be required to move out of this shelter in the near future, but she has no plans or resources for other housing.

During the early part of her treatment, Rosa does not consider her use of alcohol to be problematic—therefore, she has little or no motivation to change her drinking behavior (precontemplative stage of change). If her treatment provider insists that she immediately become abstinent from alcohol, Jùanita is likely to become defensive and may even drop out of treatment. In this instance, the treatment provider would be trying to use an intervention that is more appropriate for a client in the later stage of change (the action stage). The provider should instead identify treatment interventions that are matched to the client's stage of change.

The strategies appropriate during the engagement stage of treatment include the establishment of a working alliance with the client by providing practical assistance. In Rosa's case, she may benefit from assistance in accessing and understanding available housing programs in the city. This practical assistance may help her in establishing some sense of security in her living arrangement and provide the beginning of trust in her working relationship with her treatment provider. With the seeds of trust planted, it becomes more effective to use other interventions, such as providing information about the potential effects of alcohol in Rosa's life, without insisting on immediate changes in her drinking behavior. When treatment interventions are matched to the appropriate stage of treatment, there is a greater likelihood that the client will remain in treatment and that the interventions will be helpful in the client's recovery process.

## Use of Multiple Psychotherapeutic Modalities

Clients with dual disorders may respond to a variety of different treatment modalities, including individual, group, and family approaches. It is common to provide more than one treatment modality at a time. Individual services are helpful in developing a therapeutic alliance, exploring goals and identifying target areas for intervention. Two types of individual counseling specifically identified in this model include motivational interviewing and cognitive–behavioral therapy. Motivational interviewing is a set of techniques aimed at identifying personal goals and resolving ambivalence about behavior change (Miller & Rollnick, 2002). Many practitioners believe they are using motivational interviewing skills without having participated in proper training. However, learning the basic skills of motivational interviewing usually requires at minimum of several hours of proper training. Cognitive–behavioral therapy, as used in this model, helps clients to develop the skills necessary for a sobriety- and recovery-based lifestyle, including relapse prevention strategies, problem-solving skills, and coping skills training to deal with difficult symptoms or undesired mood states.

| Motivational interviewing

| Cognitive–behavioral therapy

The use of groups as a treatment modality in this model includes educational groups, peer groups, stage-wise treatment groups, social skills training groups, and self-help groups. Groups may provide social support and positive role models, but individual clients vary in the degree to which they are comfortable in group settings. When providing stage-wise groups, an open membership policy affords clients the opportunity to participate in groups

| Group treatment modalities

according to the individual client's changing needs. All groups should strive to address concerns about both mental health and substance use issues.

Although some consumers may find benefits in attending Alcoholics Anonymous or other community-based peer-support groups, these groups also present challenges for consumers who have difficulty with high levels of stimulation and confusion. For many consumers, support groups such as Dual Recovery Anonymous or Double Trouble may provide a more useful experience. It is helpful for program staff to attend local meetings to understand the meeting's character and help to identify the best fit for perspective consumers.

Family services may be provided in either single-family or multiple-family group formats, and usually focus on education about dual disorders and the establishment of a supportive system in the recovery process from dual disorders.

## Hope

A significant element of any successful IDDT program is the ability of staff to provide and sustain hope for recovery over the long run. Consumers with dual disorders have often had multiple episodes of both psychiatric and substance abuse treatment, and they are likely to become discouraged about the prospect of recovery. Many consumers may have lost hope of finding their way toward a meaningful life in the community. Working with consumers in hope-inducing, rather than spirit-breaking, ways is a crucial staff skill. Hope for the future is an important part of a consumer's motivation for controlling both mental illness and substance use disorders.

Clinicians and organizations need to maintain an optimistic attitude toward consumers and their potential for recovery. Treatment that is directed by the individual consumer's values and goals is empowering, increases hope, and decreases the notion that the client is helpless or unable to make positive changes. Developing ways to celebrate both the small and large successes of both the consumer and the treatment team is central to fostering optimism and increasing morale (Rapp, 1998).

In summary, the IDDT model is an evidence-based practice consisting of both organizational and treatment factors that guide a team of clinicians in providing effective treatment services to people with dual disorders.

Summary

## References

American Psychiatric Association (APA). (1994). *Diagnostic and statistical manual of mental disorders* (4th ed.). Washington, DC: Author.

Anthony, W. A. (1993). Recovery from mental illness: The guiding vision of the mental health service system in the 1990's. *Psychosocial Rehabilitation Journal, 16,* 11–23.

Becker, D. R., & Drake, R. E. (2003). *A working life for people with severe mental illness.* New York: Oxford University Press.

Biegel, D. E., Kola, L. A., Ronis, R. J., Boyle, P. E., Delos Reyes, C. M., Wieder, B., & Kubek, P. (2003). The Ohio Substance Abuse and Mental Illness Coordinating Center of Excellence: Implementation support for evidence-based practice. *Social Work Research, 13*(4), 531–545.

Connors, G. J., Donovan, D. M., & DiClemente, C. C. (2001). *Substance abuse treatment and the stages of change.* New York: Guilford Press.

Drake, R. E., McHugo, G., & Noordsy, D. L. (1993). Treatment of alcoholism among schizophrenic outpatients: Four-year outcomes. *American Journal of Psychiatry, 150,* 328–329.

Drake, R. E., Teague, G. B., & Warren, S. R. (1990). Dual diagnosis: The New Hampshire program. *Addiction and Recovery, 10,* 35–39.

Graham, H. L. Maslin, J., Copello, A., Birchwood, M., Mueser, K., McGovern, D., & Georgiou, G. (2001). Drug and alcohol problems amongst individuals with severe mental health problems in an inner city area of the UK. *Social Psychiatry and Psychiatric Epidemiology, 36,* 448–455.

Mercer-McFadden, C., Drake, R. E., Clark, R. E., Verven, N., Noordsy, D. L., & Fox, T.S. (1998). *Substance abuse treatment for people with severe mental disorders: A program manager's guide.* Concord, NH: New Hampshire–Dartmouth Psychiatric Research Center.

Miller, W. R., & Rollnick, S. (2002). *Motivational interviewing: Preparing people for change* (2nd ed.). New York: Guilford Press.

Mueser, K. T., Yarnold, P. R., Levinson, D. F., Sing, H., Bellack, A. S., Kee, K., Morrison, R. L., & Yadalam, K. G. (1990). Prevalence of substance abuse in schizophrenia: Demographic and clinical correlates. *Schizophrenia Bulletin, 16,* 31–45.

Mueser, K. T., Noordsy, D. L., Drake, R. E., & Fox, L. (2003). *Integrated treatment for dual disorders: A guide to effective practice.* New York: Guilford Press.

Osher, F. C., & Kofoed, L. L. (1989). Treatment of patients with psychiatric and psychoactive substance abuse disorders. *Hospital and Community Psychiatry, 40,* 1025–1030.

Prochaska, J. O., DiClemente, C. C., & Norcross, J. C. (1992). In search of how people change: Applications to addictive behavior. *American Psychologist, 47*(9),1102–1114.

Rapp, C. A. (1998). *The strengths model: Case management with people suffering from severe persistent mental illness.* New York: Oxford University Press.

Regier, D. A., Farmer, M. E., Rae, D. S., Locke, B. Z., Keith, S. J., Judd, L. L., & Goodwin, F. K. (1990). Comorbidity of mental disorders with alcohol and other drug abuse: Results from the epidemiologic catchment area (ECA) study. *Journal of the American Medical Association, 264,* 2511–2518.

Rosenberg, S. D., Drake, R. E., Wolford, G. L., Mueser, K. T., Oxman, T. E., Vidaver, R. M., Carreri, K. L., & Luckoor, R. (1998). The Dartmouth Assessment of Lifestyle Instrument (DALI): A substance use disorder screen for people with severe mental illness. *American Journal of Psychiatry, 155,* 232–238.

Torrey, W. C., Drake, R. E., Dixon, L., Burns, B. J., Flynn, L., Rush, A. J., Clark, R. E., & Klatzker, D. (2001). Implementing evidence-based practices for persons with severe mental illnesses. *Psychiatric Services, 52*(1), 45–50.

## SIXTEEN

# | Supported Employment

*Gary R. Bond*
*Amanda Jones*

JUST LIKE PEOPLE WITHOUT MENTAL ILLNESS, most people with severe mental illness (SMI) identify working at a regular job as an important life goal. Work helps people by providing a sense of purpose, a structure, and a daily rhythm. People often develop friendships and social relationships in the workplace. Many conversations about what movies to see, where to find a good place to live, or current events happen in the workplace. Simply put, employment enriches people's lives far beyond the value of the paycheck. Employment is a standard adult role that helps the working person derive a sense of personal meaning, expand inter-personal networks, and add structure to daily routines. When people are employed, they feel needed and counted on to be helpful and productive. Without employment, people often feel unwanted or useless. Working is impor-tant to self-esteem and often gives people confidence that they can accomplish other goals, as illustrated in this vignette.

FAITH IS A 43-YEAR-OLD AFRICAN AMERICAN WOMAN who has a bipolar illness for which she has received mental health services for more than 20 years. As a young adult, she held several jobs, working as a home health aide and as a

Importance of working

367

customer service representative. In her early 20s, Faith began to experience problems at her job. She had difficulty concentrating and had an unyielding sense that her coworkers were conspiring to do something awful to her. Her supervisor was unaware of the causes of her impairments, but was quite aware of her inability to perform her job satisfactorily. After being terminated from her employment, Faith experienced increased social isolation and symptoms of her bipolar illness that led to her being hospitalized for treatment. After discharge, Faith was referred to a community mental health center where she connected with a case manager who urged her to apply for disability benefits. Faith was found eligible and started to receive some income from Social Security Disability Insurance. She also started participating in services at the mental health center. When she informed her case manager that she wanted to work again, Faith was given a position in a sheltered workshop assembling circuit boards. She found the work to be repetitive and boring and eventually left the position. Faith struggled to find a place where she felt that she belonged. She disliked the sheltered workshop and pleaded with her mental health treatment team to help her find a job that was hers and that allowed her to be around other people who were not disabled.

With help from her case manager, Faith obtained a part-time data entry job at a local university. he recently celebrated her third year of employment at the university, and she reports that her self-esteem has improved dramatically. She feels appreciated as a member of the research staff. When another position at her workplace became available, her supervisor invited Faith to share her view on the job applicants. Faith said that being asked for her input made her feel important. "It makes me feel good to know that what I think counts. I am part of this team. I've never felt like that at a job before." During the past year Faith initiated lifestyle changes that she attributes to her success on the job. She decided to take care of herself and lost more than 70 pounds. Faith believes that her understanding supervisor and co workers and her pride in her work have motivated her to improve herself and her life. Although she still struggles with the symptoms of a mental illness, the effect of participating in the competitive job market has been profoundly positive for Faith.

Supported employment (SE), a relatively new approach to helping individuals with disabilities succeed in employment, was first defined during the 1980s. SE was formalized in federal legislation known, as the Rehabilitation Amendments of 1986, to include these features: "competitive work in an integrated work setting with ongoing support services for individuals with severe handicaps" (Federal Register, 1987, p. 30551). Evidence-based SE is more specifically defined by a set of core principles, which we discuss below.

| Origins of supported employment

The majority of consumers—at least 60%, in most surveys—say that they would like to work in competitive employment, defined as jobs for which anyone can apply, in regular places of community employment, and that pay at least minimum wage. Surveys show, however, that less than 15% of consumers are competitively employed. Moreover, many practitioners do not realize that people with SMI can work or that they want to work. Lacking this understanding, it is not surprising that many mental health centers, and even many psychiatric rehabilitation centers in the United States and elsewhere, do not provide supported employment services.

## Brief History and Context for Supported Employment

The idea that work is therapeutic is found in the "moral therapy" movement that was developed by Philippe Pinel in France and William Tuke in England in the late 18th and early 19th centuries. These reformers sought to replace the inhumane conditions of insane asylums with retreats in the countryside where individuals with SMI could be treated with respect and kindness and where productive activity was part of the daily routine. During the first half of the 20th

| Moral treatment

century, as part of the moral therapy legacy, many psychiatric hospitals developed extensive work programs for their long-term patients.

**Hospital-based work**

The most important finding from early hospital-based work programs was that, although they did help the patient combat the lethargy and passivity of hospital life, these programs did not, in fact, prepare individuals for employment outside the hospital. One study found that discharged patients who had been enrolled in a hospital-based work program were more likely to be readmitted to the hospital than those who had not worked!

**Sheltered employment and prevocational training**

Unfortunately, variations of these hospital findings have been repeated for many other types of work programs. Sheltered employment (i.e., placements restricted to people with disabilities and obtained by rehabilitation programs in jobs that pay less than minimum wage) help consumers to adjust to a sheltered workplace; prevocational training programs (i.e., unpaid training experiences intended to help people prepare for employment) may improve work behaviors within the prevocational setting, and skills training classes help consumers learn specific skills as practiced in the classroom. None of these, however, actually helps people to achieve competitive employment (Bond, Drake, Becker, & Mueser, 1999). The theory that employment skills developed in a protected work setting can transfer to real-world employment has been repeatedly debunked, yet many vocational programs continue to use this model.

**Role of federal government in rehabilitation**

The federal government's role in rehabilitation has been critical to the evolution of vocational services for people with SMI. The Rehabilitation Services Administration is the federal agency that manages the federal–state programs that fund rehabilitation services for individuals with disabilities. This program is commonly referred to as *vocational rehabilitation* (VR). Each state has its own Office of Vocational Rehabilitation Services—though they frequently have different names—and a local network of offices that provides vocational services. VR had its origins in a program created after World War I to assist returning veterans who suffered injuries that rendered them incapable of returning to their former employment. In 1920, Congress passed the Smith–Fess Act, authorizing funds to provide rehabilitation services to civilians with physical disabilities. The Barden–LaFollette Act of 1943 extended VR to mental disabilities (including both intellectual impairments and psychiatric disabilities). Historically, the state and federal bureaucracies responsible for VR have struggled with how to provide effective services to people with psychiatric disabilities. One consequence of this struggle has been a lower rate of funding approval for mental health consumers than for those with other disabilities, even though psychiatric disabilities constitute the single largest disability group in the United States.

Although many different vocational approaches have been used to help individuals with SMI, we limit our description to four models that have influenced the development of supported employment: the clubhouse model, assertive community treatment, the job-coach model, and the choose–get–keep model. These four models also offer a chronology of important milestones in the development of vocational services in the United States.

### Clubhouse Model

In the 1950s, large state psychiatric hospitals in the United States began to discharge patients in increasingly large numbers, as the length of inpatient stays was shortened dramatically. The movement of massive numbers of people with SMI from inpatient treatment to community settings, known as *deinstitutionalization*, presented a new set of challenges. Although significant planning went into moving people out of the hospitals, there was little or no planning for, and few resources directed toward, helping consumers do something meaningful once they were back in the community. Prior to deinstitutionalization, former patients in New York City had begun to meet together to help each other adjust to community living (Beard, Propst, &

Malamud, 1982). Operating outside the traditional mental health system, this self-help group became known as Fountain House and spawned the development of other clubhouses, or meeting places, at which members could socialize. Under the leadership of its director, John Beard, Fountain House developed a central focus on work and pioneered the concept of a work-ordered day, in which members were expected to do chores (e.g., prepare and serve lunches) rather than socialize or watch TV. Beard believed that members benefited from participation in the clubhouse because they felt needed for its successful functioning. Fountain House also pioneered transitional employment placements, which were temporary, entry-level, part-time community jobs designed to acclimate people with SMI to work, increase their self-confidence, and help them build their résumés. In this model, clubhouse staff workers negotiated with community employers for transitional employment positions for the members.

Emergence of philosophical cornerstone

The Fountain House program made an enormous contribution to the evolution of vocational services for people with SMI. During the 1960s and 1970s, most providers of mental health services assumed that people with SMI were generally incapable of working. They also believed that the rare consumer who was capable of working needed to be stabilized and achieve complete symptom remission before considering employment. Research has since confirmed that requiring consumers to be symptom free *before* they can start a vocational program is simply wrong. During this early era, clubhouse programs demonstrated that consumers could work and that all individuals with SMI deserved a chance to work, regardless of employment history, current symptomology, or hospitalization history. This philosophy has become the cornerstone of the supported employment model.

Disadvantages

The clubhouse vocational model, however, is not an evidence-based practice, and some experts believe that its core components have more disadvantages than advantages. The overall use and popularity of transitional employment appears to be declining, and many clubhouses are beginning to focus on SE because most consumers want to find permanent jobs.

## Assertive Community Treatment

In the 1970s, a very different model for providing community-based treatment for people with SMI, known as assertive community treatment, or ACT, was developed. This model had a profound influence on the development of supported employment. (For a comprehensive description of ACT, see Chapter 14.) ACT is an individualized approach that emphasizes helping people in natural community settings, rather than creating special segregated environments. Instead of discontinuing services after a fixed time period, ACT provides unlimited support. These components of the ACT model also are integral to supported employment. However, the most distinctive contribution of the ACT model to supported employment was the discovery that a multidisciplinary team working together is the most effective way to help people with SMI, regardless of the goals they are pursuing. Some current ACT teams have a designated employment specialist who works closely with the other professionals on the team (i.e., psychiatrist, nurses, social workers, housing specialist, substance abuse specialist) to help consumers find and keep jobs. ACT contends that work is a therapeutic activity and therefore not to be postponed until the illness is stabilized.

## Job-Coach Model

A third influence on the conceptualization of supported employment for people with SMI was the job-coach model developed by Paul Wehman (1986). In the 1980s a group of advocates for persons with developmental disabilities, dissatisfied with sheltered rehabilitation services, proposed the new approach of supported employment. It was justified as a more effective, humane, and cost-effective alternative to sheltered workshop and day programs, which were, and continue to be, the dominant forms of vocational rehabilitation in the United States. Wehman described this new model as a place–train approach, in contrast to the previous conventional train–place approach. The job-coach model targeted persons with the most severe disabilities who were often ignored by traditional vocational programs (Wehman, 1986). In the old train–place model, it was common for consumers to languish in sheltered settings for years, losing hope that they could transition to competitive work. Indeed, less than 3% made the transition to competitive work. Piloting their approach with persons with developmental disabilities, Wehman and others showed the feasibility of providing job coaches at a work site, intensively training consumers in their job duties, then gradually fading out the intensive on-site coaching. Several aspects of the job-coach model were revolutionary, including the assumption that consumers could succeed in competitive employment without preparatory training. This assumption has been proven valid. At the same time, the vocational rehabilitation field has come to accept that preparatory training actually serves to inhibit progress toward competitive jobs and, in some cases, creates an institutional dependency. A pattern of dependency has also been found for people with SMI who attend day treatment programs, even programs intended to be rehabilitative. The following vignette illustrates this point.

MARK, A 28-YEAR-OLD MALE with a long history of a major depressive illness, has been receiving services from a community mental center for the past 3 years. When Mark informed his case manager that he was interested in employment, specifically a job in the field of data entry, she had significant doubts about his ability to achieve employment and instead recommended that he develop his work skills at the mental health center. He spent hours working on the word processors in the mental health center to help improve his typing speed. But without a specific job in mind, it was hard to maintain his motivation for typing practice. Later, he was assigned the task of helping to

Severely disabled targeted

prepare the mental health center newsletter, but he had little interest in writing and was embarrassed when he could not find good stories to report. He felt he was letting down the staff. Consequently, he started to avoid the day treatment program. He was also puzzled about the purpose of the day program. Like many consumers, Mark could not understand how the activities at the day treatment program would help him to achieve his own personal goals. Mark received little hope from his treatment providers regarding his employment goals and felt that he was doing the work of day treatment staff without any pay. He eventually left the program when he moved to another state. In his new treatment program, Mark was asked about his employment goal and was given supports and encouragement to apply for a data entry position at a local bank. He was hired for the job and has since become a model employee who recently won an award for his positive attitude and excellent work.

A second feature of the job coach model is the rejection of the preplacement assessment universally used in train–place programs. Historically, standardized testing has been one of the main activities funded by VR, even though such testing typically has little or no bearing on what a person with SMI can or wants to do in terms of employment.

Rejection of the preplacement assessment model

Like the ACT model, the job-coach model emphasizes continued support without arbitrary time limits. This feature addresses the need for long-term support, which is not available in the VR system. Because VR services are provided on a time-limited basis (usually fixed at 60 or 90 days), they are discontinued after the consumer is able to obtain employment. For many consumers, however, their struggle is with keeping employment, not simply finding it. Unfortunately, the provision of many services is based on the limits and conditions of the funding sources rather than  evidence-based principles. Despite continuing expansion of supported employment over the past two decades (Wehman, Revell, & Brooke, 2003), the job-coach model has not been rigorously studied. Although the job-coach model is philosophically compatible with evidence-based supported employment for people with SMI, its emphasis on on-site job coaching is more suited to someone with an intellectual impairment. In addition, many people with SMI feel stigmatized by the presence of an on-site job coach and do not need the on-site assistance. The employment specialist can help with interpersonal difficulties outside of the workplace.

### Choose–Get–Keep Model

A fourth influence on supported employment was the person-centered philosophy articulated by Karen Danley and William Anthony, called the *choose–get–keep model* (Danley & Anthony, 1987). This model represented an early attempt to define supported employment services specifically for people with SMI. Although some of the features of this model have not been supported by research, it played a critical role in identifying the value of consumer choice in selecting, obtaining, and maintaining employment. Unlike most existing vocational approaches at that time, which gave priority to placing consumers in readily available jobs in the interest of helping them to build a work history, the choose–get–keep model focused on the consumer's perspective, including the person's preference for a particular kind of job.

## Overview of Supported Employment

In the 1990s, Deborah Becker and Robert Drake defined and systematically evaluated a model of supported employment called individual placement and support (IPS; Becker & Drake, 2003). Their conceptualization proved to be clinically sound, and the research on IPS has been uniformly positive. Consequently, the individual placement and support model has become widely accepted as synonymous with evidence-based supported employment (SE).

Supported employment is an individualized approach to helping consumers get and keep competitive jobs that fit each individual's goals, preferences, strengths, and abilities. Supported employment is effective when vocational services are integrated completely with mental health services. This integration supports a holistic approach to providing information and services to support the needs of each individual consumer. Integrated services require that employment specialists are active and equal partners with other practitioners on each consumer's mental health treatment team, thereby providing the most effective collaborative mechanism with which to identify good job matches and appropriate supports for each consumer.

A supported employment team typically consists of at least two employment specialists supervised by an experienced practitioner, although teams of eight or more are found in urban areas. Employment specialists work closely with the treatment team serving each consumer by attending treatment team meetings and interacting with case managers, therapists, and psychiatrists. These specialists assist consumers with all stages of the employment process: identifying types of jobs to pursue, developing job leads, accompanying consumers on interviews, and helping consumers solve problems on the job. If a consumer decides to switch jobs or if a job is not a good match for a consumer, an employment specialist helps the consumer to find a new job. Even jobs that do not work out are learning opportunities for the consumer and the employment specialist, helping to prepare them for making the next job more successful. In most cases consumers work part-time jobs; 5–10 hours a week is not unusual. Each employment specialist has an individual caseload of approximately 20 consumers.

Employment specialists must convey hope and the conviction that every consumer who wants to be employed can be. The employment specialist's role requires flexibility, good interpersonal skills, patience, and negotiating skills. These practitioners need to engage consumers, family members, other practitioners, VR counselors, and employers, not only in the belief that each consumer is able to work in a competitive job, but also in understanding the

*SE team*

*Employment specialists*

job-search process and the ongoing support needed after a consumer obtains employment. Most of their time is spent in their community, not in their offices. Employment specialists perform a wide variety of tasks ranging from building a hopeful and trusting relationship with consumers to problem solving and helping with the myriad of logistics associated with employment. Effective employment specialists are a blend of therapist, salesperson, and employment counselor.

## Basic Principles of SE

Supported employment is one of the more clearly defined evidence-based practices. For all practical purposes, there is a single model, not different variations of a broad model. Experts and practitioners agree on the core principles (Evans, 2002). In Box 16.1 we present seven basic principles of supported employment (Becker & Bond, 2002; Bond, 2004).

---

### BOX 16.1
### Principles of Supported Employment

- **Vocational and mental health services are integrated**. Employment specialists work closely with the treatment team (e.g., case manager, psychiatrist, social worker) and attend treatment team meetings.

- **Eligibility is based on consumer choice**. Any consumers who want to work can participate in supported employment programs, regardless of illness or employment history.

- **Competitive employment is the goal**. An agency that provides supported employment devotes its resources to helping consumers obtain and maintain competitive employment. Participation in day treatment, sheltered work, and other noncompetitive employment activities are not goals.

*Continued on following page*

---

> **BOX 16.1** (*continued*)
>
> - **The job-search process begins soon after program entry.** Lengthy pre-employment assessment, counseling, training, and intermediate work experiences are not required.
> - **Job choice follows consumer preference.** Choices and decisions about work and support are based on the consumer's preferences, strengths, and experiences.
> - **Support is provided over time, based on consumer need.** Employment specialists provide individualized supports to help consumers maintain employment or find a new job on a time-unlimited basis.
> - **Benefits counseling is provided.** Employment specialists provide ongoing planning and guidance to help consumers make well-informed decisions regarding Social Security, health insurance, and other government benefits.

These principles explain the organization for a supported employment program within an agency, as well as the program eligibility criteria, the type of employment targeted for the consumer, the consumer's role in deciding on the type of employment to target, the method of job search, and the role of the program once consumers obtain jobs. Readers seeking further information regarding the strength of the research supporting each of these principles may consult Bond (1998, 2004).

*SE principles summary*

### Vocational and Mental Health Services Are Integrated

Integration of vocational and mental health services means that supported employment programs work closely with each consumer's treatment team. To achieve integrated services, it is important that the supported employment team and the treatment team are part of the same agency. Ideally, both teams should be located in the same building to facilitate frequent contact. To ensure integration, employment specialists regularly participate in treatment team meetings (at least weekly) and interact with treatment team members outside of these meetings. Employment specialists are full-fledged members of the consumers' treatment team, although their responsibilities are focused exclusively on employment. Employment specialists do not have other duties, such as part-time case management. With the employment specialist's presence on the treatment team, vocational goals are more likely to be given high priority by everyone involved in providing services, not just the employment specialist. The treatment team meetings provide an opportunity to discuss a range of issues pertinent to work, such as symptoms, cognitive problems, medication side effects, and interpersonal problems. Different practitioners see consumers in different settings, and issues both at work and outside work are pertinent to successful employment. A further benefit of an integrated approach is that because of the coordinated attention to employment issues, consumers are less likely to drop out of supported employment (Drake, Becker, Bond, & Mueser, 2003).

*Eligibility Is Based on Consumer Choice*
The only requirement for admission to a supported employment program is a desire to work in a competitive job. Supported employment programs open their doors to all consumers who want to use their services, regardless of presumed work readiness, diagnoses, symptoms, substance use history, psychiatric hospitalizations, legal history, or level of disability. The literature on supported employment indicates that the factors used by traditional vocational programs to exclude consumers, in fact, do not predict who will succeed in employment. Many practitioners are surprised by these findings; they find it especially hard to believe that consumers who use substances do *not* have poorer work outcomes. One of the challenges for employment specialists—and all members of a consumer's mental health treatment team—is to be aware of the personal and professional biases that they may have developed regarding which consumers are capable of employment and which are not.

Exclusion factors used by traditional programs don't predict success

PAUL DRESSED POORLY, WAS POORLY GROOMED, and walked with an odd, shuffling gait. He drank heavily and showed severe symptoms of schizophrenia. He was ambivalent about working when he first met with Tim, an employment specialist. Paul did say, however, that he might be interested in cooking in a restaurant, a job he had held a decade ago. Tim used the tactic of frequenting a local restaurant with Paul and then casually suggesting to the owner that he give Paul a brief trial in the kitchen. The owner did so, but the trial was unsuccessful. The owner told Tim that Paul had the skills but was not fast enough. Tim then arranged a second job opportunity, but again Paul was too slow. Finally a third job at a nursing home led to a successful job hire. The interview was difficult, but Tim explained to the nursing home director that "Paul cooks a lot better than he interviews." (Adapted from Becker & Drake, 2003)

*Competitive Employment Is the Goal*

Many practitioners believe that consumers should be protected from excessive expectations regarding competitive employment. Their view is that consumers are fragile and must proceed very gradually toward entering competitive work. This point of view is reflected in treatment plans that cite "attending day treatment" as a treatment goal. Some agencies even require consumers to prove their ability to be serious about work by regularly attending the day treatment program groups for a predetermined amount of time. By contrast, supported employment programs steadfastly focus on the goal of helping consumers obtain their own permanent competitive jobs rather than good attendance in day treatment, sheltered workshops, skills training, or temporary jobs. The goal is not to prepare people to work, but to help them realize their dreams of holding regular jobs in the communities where they and their friends and family live and work. The following vignette suggests the drawbacks of focusing on intermediate goals.

AFTER JOINING A CLUBHOUSE PROGRAM, DIANE, a 32-year-old consumer with experience working in a variety of different jobs, was initially assigned to participate in work preparation activities and subsequently earned the right to ask for one of the available transitional employment positions. In the clubhouse procedure each consumer examines a list of available jobs posted on a bulletin board. She turned down several janitorial positions because she abhorred dirt and germs. Her first job placement was at a video store. Diane started the job, but she left after a few days because she did not watch videos and the classification system for movies was incomprehensible to her. She was then placed in a mailroom job, a position that she liked and in which she did well. However, the clubhouse program required her to leave this transitional job placement after 6 months. Diane was then back to being unemployed and searching for work again. This process repeated itself again. Diane's preferences for the type of job she wanted became secondary to working in the types of transitional placement jobs that were available to the program. Staff began to lose sight of what Diane wanted—her own job that fit with her interests and talents—not just work that was temporarily available to her. Diane's history as a successful employee prior to seeking mental health services was also lost. In fact, Diane's biggest employment need was not finding work and being hired, but rather managing her symptoms effectively once she obtained the kind of job she wanted.

**Focus on competitive employment**

Three reasons for the uncompromising focus on competitive employment are: (1) competitive employment is the goal consumers most often have in the vocational area; (2) competitive employment leads to nonvocational benefits (e.g., increased self-esteem, reduced symptoms), whereas sheltered employment does not (Bond et al., 2001); (3) what programs focus on (e.g., in their outcome monitoring, expectations for staff, and in meeting agendas) gets accomplished. Moreover, there is no evidence that work preparation actually leads to the benefits assumed by traditional vocational models.

*Job-Search Process Begins Soon after Program Entry*
Supported employment programs have a policy of responding to consumers as soon as possible after they have expressed an interest in working. There are several reasons for beginning the job-search process soon after a consumer is enrolled in supported employment. First, it demonstrates to consumers that their desire to work is taken seriously and conveys optimism that there are multiple job opportunities available in the community. Second, identifying job preferences and then engaging in a job search helps the consumer and employment specialist become increasingly specific about finding a job that matches the consumer. The process of looking for a job is more efficient than talking about employment in the abstract, as is the case in career counseling approaches. Third, the rapid job-search approach also can be helpful for consumers who are ambivalent about working. Often, consumers' fears and misconceptions about work are dispelled when they actually begin exploring possibilities. Fourth, starting the job search early makes sense, because some consumers explore many jobs before the right one is selected, and beginning this process early increases the likelihood of eventual success. In addition to these practical arguments, a powerful reason for employing a rapid job-search process is a very strong research base showing that it is superior to other approaches that provide preparatory training before consumers look for jobs (Bond, 1998). The main reason for rapid job search can be summed up in the explanation most consumers give for entering a vocational program: "I am here because I want a job, not because I want to be trained."

*Job Choice Follows Consumer Preference*
Contrary to popular belief, consumers usually have realistic job-related interests and preferences. Thus, before employment specialists begin their collaborative search with a consumer for a job, they work with the consumer to understand his or her preferences for type of job, hours of work, and location. This information, along with information

about the consumer's history of job successes and failures, helps them to develop the best job match. Often, finding an appropriate job requires employment specialists to be creative and find employers willing to adapt positions to accommodate a particular consumer's abilities and interests. Compared to simply placing a consumer in the first available job, this process requires more effort, but honoring consumer preferences leads to greater job satisfaction and longer job tenure (Becker, Drake, Farabaugh, & Bond, 1996). The following case example illustrates such a job search.

DAVID WAS AN AVID PHOTOGRAPHER who had not worked in 20 years due to his symptoms. He did not do well in groups and, in fact, left early from an informational meeting on supported employment because of this discomfort. The idea of working in a competitive job frightened him. Over time, his employment specialist was able to reframe competitive employment for David to focus it more on the use of his talents. After considerable searching, the employment specialist located a one-shot project at the YMCA, mounting photographs on posters. Eventually this project blossomed into a permanent job framing prints—a job that used his talents and did not require working in a group. (Adapted from Becker & Drake, 2003)

*Support Is Provided Over Time, Based on Consumer Need*
Because each consumer's path to recovery is unique, supported employment programs maintain a long-term commitment to the support of consumers after they have achieved employment. The nature and intensity of the support vary from consumer to consumer, but the support is universally based on a problem-solving orientation and close coordination with the treatment team. Over time, case managers may play a lead role in providing vocational support when the consumer does not need the intensive services of the employment specialist. Employment specialists also look for opportunities to strengthen natural supports (e.g., family members, friends, coworkers).

Supports vary from extensive to minor. Sometimes employment specialists provide a simple reality check, helping consumers whose poor self-esteem interferes with a realistic appraisal of their performance.

STEVE GOT A JOB AS A MEMBER OF A SOIL SURVEY team. His job involved studying details of aerial photographs, a job compatible with his academic training. After 1 week on the job, he told his employment specialist, Gail, that he was going to quit, because he could not handle his work. Gail asked if she might talk to the employer to get his perspective. The employer was surprised to hear Steve's poor self-evaluation because his supervisor was pleased with Steve's progress. When Steve was given this encouraging information, he decided to stay at his position. He continued to perform well in the job and was eventually promoted to a supervisory position within the company.

The research suggests that the most common problem encountered by consumers with SMI in the work place, and the most common reason they lose a job, concerns interpersonal relationships. The following example illustrates the type of situation that feels intolerable to a consumer, but that an employment specialist can help navigate. The most challenging part of job adjustment often is not related to the job duties but to fitting into the social culture in a workplace.

Interpersonal relationships

AT HER REAL ESTATE OFFICE JOB, MICHAELA, a 22-year-old consumer, worked as a receptionist. As part of the agency's business strategy, they held frequent receptions throughout the community. Michaela became paralyzed with anxiety whenever an office party was scheduled, and, in fact, she called in sick the day of the first event. All staff from the office were routinely expected to attend these events. Michaela was not only anxious about the challenge of talking with the rest of the staff from the agency, but she also was also panicked by the idea of driving to unfamiliar places in the community. When Michaela's employment specialist checked in with her at work regarding any concerns that Michaela had with her job situation, Michaela explained her bind. Given that the next party was still 2 weeks away, the employment specialist had time to discuss this problem with Michaela's mental health treatment team. The team was well aware of Michaela's anxiety and noted that she had been successful in the past with anxiety management strategies that involved rehearsal and planning. The employment specialist proposed to Michaela that they could map out a route to the restaurant where the next party was to be held and that they drive this route together. They also agreed that it would be useful for Michaela to see the inside of the restaurant. The employment specialist also suggested that Michaela get a map of the area and plan a route from her office to the restaurant. Together they set up a plan for the employment specialist to meet Michaela during her lunch hour. Michaela drove to the restaurant, where they had lunch. During lunch, Michaela and her employment specialist identified some simple and concrete things she could use in conversations at the upcoming office party. Although this intervention did not alleviate all of Michaela's anxieties, it did provide her with a specific plan that enabled her to attend the event.

While employment specialists continually remind consumers that support is always available, experience suggests that often the need for support decreases over time. The intent is always to find a balance between helping consumers become as independent as possible, while remaining available to provide support and assistance when needed.

*Benefits Counseling Is Provided*
A reason many consumers give for not pursuing work is their fear that if they do so, they will lose their entitlements. These entitlements may include Social Security Disability

Insurance (SSDI), Supplemental Security Income (SSI), and medical insurance (Medicaid). The often confusing and ever-changing Social Security and Medicaid rules exacerbate this fear. *Benefits counseling* refers to ongoing planning and guidance to help consumers make well-informed employment decisions regarding Social Security, health insurance, and other government benefits. The benefits counselor, who may be the employment specialist or a specially designated benefits counselor, meets with each consumer (and sometimes family members) before they start a job and whenever there is a significant change in income or change in Social Security rules. The benefits counselor provides current, easy-to-understand, and personalized information regarding the impact of earned income on their entitlements. The outcome of benefits counseling includes specific calculations of the consequences of different levels of earnings for each individual, along with a strategy on the best course of action. One study has shown that skilled benefits counseling can dramatically increase employment earnings for SSI and SSDI beneficiaries (Tremblay, Smith, Xie, & Drake, in press). A variety of work incentive programs, at the state and federal levels, enables people to work while retaining some benefits. It is important to provide knowledge about these programs to consumers and family members.

In addition to the principles outlined above, evidence-based supported employment includes other program components that are critical to program effectiveness. Employment specialists reach out to consumers in their community if they fail to keep appointments. Employment specialists assist consumers with the decision making process regarding disclosure in the workplace. *Disclosure* refers to the act of informing an employer that a person has a disability that may require some type of accommodation for the person to do the job. Spending time to discuss the benefits and risks of disclosure regarding the presence of a mental illness provides consumers with the chance to make an informed decision about how to proceed in this area.

More components of SE

## Research on the Effectiveness of Supported Employment

Several different researchers have carefully examined the evidence concerning supported employment. All have reached the same conclusion: that the evidence supporting its effectiveness for helping consumers achieve competitive employment is strong, and that no other vocational approach has this empirical support. In this section we summarize the findings from one recent review (Bond, 2004) that focused on two types of research: day treatment conversion studies and experimental studies.

### Day Treatment Conversion Studies

Historically, day treatment programs have been a very common practice and often the cornerstone of services provided by community mental health centers, even though their effectiveness has been questionable. These programs usually involved providing a series of structured groups and social activities (i.e., lunch) or recreational activities at a community mental health center. Many of these programs were based on the milieu treatment models used in psychiatric hospital settings. Four studies have examined the consequences of replacing day treatment programs with supported employment programs. Altogether, these studies included 317 consumers at six-day treatment sites that were converting to supported employment and 184 consumers at three comparison day treatment sites. In every case, sites converting to supported employment programs showed a substantial increase in competitive employment rates, whereas the control sites did not, as shown in Figure 16.1.

Overall, the percentage of consumers who was able to obtain competitive jobs nearly tripled after day treatment programs converted to supported employment, whereas competitive employment rates at centers not converting their services were unchanged. No negative outcomes were reported in any of these studies, except a small minority of consumers who reported missing the social contact they received in day treatment. Centers converting to supported employment met with overwhelmingly favorable reactions from consumers, family members, and program staff.

Success of conversion
to SE model

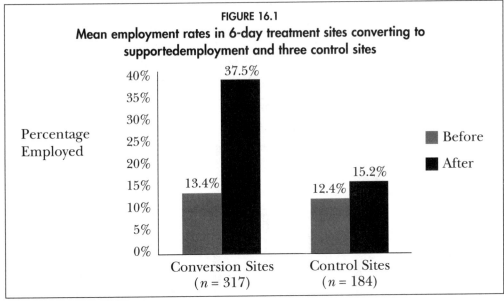

**FIGURE 16.1**
**Mean employment rates in 6-day treatment sites converting to supportedemployment and three control sites**

Adapted from Bond, 2004

## Experimental Studies

Eleven carefully controlled experimental studies have compared supported employment to traditional vocational services, including skills training, sheltered workshops, transitional employment, and referral to the state vocational rehabilitation services. All 11 studies showed significantly better competitive employment rates for consumers receiving supported employment, as Figure 16.2 shows.

Across all studies, the average competitive employment rate during the study period was 60% for consumers in supported employment programs, compared to 21% for consumers in other programs.

Other employment outcomes, such as time to first job, job tenure, and earnings from employment, all showed similar advantages in supported employment. Moreover, these studies suggest that supported employment is effective in a wide variety of communities and across a wide range of consumer characteristics. Supported employment has been shown to be effective in both large and moderately sized cities as well as in rural communities. Compared to consumers in other vocational programs, consumers receiving supported employment services were more likely to find competitive employment, regardless of gender, ethnicity, employment histories, clinical histories, or diagnoses. Consumers with co-occurring substance use disorders have also benefited more from supported employment than from other types of employment services.

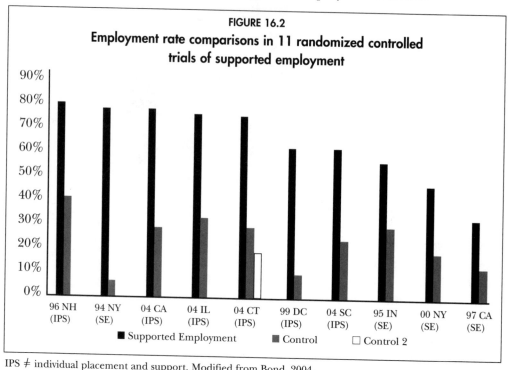

**FIGURE 16.2**

**Employment rate comparisons in 11 randomized controlled trials of supported employment**

IPS $\neq$ individual placement and support. Modified from Bond, 2004.

**Fidelity to EBP principles is important**

Among the 11 experimental studies described above, 7 followed the supported employment model, using careful monitoring procedures to ensure high fidelity to the model. Of these 7 studies, 6 attained competitive employment rates exceeding 60%. In the 4 remaining studies, the supported employment program was not as explicitly defined and lacked one or more of the above evidence-based principles. In only one of these 4 studies did the competitive employment rate exceed 60%. In the single study with a supported employment program that achieved a low competitive employment rate (27%), despite careful monitoring for evidence-based principles, consumers were enrolled in supported employment whether or not they expressed an interest in employment, perhaps explaining the low success rate.

A study of 10 community mental health centers in Vermont found that the centers that followed the principles of supported employment closely (as measured by the Supported Employment Fidelity Scale) had higher employment rates than those that did not (Becker, Smith, Tanzman, Drake, & Tremblay, 2001). In summary, the evidence indicates that vocational programs following evidence-based principles are more successful in helping consumers to obtain competitive employment.

## Future Directions

The research base is now very strong: Supported employment programs are superior to many traditional approaches in helping consumers obtain work. In addition, there is a clear set of principles describing supported employment and a scale that measures whether a program has implemented supported employment with high fidelity (i.e., whether the program is implemented as intended; Bond, Becker, Drake, & Vogler, 1997).

There continue to be opportunities to improve the supported employment model to more effectively help people with a mental illness to achieve their employment-related goals. This chapter has not discussed supported education, which is a strategy similar in philosophy to supported employment, but which aims at helping people gain further education and technical training to prepare for more advanced jobs. Many consumers are asking for more education, and it is obvious that they often are blocked from pursuing better paying and more rewarding jobs by their lack of education. Supported education is not an evidence-based practice, at least not yet, but it clearly has an important role in a program that aims to help people develop meaningful careers.

A second opportunity concerns the long-term outcomes from supported employment. We have only a handful of studies that have examined outcomes after 3 years or more. One recent study examining 10-year outcomes offers a very hopeful message: Consumers do continue to work, and some who initially were not employed later become successfully employed (Salyers, Becker, Drake, Torrey, & Wyzik, 2004).

Another area concerns those consumers who do not appear to benefit from supported employment. A fair percentage of consumers drop out of supported employment services. Some leave because they have decided that they do not want to work at this point in their lives, which is consistent with consumer choice. Many consumers later change their minds and seek work. Is there more we can do with the engagement phase of supported employment? Some experts have suggested that the principles of motivational interviewing, discussed in Chapter 15, may be productively adapted to supported employment.

Many states have benefited from developing a partnership between the state mental health system and the state vocational rehabilitation system in the supported employment area. The Johnson and Johnson–Dartmouth Community Mental Health Program provides technical and other types of assistance to a number of states to promote the implementation of supported employment in this collaborative fashion. The vocational rehabilitation system often brings specific resources and a healthy history of job development to this partnership, whereas the mental health system is able to provide information and long-term supports in the management of impairments associated with mental illness. Effective partnerships are more critical than ever in this time of funding and resource reductions and scarcity.

The ability of community mental health centers and other associated agencies to pay for the provision of supported employment services is a prominent topic. As is true for all the EBPs, access to supported employment is often limited by the lack of a dependable funding stream, especially when the goal is to implement it in a high-fidelity fashion. A recent study has suggested that supported employment services are relatively inexpensive, averaging about $2500 per year per consumer (Latimer, Bush, Becker, Drake, & Bond, 2004). Given the numerous benefits of meaningful work for people with a mental illness, it is incumbent upon public mental health systems to develop funding and incentive mechanisms for the provision of supported employment to further assist consumers in their recovery process.

| SE is cost effective as
| well as beneficial

## References

Beard, J. H., Propst, R. N., & Malamud, T. J. (1982). The Fountain House model of psychiatric rehabilitation. *Psychosocial Rehabilitation Journal, 5*(1), 47–53.

Becker, D. R., & Bond, G. R. (Eds.). (2002). *Supported employment implementation resource kit.* Rockville, MD: Substance Abuse and Mental Health Services Administration, Center for Mental Health Services.

Becker, D. R., & Drake, R. E. (2003). *A working life for people with severe mental illness.* New York: Oxford University Press.

Becker, D. R., Drake, R. E., Farabaugh, A., & Bond, G. R. (1996). Job preferences of clients with severe psychiatric disorders participating in supported employment programs. *Psychiatric Services, 47,* 1223–1226.

Bond, G. R. (1998). Principles of the individual placement and support model: Empirical support. *Psychiatric Rehabilitation Journal, 22,* 11–23.

Bond, G. R. (2004). Supported employment: Evidence for an evidence-based practice. *Psychiatric Rehabilitation Journal, 27,* 345–359.

Bond, G. R., Becker, D. R., Drake, R. E., & Vogler, K. M. (1997). A fidelity scale for the individual placement and support model of supported employment. *Rehabilitation Counseling Bulletin, 40,* 265–284.

Bond, G. R., Drake, R. E., Becker, D. R., & Mueser, K. T. (1999). Effectiveness of psychiatric rehabilitation approaches for employment of people with severe mental illness. *Journal of Disability Policy Studies, 10,* 18–52.

Bond, G. R., Resnick, S. R., Drake, R. E., Xie, H., McHugo, G. J., & Bebout, R. R. (2001). Does competitive employment improve nonvocational outcomes for people with severe mental illness? *Journal of Consulting and Clinical Psychology, 69,* 489–501.

Danley, K. S., & Anthony, W. A. (1987). The choose–get–keep model: Serving psychiatrically disabled people. *American Rehabilitation, 13*(4), 6–9, 27–29.

Drake, R. E., Becker, D. R., Bond, G. R., & Mueser, K. T. (2003). A process analysis of integrated and non-integrated approaches to supported employment. *Journal of Vocational Rehabilitation, 18,* 51–58.

Evans, L. J. (2002). *Obtaining expert consensus on the critical ingredients of supported employment programs for people with severe mental illness.* Unpublished dissertation, Indiana University–Purdue University, Indianapolis, IN.

Federal Register. (1987, August 14). Final Regulations, State Supported Employment Services Program, 34 CFR Part 363, V 52 (157).

Latimer, E., Bush, P., Becker, D. R., Drake, R. E., & Bond, G. R. (2004). How much does supported employment for the severely mentally ill cost? An exploratory survey of high-fidelity programs. *Psychiatric Services, 55,* 401–406.

Salyers, M. P., Becker, D. R., Drake, R. E., Torrey, W. C., & Wyzik, P. F. (2004). Ten-year follow-up of clients in a supported employment program. *Psychiatric Services, 55,* 302–308.

Tremblay, T., Smith, J., Xie, H., & Drake, R. E. (2004). The impact of specialized benefits counseling services on Social Security Administration disability beneficiaries in Vermont. *Journal of Rehabilitation.*

Wehman, P. (1986). Supported competitive employment for persons with severe disabilities. *Journal of Applied Rehabilitation Counseling, 17,* 24–29.

Wehman, P., Revell, W. G., & Brooke, V. (2003). Competitive employment: Has it become the "first choice" yet? *Journal of Disability Policy Studies, 14*(3), 163–173.

SEVENTEEN

# | Illness Management and Recovery

*Susan Gingerich*
*Kim T. Mueser*

PEOPLE WITH SEVERE MENTAL ILLNESS (SMI) can play a critical role in achieving their personal goals and advancing their own recovery through learning how to manage their illness. Effective illness management requires that individuals have basic information about mental illness, the principles of treatment, and strategies for coping with persistent symptoms and other problems. In this chapter, we summarize the evidence supporting interventions for helping consumers manage their mental illness, such as developing relapse prevention plans and learning strategies for coping with persistent symptoms. We begin by describing the recent shift from viewing consumers as passive recipients of mental health services to active participants and personal experts in their own recovery process. We then describe the concept of recovery and its role in helping consumers to discover or rediscover their own strengths and abilities for pursuing personal goals. We briefly review controlled research on illness management programs and then describe the illness management and recovery (IMR) program that is based on this research. We conclude by discussing future directions for research on the IMR Program.

## Background of IMR

Over the past 20 years there have been many advances in the treatment of major mental illnesses such as schizophrenia, bipolar disorder, and major depression. The discovery of effective psychotropic medications that reduce symptoms and prevent relapses has had a major impact on improving the course of psychiatric disorders. In addition to medications, some of the most significant innovations involve new practice models with an emphasis on rehabilitation and recognition of the powerful role the individual plays in achieving desired outcomes.

Hope for recovery

Severe mental illnesses, especially schizophrenia, were previously thought to have a steadily deteriorating course. As a result, practitioners often advised consumers and family members to accept that they had a chronic illness and to lower their expectations for what they could accomplish in life. Consumers were discouraged from having hope for their future and from actively working to regain control over their lives. A body of research is emerging, however, which shows a more optimistic picture. For example, a review of long-term follow-up studies of people with schizophrenia shows that between 42% and 68% of consumers with the illness experience either a full recovery or show substantial improvement in their lives (Hafner et al., 2003).

Consumer participation in treatment

In keeping with the previous pessimistic view of the course of severe mental illnesses, there was a parallel belief among practitioners that consumers were unable to participate in their own treatment, including the prevention of relapses, reducing persistent symptoms, dealing with loss of social support, and meeting challenging social roles (e.g., work, school, or parenting). Rather than helping consumers acquire the information and skills to help themselves, practitioners often focused their efforts on doing everything for the consumer. Recent research, however, and the growth and enthusiasm for the vision of recovery championed in the consumer movement, have led to the recognition that practitioners are most effective when they empower consumers to learn how to mange the symptoms of mental illnesses and increase control over their own lives.

Although recovery is a frequently cited goal by consumers and treatment providers, the term has no universal definition. Recovery means different things to different individuals (Anthony, 1993), and each person defines it in his or her own terms. For some individuals, recovery means taking on challenges, enjoying the pleasures life has to offer, pursuing personal dreams and goals, developing rewarding relationships, and learning to cope with, or grow past, the mental illness, despite symptoms or setbacks. For others it means reducing relapses, becoming free of symptoms, staying out of the hospital, or getting a job. Regardless of the personal meaning each individual develops about recovery, the overriding message is one of hope and optimism. Patricia Deegan, a leader in the consumer recovery movement, has described this message as "a conspiracy of hope":

| Recovery

> Both individually and collectively we have refused to succumb to the images of despair that so often are associated with mental illness. We are a conspiracy of hope and we are pressing back against the strong tide of oppression, which for centuries has been the legacy of those of us who are labeled with mental illness. We are refusing to reduce human beings to illnesses. . . . We share in the certainty that people labeled with mental illness are first and above all, human beings. Our lives are precious and are of infinite value. . . . Those of us with psychiatric disabilities can become experts in our own self care, can regain control over our lives and can be responsible for our own individual journey of recovery. (Deegan, 1996)

## Research on Illness Management Programs

For the purposes of this chapter, we define illness management as professional-based interventions designed to help consumers and professionals collaborate in the treatment of mental illness, reduce susceptibility to

| Definition of illness
| management

relapses, and develop effective coping strategies for the management of symptoms. There is a substantial body of controlled research addressing the effectiveness of teaching illness management skills. A variety of illness self-management programs (i.e., consumers sharing information and illness management strategies with other consumers) has also been developed (e.g., Baxter & Diehl, 1998; Copeland, 1997; Low, 1957; Spaniol, Koehler, & Hutchinson, 1994). There has been little controlled research, however, to evaluate the effects of these programs.

Components of<br>illness management<br>programs

Although illness management and recovery are intertwined, almost all of the controlled research pertains to illness management. Mueser and his colleagues (2002) reviewed 40 randomized controlled trials of illness management programs for people with schizophrenia, schizoaffective, and bipolar disorder. This review identified four specific components of illness management programs that were associated with benefits: psychoeducation, strategies for addressing medication nonadherence, relapse prevention training, and coping skills training for persistent symptoms.

## Psychoeducation

Psychoeducation involves teaching consumers basic information about their mental illness, including the diagnosis, symptoms, causes, course of the disorder, and effective treatment. Consumers need accurate information about their illness and its treatment in order to make informed decisions. Psychoeducation programs achieve this goal by imparting information through a combination of didactic and interactive teaching methods, and often employ written handouts.

Numerous studies of psychoeducation (e.g., Goldman & Quinn, 1988; Bäuml, Kissling, & Pitschel-Walz, 1996; MacPherson, Jerrom, & Hughes, 1996) have reported that it is successful at increasing consumers' knowledge about mental illness. Psychoeducation alone, however, is not associated with improved outcomes such as reduced relapses and rehospitalizations. Thus, psychoeducation can help consumers make informed decisions about their treatment, but it needs to be combined with other interventions in order to help consumers to achieve optimal outcomes.

## Strategies Addressing Medication Nonadherence

Medications are a powerful tool for reducing symptoms and risk of relapses, but many consumers do not regularly take their medication as prescribed. *Behavioral tailoring* is a system for helping consumers develop strategies for incorporating medication into their daily routine (e.g., placing medication next to one's toothbrush so it is taken before brushing one's teeth). Behavioral tailoring may also include working with the psychiatrist to simplify the medication regimen, so that the consumer takes medication once or twice a day instead of more often. Several studies of behavioral tailoring found improvements in taking medication as prescribed (Boczkowski, Zeichner, & DeSanto, 1985; Azrin & Teichner, 1998; Cramer & Rosenheck, 1999; Kelly & Scott, 1990), as has one study that evaluated simplifying the medication regimen (Razali & Yahya, 1995). Motivational interviewing (Miller & Rollnick 2003), which helps people articulate personally meaningful goals and explore how behavior changes such as taking medication may facilitate achieving those goals, has also been found to improve medication adherence (Kemp, Kirov, Everitt, Hayward, & David, 1998).

*Behavioral tailoring*

*Motivational interviewing*

## Relapse Prevention Training

Relapses of symptoms can have a significant impact on the lives of consumers and frequently interfere with the pursuit of important personal goals, such as education and employment. Taking medication regularly can help prevent relapses, but additional strategies and skills are also beneficial. Relapses happen gradually over several days or weeks and are usually preceded by subtle changes or "early warning signs" that can lead to a full-blown relapse unless there is intervention. Rapid response to, and treatment of,

*Early warning signs*

these early warning signs can avert a full-blown relapse. Relapse prevention training programs focus on helping consumers to learn how to recognize environmental triggers (e.g., stressful events) and early warning signs of relapse, and how to prevent symptoms from getting worse. These programs also teach stress management skills as a way of reducing the risk of relapse. Because a consumer may not be fully aware when a relapse is beginning to happen, including relatives or significant others in the identification of early warning signs of relapse is useful. Studies of relapse prevention training programs have shown significant decreases in relapses or rehospitalizations (Buchkremer & Fiedler, 1987; Herz et al., Lam et al., 2000; 2000; Perry, Tarrier, Morriss, McCarthy, & Limb, 1999; Scott, Garland, & Moorhead, 2001).

*Environmental triggers*

### Coping Skills Training

Although taking medication regularly and developing relapse prevention plans can provide substantial help in reducing symptoms and relapses, many consumers are still troubled by ongoing symptoms. Coping skills training is designed to increase consumers' ability to manage persistent symptoms. Research has shown that cognitive–behavioral approaches to teaching coping skills are effective in reducing symptom severity (Leclerc, Lesage, Ricard, et al., 2000; Lecomte, Cyr, Lesage, et al., 1999; Schaub, 1998). Cognitive–behavioral approaches include the systematic application of learning principles to help people acquire and use information and skills, employing techniques such as reinforcement, shaping, modeling, practice, and behavioral rehearsal (e.g., role playing). When teaching coping skills, practitioners help consumers identify a specific strategy to help them cope with a symptom, such as listening to music to reduce the effects of hearing auditory hallucinations. The consumer is then asked to practice the strategy in the session and then in his or her own environment in order to evaluate its effectiveness. If the strategy is helpful, the consumer is encouraged to use

*Cognitive–behavioral approaches*

the skill more often; if the strategy is not effective, the practitioner helps the consumer to either modify the strategy or to identify a new one.

Cognitive–behavioral therapy that employs a major focus on cognitive restructuring has also been used to treat persistent psychotic symptoms. Cognitive restructuring helps people to evaluate the accuracy of specific thoughts or beliefs, and, if these thoughts are found to be inaccurate, to identify alternative and more accurate thoughts. Several controlled studies of cognitive–behavioral therapy for people with psychosis have shown that it is effective at reducing the severity of psychotic symptoms (Gould, Mueser, Bolton, Mays, & Goff, 2001).

The research described above indicates that illness management, including psychoeducation, strategies for improving medication adherence, relapse prevention, and coping skills training, is an evidence-based practice (Mueser et al., 2002). The key findings of the research are summarized in Table 17.1.

| TABLE 17.1 |
| --- |
| **Summary of Illness Management Research** |
| • Psychoeducation improves consumers' knowledge about mental illness. |
| • Behavioral tailoring for medication helps consumers take medication as prescribed. |
| • Relapse prevention training reduces symptom relapses and rehospitalizations. |
| • Coping skills training reduces the severity and distress of persistent symptoms. |

## The Illness Management and Recovery Program

The IMR program was developed by us in collaboration with an advisory committee to combine the key components identified in the research in a comprehensive and standardized intervention (Gingerich, Mueser, & co-investigators, 2002). The program consists of a series of weekly

Congnitive restructuring

Summary

sessions during which trained practitioners help consumers to develop personalized strategies for managing their mental illness and moving forward in their lives. The program is provided in an individual or group format, and generally lasts between 4 and 8 months. In the sessions, practitioners and consumers work collaboratively as they review information, strategies, and skills that consumers can use to promote their recovery process.

Setting and pursuing personal goals

Helping consumers set and pursue personally meaningful goals is a critical component of the IMR emphasis on recovery. These goals are monitored and evaluated over the course of the IMR program. As consumers gain more mastery over their psychiatric symptoms, they are able to establish more control over their lives and become better able to realize their own vision of recovery.

Being able to set and pursue personal goals provides much of the motivation for learning and applying the information, strategies, and skills taught in IMR. Practitioners help consumers identify desired goals, and large goals are broken down into smaller goals or steps to optimize the chances for success. Goals set in IMR reflect consumers' desire to achieve specific, concrete changes in their life. Some examples of personal goals are included in Table 17.2.

| TABLE 17.2 Examples of Goals Set in IMR | |
|---|---|
| *General goals* | *Examples of specific goals* |
| Improved role functioning (such as work, school, parenting, homemaking) | • Explore jobs that involve working outdoors<br>• Having clean clothes to wear<br>• Enroll in a computer class |
| Better social relationships | • Have coffee with my sister once a week<br>• Watch a video with a friend<br>• Start a conversation with a class mate or coworker<br><br>*Continued on following page* |

| TABLE 17.2 (continued) | |
|---|---|
| Improved use of leisure time (both recreational and creative activities) | • Read the newspaper each day<br>• Join the local softball league<br>• Draw in sketchbook twice a week |
| Reduced symptom severity or distress from symptoms | • Learn a coping skill for distracting self from critical voices<br>• Learn a coping skill for distracting self<br>• Use a relaxed breathing technique to stay calm when I am stressed<br>• Participate in an outdoor recreation activity when I feel overwhelmed |
| Improved health | • Take a 15-minute walk three times per week<br>• Eat one serving of fruit each day<br>• Have a complete physical exam |
| Reduced alcohol or drug use | • Make friends with someone who doesn't use drugs<br>• Learn to recognize high-risk situations for drinking<br>• Develop strategies to sleep better that don't involve using drugs or alcohol |
| Improved living situation | • Advocate for myself with landlord about making needed repairs<br>• Find a roommate to share an apartment<br>• Apply for programs that provide housing subsidies |
| More spiritual fulfillment | • Attend services at synagogue once a month<br>• Meditate once a week<br>• Take a nature walk once a week |
| Improved finances | • Get a part-time job<br>• Learn to cook three inexpensive, nutritional meals<br>• Reduce the number of fast-food meals to one per week |

## Curriculum

The core content of the IMR program is organized into nine module topics, each of which is summarized in a handout. The handouts contain practical information and describe strategies and skills that help consumers (1) develop their own recovery goals, (2) make informed decisions about treatment, (3) increase their social support, (4) develop relapse prevention plans, (5) take medication regularly, and (6) cope effectively with symptoms. The practitioner and consumer typically spend two to four sessions working on each module. Depending on the consumer's abilities and preferences, different strategies are used to teach the materials in the modules; practitioners may read sections out loud or summarize the main points without reading directly from the handout. A corresponding series of Practitioners' Guidelines suggest specific ways practitioners can help consumers learn the material and put into practice the knowledge and strategies in each module. The practitioner encourages practice both during the session and in the consumer's everyday life. The nine topics covered in the handouts are specified in Table 17.3.

| | TABLE 17.3 Educational Handouts in IMR |
|---|---|
| **no.** | **Topic of Handout** |
| 1 | Recovery Strategies |
| 2 | Practical Facts about Mental Illness (three separate handouts about schizophrenia, bipolar disorder, and major depression) |
| 3 | The Stress-Vulnerability Model and Strategies for Treatment |
| 4 | Building Social Support |
| 5 | Using Medication Effectively |
| 6 | Reducing Relapses |
| 7 | Coping with Stress |
| 8 | Coping with Problems and Symptoms |
| 9 | Getting Your Needs Met in the Mental Health System |

1. *Recovery Strategies* sets a positive, optimistic tone about the ability of consumers to take control over their lives. The module introduces the concept of recovery, encourages consumers to explore and develop their own definitions it and helps them take steps toward realizing their goals. For example, while working with this module, one consumer defined recovery as "working and having friends." He identified three recovery goals: (1) finding a part-time job that involved working with animals, (2) joining an organization where he would have the opportunity to meet new people, (3) and working in a local community program that delivered meals to housebound senior citizens.

2. *Practical Facts about Mental Illness* provides information about schizophrenia, bipolar disorder, and major depression. The module explains how psychiatric diagnoses are established, their symptoms, how common they are, and the course of illness. Several examples are given of famous people with a psychiatric disorder who have made positive contributions to society. Learning basic facts about mental illness helps consumers to conceptualize their problems as related to a specific disorder for which effective treatments exist. One consumer working with this module found it particularly helpful to learn that difficulty concentrating was a symptom of her illness and not "laziness," as she had previously thought. She became interested in exploring coping strategies to help improve her concentration.

3. *The Stress-Vulnerability Model and Treatment Strategies* module summarizes this model of mental illness, which establishes the foundation for treatment. According to the model, psychiatric disorders are biological in nature, but their severity and course can be affected by stress. The effects of biological vulnerability and stress can be minimized, however, enabling consumers to optimize their outcome and functioning. Specifically, taking medication and not abusing substances can reduce biological vulnerability, whereas minimizing exposure to stress, improving social support, and learning coping skills can reduce the effects of stress, thereby improving functioning. Being

*Setting a positive tone*

*Learning basic facts*

*The foundation of treatment*

informed about the nature of mental illnesses and effective treatments helps engage consumers actively in the treatment process and provides the optimistic message that effective symptom management is possible. For example, when working on this module, one consumer made the connection between experiencing stress and having increased symptoms of depression. This insight led to an interest in developing strategies for reducing stress in his life.

**Relational strategies**

4. *Building Social Support* describes strategies for improving social relationships, which is an important goal for many consumers. In this module consumers evaluate their satisfaction with their social supports, identify places to meet people, and develop strategies for increasing closeness in personal relationships. Social skills training techniques are sometimes used to help consumers learn needed skills in the sessions and then practice them in the community. For example, one consumer practiced how to start conversations in several sessions and was then able to initiate a conversation with the person sitting next to her at a concert.

**Pros and cons of taking medication**

5. *Using Medication Effectively* provides information about the role of medications in treatment and how they can help people achieve their goals. The benefits and side effects of taking medications are discussed. For example, when discussing the pros and cons of taking medication, one consumer identified that he had been experiencing the side effect of drowsiness, which had led him to stop taking his medication. Not taking medication, however, had resulted in an increase in hearing voices, becoming distracted on the job, and eventually a relapse of more severe symptoms. He decided to work with his doctor regarding medication options that would have fewer side effects. Consumers who choose to take medications, but take them inconsistently, are taught strategies for incorporating medication into their daily routine (i.e., behavioral tailoring).

**Triggers and early warning signs**

6. *Reducing Relapses* involves working with the consumer to examine past experiences with relapses in order to prevent future ones. Triggers and early warning signs of relapse are identified and a specific plan for identifying and

preventing relapses is formulated. The consumer and the practitioner often use role plays to rehearse the steps of the relapse prevention plan. In this module, consumers are encouraged to include a family member or another supportive person in talking about past relapses and developing the relapse prevention plan. For example, one consumer invited his father and brother to participate in some sessions about relapse prevention. They helped him to identify early warning signs, some of which he had not recognized, such as spending increased time alone in his bedroom. As part of his relapse prevention plan he asked his family to let him know when they noticed early warning signs and to help him contact his treatment team so that he could avoid a full-blown relapse.

7. *Coping with Stress* involves helping consumers to recognize different types of stress and identify their own physical and emotional reactions to these stressors. Coping effectively with stress can decrease symptoms and distress, increase consumers' ability to manage their illness, and improve their quality of life. Several different strategies for coping with stress are taught, such as relaxation and imagery techniques. For example, one consumer reported that she experienced stress at her job and found it difficult to relax at the end of the day. She explored several different ways of coping with stress, including taking a walk in the evening to help her unwind, and learning a muscle relaxation technique, which she practiced in the session and then later used at work when she felt tense. She said she found these strategies very helpful, and as a result, experienced less stress at work.

| Relaxation and imagery techniques

8. *Coping with Problems and Symptoms* involves teaching consumers two approaches for managing difficulties: (1) a step-by-step problem-solving method, and (2) specific coping skills. Problem solving includes a six-step method: defining the problem, brainstorming possible solutions, evaluating the advantages and disadvantages of each solution, choosing the best solution or combination of solutions, planning how to implement the solution, and evaluating how well the plan worked. This problem-solving

| Step-by-step problem-solving method

method is then used in the sessions and in real-life situations to solve problems and achieve goals. One consumer, for example, used the problem-solving method to address his goal of increasing his fitness. Possible solutions he generated included joining an exercise class, lifting weights at home, or running; he decided that running was the best. His implementation plan included buying running shoes, locating a local park with a running path, walking the half-mile path three times the 1st week, alternating walking and running three times the 2nd week, and running three times the 3rd and 4th weeks. When he evaluated how well the plan was working 5 weeks later, he decided that although he was running as planned, he felt it would be more enjoyable to run with someone. He then used problem solving again to develop a plan for asking a friend to join him at least once a week. He also made plans to increase his running distance to 1 mile over the course of the next 2 months.

**Specific coping skills**    In coping skills training, consumers first review how they currently cope with symptoms and are then taught how to amplify those strategies that are working. Because research shows that the more coping skills consumers have in their repertoire, the more effective their coping efficacy (Falloon & Talbot, 1981; Mueser, Valentiner, & Agresta, 1997), new coping strategies are also developed, and practiced in the session and at home. For example, one consumer identified strategies to help him cope with hearing voices that criticize and upset him. Since listening to a Walkman had helped to distract him from voices in the past, he decided to try using that strategy more often. He also tried the strategy of getting involved in an activity that took his mind off the voices, and found that working on crossword puzzles was very helpful in reducing the impact of the voices.

**Learning the ropes**    9. *Getting Your Needs Met in the Mental Health System* provides an overview of the mental health system, including the services and programs commonly offered by community health centers and benefits to which consumers may be entitled. Many community health centers, for example, offer case management, medication services, support groups, social skills training, family psychoeducation, substance abuse treatment, and employment services. Financial benefits include SSDI (Social Security Disability Insurance), SSI (Supplemental Security Income), and public assistance; insurance benefits include Medicare and Medicaid. Eligibility requirements and application procedures can be complex, however, and many consumers benefit from help in navigating the system. Consumers are also taught strategies for advocating for themselves when they encounter problems in the mental health system.

For example, when working with this module, one consumer learned about supported employment programs. The consumer became interested in work and after learning more about supported employment she, enrolled in the program.

At the end of each IMR session, practitioners help consumers to plan how they will practice skills, review information, or share what they have learned with significant others. The practitioner and the consumer collaborate on developing home assignments related to the consumer's goal or the module topic. Some examples are provided in Table 17.4.

Home assignments

| TABLE 17.4 Examples of Home Assignments | |
|---|---|
| *General types of home assignments* | *Specific examples of home assignments* |
| Practicing a social skill | Start a conversation with the coworker who shares the same office |
| Using a coping strategy | Practice a muscle relaxation exercise at bedtime three times a week |
| Getting more information about a goal | Contact a local health club for information about joining |
| Taking a step toward a personal goal | Complete the registration form for enrolling in a class |
| Sharing a handout, checklist, or plan with a significant other | Share the handout "Practical Facts about Bipolar Disorder" with brother and identify the symptoms that have been experienced |

## Curriculum Benefits and Format

The curriculum in IMR was designed for consumers with schizophrenia, schizoaffective disorder, bipolar disorder, and major depression. IMR has been provided to a variety of different consumers, ranging from those with a recent onset of their mental illness to those who developed it many years ago, including consumers in long-term inpatient treatment facilities. Although consumers may be familiar with some of the information and skills taught in IMR, most can benefit from learning more and working closely with a practitioner in pursuing personal goals.

IMR can be taught in an individual or group format. The primary advantages of the individual format are that the practitioner can pace the material more easily to meet each consumer's needs and can devote more time to addressing his or her personal goals and specific concerns. It may also be easier to engage some people in individual treatment than in group treatment. The main advantages of the group format are that it provides consumers with more sources of support, feedback, encouragement, ideas, and role models from other consumers who have had similar experiences. Teaching in a group may also be more cost effective.

IMR services can be provided in a variety of different settings, including the mental health center, the consumer's home, the home of a family member/significant other, or even a public place such as a coffee shop. The setting should have ample lighting (to review handouts), comfortable seating, and some privacy. Regardless of the location, the practitioner should strive to create an environment that is safe, quiet, free of unnecessary distractions, and conducive to learning and practicing the material.

IMR sessions are generally scheduled weekly and last between 45 and 60 minutes, although more or less frequent sessions can be arranged. The most critical determinant of session length is the consumer's ability to remain engaged and learn the relevant material. Shorter sessions (e.g., 30–40 minutes) may be held depending on consumers' preferences and abilities. Taking a break during a session is another strategy to avoid taxing the cognitive resources of consumers. Conducting multiple sessions per week, such as in the hospital, is feasible and minimizes the loss of learned material between sessions. IMR sessions are conducted following a standardized structure, as summarized in Table 17.5.

| TABLE 17.5<br>Structure of an IMR Session | |
|---|---|
| *Step* | **Time**<br>(minutes) |
| 1.  Informal socializing | 1–3 |
| 2.  Review content of previous session | 1–3 |
| 3.  Review home assignment from previous session | 3–5 |
| 4.  Follow up on goals | 1–3 |
| 5.  Set agenda for current session | 1–2 |
| 6.  Teach new material or review previously taught material; practice new strategies or skills | 30–40 |
| 7.  Agree on home assignment to be completed before the next session | 3–5 |
| 8.  Summarize progress made in current session | 3–5 |

Consumers often benefit from involving significant others in IMR to help them learn how to better manage their mental illness and to support them in pursuing their recovery goals. Significant others may include family members, friends, roommates, neighbors, cousins, landlords, members of the clergy, or anyone else the consumer identifies as providing a supportive relationship. With the permission of the consumer, significant others can be involved in a variety of ways, such as reading the educational handouts, helping to practice specific skills, and participating in some sessions.

Involvement of significant others

## Teaching Strategies

To help consumers learn IMR and apply it to their day-to-day lives, practitioners use a combination of motivational, educational, and cognitive–behavioral teaching methods.

### Motivational Strategies

Time and effort are required to learn the information and skills taught in IMR. In order to motivate consumers to invest their energies, they need to understand the relevance of IMR to achieving their goals. Directly linking consumers' personal goals with the content of each IMR module increases motivation to learn the material and practice the skills. For example, one consumer who was working on the "Reducing Relapses" module had the goal of finding work as a floral designer. When the practitioner explored with the consumer how staying out of the hospital could help her maintain a job, she then became interested in developing an effective relapse prevention plan.

Genuine sense of hope and positive expectation

To help consumers sustain motivation, practitioners need to convey a genuine sense of hope and positive expectation regarding consumers and their abilities to achieve recovery-oriented goals. Practitioners can help consumers reframe past negative experiences in a more positive light, thereby instilling hope for the future. For example, one consumer saw past hospitalizations as a sign of personal failure and was discouraged about her ability to stay out of the hospital and pursue her goals, which included regaining custody of her children. The practitioner asked her to describe the strategies she had used to stay out of the hospital and the personal strengths she had relied on, or developed, to cope with being hospitalized. As she talked about her experiences, she started to view herself as a "survivor" who had grown stronger as a result of these experiences. With this perspective, the consumer developed a greater sense of hope and increased confidence in her ability to tackle new challenges.

## Educational Strategies

In order to impart information effectively, education must be interactive, not purely didactic. People learn information by actively processing it in discussion with someone else. This interaction involves pausing frequently when presenting information to listen actively to the consumer's reactions and perspectives, talking about what the information means to him or her, and clarifying questions that arise. The practitioner must also frequently evaluate the consumer's understanding of information. One effective way to do this is to periodically stop and ask the consumer to summarize what he or she has learned, and then to clarify any misunderstandings or fill in any gaps. Information should also be broken down into small segments. The pace of teaching varies, with some people absorbing the information faster than others.

*Interactive teaching*

## Cognitive–Behavioral Strategies

Because research shows that educational techniques alone are insufficient to improve consumers' ability to manage their mental illness (Mueser et al., 2002), other teaching strategies are needed to help them put knowledge into action. Cognitive–behavioral techniques involve the systematic application of learning principles to help people acquire and use the information and skills taught in IMR. A number of different techniques is employed to help consumers master the material, including reinforcement, shaping, modeling, role plays and practice, homework, coping skills enhancement, and cognitive restructuring.

### Reinforcement

We typically experience consequences following our behaviors, and the nature of these consequences can significantly affect the frequency of the behaviors that they follow. Consequences that increase the rate of the behavior are called *reinforcers*. When the consequences that follow a behavior involve adding something positive, we call it *positive reinforcement*. When the consequences involve removing something negative, we call it *negative reinforcement*.

Examples of positive reinforcement include providing something pleasant, such as a nice meal, money, a hug, or praise following a behavior we seek to build in frequency. Examples of negative reinforcement include decreasing something that is unpleasant, such as anxiety, sadness, boredom, stress or, distressing symptoms. When teaching IMR, the practitioner may use positive reinforcement in the form of praise, smiles, interest, and enthusiasm to help consumers learn information and skills in sessions and to motivate them to review that information and practice the newly acquired skills on their own. As consumers learn skills for managing their illness and making progress toward recovery, they experience the naturally reinforcing effects, including reduced distress, increased self-sufficiency, and attainment of their personal goals.

### Shaping

*Shaping* is the reinforcement of successive steps toward achieving a desired goal. As consumers work on learning complex skills, such as developing a relapse prevention plan, it is important for the practitioner to recognize the steps taken toward learning these skills and provide ample

**Shaping attitude**

positive feedback and encouragement. Taking a "shaping attitude" includes drawing attention to the small gains consumers make, praising their efforts, and letting them know they are making progress.

### Modeling

*Modeling* is the explicit demonstration of a skill in order to teach it. Showing people how to do something is often more powerful than simply instructing them about how to do it. When modeling a skill, the practitioner first describes the skill and then explains how he or she will demonstrate it. The practitioner then models the skill, and when completed, obtains feedback from the consumer about what he or she observed and how effective the skill appeared to be. The consumer then practices the skill in a role play (see below). For example, while working on the module "Building Social Support," one consumer wanted to improve her relationship with her roommate by complimenting her more often. The practitioner modeled how she might give a compliment to the roommate about how well she prepared a favorite dish, lasagna. She then asked the consumer how well she thought it would work if she complimented her roommate in this way.

*Role Plays and Practice*
Role plays are used to help the consumer try out a skill and receive feedback from the practitioner. Typically, role plays are conducted after a skill has first been discussed and modeled. For example, after the practitioner modeled the skill of giving a compliment to the consumer's roommate, she set up a role play for the consumer to practice how she would do so. After she completed the role play, the practitioner noted the strengths of the enactment in specific terms: how the consumer made good eye contact and was specific about what she was complimenting. The practitioner also made a suggestion about how the skill could be done even more effectively (i.e., by speaking less timidly). The role play was followed by additional practice to increase the consumer's skill and confidence before trying it out in her apartment. Practitioners can find more detailed information about teaching social skills using modeling, role plays, and practice in Bellack, Mueser, Gingerich, and Agresta (2004).

*Homework*
Homework assignments, described earlier in this chapter, are a critical component of the IMR program. Specific assignments, which are collaboratively developed, to practice skills at home are helpful after a skill has been taught and practiced in the session. The consumer should be familiar with the skill and have a specific plan for when, where, and with whom he or she would like to practice. For example, one consumer who was working on the "Coping with Stress" module practiced the muscle relaxation exercise in the session and agreed on a home assignment to practice the exercise every other evening after dinner, using a comfortable chair in the living room. The practitioner followed up with the consumer, who told him that he

found the exercise relaxing, but was having difficulty staying awake afterward. The consumer and the practitioner then used problem solving to come up with strategies for staying awake, including changing the time for doing the exercise or using a straight-back wooden chair. The consumer chose the strategy of doing the exercise before dinner and practiced it at 4:00 P.M. three times a week for his next homework assignment. The following week he reported that the change in time made it possible to experience relaxation without sleepiness.

*Coping Skills Enhancement*

Coping skills enhancement involves using cognitive–behavioral strategies to help consumers develop more effective strategies for managing distressing and persistent symptoms, such as depression, anxiety, hallucinations, and paranoia. First, a careful behavioral analysis of the consumer's symptoms and coping efforts is conducted, including identifying situations in which a symptom is most severe or distressing, noting any coping strategies that the consumer uses to deal with it, and evaluating the effectiveness of these efforts. Second, if the consumer occasionally uses some coping strategies that appear effective, plans are made to increase the use of those strategies. Third, additional coping strategies are taught to manage the symptoms. The practitioner and consumer consider possible coping strategies (described in the educational handout) and jointly select one that holds promise. The practitioner may first model that coping strategy for the consumer, who then practices it in the session. Plans are made for the consumer to practice the skill at home. As consumers learn more skills for coping with persistent symptoms, their distress related to these symptoms decreases, and they develop a greater sense of self-efficacy regarding their ability to cope with them.

*Cognitive Restructuring*

Cognitive restructuring is a technique that involves helping people to identify and change inaccurate, discouraging, or

Steps in coping skills enhancement

self-defeating beliefs into more accurate and more adaptive ways of looking at things. There are many opportunities to employ cognitive restructuring in teaching IMR. For example, in the first few sessions, practitioners may help consumers challenge the belief that having a mental illness means not being able to pursue and achieve their goals. This can be done by introducing the concept of recovery, encouraging consumers to define recovery in terms of their own goals, and identifying famous people with mental illness who have made significant contributions to society. Cognitive restructuring can also be taught more formally as a coping skill for dealing with negative emotions. The essence of this strategy is to convey the message that feelings are the byproduct of thoughts, that such thoughts are often inaccurate, and that people can decide to change their thoughts to more accurate ones based on an examination of the evidence.

The basic components of IMR are summarized in Table 17.6.

| TABLE 17.6 Summary of the IMR Program | |
|---|---|
| Overall goal | Consumers learn information, strategies, and skills for managing their mental illness and making progress in their recovery process. |
| Format | Consumers meet with practitioners for weekly sessions either individually or as part of a small group (eight consumers or less). |
| Length of sessions | 45–60 minutes |
| Length of intervention | 4–8 months (usually longer for group intervention) |
| Role of personal goals | Consumers identify and pursue personal recovery goals throughout the program. |

*Continued on following page*

| | **TABLE 17.6** (continued) |
|---|---|
| Significant others | With the person's permission, significant others are involved in the program, such as attending some sessions, reviewing educational handouts, helping the consumer complete homework assignments, collaborating on the formulation of a relapse prevention plan, and supporting the consumer in pursuing personal goals. |
| Curriculum | Educational handouts summarize the information taught in the nine modules: recovery strategies, practical facts about mental illness, the stress-vulnerability model, building social support, using medication effectively, reducing relapses, coping with stress, coping with problems and symptoms, and getting your needs met in the mental health system. |
| Teaching skills used by the practitioners | Motivational strategies, educational strategies, and cognitive–behavioral techniques |
| Role of practice | Consumers practice the skills in the sessions and as part of home assignments. |

**José**

JOSÉ IS A 22-YEAR-OLD MAN who began the IMR program 1 year after he was diagnosed with schizophrenia. When he first experienced symptoms, he was working as a library assistant and began to hear voices coming from the books he was shelving. José's parents lived in the area but had become estranged from him after he threatened them, because voices told him that they were robot-imposters of his real parents. José had five hospitalizations related to severe auditory hallucinations in the year subsequent to his first hospitalization. The repeated hospitalizations led to José's losing his job and, as a result, a number of financial difficulties. After his last hospitalization, his practitioner at the community mental health center recommended to José that they begin working on the IMR program. He told his practitioner that he was confused about his diagnosis and was discouraged about the future. He was initially reluctant to participate in the IMR program until the practitioner explained that they would be working together to help him identify and pursue personal goals. They spent a session establishing the following personal goals:

- Avoid going back to the hospital.
- Find a job.
- Improve José's relationship with his parents.

José initially refused to let the practitioner contact his parents, given his fears about them. The practitioner, however, spent some time discussing José's concerns and reviewed the pros and cons of involving his parents. After some hesitation, José agreed that the practitioner could contact his family members, but only to let them know about the program and send them copies of some of the educational handouts.

The practitioner referred to at least one of José's goals in every session, to enhance his motivation to work on the information and skills covered in IMR. For example, José's goal of avoiding rehospitalization motivated him to learn practical facts about schizophrenia and strategies for reducing relapses. Homework assignments were tailored to address his goals as well, such as developing a relapse prevention plan that included an awareness of early warning signs that his symptoms might be returning. He agreed to let the practitioner send his parents the "Practical Facts about Schizophrenia" handout and later agreed that they could attend some of the sessions that focused on reducing relapses. His parents became more understanding of his situation after they realized that his previous threatening behavior had been the result of his illness. They were also able to help José identify some early warning signs of relapse, such as increased irritability and distractibility, which he had not recognized in himself.

The "Recovery Strategies" module was encouraging to José as he contemplated his goal of returning to work, and he decided to start looking for a part-time job working with books. José identified that he was very anxious about interviewing for jobs again, given his previous experience with losing his job. José's practitioner discussed the potential value of the "Coping with Stress" module in helping José identify ways to manage his anxiety. He agreed that this module would be helpful for him. The practitioner used cognitive–behavioral teaching strategies by modeling the muscle relaxation exercise and then gave José an opportunity to practice it in the sessions. Homework assignments included doing the muscle relaxation exercise three times a week.

José also said that he felt anxious around his parents because of previous incidents related to his illness (e.g., calling his parents robots). To address this issue, José and his practitioner identified and practiced conversational skills for interacting pleasantly with his parents, based on the "Building Social Support" module. After developing more confidence in his ability to converse with his parents, José was successful in his home assignment of attending a family dinner and carrying on a pleasant conversation. In response to his desire for more friends, the practitioner also helped José to practice starting conversations with new people and identify good places for meeting people.

As José began to pursue his goal of employment, the "Coping with Problems and Symptoms" module was especially helpful in developing specific coping strategies for the persistent auditory hallucinations that often interfered with his concentration. José found that the best strategy for him was to use positive self-talk, such as telling himself, "I'm going to stay cool and not let these voices get to me," which he practiced in sessions and at home. He also practiced the strategy of listening to music on a personal compact disc player to help distract him from the voices.

After 28 sessions, José had completed the nine modules and had made significant progress toward his goals. With the help of his parents, he had developed a written relapse prevention plan that included what to do if he experienced early warning signs and letting his parents know when he needed help. He was participating in a supported employment program to help him find work and had scheduled an interview for a part-time job at a bookstore. His relationship with his parents was improving, and he was planning to attend Thanksgiving dinner at their house. At his last session of IMR, he told the practitioner, "I don't feel helpless anymore. There are things I can do to make a difference. I'm much more optimistic about the future and what I can accomplish."

## Directions for Future Research of IMR

The IMR program was developed in order to incorporate evidence-based practices for the management of mental illness into a cohesive package, including psychoeducation, strategies for improving medication adherence, relapse prevention training, and coping skills enhancement. Although each of these treatment components is supported by extensive research, IMR as a program has not been systematically evaluated and should be a focus of research to test the hypotheses that IMR can facilitate a variety of outcomes, including prevention of relapse and rehospitalizations, reduction in symptom severity, enhanced knowledge of mental illness, medication adherence, coping self-efficacy, progress toward personal goals, hopefulness and optimism, perceived social support, and treatment alliance with mental health professionals.

IMR hypotheses to be tested

Another area worthy of research concerns the timing of providing IMR. Although IMR may be effective for consumers at any point in the course of their illness, it may be especially helpful soon after the onset of a mental illness, when consumers and their significant others could have an opportunity to develop a positive outlook about managing the illness and the ability to achieve meaningful personal goals. Learning the fundamentals of illness management and developing a personal concept of recovery may help consumers prevent the relapses and hospitalizations that often interrupt important life events, such as education and employment, and that contribute to feelings of helplessness and low self-esteem.

Finally, research is needed to compare the individual approach with the group format of IMR in order to determine whether one format is more effective than the other for some consumers and to evaluate the relative cost-effectiveness of each.

## References

Anthony, W. A. (1993). Recovery from mental illness: The guiding vision of the mental health service system in the 1990s. *Psychosocial Rehabilitation Journal, 16*, 11–23.

Azrin, N. H., & Teichner, G. (1998). Evaluation of an instructional program for improving medication compliance for chronically mentally ill outpatients. *Behaviour Research and Therapy, 36*, 849–861.

Bäuml, J., Kissling, W., & Pitschel-Walz, G. (1996). Psychoedukative gruppen für schizophrene patienten: Einfluss auf wissensstand und compliance [Psychoeducational groups for schizophrenic patients: Effects on Knowledge and compliance. *Nervenheilkunde, 15*, 145–150.

Baxter, E. A., & Diehl, S. (1998). Emotional stages: Consumers and family members recovering from the trauma of mental illness. *Psychiatric Rehabilitation Journal 21*, 349–355.

Bellack, A., Mueser, K., Gingerich, S., & Agresta, J. (2004). *Social skills training for schizophrenia: A step-by-step guide.* New York: Guilford Press.

Boczkowski, J., Zeichner, A., & DeSanto, N. (1985). Neuroleptic compliance among chronic schizophrenic outpatients: An intervention outcome report. *Journal of Consulting and Clinical Psychology, 53*, 666–671.

Buchkremer, G., & Fiedler, P. (1987). Kognitive vs. Handlungsorientierte Therapie [Cognitive vs. action-oriented treatment]. *Nervenarzt, 58*, 481–488.

Copeland, M. E. (1997). *Wellness recovery action plan.* Brattleboro, VT: Peach Press.

Cramer, J. A., & Rosenheck, R. (1999). Enhancing medication compliance for people with serious mental illness. *The Journal of Nervous and Mental Disease, 187*, 53–55.

Deegan, P. (1996, September). *Recovery and the conspiracy of hope.* Paper presented at the Sixth Annual Mental Health Conference of Australia and New Zealand, Brisbane, Australia. (Note: This paper is also available at *www.intentionalcare.org.*)

Falloon, I. R. H., & Talbot, R. E. (1981). Persistent auditory hallucinations: Coping mechanisms and implications for management. *Psychological Medicine, 11*, 329–339.

Gingerich, S., Mueser, K. T., & co-leaders of the development team. (2002). *Illness management and recovery: Implementation resource kit.* Rockville, MD: Substance Abuse and Mental Health Services Administration.

Goldman, C. R., & Quinn, F. L. (1988). Effects of a patient education program in the treatment of schizophrenia. *Hospital and Community Psychiatry, 39*, 282–286.

Gould, R. A., Mueser, K. T., Bolton, E., Mays, V., & Goff, D. (2001). Cognitive therapy for psychosis in schizophrenia: A preliminary meta-analysis. *Schizophrenia Research, 48*, 335–342.

Hafner, H., Maurer, K., Laffler, W., an der Heiden, W., Hambrecht, M., & Schultze-Lutter, F. (2003). Modeling the early course of schizophrenia. *Schizophrenia Bulletin, 29*, 325–340.

Herz, M. I., Lamberti, J. S., Mintz, J., Scott, R., O'Dell, S. P., McCartan, L., et al. (2000). A program for relapse prevention in schizophrenia: A controlled study. *Archives of General Psychiatry, 57*, 277–283.

Kelly, G. R., & Scott, J. E. (1990). Medication compliance and health education among outpatients with chronic mental disorders. *Medical Care, 28*, 1181–1197.

Kemp, R., Kirov, G., Everitt, B., Hayward, P., & David, A. (1998). Randomized controlled trial of compliance therapy: 18-month follow-up. *British Journal of Psychiatry, 173*, 271–272.

Lam, D. H., Bright, J., Jones, S., Hayward, P., Schuck, N., Chisholm, D., & Sham, P. (2000). Cognitive therapy for bipolar illness: A pilot study of relapse prevention. *Cognitive Therapy and Research, 24*, 503–520.

Leclerc, C., Lesage, A. D., Ricard, N., Lecomte, T., & Cyr, M. (2000). Assessment of a new rehabilitative coping skills module for persons with schizophrenia. *American Journal of Orthopsychiatry, 70*, 380–388.

Lecomte, T., Cyr, M., Lesage, A. D., Wilde, J. Leclerc, C., & Ricard, N. (1999). Efficacy of a self-esteem module in the empowerment of individuals with schizophrenia. *Journal of Nervous and Mental Disease, 187*, 406–413.

Low, A. A. (1957). *Mental health through will-training: A system of self Help in psychotherapy as practiced by recovery*, (7th ed.). Boston: Christopher Publishing House.

MacPherson, R., Jerrom, B., & Hughes, A. (1996). A controlled study of education about drug treatment in schizophrenia. *British Journal of Psychiatry, 168*, 709–717.

Miller, W., & Rollnick, S. (2003). *Motivational interviewing: Preparing people to change addictive behavior.* New York: Guilford Press.

Mueser, K. T., & Gingerich, S. (in press). *Coping with schizophrenia: A guide for families.* New York: Guilford Press.

Mueser, K. T., Corrigan, P. W., Hilton, D. W., Tanzman, B., Schaub, A., & Gingerich, S., (2002). Illness management and recovery: A review of the research. *Psychiatric Services, 53,* 1272–1284. (Note: This paper is also available at *www.mental-healthpractices.org.*)

Mueser, K. T., Valentiner, D. P., & Agresta, J. (1997). Coping with negative symptoms of schizophrenia: Patient and family perspectives. *Schizophrenia Bulletin, 23,* 329–339.

Perry, A., Tarrier, N., Morriss, R., McCarthy, E., & Limb, K. (1999). Randomised controlled trial of efficacy of teaching patients with bipolar disorder to identify early symptoms of relapse and obtain treatment. *British Medical Journal, 318,* 149–153.

Razali, M. S., & Yahya, H. (1995). Compliance with treatment in schizophrenia: A drug intervention program in a developing country. *Acta Psychiatrica Scandinavica, 91,* 331–335.

Schaub, A., & Mueser, K. T. (2000, November). *Coping-oriented treatment of schizophrenia and schizoaffective disorder: Rationale and preliminary results.* Paper presented at the 34th Annual Convention of the Association for the Advancement of Behavior Therapy, New Orleans.

Scott, J., Garland, A., & Moorhead, S. (2001). A pilot study of cognitive therapy in bipolar disorders. *Psychological Medicine 31,* 459–467.

Spaniol, L., Koehler, M., & Hutchinson, D. (1994). *The recovery workbook: Practical coping and empowerment strategies for people with psychiatric disability.* Boston: Boston University, Center for Psychiatric Rehabilitation, Sargent College of Allied Health Professions.

# EIGHTEEN

# Evidence-Based Practices for Families of Individuals with Severe Mental Illness

*Aaron Murray-Swank*
*Lisa Dixon*

MANY PEOPLE WITH SEVERE MENTAL ILLNESS (SMI) rely on family members for assistance and support. Over half of adults who have SMI live with their families, who often provide emotional support, financial assistance, advocacy, and treatment coordination for their ill relative (Solomon & Draine, 1995). Unfortunately, family members, or other persons who are supportive to people with SMI, often have difficulty finding information and resources to help them navigate these multiple roles. Over the past 25 years, a number of effective evidenced-based approaches have been developed to include family members of consumers in treatment and meet their needs for information, clinical guidance, and support. Our primary aim is to present these approaches, to provide a summary of the research evidence regarding these interventions, and to offer guidance on the implementation of family interventions.

## Family Interventions for People with SMI:
## A Brief History

In an earlier era of mental health treatment, disruptions in family dynamics were believed to play a major role in

Stress–diathesis model

causing disorders such as schizophrenia. Thus, family therapies in the 1950s and 1960s attempted to work with families to correct supposedly dysfunctional interaction patterns. Since then, decades of research have discredited the idea that family interactions play a primary role in causing schizophrenia. The current scientific consensus is that schizophrenia and other severe mental illnesses are primarily biologically based conditions that can be understood within a stress–diathesis framework. The Stress–diathesis model indicates that both biology and environmental stress play a role in mental illness. Persons with SMI have a genetic vulnerability to develop psychiatric problems, and life stressors influence the course of the disorder over time. Following from the basic tenets of this model, providing both medication and psychosocial services (e.g., family support, rehabilitation) are necessary for optimal treatment and recovery. Although environment is clearly important, the focus on family interactions as a driving environmental causal force has not been supported. Furthermore, there is no evidence that therapeutic approaches based on a "family dysfunction" model were useful in helping consumers and their families. Unfortunately, these interventions also alienated families from the mental health system. In sum, interventions based in the idea that family interactions cause schizophrenia have been found to be ineffective and even harmful to consumers and their families.

**Expressed emotion**    The concept of expressed emotion (EE) has been important in the development of family psychoeducational programs. This concept grew out of research attempting to understand the relationship between emotions, behaviors, and attitudes of family members and the course of schizophrenia. EE refers to the level of criticism and emotional overinvolvement directed toward a consumer by family members; it has been measured by an interview that assesses these behaviors (the Camberwell Family Interview; Vaughn & Leff, 1976). It is important to note that research has not focused on EE as the *cause* of schizophrenia. Instead, investigators have explored the association between EE and risk of an acute relapse after the illness has developed. A comprehensive review of 25 studies on EE found that high levels of EE in the family are strongly associated with consumer relapse rates. For example, combining data collected from 1,346 families, Bebbington and Kuipers (1994) found that the 1-year relapse rate in high-EE families averaged 50.1%, whereas it was only 21.1% in low-EE families. Recently researchers have suggested that the risk posed by EE may be rooted in biological deficits, because individuals with schizophrenia show particular difficulty processing criticism and regulating arousal due to brain dysfunction in systems that perform these tasks (McFarlane, 2002b).

A few key points regarding EE research and family interventions should be noted. Initially, family psychoeducational programs were targeted to reduce EE and were offered only to families high in EE. However, research has failed to show that reductions in EE account for the effectiveness of family interventions. It is likely that a number of other processes of family psychoeducation, beyond reducing EE, account for its effectiveness. Furthermore, subsequent research has shown that family psychoeducation is helpful for families low in EE (McFarlane et al., 1995), again suggesting that the sole target of family interventions should not be simply reducing EE. Finally, many family members have experienced the idea of EE as another form of blaming family members for their relatives' illness (Hatfield, Spaniol, & Zipple, 1987), although EE researchers did not intend to communicate this message. In sum, research on EE highlights important factors that may help avoid relapse and maintain well-being for consumers with schizophrenia. In particular, environments that are calm, low-key, and limit intense expression of criticism and negative emotion appear to facilitate better outcomes for recovery. More research on the role and meaning of EE in different cultural contexts is needed.

## General Goals and Principles of Evidence-Based Family Interventions

Concept of family

The concept of family should be broadly considered when designing and conducting interventions. Families may include parents, siblings, spouses, partners, grandparents, aunts, uncles, and other extended family members. Family may also include individuals who are not blood relatives, such as friends and other important people in the lives of consumers. For the purposes of family interventions, family has been defined as "anyone committed to the care and support of the person with mental illness" (Dartmouth Psychiatric Research Center, 2002, p. 1).

Effective ingredients of successful family interventions

Before presenting the primary models of family intervention, it is important to consider some general principles of working with families of consumers. A variety of clinical programs, typically referred to as family psychoeducational programs, have been developed. These programs are offered as part of overall mental health services, and they have focused mainly on supporting the well-being and functioning of the consumer (however, improved family well-being is an important intermediate and additional benefit).

Family psychoeducation

Models of family psychoeducation differ in how they are presented. For example, some are designed to work with one family at a time (Anderson, Reiss, & Hogarty, 1986; Falloon, Boyd, & McGill, 1984), whereas others involve multiple families in a group format (McFarlane, 2002a). Although the models of intervention differ, they all share common threads. These common threads prompted the World Schizophrenia Fellowship (1998) to identify effective ingredients of successful family interventions. According to this international panel of experts, treatments that have been found to be successful accomplish the following tasks in working with consumers and their families:

- Coordinate all elements of treatment and rehabilitation to ensure that everyone is working toward the same goals in a collaborative, supportive partnership.

- Pay attention to both the social and clinical needs of the consumer.
- Provide optimum medication management.
- Listen to families' concerns and involve them as equal partners in the planning and delivery of treatment.
- Explore family members' expectations of the treatment program and expectations for the consumer.
- Assess the strengths and limitations of the family's ability to support the consumer.
- Help resolve family conflict by responding sensitively to emotional distress.
- Address feelings of loss.
- Provide relevant information for the consumer and his or her family at appropriate times.
- Provide an explicit crisis plan and professional response.
- Help improve communication among family members.
- Provide training for the family in structured problem-solving techniques.
- Encourage family members to expand their social support networks—for example, to participate in family support organizations such as the National Alliance for the Mentally Ill (NAMI).
- Be flexible in meeting the needs of the family.

Over the past 25 years, clinicians and researchers have developed a number of specific models reflecting these principles identified by the World Schizophrenia Fellowship. The Schizophrenia Patient Outcomes Research Team (PORT) conducted another review of evidence-based principles of family intervention. The purpose of the PORT is to conduct a rigorous review of the research on medical and psychosocial treatments for schizophrenia, and to offer specific, evidence-based recommendations (Lehman et al., 1998). With regard to family intervention, the PORT recommends that persons with schizophrenia and their families, who have ongoing contact with each other, should

PORT
recommendations

be offered a family intervention. The key elements of this intervention include a duration of at least 9 months, mental illness education, crisis intervention, emotional support, and training in how to cope with illness symptoms and related problems (Lehman et al., 2003). Program length is emphasized by the PORT recommendation, based on research that has shown that programs lasting 6 months or less have little effect, whereas the evidence supporting programs lasting 9 months or longer is quite strong (Pitschel-Waltz, Leucht, Bauml, Kissling, & Engel, 2001).

## Models of Family Psychoeducation

Overview | Although evidence-based models of family psychoeducation share a number of common key ingredients, they also differ in format and emphasis in working with the consumer and their family. Fortunately, the clinicians and researchers who have developed each of these models have also conducted well-controlled research on their effects. We now present overviews of the major models of family psychoeducation, including some examples of what they look like in practice. We also provide a brief summary of the research supporting each model as an evidence-based practice (EBP).

### Behavioral Family Management

In the behavioral family management (BFM) model developed by Ian Falloon and his colleagues (Falloon et al., 1984), interventions are tailored to the strengths and needs of the consumer and each family member through a focused assessment. Falloon (2002) recommended interviewing family members individually and also observing the family interacting together to complete the initial assessment. One focus of the assessment is to conduct "problem analysis" by identifying areas of particular concern for the consumer and family (Falloon, 2002). Following the comprehensive assessment, BFM uses presentation, handouts, and discussion to teach the consumer and the family important facts about the nature of schizophrenia and its treatments. After this basic education is provided, interventions are then directed at developing problem-solving skills in the family and teaching strategies for effective communication, with an eye to the issues identified in the assessment process and ongoing assessment of goals. In the BFM approach, individual family sessions are typically conducted in the home, and sessions continue for at least 1–2 years, depending on the needs and circumstances of the consumer and the family (Falloon, 2002).

*Assessment* refers to the process of initially meeting with the consumer and family to collect information and pinpoint the goals of the intervention. For example, some important information to learn about during the assessment includes (1) the course of illness and treatment; (2) each family member's thoughts, feelings, and goals in relation to the presence of the consumer's mental illness-related difficulties; (3) what each family member views as problems and concerns; and (4) the individual goals of the consumer and each family member.

| Assessment

*Problem analysis*, a behavioral therapy technique used to examine important problems identified by family members, involves two basic steps. First, the clinician helps family members specifically identify and describe the problem. For example, if a family talks about "conflict" as a problem, the task of the clinician would be to learn which behaviors constitute a conflict in the family (e.g., arguing, yelling, hitting, avoiding each other). This step would also involve learning exactly where, when, and how often conflict tends to occur. Second, once the problem has been specifically identified, the clinician helps the family look closely at what comes *immediately before* and *immediately after* the identified problem behaviors. If the identified problem were frequent family arguments, the clinician would work with family members to identify what kinds of behaviors trigger arguments, how family members cope with arguments, and what happens in their aftermath. The ultimate goal of the problem analysis is to engage the consumer and family

| Problem analysis

members in collaborative problem solving to accomplish their identified goals. For example, if reducing arguing is a family goal, then the clinician may help family members to recognize what triggers arguments and help them to develop alternative ways of communicating.

**Effectiveness of BFM**

The effectiveness of the BFM approach was first tested in a randomized control trial (RCT) with 36 consumers with schizophrenia and their families, which were identified as high EE (Falloon & Penderson, 1985). Consumers were randomized to individual treatment or BFM. Consumers in the family intervention condition had significantly lower relapse rates than those provided individual treatment. Furthermore, consumers in the family intervention showed less behavioral disturbance and reported that they had better family relationships and more friendships. Additionally, families in the family intervention condition reported less family stress and more satisfaction with the consumer's behavior, compared with families of consumers in the individual treatment condition. Further controlled studies testing the effectiveness of behavioral family management have yielded similarly positive results (Randolph et al., 1994; Zastowny, Lehman, Cole, & Kane, 1992).

### Family Psychoeducation

**Principles of initial contact**

The family psychoeducational approach developed by Carol Anderson and her colleagues (Anderson et al., 1986) involves a gradual treatment effort that first focuses on individually reaching out to the family and providing support. Anderson et al. (1986) outlined a number of important principles to guide the initial contact with families: (1) being immediately available, (2) focusing first on the present crisis, (3) avoiding treating the family as the "patient," (4) attending to family supports and stresses, and (5) establishing the clinician as the family representative.

**Family psychoeducation vignette**

When initially establishing a connection with the family, the clinician must communicate empathy and an atmosphere of collaboration. Care must be taken to avoid criticism and judgment of family members. In their treatment manual, Anderson and colleagues (1986) provided an example of establishing connection with a family in crisis. In this example, the clinician is meeting with the family members for the first time in the psychiatric emergency room. The parents have contacted the police, seeking an involuntary hospitalization for their son. They are upset by their son's anger at them, and they are also feeling guilty about bringing him to the hospital against his will. The family representative met with the family while the consumer was being seen in the emergency room.

CLINICIAN: While Dr. S is seeing your son, I'd like to get your views on what just happened.

Father: Well, it just got so bad; we had to call the police.

MOTHER: I don't even know if I can tell you. It's all been so confusing. He's been acting strange for days, but these last few weeks . . .

FATHER: (*interrupting*) He's been up all night for weeks—laughing and talking to himself. First, he just told us that God was talking to him. Then, he started talking about how people were out to get him. When he asked where I kept my gun, I really got scared. I knew there was no way this was going to settle down.

MOTHER: I've tried to get him to call his old therapist, but he wouldn't. He needs help.

FATHER: So, I told him, "You have to come with us to the hospital," and he swung at me and locked himself in his room.

MOTHER: When he is himself, he is very gentle, but when he gets like this, we get scared.

CLINICIAN: I'm sure you do. So this has been getting worse for weeks?

MOTHER: At least. We've put up with a lot, you know. We don't like to do this to him.

CLINICIAN: I guess you wouldn't have gotten the police involved unless things were really bad.

FATHER: He was talking about "getting even" with the CIA.

MOTHER: We don't know exactly what he means, but we get scared. Now, he blames us for everything. He says the CIA is controlling our minds. I'm afraid he might hurt us. Hurt himself, too.

CLINICIAN: Clearly, you have been through a lot in the past few weeks and particularly tonight. It must be tough when he blames you.

MOTHER: It's terrible, and you know, no one ever understands. He's had problems for 6 years, and no one has ever really helped him.

FATHER: (*angrily*) And now you can't get him in the hospital unless he is out of control. I got him to come down 2 weeks ago before things were so bad, but when he wouldn't sign himself in, they just let him go. They could see he was crazy.

MOTHER: It's the law, Joe. They can't make him stay unless he's dangerous.

FATHER: What kind of law is that? Do they think we want to see him in a hospital just for the fun of it?

CLINICIAN: It must be really frustrating to see someone you love getting worse and not be able to do anything about it, not be able to get anyone to help.

FATHER: It sure is. I've about had it. And I'm still not sure we did the right thing.

MOTHER: I know—he'll blame us for making him come down here, and it will be more trouble.

CLINICIAN: Really, it sounds as though you did the only thing you could under the circumstances. You coped as well as anyone for as long as you could.

MOTHER: I guess so, but it breaks my heart to see him go through it again. (Anderson et al., 1986, pp. 35–36)

As the interview continued, the clinician continued to collect information about recent events and to allow the family to express their thoughts and feelings about what had happened. The transcript from this initial part of the meeting illustrates a few key points as this clinician begins to build a connection with the family. First, the parents have the opportunity to express their feelings without encountering any initial judgment or evaluation from the clinician. Second, as noted by Anderson and associates (1986), the clinician does not provide false reassurances to the family (e.g., "Everything will be fine"). Finally, the clinician communicates that the parents are doing the best that they can in their present difficult circumstances. This message helps to establish an atmosphere of mutual respect and collaboration.

Once a firm connection with the family is established, the clinician works toward establishing a *treatment contract* with the family and consumer. The contract provides a roadmap of the goals and plan of the intervention. Next, family members attend a psychoeducational workshop with other families. The workshop focuses on mental illness education, treatment resources, preventing relapse, and information about social and vocational rehabilitation. Following the educational workshop, the clinician meets regularly with the family and the consumer, using a practical problem-solving approach, to help them navigate the recovery process. The clinician is also available for phone calls, as-needed crisis support, and coordination with other treatment providers to help the family navigate the mental health system. The family psychoeducational approach stresses a few *key concepts*. First, there is a careful effort to establish gradual, realistic goals with the consumer in the recovery process. Second, the family is taught to create an ideal atmosphere to support recovery in the home, one that is quieter, slower, and less intense. The purpose of this guideline is to create an atmosphere that compensates for the difficulties that people with schizophrenia often have with emotionally charged and complex environments, especially in the immediate months following a relapse. Finally, after the consumer has experienced a significant period of stability, efforts are directed toward introducing gradual social and vocational rehabilitation activities.

| Treatment contract

| Key concepts

Effectiveness of family psychoeducation

The effectiveness of the family psychoeducational approach was initially tested in studies by Hogarty and his colleagues (Hogarty et al., 1986; Hogarty et al., 1991). These studies supported the effectiveness of this approach: The program significantly reduced consumer relapses during the 2-year period in which families participated in the intervention. These studies are unique in that they compared the outcomes of family psychoeducation with those of an individual social skills intervention with consumers, and a combination of family and individual treatment (all consumers received standard medication treatment). After 2 years, the relapse rates were 29% for consumers in the family psychoeducational condition, 25% for consumers in the family psychoeducational plus social skills condition, 50% in the individual social skills condition, and 62% for consumers who received only medication and support.

*Relatives Groups*
As the family psychoeducation and BFM models emerged in the United States, the relatives group model was developed and tested by Leff and his colleagues in the United Kingdom (Leff, 1994). Like other models, the format of the relatives group first involves educational presentations that take place in the home with the family. Following the educational sessions, biweekly sessions are held in the home with the consumer and family members. These sessions focus on improving communication, teaching problem solving, and helping the family cope more effectively. Alongside the individual family sessions, family members also have the opportunity to attend biweekly relatives groups (which do not include consumers). Group sessions focus on discussion and problem solving for family members. The rationale for the relatives groups is strongly rooted in research on EE; groups are structured to include families of both high and low EE, with a goal of mutual modeling. Overall, in RCTs, programs based on this model that last a year or more have been found to reduce consumers'

relapse rates significantly (Leff et al., 1989, 1990). Some of these studies tested which component of the model is more effective (relatives group vs. individual family sessions) and found no differential effects on relapse rates (Leff et al., 1989, 1990).

## Psychoeducational Multifamily Groups (PMFG)

The psychoeducational multifamily group (PMFG) was developed by William McFarlane and colleagues to combine the best elements of behavioral family manage-ment, family psychoeducation, and multiple-family approaches. The PMFG model of intervention involves three phases. Initially, efforts are focused on joining and forming a connection with each family member individu-ally. Once a connection has been established, the family attends a multifamily educational workshop. In the next phase of treatment, families attend multifamily group sessions, with a particular emphasis on gradual increases in consumers' community functioning. In these sessions, clinicians work to promote group problem solving around issues and challenges that arise in the consumers' recovery processes. In the final phase of the PMFG, the goal of the group is to evolve into a social network for both families and consumers, as well as a forum for continued clinical monitoring. This phase highlights a unique and potentially beneficial aspect of PMFG: the opportunity for family and consumer to obtain ongoing social support though rela-tionships with others in the multifamily group (McFarlane et al., 2002).

> Phases of treatment

All successful family psychoeducational programs involve structured problem-solving interventions. In PFMG these are conducted either with individual families or with multifamily groups. In either case, the essential steps of problem solving, as initially applied with individual families by Falloon (Fallon et al., 1984), are the same:

> Group problem-solving steps

1. Define the problem and goal.
2. List all the possible solutions.

3. Discuss the advantages and disadvantages of each.
4. Choose the solution that best fits the situation.
5. Plan how to carry out the solution, in detail.
6. Review implementation of the solution.

The overall goal of problem solving with families is to build on their strengths and resources to help them find and implement practical solutions to cope with illness-related difficulties. During the initial part of each session of the PMFG, the group facilitators identify one problem presented by a family as a focus for the session. All family members in the group help generate solutions and identify potential advantages and disadvantages of each. The family members then select the solution that best fits the situation and plan how they implement it. In the following session, the group leaders check back with the family to review how things went in implementing the solution at home (McFarlane et al., 2002).

PFMG research findings | Research has provided strong support for the effectiveness of the PMFG model. In one large-scale study (McFarlane et al., 1995) of the PMFG treatment, 172 consumers/families were randomly assigned to 2 years of participation in (1) single-family treatment that combined family psychoeducation and behavioral family management; or (2) a group following the PMFG model. In this study, the PMFG was shown to be more effective in preventing relapse over a 2-year period (although both treatment groups showed reduced relapse compared with standard rates). Overall, research comparing single-family and multiple-family approaches has found that multifamily groups are particularly effective with consumers who are experiencing their first acute episode of the mental illness and in families with high levels of EE. In contrast, research suggests that families low in EE and consumers with unusually good medication response may fare better in single-family formats. Also, the PMFG approach has been integrated with another EBP, assertive community treatment (ACT), including its supported employment component, to create a model called family-aided assertive community treatment, or FACT. In an RCT comparing FACT with standard vocational rehabilitation, it was found that FACT helped consumers to improve their employment rates (McFarlane et al., 2000). FACT also has been shown to reduce family stress and increase family members' satisfaction with their ill relative (McFarlane, 2002a).

### Other Disorders

Most of this discussion has been focused on family psychoeducational programs designed for consumers and families of individuals diagnosed with schizophrenia and related disorders, because much of the research on family interventions has been conducted in this area. It should be noted, however, that family interventions have been shown to be helpful in the treatment of consumers with other mental illnesses, including bipolar disorder (Miklowitz & Goldstein, 1997), major depression (Emanuels-Zuurvenn & Emmelkamp, 1997), obsessive–compulsive disorder (Van Noppen, 1999), and borderline personality disorder (Gunderson, Berkowitz, & Ruizsancho, 1997).

For example, one approach to working with families of consumers with bipolar disorder has been offered by David Miklowitz and his colleagues (Miklowitz & Goldstein, 1997). This approach, called family-focused treatment (FFT), contains similar elements to psychoeducational programs for schizophrenia, with appropriate modifications for consumers with bipolar disorder and their families. The treatment involves an initial effort to connect with family members to engage them in the intervention, which often occurs during an active episode of the illness. Next, the consumer and family are provided with educational information about bipolar disorder, focusing on the symptoms of the disorder and a vulnerability–stress model to explain its development and course. After the consumer has stabilized from the active episode, efforts in FFT are directed

Family-focused treatment for bipolar disorder

toward increasing effective coping within the family, improving communication, and structured problem-solving interventions through individual meetings with the consumer and family. Controlled clinical trials have found that FFT significantly reduced risk of relapse in consumers with bipolar disorder, compared with a crisis management intervention (Miklowitz, George, Richards, Simoneau, & Suddath, 2003) and an individually focused consumer treatment (Rea et al., 2003).

### Briefer Family Interventions

In addition to the models of family psychoeducation discussed, briefer interventions have been proposed to educate family members about mental illness and help them develop coping skills. For example, Solomon, Draine, Mannion, and Meisel (1996) have developed and evaluated short-term group education and individual consultation programs for family members. In a controlled study, these programs were shown to help family members feel better able to cope with the effects of their relative's mental illness. Additionally, Wynne (1994) has proposed a family consultation model in which individual families meet periodically with a professional involved in the consumer's treatment (most often, the psychiatrist or primary clinician). This flexible model may be particularly well suited for families who would have difficulty participating in a longer intervention or for families who are coping relatively well.

Family education versus family psychoeducation

Alternatively, individual consultation may also be particularly beneficial in times of crisis. These briefer interventions have been called *family educational* programs, in contrast to the comprehensive *family psychoeducational* programs discussed above. Although these education programs have useful benefits, it is important to note that they have not been shown to have the same effects on relapse rates as longer and more intensive interventions.

### Family-to-Family Education Program

Thus far, we have focused on family psychoeducational and educational programs delivered by mental health profes-

sionals. However, in addition to these interventions, volun-
tary, peer-led family educational programs have been developed. The most widespread and well-known program is the
Family-to-Family Education Program (FFEP), sponsored by
the National Alliance for the Mentally Ill (NAMI; Burland,
1998). This program is facilitated and led by trained volun-
teers from families of individuals with mental illness. The
program progresses through a series of 12 weekly, 2–3-hour
classes focusing on the following areas: (1) information
about mental illnesses and treatments; (2) self-care,
problem-solving, and communication skills; (3) emotional
insight into responses to mental illness; and (4) information about advocacy efforts. Family-to-family classes are
open to anyone with a family member who has an SMI and
are free to participants. FFEP may be a particularly valuable
resource for families of individuals who are not in treatment. Also, like multiple-family groups, the FFEP provides
a forum for socialization and mutual support between families who face similar struggles and difficulties. Recently
conducted studies have indicated that participation in
family-to-family classes is helpful to relatives of individuals
with SMI in the following areas: increasing knowledge and
understanding of SMI and the mental health system;
increasing family empowerment; reducing subjective
burden and worry; and improving family members' self-
care (Dixon et al., in press; 2001).

Peer-led interventions have unique advantages, particularly in fostering a sense of empowerment and mutual
support among family members. One potentially fruitful
direction for the design of future services may be integrating peer-led elements into family psychoeducational
programs. For example, family members and consumers
could provide the educational component of family
psychoeducation together, or perhaps lead multifamily
groups together. In sum, evidence suggests that peer-led
programs such as FFEP represent a particularly important
component of services for families, and the processes associated with these programs may offer unique benefits for
family members of individuals with SMI.

| Advantages of peer-led interventions

## Research Summary and Synthesis

Relapse rates

Over the past two decades, more than 30 RCTs have indicated that family psychoeducation is a highly effective EBP, particularly in reducing relapse rates for consumers with schizophrenia and schizoaffective disorder. On the whole, research studies have shown that the relapse rates for consumers in families who received family interventions have averaged approximately 15% per year during the intervention, compared to an average of 30%–40% for individual therapy and medication or medication alone (McFarlane, Dixon, Lukens, & Lucksted, 2003). This finding is especially significant, since fewer relapses often mean a better long-term course and higher levels of functional recovery for consumers. In reviewing these findings, McFarlane and colleagues (2003, p. 231) remarked that "these differences in outcome are some of the most substantial and consistent empirical effects achieved by any treatment in the mental health domain," underscoring the established track record of effectiveness for family interventions.

Positive effect on social relations, employment, and well-being

There is also evidence that family psychoeducation may improve other aspects of both consumers' and family members' lives. For example, in controlled studies, interventions have resulted in improved social relationships (Montero et al., 2001) and better employment rates for consumers (McFarlane et al., 2000). Also, a number of studies has documented improvements in family member well-being and decreased feelings of stress among family members as a result of family psychoeducation (Cuijpers, 1999; Falloon & Penderson, 1985). More research is needed to determine how family interventions impact the lives of consumers and families in important areas of recovery beyond the well-documented effects on relapse rates.

Cross-cultural findings

A number of studies has examined the effects of family psychoeducational programs when they are applied in different countries and cultural groups. For example, in RCTs in China, family psychoeducational programs have demonstrated success in reducing consumer relapse and in

facilitating consumers' employment status and overall functioning (Mingyuan et al., 1993; Xiang, Ran, & Li, 1994).
Studies in Spain, Scandinavia, and Britain (McFarlane et al.,
2003) have shown that family psychoeducational programs
also reduce relapse rates. One study by Telles and associates
(1995) underscores the importance of cultural factors in
the practice of family psychoeducation. In this study, 40
Spanish-speaking consumers and their families were
assigned to BFM or standard case management services.
Most participants were first-generation immigrants to the
United States, varying in their degree of acculturation. The
authors found that BFM did not have significant effects. In
fact, BFM was related to increased risk of symptom
increases in consumers least assimilated to United States
culture. Thus, acculturation status appears to be an important factor to consider in practicing family psychoeducational interventions. However, given the widespread tests of
family interventions across cultures, it is expected that they
would be successful in cross-cultural implementation, given
appropriate adaptations. Along these lines, Bae and Kung
(2000) have proposed a model of family psychoeducation
specifically designed for Asian Americans, with adaptations
for differing value orientations and cultural characteristics.

## Recommendations for Implementation and Dissemination

Despite the large body of research supporting the effectiveness of family psychoeducational programs, these programs
are rarely provided as part of the usual mental health treatment services. More generally, research has shown that
treatment in many community-based and public settings
typically involves low levels of contact between
programs/staff and family members. For example, in one
survey of 539 consumers in a community mental health
center who had contact with their family, only 31% of
consumers reported that their family received clinical information, advice, or support during their treatment (Young,

Extreme underuse of
family programs

Sullivan, & Burnam, 1998), let alone a comprehensive family psychoeducational program. Barriers to implementation generally fall into two categories: (1) barriers related to clinicians and mental health systems' and (2) factors related to consumers and families.

### Barriers Related to Clinicians and Mental Health Systems

In terms of clinician and mental health system barriers, there are a number of reasons why family psychoeducation programs have not been widely adopted. First, there is evidence that clinicians and program administrators may be unaware of the strong evidence supporting the use of family psychoeducational programs (Dixon & Lehman, 1995). Second, concerns about consumer confidentiality have been cited as a reason that clinicians may be reticent to introduce family psychoeducation in clinical settings (Bogart & Solomon, 1999). Third, there are also system-wide and organizational factors that limit implementation efforts (e.g., workload, typical agency policies and practices; Wright, 1997). Finally, and perhaps most importantly, reimbursement is a clear barrier for dissemination. Family psychoeducation will not be provided unless it is a reimbursed service.

Overcoming
barriers

A first step toward overcoming these barriers is to increase the awareness of the benefits of family psychoeducational programs among all concerned stakeholders (i.e., public mental health system administrators, agency administrators, clinicians, funding sources, consumers, family members). In addition to benefits in improving consumer and family functioning, family psychoeducation has also been shown to have long-term cost-saving effects. In an experimental study of multifamily groups in New York, McFarlane and associates (1995) estimated that for every $1 invested to conduct the groups, there was a $34 savings due to reduced hospitalization during the second year of treatment. In order for family psychoeducation to be practiced, those who fund mental health services must create mechanisms for financial reimbursement of these services. Efforts must also be made to help community mental health centers and clinicians adapt and apply family psychoeducational models to their unique setting, while maintaining an adequate degree of fidelity to the original models. Administrators and others attempting to disseminate family psychoeducation must provide a clear rationale for these programs in terms of advantages that are relevant and meaningful to clinicians. Such advantages may include reduced crises for consumers, more efficient case management, gratitude from consumers and families, and more interesting and rewarding work (McFarlane et al., 2003).

A few points are noteworthy in terms of confidentiality issues. Consistent with guidelines of ethical practice, confidential information should not be released to family members without the consent of the consumer. It should be noted, however, that general, nonconfidential information could be shared with family members. For example, if a consumer's mother calls a clinician asking for information about her son's treatment (and the son has not provided consent for release), the clinician must explain that he or she cannot verify whether the son is in treatment at the clinic. However, the clinician could share general information about mental illnesses and their treatment, services provided by the agency, and other community resources. Also, the clinician could listen to the mother's concerns and receive information about her son without violating confidentiality.

| Confidentiality issues

An important task for providers involves talking with consumers about the potential benefits of including their family in supporting their goal of recovery, as well as discussing consumers' concerns about family involvement. In addressing consumers' concerns, it can be important to point out that release of information is not an "all or nothing" proposition. For example, a consumer may be open to having information about his diagnosis of schizophrenia and medications shared with his family, but may want other personal information to be kept confidential. In this case, the clinician works with the consumer to specify

| Benefits of family involvement

and document which information will be shared and the purpose of this disclosure. Bogart and Solomon (1999) described procedures to address confidentiality issues concerning family interventions for SMI, and suggest a helpful approach and practical suggestions for integrating these into routine practice.

**Implementation challenges**

In terms of system-level factors, the movement toward briefer and less frequent hospitalizations for individuals with SMI has presented new challenges for the implementation of family interventions. In much of the research cited above, families entered psychoeducational programs while their relative with SMI was hospitalized. With the shift to more outpatient-based models of illness management, clinicians and administrators need to find creative ways to engage families and weave family psychoeducation into routine mental health services. In studies by Dyck and his colleagues (Dyck, Hendryx, Short, Voss, & McFarlane, 2002; Dyck et al., 2000), the multi-family group model was successfully integrated into services at a community mental health center in Spokane, Washington. Consumers and families were recruited through agency case managers, who reviewed their caseloads to find consumers with family involvement. In these randomized clinical trials, the PMFG treatment resulted in decreased hospital utilization (Dyck et al., 2002) and improved negative symptoms (Dyck et al., 2000), compared with a control standard care condition. Overall, these studies indicate that family psychoeducation can be successfully adopted into community mental health services.

### Barriers Related to Families and Consumers

A number of factors hinders families from participating in family psychoeducational programs. First, stigma surrounding mental illness or past negative experiences with the mental health system (e.g., being blamed or treated as the problem) may result in families' reluctance to become involved in treatment. Second, family members may be wary of programs, especially if they hold the belief that participation will result in increased care-giving responsibilities. Third, consumers and family members may feel hopeless, resulting in skepticism that family psychoeducation could be helpful to them. Finally, practical problems such as transportation and limited time and energy are common barriers (Solomon, 1996).

Several strategies can be used to minimize the impact of these barriers to participation. At the outset, it may be important to clarify that family psychoeducation is designed to improve the lives of all family members, including the person with SMI. For example, in a number of studies, programs have been shown to reduce subjective feelings of burden among family members (Cuijpers, 1999). To overcome practical barriers, flexibility in scheduling and offering to hold family sessions in the home are helpful. Initially, education might be provided to combat stigma regarding mental illness, as well as false beliefs or expectations that families may have regarding family psychoeducation. For example, based on their past negative experiences, family members may fear blame from clinicians for their relative's illness. In this case, it may be helpful to educate the family on recent scientific knowledge about the biological basis of mental illness and also to communicate respect, empathy, and a collaborative spirit with family members. Finally, when developing and disseminating family intervention programs, it has been shown to be helpful to include consumers and family members as active partners in dissemination efforts (McFarlane et al., 2003).

Strategies to overcome barriers

## Summary and Conclusions

This chapter has reviewed a number of effective evidence-based practices that include the family of individuals with SMI. These services significantly reduce relapse rates and offer promise of helping to improve employment rates, social functioning of consumers, and family relationships. Experiences in applying these models indicate that families are typically appreciative of the support of professionals as they face the difficult experience of caring for a loved one with SMI. Mutual support from others, through peer-based programs or multifamily groups, also offers the potential of creating experiences of sharing and understanding for consumers and their families. Overall, effective family programs combine education, skills training, and practical guidance within the context of an ongoing empathic, respectful, supportive relationship. To best support the recovery process for consumers and families, it is essential that those who provide services integrate these key ingredients into their work.

## References

Anderson, C. M., Reiss, D. J., & Hogarty, G. E. (1986). *Schizophrenia and the family.* New York: Guilford Press.

Bebbington, P., & Kuipers, L. (1994). The predictive utility of expressed emotion in schizophrenia: An aggregate analysis. *Psychological Medicine, 24,* 707–718.

Bogart, T., & Solomon, P. (1999). Procedures to share treatment information among mental health providers, consumers, and families. *Psychiatric Services, 50,* 1321–1325.

Burland, J. F. (1998). Family-to-family: A trauma and recovery model of family education. *New Directions for Mental Health Services, 77,* 33–44.

Cuijpers, P. (1999). The effects of family intervention on relatives' burden: A meta-analysis. *Journal of Mental Health, 8,* 275–285.

Dartmouth Psychiatric Research Center. (2002). *Family psychoeducation: Information for practitioners and clinical supervisors.* Retrieved September 15, 2003, from *http://www.mentalhealthpractices.org/fam_pcs.html.*

Dixon, L., & Lehman, A. (1995). Family interventions for schizophrenia. *Schizophrenia Bulletin, 21,* 631–643.

Dixon, L., Lucksted, A., Stewart, B., Burland, J., Postrado, L., McGuire, C., et al. (in press). Outcomes of the peer-taught 12-week family-to-family education program for severe mental illness. *Acta Psychiatrica Scandinavia.*

Dixon, L., Stewart, B., Burland, J., Delahanty, J., Lucksted, A., & Hoffman, M. (2001). Pilot study of the effectiveness of the family-to-family education program. *Psychiatric Services, 52,* 965–967.

Dyck, D. G., Hendryx, M. S., Short, R. A., Voss, W. D., & McFarlane, W. R. (2002). Service use among consumers with schizophrenia in psychoeducational multiple-family group treatment. *Psychiatric Services, 53,* 749–754.

Dyck, D. G., Short, R. A., Hendryx, M. S., Norell, D., Myers, M., & Patterson, T., et al. (2000). Management of negative symptoms among consumers with schizophrenia attending multiple family groups. *Psychiatric Services, 51,* 513–519.

Emanuels-Zuurveen, L., & Emmelkamp, P. (1997). Spouse-aided therapy with depressed consumers. *Behavior Modification, 21,* 62–77.

Falloon, I. R. H. (2002). Cognitive-behavioral family and educational interventions for schizophrenic disorders. In S. G. Hofmann & M. G. Thompson (Eds.). *Treating chronic and severe mental disorders* (pp. 3–17). New York: Guilford Press.

Falloon, I. R. H., Boyd, J., & McGill, C. (1984). *Family care of Schizophrenia.* New York: Guilford Press.

Falloon, I. R. H., & Penderson, J. (1985). Family management in the prevention of morbidity of schizophrenia: The adjustment of the family unit. *Archives of General Psychiatry, 147,* 156–163.

Gunderson, J. G., Berkowitz, C., & Ruizancho, A. (1997). Families of borderline consumers: A psychoeducational approach. *Bulletin of the Menninger Clinic, 61,* 446–457.

Hatfield, A. B., Spaniol, L., & Zipple, A. M. (1987). Expressed emotion: A family perspective. *Schizophrenia Bulletin, 13,* 221–226.

Hogarty, G. E., Anderson, C. M., Reiss, D. J., Kornblith, S. J., Greenwald, D. P., Javna, C. D., et al. (1986). Family psychoeducation, social skills training, and maintenance chemotherapy in the aftercare treatment of schizophrenia: I. One-year effects of a controlled study on relapse and expressed emotion. *Archives of General Psychiatry, 34,* 633–642.

Hogarty, G. E., Anderson, C. M., Reiss, D. J., Kornblith, S. J., Greenwald, D. P., Ulrich, R. F., et al. (1991). Family psychoeducation, social skills training, and maintenance chemotherapy in the aftercare treatment of schizophrenia: II. Two-year effects of a controlled study on relapse and adjustment. *Archives of General Psychiatry, 48,* 340–347.

Leff, J. (1994). Working with families of schizophrenic consumers. *British Journal of Psychiatry, 164*(Suppl. 23), 71–76.

Leff, J., Berkowitz, R., Shavit, N., Strachan, A., Glass, I., & Vaughn, C. (1989). A trial of family therapy v. a relatives group for schizophrenia. *British Journal of Psychiatry, 154,* 58–66.

Leff, J., Berkowitz, R., Shavit, N., Strachan, A., Glass, I., & Vaughn, C. (1990). A trial of family therapy v. a relatives group for schizophrenia: two year follow-up. *British Journal of Psychiatry, 157,* 571–577.

Lehman, A. F., Kreyenbuhl, J., Buchanan, R., Dickerson, F., Dixon, L, Goldberg, R., et al. (2003). *The Schizophrenia Consumer Outcomes Research Team (PORT): Updated treatment recommendations 2003.* Manuscript submitted for publication.

Lehman, A. F., Steinwachs, D. M., Buchanan, R., Carpenter, W. T., Dixon, L. B., Fahey, M., et al. (1998). Translating research into practice: The Schizophrenia Consumer Outcomes Research Team (PORT) treatment recommendations. *Schizophrenia Bulletin, 24,* 1–10.

McFarlane, W. R. (2002a). Empirical studies of outcome in multifamily groups. In W. R. McFarlane (Ed.), *Multifamily groups in the treatment of severe psychiatric disorders* (pp. 49–70). New York: Guilford Press.

McFarlane, W. R. (2002b). The psychobiology of schizophrenia. In W. R. McFarlane (Ed.), *Multifamily groups in the treatment of severe psychiatric disorders* (pp. 3–17). New York: Guilford Press.

McFarlane, W. R., Dixon, L., Lukens, E., & Lucksted, A. (2003). Family psychoeducation and schizophrenia: A review of the literature. *Journal of Marital and Family Therapy, 29,* 223–245.

McFarlane, W. R., Dushay, R. A., Statsny, P., Deakins, S. M., Stastny, P., Lukens, E., et al. (2000). Employment outcomes in family-aided assertive community treatment. *American Journal of Orthopsychiatry, 70,* 203–214.

McFarlane, W. R., Gingerich, S., Deakins, S. M., Dunne, E., Horen, B. T., & Newmark, M. (2002). Problem solving in multifamily groups: A psychoeducational approach to treatment and rehabilitation. In W. R. McFarlane (Ed.), *Multifamily groups in the treatment of severe psychiatric disorders* (pp. 127–141). New York: Guilford Press.

McFarlane, W. R., Lukens, E., Link, B., Dushay, R., Deakins, S. A., Newmark, M., et al. (1995). Multiple-family groups and psychoeducation in the treatment of schizophrenia. *Archives of General Psychiatry, 52,* 679–687.

Miklowitz, D. J., George, E. L., Richards, J. A., Simoneau, T. L., & Suddath, R. L. (2003). A randomized study of family-focused psychoeducation and pharmacotherapy in the outconsumer management of bipolar disorder. *Archives of General Psychiatry, 60,* 904–912.

Miklowitz, D. J., & Goldstein, M. J. (1997). *Bipolar disorder: A family focused approach.* New York: Guilford Press.

Mingyuan, Z., Heqin, Y., Chengde, Y., Jianlin, Y., Quingfeng, Y., Peijun, C., et al. (1993). Effectiveness of psychoeducation of relatives of schizophrenic consumers: A prospective cohort study in five cities of China. *International Journal of Mental Health, 22,* 47–59.

Montero, I., Asencio, A., Hernandez, I., Masanet, M. S. J., Lacruz, M., Bellver, F., et al. (2001). Two strategies for intervention in schizophrenia. *Schizophrenia Bulletin, 27*(4), 661–670.

Pitschel-Waltz, G., Leucht, S., Bauml, J., Kissling, W., & Engel, R. R. (2001). The effect of family interventions in relapse and rehospitalization rates in schizophrenia: A meta-analysis. *Schizophrenia Bulletin, 27*(1), 73–92.

Randolph, E. T., Eth, S., Glynn, S. M., Paz, G. G., Leong, G. B., Shaner, A. L., et al. (1994). Behavioural family management in schizophrenia: Outcome of a clinic-based intervention. *British Journal of Psychiatry, 164*(4), 501–506.

Rea, M. M., Tompson, M. C., Miklowitz, D. G., Goldstein, M. J., Hwang, S., & Mintz, J. (2003). Family focused treatment versus individual treatment for bipolar disorder: Results of a randomized clinical trial. *Journal of Consulting and Clinical Psychology, 71*(3), 482–492.

Solomon, P. (1996). Moving from psychoeducation to family education for families of adults with serious mental illness. *Psychiatric Services, 47,* 1364–1370.

Solomon, P., & Draine, J. (1995). Subjective burden among family members of mentally ill adults. *American Journal of Orthopsychiatry, 65,* 419–427.

Solomon, P., Draine, J., Mannion, E., & Meisel, M. (1996). Impact of brief family psychoeducation on self-efficacy. *Schizophrenia Bulletin, 22*(1), 41–50.

Telles, C., Karno, M., Mintz, J., Paz, G., Arias, M., Tucker, D., et al. (1995). Immigrant families coping with schizophrenia: Behavioral family intervention v. case management with a low-income, Spanish speaking population. *British Journal of Psychiatry, 167,* 473–479.

Van Noppen, B. (1999). Multi-family behavioral treatment (MFBT) for OCD crisis intervention and time-limited treatment. *Crisis Intervention and Time-Limited Treatment, 5,* 3–24.

Vaughn, C. E., & Leff, J. P. (1976). The influence of family and social factors on the course of psychiatric illness: A comparison of schizophrenic and depressed neurotic consumers. *British Journal of Psychiatry, 15,* 157–165.

World Schizophrenia Fellowship (1998). *Families as partners in care: A document developed to launch a strategy for the implementation of family education, training, and support.* Toronto: Author.

Wright, E. R. (1997). The impact of organizational factors on mental health professionals' involvement with families. *Psychiatric Services, 48,* 921–927.

Wynne, L. C. (1994). The rationale for consultation with the families of schizophrenic consumers. *Acta Psychiatrica Scandinavia, Supplemenum, 90,* 125–132.

Xiang, M. G., Ran, M. S., & Li, S. G. (1994). A controlled evaluation of psychoeducational family intervention in a rural Chinese community. *British Journal of Psychiatry, 165,* 544–548.

Young, A. S., Sullivan, G., Burnam, A., & Brook, R. H. (1998). Measuring the quality of outpatient treatment for schizophrenia. *Archives of General Psychiatry, 55,* 611–617.

Zastowny, T. R., Lehman, A. F., Cole, R. E., & Kane, C. (1992). Family management of schizophrenia: A comparison of behavioral and supportive family treatment. *Psychiatric Quarterly, 63,* 159–186.

NINETEEN

# | Medications

*Alexander L. Miller*

MEDICATIONS ARE OF PROVEN BENEFIT for almost all psychiatric disorders (Janicak, Davis, Preskorn, & Ayd, 1997), but understanding the appropriate use of medications is far more complex than simply learning about the effects of medications on the symptoms of a mental illness. The interactions between practitioner and consumer concerning medications have multiple dimensions, all of which impact medication selection and the likelihood that medications will be effective. Moreover, over the course of time, consumers typically receive medications from multiple practitioners and often different health care systems. Medication management is an ongoing process in which new information, including ongoing assessments, is constantly being generated. This information must be accurately recorded and readily accessible to optimize collaborative medication decision making and facilitate desired outcomes.

| Complexity of medication management

Imagine a trip to the doctor's office for recent problems with headaches. During the visit your blood pressure is found to be moderately elevated. Nothing else to explain the headaches is found in a series of tests. You are going through a stressful period in your life. Does stress explain

| Blood pressure analogy

453

the headaches? Are they due to the high blood pressure? The doctor prescribes a pain medicine for the headaches and rechecks your blood pressure. It is still high. She asks you to return in a month for follow-up. The headaches respond to the medicine and you have not needed it for several weeks, but your blood pressure is still elevated. She recommends that you begin a blood pressure medicine, after explaining that untreated high blood pressure increases the likelihood of stroke and heart attack. Your father died 5 years ago at age 59 of a heart attack. She discusses the medication choices, listing the side effects and risks of each. You have concerns about having to take medicines. You are unhappy that even though your original problem is now gone, you have been diagnosed with a problem that requires long-term treatment. You ask if diet, exercise, relaxation procedures, or anything other than medication could help. She gives you reading materials about each of these approaches to blood pressure control.

You review them before your next appointment and discuss them with your spouse. Will they fit in with your lifestyle and eating habits? Do you have time to do them regularly? Your blood pressure is still up. You decide to try diet and exercise. You feel better, but your blood pressure is only marginally improved. It is very disappointing that, despite your best efforts, the problem is not resolved. You and your spouse discuss it and agree that you will start a medication for the blood pressure. The doctor prescribes one that makes you feel sluggish and tired, though it controls your blood pressure well. She listens to your complaints about not feeling right and switches you to a different medicine. This time, the side effects of the medication are not bothersome to you. Your blood pressure returns to the normal range. All is well for the next 10 years, and then your blood pressure rises again. The doctor recommends an increased dosage of the medication, but this does not lower your blood pressure. Your doctor recommends starting a second medicine. She discusses the increased risk of strokes and heart attacks with high blood pressure. You wonder why the medicine is no longer totally effective. She tells you this is quite common. You ask about a new hypertension treatment, nighttime transcranial magnetic therapy, that you recently saw in a news report. She gives you a DVD that reviews this and other newer blood pressure treatments. You discuss it with your spouse. . .

This brief vignette illustrates many issues that arise in the course of medication management for both psychiatric and nonpsychiatric illnesses. The symptoms that the consumer is seeking to manage may not be the only factors that a physician must consider in prescribing medications. The value of long-term treatment may not be evident once the symptoms are gone. Relating the problem to personally meaningful events or goals in the consumer's life helps achieve collaboration with treatment. The treatment options may include both pharmacological and nonpharmacological approaches. Effective psychiatric treatment approaches may also integrate information and involvement of a consumer's family members or significant supportive others. The idea of needing to take medications over the long term engenders feelings about loss of control. There are often multiple medication choices for an illness, and sometimes the biggest difference between them involves side effects. The prescribed medications may lose their effectiveness for the consumer over time, and therefore may need to be augmented with other medications or changed completely. The questions of whether or not to take medications and the usefulness of medications in the management of symptoms should be routinely reviewed and revisited collaboratively by the prescriber and the consumer.

*Collaborative approaches to multiple medication issues*

Each of these issues has an evidence base to support particular interventions that address it. The purpose of this chapter is to explain the evidence base for medication management of the symptoms of major psychiatric illnesses. Entire textbooks are devoted to the field of psychopharmacology. In this brief chapter, it is not possible to cover all psychiatric illnesses. Rather, I use examples to illustrate the effective use of the evidence base to guide the use of medications.

*Evidence guiding medication usage*

## How Do Medications Get Approved?

Rigorous FDA
approval process

It is important to have some understanding of how we develop evidence that a medication is safe and effective, because the process is also designed to weed out medications that are not safe and effective. Drug treatments that have not been through this rigorous evaluation process are unproven. Some unproven treatments are available over the counter or in health food stores, but doctors are understandably reluctant to recommend them. The role of the Food and Drug Administration (FDA) is to evaluate the evidence about a medication's safety and effectiveness. Pharmaceutical companies typically gather this evidence, using criteria set down by the FDA. The FDA asks internal and external experts to assess the evidence. The FDA also provides spot checks of some of the sites where the evidence has been obtained to verify its accuracy and to ensure that proper procedures have been followed.

Randonmized
controlled trials

Placebo

Most of the evidence comes from randomized controlled trials that compare the new drug with other treatments or no treatment (placebo). This method of testing means that consumers and doctors who participate in a study do not choose which treatment they will receive. It avoids the biases that would inevitably occur if, for example, everyone got to decide whether they would take the new, experimental drug or an already approved medication. In the case of medications for psychiatric illnesses, the studies intended to show the usefulness of a medication almost always include comparisons with a placebo (e.g., sugar pill) and with an FDA-approved medication for the disorder. The use of placebos can be controversial, but the justification for using them is especially strong when it is known that many persons with an illness are likely to get better even with placebo treatments. In trials of antidepressant medications, for example, up to half the participants with depression respond to a placebo. For the FDA to approve a treatment for depression, it must prove that it is more effective than placebo and at least as good as an existing treatment.

Aside from the question of whether a medication works, a key role of the FDA approval process is to test the safety of the medication. Virtually all medications have side effects that are troublesome for many of the consumers who take them, but if the benefits are great enough, the consumer may choose to live with the side effects. Some medications have dangerous side effects and the question becomes whether the benefits outweigh the risks for the individual. If there are dangerous side effects and there are already approved medications for the condition that are just as effective and are less dangerous, the medication will not be approved by the FDA. Sometimes, however, there are no good treatments without dangerous side effects, and the medication is approved along with recommendations or rules about how to monitor or prevent the dangerous side effects. This is frequently the situation with anti-cancer drugs, but it also occurs with psychiatric medications. For example, clozapine, which is used to treat schizophrenia, can cause the bone marrow to stop making white blood cells in about 1% of consumers who take it. If the condition is not recognized early, it can result in very severe infections leading to death. Clozapine was not approved because of this rare complication, until it was shown that some people with schizophrenia responded *only* to clozapine (Kane, Honigfeld, Singer, & Meltzer, 1988). For these consumers, clozapine was their only hope for improving a lifetime afflicted by a devastating illness. Thus, the FDA approved clozapine for treatment of schizophrenia and, at the same time, established rules for frequent monitoring of blood counts in persons taking it. These rules have proven to be very effective. Only about one in 10,000 consumers who has taken clozapine in the United States have died from this complication (*Physicians' Desk Reference*, 2004), whereas about half who have used it get major benefits from it (Lieberman et al., 1994). Moreover, there is good evidence that clozapine reduces the high risk of suicide (about 10%) in consumers with schizophrenia (Meltzer et al., 2003), so its net effect has been to save lives, in addition to enriching them.

Effectiveness and safety

Indicated versus
nonindicated
medication uses

The FDA approves a medication for a specific indication, such as treating a major depressive disorder. Doctors, however, may choose to prescribe the medication for any purpose that they think is clinically warranted. In fact, after FDA approval, medications are often used, at doctors' discretion, for disorders other than the approved one. Clinically useful and important discoveries occur in this way. Some antidepressants, for example, have been shown to be very helpful for anxiety disorders such as panic disorder and obsessive–compulsive disorder. Sometimes pharmaceutical manufacturers seek FDA approval of a new indication for a medication (e.g., an antidepressant for panic disorder). This stamp of approval is helpful because it allows the pharmaceutical company to market the medication for the new indication, but the real question for clinicians is whether the evidence base for using the medication in other conditions is sufficiently strong. Clinicians can get information about this evidence directly from the medical literature and from articles by experts who have reviewed the medical literature. The information about the medication that the FDA requires the manufacturer to make public is contained in the package insert about the drug, which consumers can obtain from the pharmacist. The *Physicians' Desk Reference* (*PDR*) is published annually (and updated more frequently). The *PDR* contains package inserts on most FDA-approved medications. Changing the package insert is an arduous process, sometimes initiated by the manufacturer and sometimes by the FDA (usually in response to new information about safety). The package insert is not a review of all relevant information about a medication and does not list all the appropriate uses of a medication.

PDR as information
source

Complementarity of
medication and
nonmedication
treatments

## How Do Medication Treatments Relate to Other Treatments?

Because of the FDA approval process and the profit motive for pharmaceutical companies in marketing drugs, the evidence base about prescription medications in psychiatry and all other branches of medicine is voluminous and often confusing, especially in comparison to nonmedication treatments. The size of the evidence base is not, however, an indicator of the relative value of medication treatments compared to other interventions for a particular disorder or problem. In some illnesses, such as schizophrenia and bipolar disorder, the evidence is overwhelming that medications can be an essential component of effective treatment for almost everyone with the illnesses. In other illnesses, such as depression, there is strong evidence that nonmedication treatments (e.g., cognitive therapies) can be just as effective as medications (Sadock & Sadock, 2003). Thus, there is sometimes an important decision to be made as to which type of evidence-based treatment a consumer will use: medication treatments, nonmedication treatments, or a combination. In reality, almost all studies that have compared medication and nonmedication treatments for a wide range of psychiatric disorders end up concluding that the combination of the two is somewhat superior to either one alone. The reasons for not using both together typically relate to the expense of delivering two treatments and the time and effort involved for consumers. Nonetheless, these sorts of studies illustrate a very important point: medication and nonmedication evidence-based treatments usually complement one another. Optimizing clinical treatment usually means combining evidence-based treatments, as necessary, to provide effective treatment of specific disorders.

## What Are Medications Used to Treat?

Medications for psychiatric consumers can be used to achieve multiple goals, and the issues regarding medication selection depend on the goal of the treatment. We can use three broad categories of goals for medication treatment: acute treatment of an illness, maintenance treatment, and symptom relief.

Multiple purposes

Carlos | CARLOS IS A 28-YEAR-OLD MALE who has a bipolar disorder and is currently experiencing an acute manic episode. Carlos's mood is elated, and he is delusional about his financial situation (he thinks he is a financial genius who has billions of dollars, but actually has nothing left after a series of extremely risky investments in the last month). He has had recent difficulty with sleeping; in fact, he has slept only 2–3 hours per night for several weeks. He has also made threatening statements toward family members who have tried to keep him from spending all of his savings.

Based on Carlos's particular presentation and on the evidence, his doctor recommends that Carlos be hospitalized to begin treating the symptoms and impairments of the bipolar disorder with a mood stabilizer, an antipsychotic medication, and a medication to help Carlos get some sleep. The mood stabilizer is intended to treat the current episode as well as to prevent recurrences of the severe symptoms of the bipolar illness. With Carlos's consent, the medication treatment plan notes that the mood stabilizer will be used for long-term treatment. The antipsychotic is intended to help resolve the delusional symptoms that Carlos is experiencing and to help with the management of the associated anxiety. With Carlos's consent, this medication may be used after the psychotic symptoms abate, because of the evidence that early discontinuation of this treatment can lead to a recurrence of symptoms. Until the past decade of the 1990s, the unpleasant side effects of antipsychotics, and one of their long-term risks (tardive dyskinesia, a disfiguring disorder characterized by involuntary movements, often in the facial area), meant that they were seldom used for maintenance treatment of bipolar disorder, even though there was evidence for their usefulness in this regard. Newer antipsychotics, however, are generally better tolerated and appear to have much less risk of causing tardive dyskinesia than older antipsychotics, so they are now being used for preventing relapses, either in combination with a mood stabilizer or by themselves. The sleeping medication is intended to be used only for a short time to provide relief from the symptom of insomnia that Carlos is currently experiencing, and the use of this medication would be discontinued when this symptom is no longer present.

## Which Medication?

In the case of Carlos, as in most cases in which a person experiences a psychiatric illness, there are multiple medication choices for treatment of the illness and for associated symptoms, such as anxiety. How is a decision made as to which medications to use? Which mood stabilizer? Which antipsychotic? Which sleeping medication? Sometimes there is a clear choice in terms of efficacy (e.g., see the discussion of clozapine above), but more often it is the short- and long-term side-effect and risk profiles that are different between the medication choices. Most of us are familiar with the practice of the doctor or nurse informing us of possible risks and side effects of the medication we have just been prescribed. Recent work, however, has found that consumer participation in medication selection and use leads to better outcomes (Kemp, Kirov, Everitt, Hayward, & David, 1998; Mueser et al., 2002). The collaborative management of side effects and associated medication risks is a core principle in this work. For one person, possible weight gain might be a major issue, whereas for another person, the level of sedation might be a critical decision factor. Weighing and dealing with these alternatives is the ongoing task of both the prescriber and the consumer. Medications that are not taken clearly do not work. Therefore, it is critical that consumers are motivated to take effective medications, and that when consumers experience problematic side effects, they are empowered to discuss them with the prescriber and make collaborative decisions.

For a multitude of reasons, many of us would prefer not to take medications, especially for long periods of time. Moreover, when distressing symptoms, such as anxiety or

Consumer–doctor decision

Medication noncompliance

difficulty with concentration, complicate our lives, it is easy to forget to take medicines. Failing to take medications as prescribed is common in medicine and is a major cause of relapse. These problems are compounded in some psychiatric illnesses, such as schizophrenia and bipolar disorder, when recurrence of the illness may impair a person's judgment or cognition about the need for taking medications. When a person is in the midst of a manic episode, for example, believing that he or she possesses special healing powers, it can be difficult to persuade that person that using a medication will be helpful.

**Partial solutions to noncompliance**

The research to find better ways of dealing with the problems associated with medication noncompliance has followed two different paths. First, long-acting oral or injectable forms of medications have been developed, often for the treatment of people with schizophrenia and substance abuse disorders (Schatzberg & Nemeroff, 1998). These simplify treatment, in that they reduce how often consumers must remember *and decide* to take these medications, and studies do show that they produce better adherence. For technical reasons, there are relatively few such medications, so that the options are limited. Moreover, the consumer still must receive and take the medication, albeit less frequently.

**Linking medication to consumer goals**

The second area of investigation has examined the psychological and environmental factors that promote or deter medication adherence. Simply providing educational materials or programs is often insufficient to improve consistency in medication taking (Zygmunt, Olfson, Boyer, & Mechanic, 2002). The psychology of taking medications is clearly very complex, but recent research has shown that one effective way to increase medication adherence is to learn about the consumer's goals and aspirations and relate them to the purposes for which the medication is being used (Kemp et al., 1998). For example, if the person wants to get along better with family members, the clinician can explore the role of past illness episodes in straining family relationships and help the consumer to achieve the goal of preventing future episodes by using medication regularly. This linking of medication usage to the consumer's individual goals has been shown to be effective.

Another approach to improving medication adherence has been developed for working with consumers who have schizophrenia, many of whom have cognitive impairments that reduce the likelihood of remembering to take medications regularly and as prescribed (Velligan et al., 2000). In this approach, therapists regularly visit the consumers in their usual living situations and assist them in developing and using prompts to remind them to take medications as they are prescribed. For example, setting up a medication reminder near a consumer's food supply for her cat may remind her to take her medications each time that she feeds her cat in the morning and at dinnertime.

| Creating medication prompts

## How Do We Measure Effects of Medications?

In the case of the person with hypertension described at the beginning of this chapter, we know how to measure the severity of the problem (i.e., the level of blood pressure), and we have a large amount of data about the range of normal blood pressure and the risks of blood pressure that is above normal. The doctor prescribing medication for blood pressure thus has precise measurements and clear target outcomes to guide medication selection and dosing. Many of the problems encountered in medicine are not measurable with this level of objective precision, and the goals of treatment cannot be so exactly defined. For problems such as headaches, pain, anxiety or depression, we rely almost entirely on the consumer's self-report to gauge the severity of the problem and the effectiveness of treatments for it. Even for the management of complicated symptoms such as auditory hallucinations (i.e.,hearing voices or other sounds in the absence of an actual voice or sound), we have had to rely solely on self-report until the development of highly sophisticated brain-imaging techniques that reveal the brain activity associated with the experience of halluci-

| Reliance on self-report

nations (Jones et al., 1996). In daily community mental health center practice, the clinician is almost entirely dependent on the consumer and on those who have an opportunity to observe him or her closely, such as case managers, family members, or significant others, for reports about symptoms.

Quantitative, objective measures of medication effects

A good deal of medical training is devoted to teaching doctors to share a common vocabulary in describing their clinical observations of skin rashes, heart murmurs, prostate characteristics, and so on. The purpose is, in part, to record information in ways that are meaningful to other doctors, who can compare their assessments of the nature and severity of the problem to earlier assessments by others. In psychiatry, clinical training places a heavy emphasis on descriptive terminology for diagnoses, symptoms, side effects, and so on. The quantification of some aspects of psychiatric illnesses, such as the presence of symptoms, associated impairments, and medication side effects, has largely been the domain of researchers. Recent work has gone into adapting these research measures for use in busy clinical settings (Shores-Wilson et al., 2002). This adaptation requires shortening the measures and training nonphysicians in their use, so that the personnel costs of obtaining the measures are not excessive. The main advantages to obtaining quantitative, objective measures of medication effects include (1) tracking results of medications over time, to help make informed decisions about the most effective dosages and types of medications for the individual; (2) creating a medical record that conveys clear information about medication benefits, effects, and side effects for other providers (e.g., in the emergency room) who see the consumer; and (3) the involvement of other members of the mental health treatment team in the processes of observing and evaluating medication effects.

Need for treatment team collaboration

For example, feedback from an employment specialist to the consumer's psychiatrist about the early-morning oversedating effects that a medication has on the consumer's ability to perform his or her job is critical. The psychiatrist can then create a different dosage schedule with the consumer to achieve maximum benefit with minimum interference in the person's daily functioning. The latter point is important. Because medications are mainstays of treatment of most psychiatric disorders, their management must be integrated with other modes of treatment for each consumer. It is not helpful for providers to practice in isolation, acting as though each treatment modality is independent of the other and assuming that medications are the sole purview of the doctor. In reality, good medication management lays the groundwork for effective use of other interventions in many serious mental illnesses, so that all providers have an interest and potential role in improving medication management. To the extent that everyone involved, including the consumer, family members, and treatment team members, has an understanding of what medicines do and do not do, and to the extent that they can learn to make precise observations of medication effects and share that information, overall treatment effectiveness for the consumer will benefit.

## Why and When Are Medications Chosen, Adjusted, or Changed?

What do we do with the results of these assessments? How do we know when the maximum benefit from a medication has been achieved? When is it appropriate to change the dose? Add another medication? Switch to a new medication? The answers to these questions are unique for each individual person. Nonetheless, a large body of scientific literature marks the paths to the answers.

First, each mental illness has a different set of cardinal symptoms and associated impairments, and a different evidence base associated with medication usage. For example, whereas the symptoms of some illnesses may remit from an acute stage rather quickly, people who experience schizophrenia almost always require some form of antipsychotic medication treatment to obtain symptom improvements. Knowledge of the prognosis of the illness and the

Knowledge of prognosis and medication benefits

usual benefits from various medications is a tremendously important factor in medication treatment decisions. It is equally important that the actual medication treatments are customized to the individual consumer's goals, preferences, and unique characteristics. Providing information about potential medication benefits to the consumer and family members helps to engage everyone in informed decision making.

*Individualizing treatments*

Second, there is a large body of knowledge about each FDA-approved medication and about the class of medications to which it belongs. This includes usual dosing, side effects, safety concerns, symptoms for which the medication is likely to be helpful, and time to respond after beginning treatment. For example, the benzodiazepine group of antianxiety agents (Valium, Xanax, and many others) starts to exert therapeutic effects with the initial dose, in less than an hour and they stop working within a day after discontinuation. The antidepressants (Prozac, Paxil, and many others), by contrast, often require 4–6 weeks to take full effect. Again, a shared knowledge of these medication characteristics is critical for prescriber, consumer, and family members alike. Final selection of the exact dose and the exact medication must be based on the individual's responses, but it is incumbent upon clinicians to know and prescribe medications that have a strong evidence base before using medications (or combinations of medications) with weaker evidence bases.

*Selection based on individual response and evidence of effectiveness*

Finally, although the first medication chosen may be completely effective with few documented undesirable side effects, the response for a particular person may be less than satisfactory or there may be bothersome side effects. As already noted, each medication has a somewhat different side-effect profile. The troublesome side effects produced by medications are often the main issue for consumers; fortunately, it is usually possible to switch to another medication in the same general class that has a more acceptable profile. If symptom reduction is less than desired, it may be worthwhile switching to a second medication—and if that is inadequate, a third. Or, the evidence

*Frequent need for two or more medication trials*

may suggest that an adjunctive medication added to the first can enhance the response. It is helpful for clinicians to be informed by medication guidelines or algorithms that incorporate current evidence and expert consensus into recommendations for sequential treatment options. Guidelines and algorithms are developed through similar processes, although algorithms are more specific in their recommendations. The use of medication guidelines and algorithms by community mental health organizations has the potential to improve consistency and to ensure that treatment of each consumer is informed by the most current evidence.

Although guidelines for treatment of psychiatric disorders have been available for over a decade, experience has shown that even when they are adopted at the level of the organization (e.g., health maintenance organization), adherence to them at the practitioner level is extremely variable (Bauer, 2002). Part of the problem in implementation can be lack of sufficient specificity of the recommendations. If the recommendations are vague or if each step in treatment contains many different alternatives, there is insufficient practical guidance for the practitioner. Even if the recommendations are sufficiently specific, users need training and consistent organizational support in applying them. One project attempted to implement medication algorithms as a central component of a disease management approach for depression, bipolar disorder, and schizophrenia: the Texas Medication Algorithm Project (TMAP; Miller et al., 1999; Rush et al., 1999). Results of this project are still being analyzed, but it does appear that consumers who received the algorithm-guided set of interventions did better clinically, especially early on. after their entry into the program.

| Use of guidelines and algorithims

| Texas Medication Algorithim Project

## Who Manages Medications?

Whose responsibility is it to manage medication treatments in psychiatry? Physicians are, of course, ultimately responsible for which medications are prescribed. Because good medication management for many psychiatric disorders

| Need for precise reporting

requires collaboration, it is the responsibility of all members of the mental health treatment team, including the consumer and his or her family, to contribute to the process of optimizing medication treatment. Most helpful are observations that provide the physician with accurate information about medication effects. Providing accurate information requires training of the observers and, very importantly, an ongoing dialogue between the physician, other treatment providers, and the consumer and family members. For example, a common side effect of conventional antipsychotics is akathisia; persons who experience akathisia feel a great sense of inner restlessness, which may lead to continuous pacing, and not surprisingly, to a more irritable mood. To the untrained observer, the consumer may simply appear nervous; the communication from a case manager to the psychiatrist might be, "Helen seems anxious today—I think she is worried about something." This report could actually mislead the psychiatrist, especially if the pacing is not evident when Helen is seated during her 15-minute meeting with the psychiatrist. The trained observer, on the other hand, might note: "Helen was pacing about her apartment when I went to visit her yesterday, and she was also pacing back and forth outside in the hall before this meeting. This is a change in Helen's behavior since she started the new medicine a few weeks ago." This latter report would help to identify akathisia, which can be alleviated in several ways once it is correctly diagnosed.

## Summary

1. Medications can be helpful to consumers in the treatment of symptoms for most mental illnesses, and they are a critical part of treatment for many illnesses.
2. The consumer benefits most from medication treatment when that treatment is integrated with all other mental health interventions.
3. Finding the correct medication at the correct dose for each individual consumer is a complex and ongoing

process, involving all members of the treatment team, the consumer, and, when appropriate, family members and significant others. The process is guided by a very large body of information about the nature of the illness and the usual benefits and side effects of medications.

4. The approval processes of the FDA generate a large amount of evidence about new drugs to show that they are safe and effective treatments for at least one aspect of one psychiatric disorder.

5. The FDA-approval processes do not identify the full range of clinical uses of new medications and may not identify very rare safety problems. This information comes from post-approval clinical experience, clinical trials, and widespread use of the medication.

## References

Bauer, M. S. (2002). A review of quantitative studies of adherence to mental health clinical practice guidelines. *Harvard Review of Psychiatry, 10*, 138–153.

Janicak, P. G., Davis, J. M., Preskorn, S. H., & Ayd, F. J. (1997). *Principles and practice of psychopharmacotherapy* (2nd ed.). Baltimore: Williams & Wilkins.

Jones, T., Silbersweig, D. A., Stern, E., Schnorr, L., Seaward, J., Clark, J.C., Lammertsma, A. A., & Grootoonk, S. (1996). The development of in vivo tracer methods to obtain new information about human disease: A study of the hallucinating brain. *European Journal of Nuclear Medicine, 23*(3), 332–335.

Kane, J., Honigfeld, G., Singer, J., & Meltzer, H. (1988). Clozapine for the treatment-resistant schizophrenic: A double-blind comparison versus chlorpromazine/benztropine. *Archives of General Psychiatry, 45*, 789–796.

Kemp, R., Kirov, G., Everitt, B., Hayward, P., & David, A. (1998). Randomised controlled trial of compliance therapy: 18 month follow-up. *British Journal of Psychiatry, 172*, 413–419.

Lieberman, J. A., Safferman, A. Z., Pollack, S., Szymanski, S., Johns, C., Howard, A., et al. (1994). Clinical effects of clozapine in chronic schizophrenia: Response to treatment and predictors of outcome. *American Journal of Psychiatry, 151*, 1744–1752.

Meltzer, H. Y., Alphs, L. D., Green, A. I., Altamura, A. C., Anand, R., Bertoldi, A., et al. (2003). Clozapine treatment for suicidality in schizophrenia: International suicide prevention trial (InterSePT). *Archives of General Psychiatry, 60*(1), 82–91.

Miller, A. L., Chiles, J. A., Chiles, J. K., Crismon, M. L., Shon, S. P., & Rush, A. J. (1999). The Texas Medication Algorithm Project (TMAP) schizophrenia algorithms. *Journal of Clinical Psychiatry, 60*(10), 649–657.

Mueser, K. T., Corrigan, P. W., Hilton, D. W., Tanzman, B., Schaub, A., Gingerich, S., et al. (2002). Illness management and recovery: A review of the research. *Psychiatric Services, 53*(10), 1272–1284.

*Physicians' Desk Reference* (58th ed.). (2004). Montvale, CA: Thomson PDR.

Rush, A. J., Rago, W. V., Crismon, M. L., Toprac, M. G., Shon, S. P., Suppes, T., et al. (1999). Medication treatment for the severely and persistently mentally ill: The Texas Medication Algorithm Project. *Journal of Clinical Psychiatry, 60*, 284–291.

Sadock, B. J., & Sadock, V. A. (2003). *Kaplan & Sadock's synopsis of psychiatry: Behavioral sciences/clinical psychiatry* (9th ed.). Philadelphia: Lippincott, Williams & Wilkins.

Schatzberg, A. F., & Nemeroff, C. B. (1998). *The American psychiatric press textbook of psychopharmacology.* Washington, DC: American Psychiatric Association.

Shores-Wilson, K., Biggs, M. M., Miller, A. L., Carmody, T. J., Chiles, J. A., Rush, A.J., et al. (2002). Itemized clinician ratings versus global ratings of symptom severity in patients with schizophrenia. *International Journal of Methods in Psychiatric Research, 11*, 45–53.

Velligan, D. I., Bow-Thomas, C. C., Huntzinger, C. D., Ritch, J., Ledbetter, N., Prihoda, T. J., et al. (2000). Randomized controlled trial of the use of compensatory strategies to enhance adaptive functioning in outpatients with schizophrenia. *The American Journal of Psychiatry, 157*, 1317–1323.

Zygmunt, A., Olfson, M., Boyer, C. A., & Mechanic, D. (2002). Interventions to improve medication adherence in schizophrenia. *The American Journal of Psychiatry, 159*, 1653–1664.

Epilogue

# The Future of Evidence-Based Practices in Mental Health

*Robert E. Drake*
*Matthew R. Merrens*
*David W. Lynde*

EVIDENCE-BASED APPROACHES TO MENTAL HEALTH CARE are an extension of a larger movement in general health care that have a rapidly expanding philosophical, practical, and empirical foundation. According to the Institute of Medicine, evidence-based practice is "the integration of best research evidence with clinical expertise and patient values" (Institute of Medicine, 2001, p. 47). This definition resonates in the mental health field because it balances the need for scientific rigor that is at the heart of evidence-based practice with comprehensive assessment, clinical judgment, individualized treatment, flexibility, patient preferences, personal choice, and self-determination.

This book has introduced the current concepts and approaches of evidence-based practice for people with severe mental illnesses. There is, however, one final question. How will evidence-based practices change mental health care in the future? Many aspects of the health field are changing and will continue to change even more rapidly in the next few years. In closing this book, we offer several educated guesses about the future.

## Scientific Evidence

Scientific evidence on the causes, course, and treatment of mental disorders will undoubtedly continue to expand dramatically. In the near future, the biological, psychological, and social underpinnings of specific disorders, including genetic factors that influence vulnerability and multiple factors that influence heterogeneity and differential treatment response, will be better understood. This knowledge will lead to mental health interventions that are more specific and more effective. Thus, using treatments that correspond to the evidence will become increasingly critical over the next few years. Clinical computing will permit the aggregation of extensive data on routine care, the instant availability of risk adjustments for individual consumers, and decision-support systems to facilitate accurate selection of interventions. Further studies of evidence-based practices for consumers with specific characteristics, such as minority groups and women, will also help to expand the available information base and the choice of optimal interventions. Computerized systems for improving individualized treatment decisions are already available for many medical disorders, and this technology will soon be extended to mental health treatments.

In the more distant future, interventions that are curative rather than palliative may become prominent for the first time. That is, mental health interventions will target underlying etiological abnormalities rather than just symptoms. Furthermore, the human genome project presents the possibility that science will transform health care to a more preventive orientation; efforts based on the insertion of corrective genetic material are already being tested in many areas of medicine.

## Consumer Preferences

As the rate of change and the total amount of scientific information increases, information technology will enable rapid synthesis and availability of scientific data. Consumers will have greater access to current evidence and to their own psychiatric records. They will be able to access personally adjusted information on treatment options, including outcomes and side effects, via electronic portals, before they meet with their mental health treatment team to make treatment decisions. Information directly available to consumers will include the latest scientific evidence as well as opportunities to participate in current clinical trials of new interventions, much like the national networks that exist for cancer treatment.

The mental health field will continue to experience shifts in ideas, values, finances, and culture. For example, community mental health providers will be strongly influenced by evolving concepts regarding choice, self-determination, community integration, self-management, cultural competence, self-help, and recovery. We expect that these social and cultural changes will continue to move in the direction of choice and autonomy.

To advance shared decision making practices in mental health, several controversial issues will need to be studied and resolved. Practitioners have a significant amount of work to do in better understanding consumers' awareness of mental illness, effective ways to ensure informed and competent decision making, risk factors for violence, and the use of coercive interventions. Scientific research will facilitate progress in these areas as well. In mental health, as opposed to other areas of health care, we have not yet studied carefully patients' interest, willingness, and ability to participate in decision making.

## Clinical Expertise

Many educational and attitudinal barriers currently inhibit practitioners. Current practitioners in mental health have some ambivalence regarding evidence-based practices and shared decision making process. Many practitioners lack the skills and understanding of recovery-oriented services needed to participate fully this directional shift. Similar themes are common in the history of medicine. For example, surgeons in the United States debunked Pasteur's ideas about germs and vigorously resisted Lister's development of antiseptic surgery. But history suggests that scientific evidence eventually prevails, and the current speed and accessibility of information permits scientific progress to influence practice more rapidly.

Mental health clinicians will need new skills to deliver evidence-based practices. The movement to teach these skills in preservice education, professional training, continuing education, and workforce retraining is just beginning. Clinical expertise is critical for asking the right question; finding the best available evidence; individualizing the evidence for a particular consumer and situation; sharing information with the consumer; assessing the consumer's preferences for outcomes, treatments, and engaging in shared decision making; and reviewing treatment and making further decisions in a progressive, collaborative fashion. With developments in information technology, many of these techniques will be ingrained and reinforced through decision-support systems built into electronic records. Relevant information will be available in real time, while the clinician is conducting an assessment, adjusting risk information, presenting information to the consumer, considering alternatives, making decisions, doing follow-ups, and so forth. Prompts, cues, warnings, and other aids not only help the clinician and the consumer to make optimal decisions but also provide a relevant, time-sensitive, educational experience. Basic education and training will not only emphasize the need for evidence-based practitioners but also the use of decision-support systems.

## Public Awareness

As the scientific understanding of mental disorders and effective treatments becomes more available, stigma related to mental illness will decline. This decline has occurred reliably in other areas of medicine (e.g., leprosy, cancer) and will inevitably occur in the mental health field. The public will understand that mental illnesses are similar to other medical illnesses. The differences between science-based practice and nonscientific practice will be greater than ever before, just as it now is in cancer treatment. The public will demand access to safe and effective treatments.

## Implementation

At this point, implementation of evidence-based practices in routine mental health settings remains an enormous challenge. As many authors in this book have pointed out, we know a significant amount regarding effective mental health services, but much less about how to make such services available. Nevertheless, public mental health programs are beginning to experiment with approaches to widespread implementation, and nearly every state has an explicit plan for implementing evidence-based practices. Over the next few years, we will continue to learn more about the process of implementation, and technological advances may enable more successful attempts. Public and private health care systems will need to develop the infrastructure to promote implementation of evidence-based practices—for consensus development, planning, training, monitoring, evaluation, improvements, consultation, and technical assistance. Sustaining new practices and improving them over time, as the evidence expands, will be as difficult as implementing them in the first place.

## Public Policy

Policymakers are just beginning to struggle with how evidence-based practices fit into the political process. The basic notion that science can be used to shift the field away from practices that result in more harm than good and toward practices that produce more good than harm is incontrovertible. Too often, however, guild organizations, some providers, and other special–interest groups that are invested in preserving the status quo reframe the issue. Financing mechanisms are critical, and changes at the level of Medicare, Medicaid, and other funding sources will strongly influence the success of evidence-based mental health.

Significant changes in the national economy have created a new paradigm in the financing of mental health services. The debate and discussion in federal and many state systems has shifted from a total focus on financial appropriations to the constant evaluation of the efficient allocation of financial resources in providing services with demonstrated effectiveness.

## Dynamic Health–Care System

The long-term goal of the evidence-based practice movement is not simply to establish a new set of interventions that outlive their usefulness. Rather, the goal is to produce a dynamic health-care system that is capable of continuous self-renewal, in congruence with scientific evidence, in order to provide the most effective services to the widest range of people who need them. Fundamental changes in education, health-care funding, and accountability will be required to ensure success.

## Conclusions

The values and recommendations discussed here are prominently featured in the President's New Freedom Commission on Mental Health (2003). It is our hope that these recommendations will be implemented thoughtfully and thoroughly. If they are, evidence-based practices will benefit individuals who experience mental disorders, their families and friends, and the broader society. As science progresses in the future, the benefits of adopting evidence-based practices will increase rapidly.

## References

Institute of Medicine (IOM). (2001). *Crossing the quality chasm: A new health system for the 21st century.* Washington, DC: National Academy Press.

The President's New Freedom Commission on Mental Health (2003). *Achieving the promise: Transforming mental health care in America.* DHHS Publication No. SMA-03-3832, Rockville, MD.

# Introductory Evidence-Base Practices DVD

We are happy to make available a DVD that presents an introduction to the evidence-based practices currently being evaluated in the Implementing Evidence-Based Practices Project and discussed in separate chapters within this text. The DVD presents an introduction to the following evidence-based practices:

- Assertive Community Treatment (16 minutes, 27 seconds)
- Integrated Dual-Disorder Treatment (18 minutes, 13 seconds)
- Supported Employment (17 minutes, 5 seconds)
- Illness Management and Recovery (14 minutes, 9 seconds)
- Family Psychoeducation (11 minutes, 33 seconds)
- Medication Management (16 minutes, 44 seconds.)

This introductory DVD is a component of the Evaluation Edition of the Implementation Resource Kit and was funded by Substance Abuse and Mental Health Services Administration (SAMHSA). The material is in the public domain and cannot be distributed for a charge. Our fee for providing the DVD covers the cost of preparing the DVD, handling and postage.

The DVD may be ordered by sending a $15 check (made payable to Dartmouth College) to:

Karen Dunn
NH-Dartmouth PRC
2 Whipple Street, Suite 202
Lebanon, NH 03766

Be sure to include your mailing address.

# Index

481

Pg 36 - Definition of EB?